GO!

with Microsoft®

Access 2007

Brief

Shelley Gaskin and Suzanne Marks

PEARSON

Prentice Hall

Upper Saddle River, New Jersey

This book is dedicated to my students, who inspire me every day, and to my husband, Fred Gaskin.
—Shelley Gaskin

*This book is dedicated with much love to my husband Phil, who is my everything; and to my children
Jeff and Laura, who are the center of my universe.*
—Suzanne Marks

Library of Congress Cataloging-in-Publication Data

Gaskin, Shelley.
  Go! with. Access 2007 : brief / Shelley Gaskin and Suzanne Marks.
    p. cm.
  ISBN 0-13-244816-5
  1. Microsoft Access. 2. Database management. I. Marks, Suzanne. II. Title.
  QA76.9.D3G3865 2007
  005.75'65--dc22

                                   2007011743

Vice President and Publisher: Natalie E. Anderson
Associate VP/Executive Acquisitions Editor,
  Print: Stephanie Wall
Executive Acquisitions Editor, Media: Richard Keaveny
Product Development Manager: Eileen Bien Calabro
Senior Editorial Project Manager: Laura Burgess
Development Editor: Ginny Munroe
Editorial Assistants: Becky Knauer, Lora Cimiluca
Executive Producer: Lisa Strite
Content Development Manager: Cathi Profitko
Senior Media Project Manager: Steve Gagliostro
Production Media Project Manager: Lorena Cerisano
Director of Marketing: Margaret Waples
Senior Marketing Manager: Jason Sakos
Marketing Assistants: Angela Frey, Kathryn Ferranti
Senior Sales Associate: Rebecca Scott

Managing Editor: Lynda J. Castillo
Manufacturing Production Project Manager:
Wanda Rockwell
Production Editor: GGS Book Services
Photo Researcher: GGS Book Services
Manufacturing Buyer: Natacha Moore
Production/Editorial Assistant: Sandra K. Bernales
Design Director: Maria Lange
Art Director/Interior Design: Blair Brown
Cover Photo: Courtesy of Getty Images, Inc./Marvin
  Mattelson
Composition: GGS Book Services
Project Management: GGS Book Services
Cover Printer: Phoenix Color
Printer/Binder: RR Donnelley/Willard

Credits and acknowledgments borrowed from other sources and reproduced, with permission, in this textbook are as
follows or on the appropriate page within the text.

  Page 2: Index Stock Imagery, Inc.; and page 98: Getty Images, Inc. – Liaison.

10 9 8 7 6 5 4 3 2 1
ISBN 0-13-244816-5

Contents in Brief

Table of Contents

Letter from the Editor

Dear Instructors and Students,

The primary goal of the *GO!* Series is two-fold. The first goal is to help instructors teach the course they want in less time. The second goal is to provide students with the skills to solve business problems using the computer as a tool, for both themselves and the organization for which they might be employed.

The *GO!* Series was originally created by Series Editor Shelley Gaskin and published with the release of Microsoft Office 2003. Her ideas came from years of using textbooks that didn't meet all the needs of today's diverse classroom and that were too confusing for students. Shelley continues to enhance the series by ensuring we stay true to our vision of developing quality instruction and useful classroom tools.

But we also need your input and ideas.

Over time, the *GO!* Series has evolved based on direct feedback from instructors and students using the series. *We are the publisher that listens.* To publish a textbook that works for you, it's critical that we continue to listen to this feedback. It's important to me to talk with you and hear your stories about using *GO!* Your voice can make a difference.

My hope is that this letter will inspire you to write me an e-mail and share your thoughts on using the *GO!* Series.

Stephanie Wall
Executive Editor, *GO!* Series
stephanie_wall@prenhall.com

GO! System Contributors

We thank the following people for their hard work and support in making the *GO!* System all that it is!

Additional Author Support

Coyle, Diane	Montgomery County Community College
Fry, Susan	Boise State
Townsend, Kris	Spokane Falls Community College
Stroup, Tracey	Amgen Corporation

Instructor Resource Authors

Amer, Beverly	Northern Arizona University	Paterson, Jim	Paradise Valley Community College
Boito, Nancy	Harrisburg Area Community College	Prince, Lisa	Missouri State
Coyle, Diane	Montgomery County Community College	Rodgers, Gwen	Southern Nazarene University
Dawson, Tamara	Southern Nazarene University	Ruymann, Amy	Burlington Community College
Driskel, Loretta	Niagara County Community College	Ryan, Bob	Montgomery County Community College
Elliott, Melissa	Odessa College		
Fry, Susan	Boise State	Smith, Diane	Henry Ford Community College
Geoghan, Debra	Bucks County Community College	Spangler, Candice	Columbus State Community College
Hearn, Barbara	Community College of Philadelphia	Thompson, Joyce	Lehigh Carbon Community College
Jones, Stephanie	South Plains College	Tiffany, Janine	Reading Area Community College
Madsen, Donna	Kirkwood Community College	Watt, Adrienne	Douglas College
Meck, Kari	Harrisburg Area Community College	Weaver, Paul	Bossier Parish Community College
Miller, Cindy	Ivy Tech	Weber, Sandy	Gateway Technical College
Nowakowski, Tony	Buffalo State	Wood, Dawn	
Pace, Phyllis	Queensborough Community College	Weissman, Jonathan	Finger Lakes Community College

Super Reviewers

Brotherton, Cathy	Riverside Community College	Maurer, Trina	Odessa College
Cates, Wally	Central New Mexico Community College	Meck, Kari	Harrisburg Area Community College
		Miller, Cindy	Ivy Tech Community College
Cone, Bill	Northern Arizona University	Nielson, Phil	Salt Lake Community College
Coverdale, John	Riverside Community College	Rodgers, Gwen	Southern Nazarene University
Foster, Nancy	Baker College	Smolenski, Robert	Delaware Community College
Helfand, Terri	Chaffey College	Spangler, Candice	Columbus State Community College
Hibbert, Marilyn	Salt Lake Community College	Thompson, Joyce	Lehigh Carbon Community College
Holliday, Mardi	Community College of Philadelphia	Weber, Sandy	Gateway Technical College
Jerry, Gina	Santa Monica College	Wells, Lorna	Salt Lake Community College
Martin, Carol	Harrisburg Area Community College	Zaboski, Maureen	University of Scranton

Technical Editors

Janice Snyder
Joyce Nielsen
Colette Eisele
Janet Pickard
Mara Zebest
Lindsey Allen
William Daley

Student Reviewers

Allen, John	Asheville-Buncombe Tech Community College	Erickson, Mike	Ball State University
		Gadomski, Amanda	Northern Michigan University
Alexander, Steven	St. Johns River Community College	Gyselinck, Craig	Central Washington University
Alexander, Melissa	Tulsa Community College	Harrison, Margo	Central Washington University
Bolz, Stephanie	Northern Michigan University	Heacox, Kate	Central Washington University
Berner, Ashley	Central Washington University	Hill, Cheretta	Northwestern State University
Boomer, Michelle	Northern Michigan University	Innis, Tim	Tulsa Community College
Busse, Brennan	Northern Michigan University	Jarboe, Aaron	Central Washington University
Butkey, Maura	Central Washington University	Klein, Colleen	Northern Michigan University
Christensen, Kaylie	Northern Michigan University	Moeller, Jeffrey	Northern Michigan University
Connally, Brianna	Central Washington University	Nicholson, Regina	Athens Tech College
Davis, Brandon	Northern Michigan University	Niehaus, Kristina	Northern Michigan University
Davis, Christen	Central Washington University	Nisa, Zaibun	Santa Rosa Community College
Den Boer, Lance	Central Washington University	Nunez, Nohelia	Santa Rosa Community College
Dix, Jessica	Central Washington University	Oak, Samantha	Central Washington University
Moeller, Jeffrey	Northern Michigan University	Oertii, Monica	Central Washington University
Downs, Elizabeth	Central Washington University	Palenshus, Juliet	Central Washington University

Pohl, Amanda	Northern Michigan University
Presnell, Randy	Central Washington University
Ritner, April	Northern Michigan University
Rodriguez, Flavia	Northwestern State University
Roberts, Corey	Tulsa Community College
Rossi, Jessica Ann	Central Washington University
Shafapay, Natasha	Central Washington University
Shanahan, Megan	Northern Michigan University
Teska, Erika	Hawaii Pacific University
Traub, Amy	Northern Michigan University
Underwood, Katie	Central Washington University
Walters, Kim	Central Washington University
Wilson, Kelsie	Central Washington University
Wilson, Amanda	Green River Community College

Series Reviewers

Abraham, Reni	Houston Community College
Agatston, Ann	Agatston Consulting Technical College
Alexander, Melody	Ball Sate University
Alejandro, Manuel	Southwest Texas Junior College
Ali, Farha	Lander University
Amici, Penny	Harrisburg Area Community College
Anderson, Patty A.	Lake City Community College
Andrews, Wilma	Virginia Commonwealth College, Nebraska University
Anik, Mazhar	Tiffin University
Armstrong, Gary	Shippensburg University
Atkins, Bonnie	Delaware Technical Community College
Bachand, LaDonna	Santa Rosa Community College
Bagui, Sikha	University of West Florida
Beecroft, Anita	Kwantlen University College
Bell, Paula	Lock Haven College
Belton, Linda	Springfield Tech. Community College
Bennett, Judith	Sam Houston State University
Bhatia, Sai	Riverside Community College
Bishop, Frances	DeVry Institute—Alpharetta (ATL)
Blaszkiewicz, Holly	Ivy Tech Community College/Region 1
Branigan, Dave	DeVry University
Bray, Patricia	Allegany College of Maryland
Brotherton, Cathy	Riverside Community College
Buehler, Lesley	Ohlone College
Buell, C	Central Oregon Community College
Byars, Pat	Brookhaven College
Byrd, Lynn	Delta State University, Cleveland, Mississippi
Cacace, Richard N.	Pensacola Junior College
Cadenhead, Charles	Brookhaven College
Calhoun, Ric	Gordon College
Cameron, Eric	Passaic Community College
Carriker, Sandra	North Shore Community College
Cannamore, Madie	Kennedy King
Carreon, Cleda	Indiana University—Purdue University, Indianapolis
Chaffin, Catherine	Shawnee State University
Chauvin, Marg	Palm Beach Community College, Boca Raton
Challa, Chandrashekar	Virginia State University
Chamlou, Afsaneh	NOVA Alexandria
Chapman, Pam	Wabaunsee Community College
Christensen, Dan	Iowa Western Community College
Clay, Betty	Southeastern Oklahoma State University
Collins, Linda D.	Mesa Community College
Conroy-Link, Janet	Holy Family College
Cosgrove, Janet	Northwestern CT Community
Courtney, Kevin	Hillsborough Community College
Cox, Rollie	Madison Area Technical College
Crawford, Hiram	Olive Harvey College
Crawford, Thomasina	Miami-Dade College, Kendall Campus
Credico, Grace	Lethbridge Community College
Crenshaw, Richard	Miami Dade Community College, North
Crespo, Beverly	Mt. San Antonio College
Crossley, Connie	Cincinnati State Technical Community College
Curik, Mary	Central New Mexico Community College
De Arazoza, Ralph	Miami Dade Community College
Danno, John	DeVry University/Keller Graduate School
Davis, Phillip	Del Mar College
DeHerrera, Laurie	Pikes Peak Community College
Delk, Dr. K. Kay	Seminole Community College
Doroshow, Mike	Eastfield College
Douglas, Gretchen	SUNYCortland
Dove, Carol	Community College of Allegheny
Driskel, Loretta	Niagara Community College
Duckwiler, Carol	Wabaunsee Community College
Duncan, Mimi	University of Missouri-St. Louis
Duthie, Judy	Green River Community College
Duvall, Annette	Central New Mexico Community College
Ecklund, Paula	Duke University
Eng, Bernice	Brookdale Community College
Evans, Billie	Vance-Granville Community College
Feuerbach, Lisa	Ivy Tech East Chicago
Fisher, Fred	Florida State University
Foster, Penny L.	Anne Arundel Community College
Foszcz, Russ	McHenry County College
Fry, Susan	Boise State University
Fustos, Janos	Metro State
Gallup, Jeanette	Blinn College
Gelb, Janet	Grossmont College
Gentry, Barb	Parkland College
Gerace, Karin	St. Angela Merici School
Gerace, Tom	Tulane University
Ghajar, Homa	Oklahoma State University
Gifford, Steve	Northwest Iowa Community College
Glazer, Ellen	Broward Community College
Gordon, Robert	Hofstra University
Gramlich, Steven	Pasco-Hernando Community College
Graviett, Nancy M.	St. Charles Community College, St. Peters, Missouri
Greene, Rich	Community College of Allegheny County
Gregoryk, Kerry	Virginia Commonwealth State
Griggs, Debra	Bellevue Community College
Grimm, Carol	Palm Beach Community College
Hahn, Norm	Thomas Nelson Community College
Hammerschlag, Dr. Bill	Brookhaven College
Hansen, Michelle	Davenport University
Hayden, Nancy	Indiana University—Purdue University, Indianapolis

Hayes, Theresa	Broward Community College	Lord, Alexandria	Asheville Buncombe Tech
Helfand, Terri	Chaffey College	Lowe, Rita	Harold Washington College
Helms, Liz	Columbus State Community College	Low, Willy Hui	Joliet Junior College
Hernandez, Leticia	TCI College of Technology	Lucas, Vickie	Broward Community College
Hibbert, Marilyn	Salt Lake Community College	Lynam, Linda	Central Missouri State University
Hoffman, Joan	Milwaukee Area Technical College	Lyon, Lynne	Durham College
Hogan, Pat	Cape Fear Community College	Lyon, Pat Rajski	Tomball College
Holland, Susan	Southeast Community College	MacKinnon, Ruth	Georgia Southern University
Hopson, Bonnie	Athens Technical College	Macon, Lisa	Valencia Community College, West Campus
Horvath, Carrie	Albertus Magnus College		
Horwitz, Steve	Community College of Philadelphia	Machuca, Wayne	College of the Sequoias
Hotta, Barbara	Leeward Community College	Madison, Dana	Clarion University
Howard, Bunny	St. Johns River Community	Maguire, Trish	Eastern New Mexico University
Howard, Chris	DeVry University	Malkan, Rajiv	Montgomery College
Huckabay, Jamie	Austin Community College	Manning, David	Northern Kentucky University
Hudgins, Susan	East Central University	Marcus, Jacquie	Niagara Community College
Hulett, Michelle J.	Missouri State University	Marghitu, Daniela	Auburn University
Hunt, Darla A.	Morehead State University, Morehead, Kentucky	Marks, Suzanne	Bellevue Community College
		Marquez, Juanita	El Centro College
Hunt, Laura	Tulsa Community College	Marquez, Juan	Mesa Community College
Jacob, Sherry	Jefferson Community College	Martyn, Margie	Baldwin-Wallace College
Jacobs, Duane	Salt Lake Community College	Marucco, Toni	Lincoln Land Community College
Jauken, Barb	Southeastern Community	Mason, Lynn	Lubbock Christian University
Johnson, Kathy	Wright College	Matutis, Audrone	Houston Community College
Johnson, Mary	Kingwood College	Matkin, Marie	University of Lethbridge
Johnson, Mary	Mt. San Antonio College	McCain, Evelynn	Boise State University
Jones, Stacey	Benedict College	McCannon, Melinda	Gordon College
Jones, Warren	University of Alabama, Birmingham	McCarthy, Marguerite	Northwestern Business College
Jordan, Cheryl	San Juan College	McCaskill, Matt L.	Brevard Community College
Kapoor, Bhushan	California State University, Fullerton	McClellan, Carolyn	Tidewater Community College
Kasai, Susumu	Salt Lake Community College	McClure, Darlean	College of Sequoias
Kates, Hazel	Miami Dade Community College, Kendall	McCrory, Sue A.	Missouri State University
		McCue, Stacy	Harrisburg Area Community College
Keen, Debby	University of Kentucky	McEntire-Orbach, Teresa	Middlesex County College
Keeter, Sandy	Seminole Community College	McLeod, Todd	Fresno City College
Kern-Blystone, Dorothy Jean	Bowling Green State	McManus, Illyana	Grossmont College
		McPherson, Dori	Schoolcraft College
Keskin, Ilknur	The University of South Dakota	Meiklejohn, Nancy	Pikes Peak Community College
Kirk, Colleen	Mercy College	Menking, Rick	Hardin-Simmons University
Kleckner, Michelle	Elon University	Meredith, Mary	University of Louisiana at Lafayette
Kliston, Linda	Broward Community College, North Campus	Mermelstein, Lisa	Baruch College
		Metos, Linda	Salt Lake Community College
Kochis, Dennis	Suffolk County Community College	Meurer, Daniel	University of Cincinnati
Kramer, Ed	Northern Virginia Community College	Meyer, Marian	Central New Mexico Community College
Laird, Jeff	Northeast State Community College	Miller, Cindy	Ivy Tech Community College, Lafayette, Indiana
Lamoureaux, Jackie	Central New Mexico Community College		
		Mitchell, Susan	Davenport University
Lange, David	Grand Valley State	Mohle, Dennis	Fresno Community College
LaPointe, Deb	Central New Mexico Community College	Monk, Ellen	University of Delaware
		Moore, Rodney	Holland College
Larson, Donna	Louisville Technical Institute	Morris, Mike	Southeastern Oklahoma State University
Laspina, Kathy	Vance-Granville Community College		
Le Grand, Dr. Kate	Broward Community College	Morris, Nancy	Hudson Valley Community College
Lenhart, Sheryl	Terra Community College	Moseler, Dan	Harrisburg Area Community College
Letavec, Chris	University of Cincinnati	Nabors, Brent	Reedley College, Clovis Center
Liefert, Jane	Everett Community College	Nadas, Erika	Wright College
Lindaman, Linda	Black Hawk Community College	Nadelman, Cindi	New England College
Lindberg, Martha	Minnesota State University	Nademlynsky, Lisa	Johnson & Wales University
Lightner, Renee	Broward Community College	Ncube, Cathy	University of West Florida
Lindberg, Martha	Minnesota State University	Nagengast, Joseph	Florida Career College
Linge, Richard	Arizona Western College	Newsome, Eloise	Northern Virginia Community College Woodbridge
Logan, Mary G.	Delgado Community College		
Loizeaux, Barbara	Westchester Community College	Nicholls, Doreen	Mohawk Valley Community College
Lopez, Don	Clovis-State Center Community College District	Nunan, Karen	Northeast State Technical Community College

Odegard, Teri	Edmonds Community College
Ogle, Gregory	North Community College
Orr, Dr. Claudia	Northern Michigan University South
Otieno, Derek	DeVry University
Otton, Diana Hill	Chesapeake College
Oxendale, Lucia	West Virginia Institute of Technology
Paiano, Frank	Southwestern College
Patrick, Tanya	Clackamas Community College
Peairs, Deb	Clark State Community College
Prince, Lisa	Missouri State University-Springfield Campus
Proietti, Kathleen	Northern Essex Community College
Pusins, Delores	HCCC
Raghuraman, Ram	Joliet Junior College
Reasoner, Ted Allen	Indiana University—Purdue
Reeves, Karen	High Point University
Remillard, Debbie	New Hampshire Technical Institute
Rhue, Shelly	DeVry University
Richards, Karen	Maplewoods Community College
Richardson, Mary	Albany Technical College
Rodgers, Gwen	Southern Nazarene University
Roselli, Diane	Harrisburg Area Community College
Ross, Dianne	University of Louisiana in Lafayette
Rousseau, Mary	Broward Community College, South
Samson, Dolly	Hawaii Pacific University
Sams, Todd	University of Cincinnati
Sandoval, Everett	Reedley College
Sardone, Nancy	Seton Hall University
Scafide, Jean	Mississippi Gulf Coast Community College
Scheeren, Judy	Westmoreland County Community College
Schneider, Sol	Sam Houston State University
Scroggins, Michael	Southwest Missouri State University
Sever, Suzanne	Northwest Arkansas Community College
Sheridan, Rick	California State University-Chico
Silvers, Pamela	Asheville Buncombe Tech
Singer, Steven A.	University of Hawai'i, Kapi'olani Community College
Sinha, Atin	Albany State University
Skolnick, Martin	Florida Atlantic University
Smith, T. Michael	Austin Community College
Smith, Tammy	Tompkins Cortland Community Collge
Smolenski, Bob	Delaware County Community College
Spangler, Candice	Columbus State
Stedham, Vicki	St. Petersburg College, Clearwater
Stefanelli, Greg	Carroll Community College
Steiner, Ester	New Mexico State University
Stenlund, Neal	Northern Virginia Community College, Alexandria
St. John, Steve	Tulsa Community College

Sterling, Janet	Houston Community College
Stoughton, Catherine	Laramie County Community College
Sullivan, Angela	Joliet Junior College
Szurek, Joseph	University of Pittsburgh at Greensburg
Tarver, Mary Beth	Northwestern State University
Taylor, Michael	Seattle Central Community College
Thangiah, Sam	Slippery Rock University
Thompson-Sellers, Ingrid	Georgia Perimeter College
Tomasi, Erik	Baruch College
Toreson, Karen	Shoreline Community College
Trifiletti, John J.	Florida Community College at Jacksonville
Trivedi, Charulata	Quinsigamond Community College, Woodbridge
Tucker, William	Austin Community College
Turgeon, Cheryl	Asnuntuck Community College
Turpen, Linda	Central New Mexico Community College
Upshaw, Susan	Del Mar College
Unruh, Angela	Central Washington University
Vanderhoof, Dr. Glenna	Missouri State University-Springfield Campus
Vargas, Tony	El Paso Community College
Vicars, Mitzi	Hampton University
Villarreal, Kathleen	Fresno
Vitrano, Mary Ellen	Palm Beach Community College
Volker, Bonita	Tidewater Community College
Wahila, Lori (Mindy)	Tompkins Cortland Community College
Waswick, Kim	Southeast Community College, Nebraska
Wavle, Sharon	Tompkins Cortland Community College
Webb, Nancy	City College of San Francisco
Wells, Barbara E.	Central Carolina Technical College
Wells, Lorna	Salt Lake Community College
Welsh, Jean	Lansing Community College Nebraska
White, Bruce	Quinnipiac University
Willer, Ann	Solano Community College
Williams, Mark	Lane Community College
Wilson, Kit	Red River College
Wilson, Roger	Fairmont State University
Wimberly, Leanne	International Academy of Design and Technology
Worthington, Paula	Northern Virginia Community College
Yauney, Annette	Herkimer County Community College
Yip, Thomas	Passaic Community College
Zavala, Ben	Webster Tech
Zlotow, Mary Ann	College of DuPage
Zudeck, Steve	Broward Community College, North

About the Authors

Shelley Gaskin, Series Editor, is a professor of business and computer technology at Pasadena City College in Pasadena, California. She holds a master's degree in business education from Northern Illinois University and a doctorate in adult and community education from Ball State University. Dr. Gaskin has 15 years of experience in the computer industry with several Fortune 500 companies and has developed and written training materials for custom systems applications in both the public and private sector. She is also the author of books on Microsoft Outlook and word processing.

Suzanne Marks is a faculty member in Business Technology Systems at Bellevue Community College, Bellevue, Washington. She holds a bachelor's degree in business education from Washington State University, and was project manager for the first IT Skills Standards in the United States.

Visual Walk-Through of the *GO!* System

The *GO!* System is designed for ease of implementation on the instructor side and ease of understanding on the student. It has been completely developed based on professor and student feedback.

The *GO!* System is divided into three categories that reflect how you might organize your course— **Prepare**, **Teach**, and **Assess**.

Prepare

NEW

Transition Guide

New to *GO!*—We've made it quick and easy to plan the format and activities for your class.

GO!

Because the GO! System was designed and written by instructors like yourself, it includes the tools that allow you to Prepare, Teach, and Assess in your course. We have organized the GO! System into these three categories that match how you work through your course and thus, it's even easier for you to implement.

To help you get started, here is an outline of the first activities you may want to do in order to conduct your course.

There are several other tools not listed here that are available in the GO! System so please refer to your GO! Guide for a complete listing of all the tools.

Prepare
1. Prepare the course syllabus
2. Plan the course assignments
3. Organize the student resources

Teach
4. Conduct demonstrations and lectures

Assess
5. Assign and grade assignments, quizzes, tests, and assessments

PREPARE

1. Prepare the course syllabus

A syllabus template is provided on the IRCD in the **go07_syllabus_template** folder of the main directory. It includes a course calendar planner for 8-week, 12-week, and 16-week formats. Depending on your term (summer or regular semester) you can modify one of these according to your course plan, and then add information pertinent to your course and institution.

2. Plan course assignments

For each chapter, an Assignment Sheet listing every in-chapter and end-of-chapter project is located on the IRCD within the **go01_go!office2007intro_instructor_resources_by_chapter** folder. From there, navigate to the specific chapter folder. These sheets are Word tables, so you can delete rows for the projects that you choose not to assign or add rows for your own assignments—if any. There is a column to add the number of points you want to assign to each project depending on your grading scheme. At the top of the sheet, you can fill in the course information.

Transitioning to GO! Office 2007   Page 1 of 1

Syllabus Template

Includes course calendar planner for 8-, 12-, and 16-week formats.

GO! with Microsoft Office 2007 Introductory
SAMPLE SYLLABUS (16 weeks)

I. COURSE INFORMATION

Course No.:   Semester:
Course Title: Credits:
Course Hours:

Instructor: Office:
Office Hours:
Email: Phone:

II. TEXT AND MATERIALS

Before starting the course, you will need the following:

➢ GO! with Microsoft Office 2007 Introductory by Shelley Gaskin, Robert L. Ferrett, Alicia Vargas, Suzanne Marks ©2007, published by Pearson Prentice Hall. ISBN 0-13-167990-6

➢ Storage device for saving files (any of the following: multiple diskettes, CD-RW, flash drive, etc.)

III. WHAT YOU WILL LEARN IN THIS COURSE

This is a hands-on course where you will learn to use a computer to practice the most commonly used Microsoft programs including the Windows operating system, Internet Explorer for navigating the Internet, Outlook for managing your personal information and the four most popular programs within the Microsoft Office Suite (Word, Excel, PowerPoint and Access). You will also practice the basics of using a computer, mouse and keyboard. You will learn to be an intermediate level user of the Microsoft Office Suite.

Within the Microsoft Office Suite, you will use Word, Excel, PowerPoint, and Access. Microsoft Word is a word processing program with which you can create common business and personal documents. Microsoft Excel is a spreadsheet program that organizes and calculates accounting-type information. Microsoft PowerPoint is a presentation graphics program with which you can develop slides to accompany an oral presentation. Finally, Microsoft Access is a database program that organizes large amounts of information in a useful manner.

GO! with Microsoft Office 2007 Introductory

Assignment Sheet for GO! with Microsoft Office 2007 Introductory
Chapter 5

Instructor Name: _____
Course Information: _____

Do This (✓ when done)	Then Hand in This Check each Project for the elements listed on the Assignment Tag. Attach the Tag to your Project.	Submit Printed Formulas	By This Date	Possible Points	Your Points
Study the text and perform the steps for Activities 5.1 – 5.11	Project 5A Application Letter				
Study the text and perform the steps for Activities 5.12 – 5.23	Project 5B Company Overview				
End-of-Chapter Assessments					
Complete the Matching and Fill-in-the-Blank questions	As directed by your instructor				
Complete Project 5C	Project 5C Receipt Letter				
Complete Project 5D	Project 5D Marketing				
Complete Project 5E	Project 5E School Tour				
Complete Project 5F	Project 5F Scouting Trip				
Complete Project 5G	Project 5G Contract				
Complete Project 5H	Project 5H Invitation				
Complete Project 5I	Project 5I Fax Cover				
Complete Project 5J	Project 5J Business Running Case				
Complete Project 5K	Project 5K Services				
Complete Project 5L	Project 5L Survey Form				
Complete Project 5M	Project 5M Press Release				

Copyright © 2008 Pearson Prentice Hall

Page 1 of 1

Assignment Sheet

One per chapter. Lists all possible assignments; add to and delete from this simple Word table according to your course plan.

File Guide to the *GO!* Supplements

Tabular listing of all supplements and their file names.

NEW

Assignment Planning Guide

Description of *GO!* assignments with recommendations based on class size, delivery mode, and student needs. Includes examples from fellow instructors.

GO! with Microsoft Office 2007 Introductory
Assignment Planning Guide

Planning the Course Assignments

For each chapter in GO!, an Assignment Sheet listing every in-chapter and end-of-chapter project is located on the IRCD. These sheets are Word tables, so you can delete rows for the projects that you will not assign, and then add rows for any of your own assignments that you may have developed. There is a column to add the number of points you want to assign to each project—depending on your grading scheme. At the top of the sheet, you can fill in your course information.

Additionally, for each chapter, student Assignment Tags are provided for every project (including Problem Solving projects)—also located on the IRCD. These are small scoring checklists on which you can check off errors made by the student, and with which the student can verify that all project elements are complete. For campus classes, the student can attach the tags to his or her paper submissions. For online classes, many GO! instructors have the student include these with the electronic submission.

Deciding What to Assign

Front Portion of the Chapter—Instructional Projects: The projects in the front portion of the chapter, which are listed on the first page of each chapter, are the instructional projects. Most instructors assign all of these projects, because this is where the student receives the instruction and engages in the active learning.

End-of-Chapter—Practice and Critical Thinking Projects: In the back portion of the chapter (the gray pages), you can assign on a prescriptive basis; that is, for students who were challenged by the instructional projects, you might assign one or more projects from the two *Skills Reviews*, which provide maximum prompting and a thorough review of the entire chapter. For students who have previous software knowledge and who completed the instructional projects easily, you might assign only the *Mastery Projects*.

You can also assign prescriptively by Objective, because each end-of-chapter project indicates the Objectives covered. So you might assign, on a student-by-student basis, only the projects that cover the Objectives with which the student seemed to have difficulty in the instructional projects.

The five Problem Solving projects and the You and GO! project are the authentic assessments that pull together the student's learning. Here the student is presented with a "messy real-life situation" and then uses his or her knowledge and skill to solve a problem, produce a product, give a presentation, or demonstrate a procedure. You might assign one or more of the Problem

GO! Assignment Planning Guide

Page 1 of 1

Student Data Files

Music School Records discovers, launches, and and develops the careers of young artists in classical, jazz, and contemporary music. Our philosophy is to not only shape, distribute, and sell a music product, but to help artists create a career that can lats a lifetime. too often in the music industry, artists are forced to fit their music to a trend that is short-lived. Music School Records doesn't just follow trends, we take a long-term view of the music industry and help our artists develop a style and repertiore that is fluid and flexible and that will appeal to audiences for years and even decades.

The music industry is constantly changing, but over the last decade the changes have been enormous. New forms of entertainment such as DVDs, video games, and the Internet mean there are more competition for the leisure dollar in the market. New technologies give consomers more options for buying and listening to music, and they are demanding high quality recordings. Young consomers are comfortable with technology and want the music they love when and where they want it, no matter where they are or what they are doing.

Music School Records embraces new technologies and the sophisticated market of young music lovers. We believe that providing high quality recordings of truly talented artists make for more discerning listeners who will cherish the gift of music for the rest of their lives. The expertise of Music School Records includes:

- Insight into our target market and the ability to reach the desired audience
- The ability to access all current sources of music income
- A management team with years of experience in music commerce
- Innovative business strategies and artist development plans
- Investment in technology infrastructure for high quality recordings and business services
- Initiative and proactive management of artist careers

Online Study Guide for Students

Interactive objective-style questions based on chapter content.

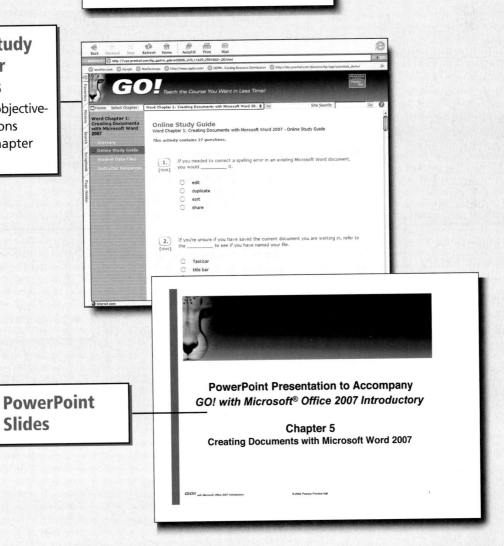

PowerPoint Slides

PowerPoint Presentation to Accompany
GO! with Microsoft® Office 2007 Introductory

Chapter 5
Creating Documents with Microsoft Word 2007

Teach

Student Textbook

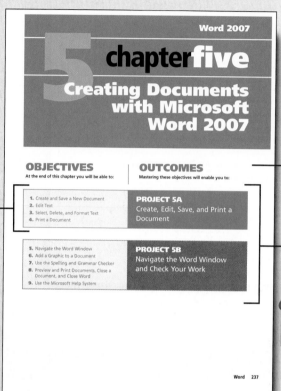

Word 2007

5 chapter five

Creating Documents with Microsoft Word 2007

OBJECTIVES
At the end of this chapter you will be able to:

1. Create and Save a New Document
2. Edit Text
3. Select, Delete, and Format Text
4. Print a Document

OUTCOMES
Mastering these objectives will enable you to:

PROJECT 5A
Create, Edit, Save, and Print a Document

5. Navigate the Word Window
6. Add a Graphic to a Document
7. Use the Spelling and Grammar Checker
8. Preview and Print Documents, Close a Document, and Close Word
9. Use the Microsoft Help System

PROJECT 5B
Navigate the Word Window and Check Your Work

Word 237

Learning Objectives and Student Outcomes

Objectives are clustered around projects that result in student outcomes. They help students learn how to solve problems, not just learn software features.

Project-Based Instruction

Students do not practice features of the application; they create real projects that they will need in the real world. Projects are color coded for easy reference and are named to reflect skills the students will be practicing.

NEW

A and B Projects

Each chapter contains two instructional projects—A and B.

Music School Records

Music School Records was created to launch young musical artists with undiscovered talent in jazz, classical, and contemporary music. The creative management team searches internationally for talented young people, and has a reputation for mentoring and developing the skills of its artists. The company's music is tailored to an audience that is young, knowledgeable about music, and demands the highest quality recordings. Music School Records releases are available in CD format as well as digital downloads.

Getting Started with Microsoft Office Word 2007

A word processor is the most common program found on personal computers and one that almost everyone has a reason to use. When you learn word processing you are also learning skills and techniques that you need to work efficiently on a personal computer. You can use Microsoft Word to perform basic word processing tasks such as writing a memo, a report, or a letter. You can also use Word to complete complex word processing tasks, such as those that include sophisticated tables, embedded graphics, and links to other documents and the Internet. Word is a program that you can learn gradually, and then add more advanced skills one at a time.

Each chapter opens with a story that sets the stage for the projects the student will create; the instruction does not force the student to pretend to be someone or make up a scenario.

Each chapter has an introductory paragraph that briefs students on what is important.

Teach (continued)

Visual Summary
Shows students upfront what their projects will look like when they are done.

Project Summary
Stated clearly and quickly in one paragraph.

NEW

File Guide
Clearly shows students which files are needed for the project and the names they will use to save their documents.

Objective
The skills the student will learn are clearly stated at the beginning of each project and color coded to match projects listed on the chapter opener page.

Teachable Moment
Expository text is woven into the steps—at the moment students need to know it—not chunked together in a block of text that will go unread.

NEW

Screen Shots
Larger screen shots.

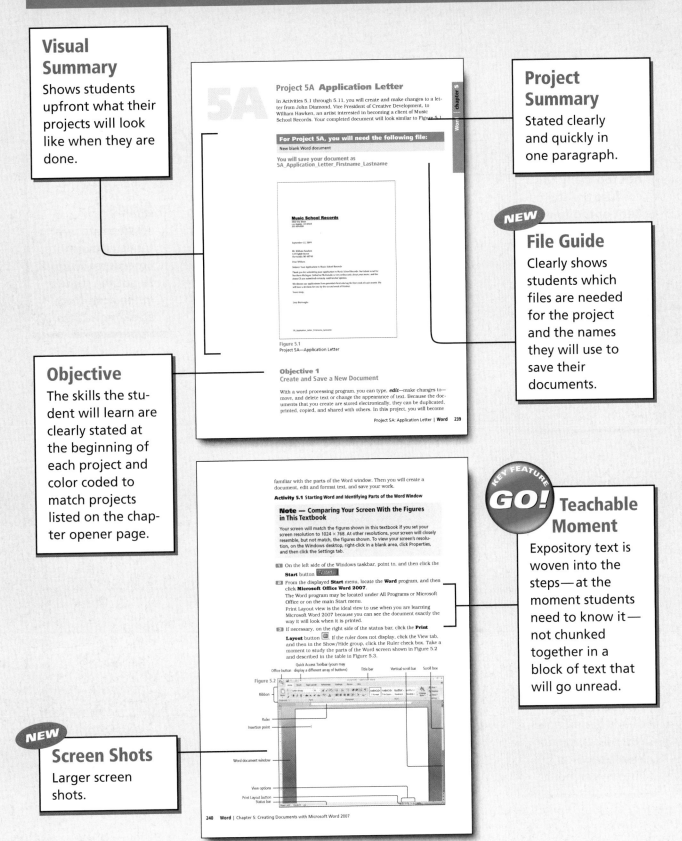

Steps

Color coded to the current project, easy to read, and not too many to confuse the student or too few to be meaningless.

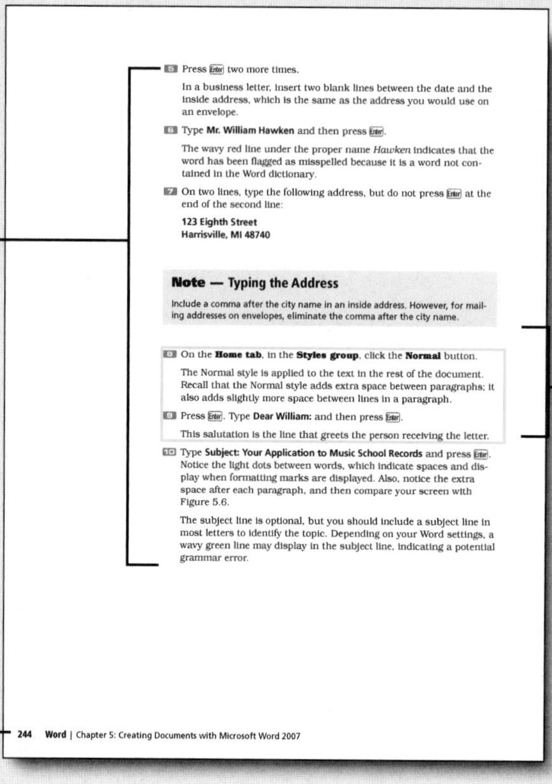

GO! KEY FEATURE
Sequential Pagination

No more confusing letters and abbreviations.

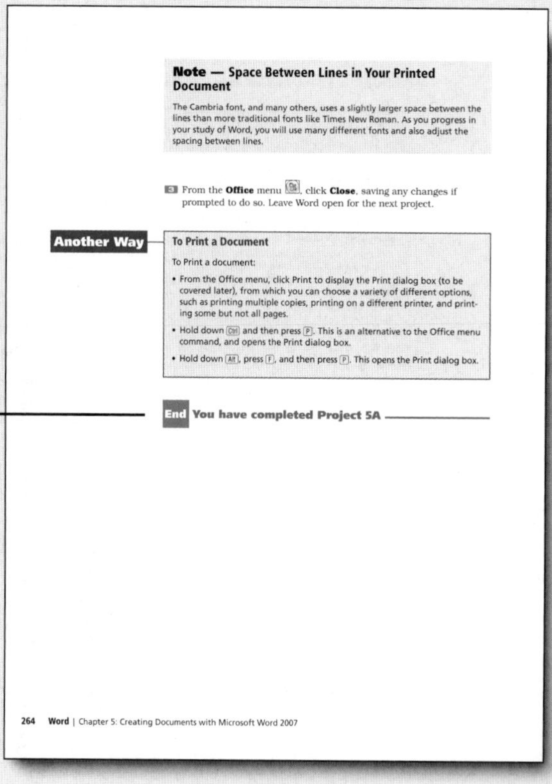

End-of-Project Icon

All projects in the *GO! Series* have clearly identifiable end points, useful in self-paced or on-line environments.

(Sample textbook page, page 244)

▸ Press Enter two more times.

In a business letter, insert two blank lines between the date and the inside address, which is the same as the address you would use on an envelope.

▸ Type **Mr. William Hawken** and then press Enter.

The wavy red line under the proper name *Hawken* indicates that the word has been flagged as misspelled because it is a word not contained in the Word dictionary.

▸ On two lines, type the following address, but do not press Enter at the end of the second line:

123 Eighth Street
Harrisville, MI 48740

Note — Typing the Address

Include a comma after the city name in an inside address. However, for mailing addresses on envelopes, eliminate the comma after the city name.

▸ On the **Home tab**, in the **Styles group**, click the **Normal** button.

The Normal style is applied to the text in the rest of the document. Recall that the Normal style adds extra space between paragraphs; it also adds slightly more space between lines in a paragraph.

▸ Press Enter. Type **Dear William:** and then press Enter.

This salutation is the line that greets the person receiving the letter.

▸ Type **Subject: Your Application to Music School Records** and press Enter. Notice the light dots between words, which indicate spaces and display when formatting marks are displayed. Also, notice the extra space after each paragraph, and then compare your screen with Figure 5.6.

The subject line is optional, but you should include a subject line in most letters to identify the topic. Depending on your Word settings, a wavy green line may display in the subject line, indicating a potential grammar error.

244   **Word** | Chapter 5: Creating Documents with Microsoft Word 2007

GO! KEY FEATURE
Microsoft Procedural Syntax

All steps are written in Microsoft Procedural Syntax to put the student in the right place at the right time.

(Sample textbook page, page 264)

Note — Space Between Lines in Your Printed Document

The Cambria font, and many others, uses a slightly larger space between the lines than more traditional fonts like Times New Roman. As you progress in your study of Word, you will use many different fonts and also adjust the spacing between lines.

▸ From the **Office** menu, click **Close**, saving any changes if prompted to do so. Leave Word open for the next project.

Another Way | **To Print a Document**

To Print a document:

- From the Office menu, click Print to display the Print dialog box (to be covered later), from which you can choose a variety of different options, such as printing multiple copies, printing on a different printer, and printing some but not all pages.
- Hold down Ctrl and then press P. This is an alternative to the Office menu command, and opens the Print dialog box.
- Hold down Alt, press F, and then press P. This opens the Print dialog box.

End You have completed Project 5A

264   **Word** | Chapter 5: Creating Documents with Microsoft Word 2007

Teach (continued)

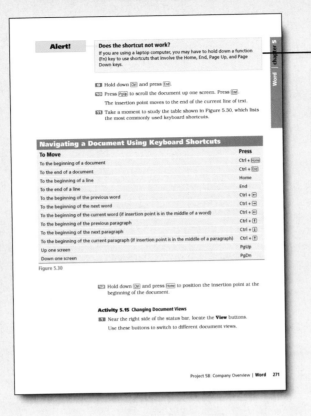

Alert! | **Does the shortcut not work?**
If you are using a laptop computer, you may have to hold down a function (Fn) key to use shortcuts that involve the Home, End, Page Up, and Page Down keys.

Hold down Ctrl and press End.

Press PgUp to scroll the document up one screen. Press End.
The insertion point moves to the end of the current line of text.

Take a moment to study the table shown in Figure 5.30, which lists the most commonly used keyboard shortcuts.

Navigating a Document Using Keyboard Shortcuts

To Move	Press
To the beginning of a document	Ctrl + Home
To the end of a document	Ctrl + End
To the beginning of a line	Home
To the end of a line	End
To the beginning of the previous word	Ctrl + ←
To the beginning of the next word	Ctrl + →
To the beginning of the current word (if insertion point is in the middle of a word)	Ctrl + ←
To the beginning of the previous paragraph	Ctrl + ↑
To the beginning of the next paragraph	Ctrl + ↓
To the beginning of the current paragraph (if insertion point is in the middle of a paragraph)	Ctrl + ↑
Up one screen	PgUp
Down one screen	PgDn

Figure 5.30

Hold down Ctrl and press Home to position the insertion point at the beginning of the document.

Activity 5.15 Changing Document Views

Near the right side of the status bar, locate the **View** buttons.
Use these buttons to switch to different document views.

Project 5B: Company Overview | **Word** 271

Alert box
Draws students' attention to make sure they aren't getting too far off course.

Another Way box
Shows students other ways of doing tasks.

More Knowledge box
Expands on a topic by going deeper into the material.

Note box
Points out important items to remember.

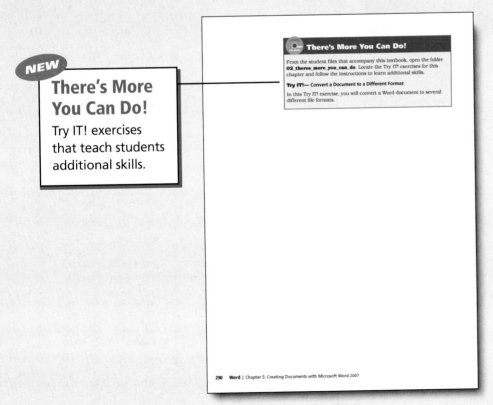

There's More You Can Do!

From the student files that accompany this textbook, open the folder **02_theres_more_you_can_do**. Locate the Try IT! exercises for this chapter and follow the instructions to learn additional skills.

Try IT!— Convert a Document to a Different Format

In this Try IT! exercise, you will convert a Word document to several different file formats.

NEW

There's More You Can Do!
Try IT! exercises that teach students additional skills.

290 **Word** | Chapter 5: Creating Documents with Microsoft Word 2007

End-of-Chapter Material

Take your pick! Content-based or Outcomes-based projects to choose from. Below is a table outlining the various types of projects that fit into these two categories.

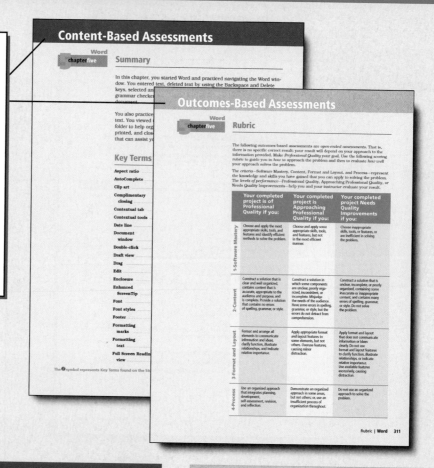

Content-Based Assessments

(Defined solutions with solution files provided for grading)

Project Letter	Name	Objectives Covered
N/A	Summary and Key Terms	
N/A	Multiple Choice	
N/A	Fill-in-the-blank	
C	Skills Review	Covers A Objectives
D	Skills Review	Covers B Objectives
E	Mastering Excel	Covers A Objectives
F	Mastering Excel	Covers B Objectives
G	Mastering Excel	Covers any combination of A and B Objectives
H	Mastering Excel	Covers any combination of A and B Objectives
I	Mastering Excel	Covers all A and B Objectives
J	Business Running Case	Covers all A and B Objectives

Outcomes-Based Assessments

(Open solutions that require a rubric for grading)

Project Letter	Name	Objectives Covered
N/A	Rubric	
K	Problem Solving	Covers as many Objectives from A and B as possible
L	Problem Solving	Covers as many Objectives from A and B as possible.
M	Problem Solving	Covers as many Objectives from A and B as possible.
N	Problem Solving	Covers as many Objectives from A and B as possible.
O	Problem Solving	Covers as many Objectives from A and B as possible.
P	You and GO!	Covers as many Objectives from A and B as possible
Q	GO! Help	Not tied to specific objectives
R	* Group Business Running Case	Covers A and B Objectives

* This project is provided only with the *GO! with Microsoft Office 2007 Introductory* book.

Objectives List

Most projects in the end-of-chapter section begin with a list of the objectives covered.

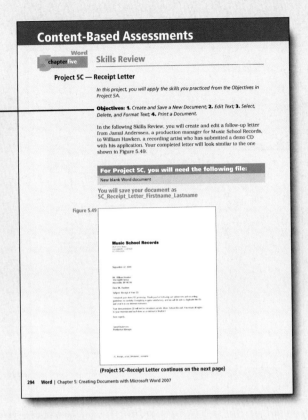

Content-Based Assessments

Word
chapter five   **Skills Review**

Project 5C — Receipt Letter

In this project, you will apply the skills you practiced from the Objectives in Project 5A.

Objectives: 1. *Create and Save a New Document;* **2.** *Edit Text;* **3.** *Select, Delete, and Format Text;* **4.** *Print a Document.*

In the following Skills Review, you will create and edit a follow-up letter from Jamal Anderssen, a production manager for Music School Records, to William Hawken, a recording artist who has submitted a demo CD with his application. Your completed letter will look similar to the one shown in Figure 5.49.

For Project 5C, you will need the following file:

New blank Word document

You will save your document as
5C_Receipt_Letter_Firstname_Lastname

Figure 5.49

Music School Records

September 27, 2009

Mr. William Hawken
332 Eighth Street
Marionville, IN 38790

Dear Mr. Hawken

Subject: Receipt of Your CD

(Project 5C–Receipt Letter continues on the next page)

294   **Word** | Chapter 5: Creating Documents with Microsoft Word 2007

Content-Based Assessments

Word
chapter five   **Skills Review**

(Project 5C–Receipt Letter continued)

14. Save the changes you have made to your document. Press Ctrl + A to select the entire document. On the **Home tab**, in the **Font group**, click the **Font button arrow**. Scroll as necessary, and watch Live Preview change the document font as you point to different font names. Click to choose **Tahoma**. Recall that you can type T in the Font box to move quickly to the fonts beginning with that letter. Click anywhere in the document to cancel the selection.

15. Select the entire first line of text—*Music School Records*. On the Mini toolbar, click the **Font button arrow**, and then click **Arial Black**. With the Mini toolbar still displayed, click the **Font Size button arrow**, and then click **20**. With the Mini toolbar still displayed, click the **Bold** button.

16. Select the second, third, and fourth lines of text, beginning with *2620 Vine Street* and ending with the telephone number. On the Mini toolbar, click the **Font button arrow**, and then click **Arial**. With the Mini toolbar still displayed, click the **Font Size button arrow**, and then click **10**. With the Mini toolbar still displayed, click the **Italic** button.

17. In the paragraph beginning *Your demonstration*, select the text *Music School Records*. On the Mini toolbar, click the **Italic** button, and then click anywhere to deselect the text.

18. Click the **Insert tab**. In the **Header & Footer group**, click the **Footer** button,

and then click **Edit Footer**. On the **Design tab**, in the **Insert group**, click the **Quick Parts** button, and then click **Field**. In the **Field** dialog box, under **Field names**, scroll down and click to choose **FileName**, and then click **OK**. Double-click anywhere in the document to leave the footer area.

19. Click the **Page Layout tab**. In the **Page Setup group**, click the **Margins** button to display the Margins gallery. At the bottom of the **Margins gallery**, click **Custom Margins** to display the **Page Setup** dialog box. Near the top of the **Page Setup** dialog box, click the **Layout tab**. Under **Page**, click the **Vertical alignment arrow**, click **Center**, and then click **OK**.

20. From the **Office** menu, point to the **Print arrow**, and then click **Print Preview** to make a final check of your letter. Follow your instructor's directions for submitting this file. Check your *Chapter Assignment Sheet* or *Course Syllabus* or consult your instructor to determine if you are to submit your assignments on paper or electronically. To submit electronically, go to Step 22, and then follow the instructions provided by your instructor.

21. On the **Print Preview tab**, in the **Print group**, click the **Print** button. Collect your printout from the printer and submit it as directed.

22. From the **Office** menu, click **Exit Word**, saving any changes if prompted to do so.

End You have completed Project 5C

296   **Word** | Chapter 5: Creating Documents with Microsoft Word 2007

End of Each Project Clearly Marked

Clearly identified end points help separate the end-of-chapter projects.

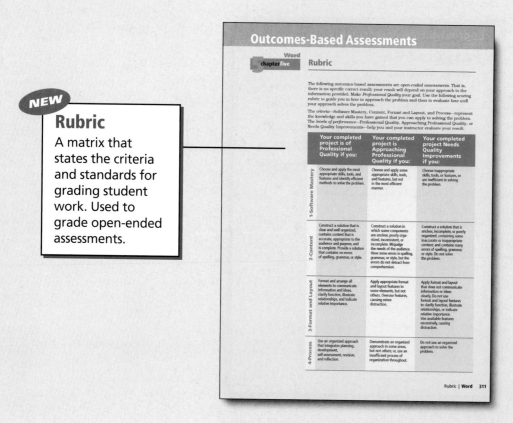

NEW

Rubric

A matrix that states the criteria and standards for grading student work. Used to grade open-ended assessments.

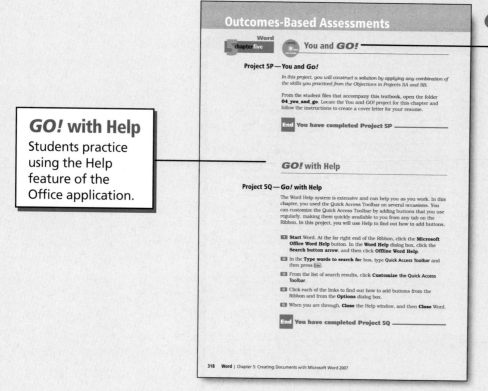

GO! with Help

Students practice using the Help feature of the Office application.

NEW

You and GO!

A project in which students use information from their own lives and apply the skills from the chapter to a personal task.

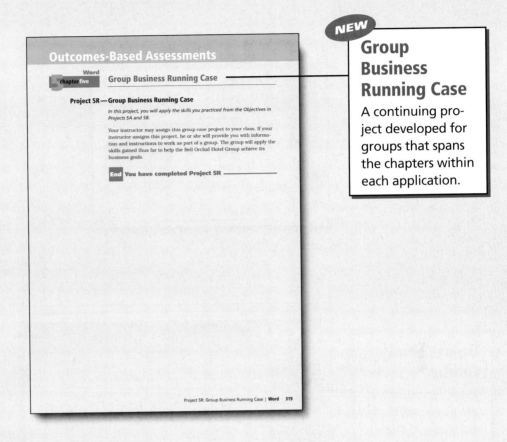

Outcomes-Based Assessments

Word
chapter five   Group Business Running Case

Project 5R — Group Business Running Case

In this project, you will apply the skills you practiced from the Objectives in Projects 5A and 5B.

Your instructor may assign this group case project to your class. If your instructor assigns this project, he or she will provide you with information and instructions to work as part of a group. The group will apply the skills gained thus far to help the Bell Orchid Hotel Group achieve its business goals.

End You have completed Project 5R

Project 5R: Group Business Running Case | **Word**   **319**

NEW
Group Business Running Case

A continuing project developed for groups that spans the chapters within each application.

Student CD includes:

- Student Data Files
- There's More You Can Do!
- Business Running Case
- You and *GO!*

Student Resource
CD-ROM

See readme file on this CD-ROM for usage instructions.

PEARSON
Prentice Hall

©2008 Pearson Prentice Hall
Upper Saddle River, NJ 07458

0-13-221718-X

Technical Support:
http://247.prenhall.com

diSC
COMPACT
DIGITAL DATA

GO!
with Microsoft®

Office 2007
Introductory

www.prenhall.com/go

Companion Web site

An interactive Web site to further student leaning.

Online Study Guide

Interactive objective-style questions to help students study.

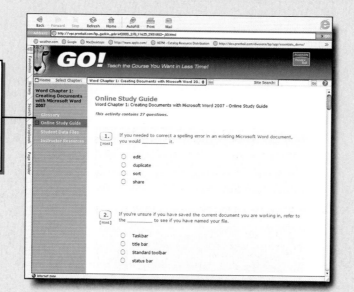

Annotated Instructor Edition

The Annotated Instructor Edition contains a full version of the student textbook that includes tips, supplement references, and pointers on teaching with the *GO!* instructional system.

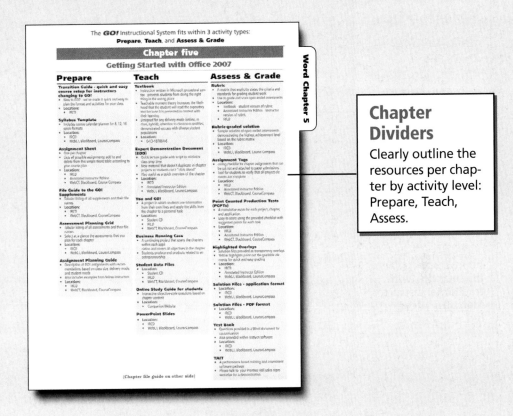

Chapter Dividers

Clearly outline the resources per chapter by activity level: Prepare, Teach, Assess.

Instructor File Guide

Complete list of all Student Data Files and instructor Solution Files needed for the chapter.

Helpful Hints, Teaching Tips, Expand the Project

References correspond to what is being taught in the student textbook.

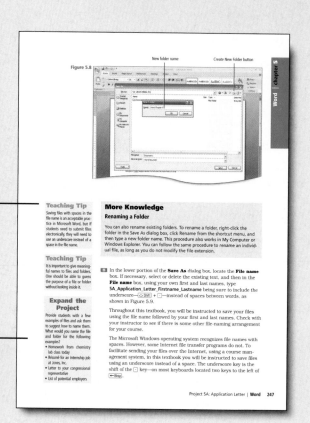

Teaching Tip

Saving files with spaces in the file name is an acceptable practice in Microsoft Word, but if students need to submit files electronically, they will need to use an underscore instead of a space in the file name.

Teaching Tip

It is important to give meaningful names to files and folders. One should be able to guess the purpose of a file or folder without looking inside it.

Expand the Project

Provide students with a few examples of files and ask them to suggest how to name them. What would you name the file and folder for the following examples?
- Homework from chemistry lab class today
- Résumé for an internship job at Jones, Inc.
- Letter to your congressional representative
- List of potential employers

More Knowledge
Renaming a Folder

You can also rename existing folders. To rename a folder, right-click the folder in the Save As dialog box, click Rename from the shortcut menu, and then type a new folder name. This procedure also works in My Computer or Windows Explorer. You can follow the same procedure to rename an individual file, as long as you do not modify the file extension.

8 In the lower portion of the **Save As** dialog box, locate the **File name** box. If necessary, select or delete the existing text, and then in the **File name** box, using your own first and last names, type **5A_Application_Letter_Firstname_Lastname** being sure to include the underscore—⇧ Shift + −—instead of spaces between words, as shown in Figure 5.9.

Throughout this textbook, you will be instructed to save your files using the file name followed by your first and last names. Check with your instructor to see if there is some other file-naming arrangement for your course.

The Microsoft Windows operating system recognizes file names with spaces. However, some Internet file transfer programs do not. To facilitate sending your files over the Internet, using a course management system, in this textbook you will be instructed to save files using an underscore instead of a space. The underscore key is the shift of the − key—on most keyboards located two keys to the left of ← Bksp.

Project 5A: Application Letter | **Word** 247

NEW

Full-Size Textbook Pages

An instructor copy of the textbook with traditional Instructor Manual content incorporated.

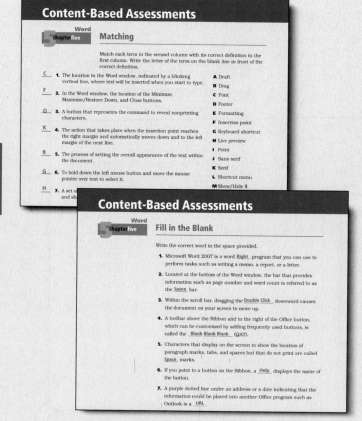

Content-Based Assessments

Word
chapter **five**   Matching

Match each term in the second column with its correct definition in the first column. Write the letter of the term on the blank line in front of the correct definition.

C 1. The location in the Word window, indicated by a blinking vertical line, where text will be inserted when you start to type.

F 2. In the Word window, the location of the Minimize, Maximize/Restore Down, and Close buttons.

Q 3. A button that represents the command to reveal nonprinting characters.

K 4. The action that takes place when the insertion point reaches the right margin and automatically moves down and to the left margin of the next line.

B 5. The process of setting the overall appearance of the text within the document.

G 6. To hold down the left mouse button and move the mouse pointer over text to select it.

H 7. A set of... and sh...

A Draft
B Drag
C Font
D Footer
E Formatting
F Insertion point
G Keyboard shortcut
H Live preview
I Point
J Sans serif
K Serif
L Shortcut menu
M Show/Hide ¶

Content-Based Assessments

Word
chapter **five**   Fill in the Blank

Write the correct word in the space provided.

1. Microsoft Word 2007 is a word _Right_ program that you can use to perform tasks such as writing a memo, a report, or a letter.

2. Located at the bottom of the Word window, the bar that provides information such as page number and word count is referred to as the _Space_ bar.

3. Within the scroll bar, dragging the _Double Click_ downward causes the document on your screen to move up.

4. A toolbar above the Ribbon and to the right of the Office button, which can be customized by adding frequently used buttons, is called the _Blank Blank Blank_ (QAT).

5. Characters that display on the screen to show the location of paragraph marks, tabs, and spaces but that do not print are called _Space_ marks.

6. If you point to a button on the Ribbon, a _Help_ displays the name of the button.

7. A purple dotted line under an address or a date indicating that the information could be placed into another Office program such as Outlook is a _URL_

End-of-Chapter Concepts Assessments contain the answers for quick reference.

NEW

Rubric

A matrix to guide the student on how they will be assessed is reprinted in the Annotated Instructor Edition with suggested weights for each of the criteria and levels of performance. Instructors can modify the weights to suit their needs.

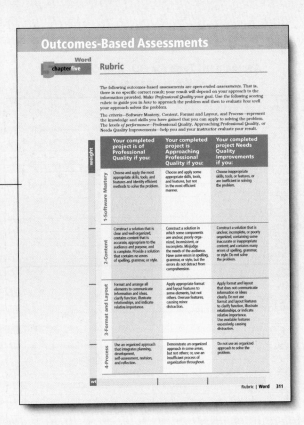

Assess

Assignment Tags

Scoring checklist for assignments. Now also available for Problem-Solving projects.

NEW

Highlighted Overlays

Solution files provided as transparency overlays. Yellow highlights point out the gradable elements for quick and easy grading.

GO! with Microsoft® Office 2007

Assignment Tags for GO! with Office 2007
Word Chapter 5

Name: Professor:	Project: Course:	5A		Name: Professor:	Project: Course:	5B

Task	Points	Your Score		Task	Points	Your Score
Center text vertically on page	2			Insert the file w05B_Music_School_Records	4	
Delete the word "really"	1			Insert the Music Logo	4	
Delete the words "try to"	1			Remove duplicate "and"	2	
Replace "last" with "first"	1			Change spelling and grammar errors (4)	8	
Insert the word "potential"	1			Correct/Add footer as instructed	2	
Replace "John W. Diamond" with "Lucy Burrows"	2			Circled information is incorrect or formatted incorrectly		
Change entire document to the Cambria font	2					
Change the first line of text to Arial Black 20 pt. font	2					
Bold the first line of text	2					
Change the 2nd through 4th lines to Arial 10 pt.	2					
Italicize the 2nd through 4th lines of text	2					
Correct/Add footer as instructed	2					
Circled information is incorrect or formatted incorrectly						
Total Points	**20**	**0**		**Total Points**	**20**	**0**

Name: Professor:	Project: Course:	5C		Name: Professor:	Project: Course:	5D

Task	Points	Your Score		Task	Points	Your Score
Add four line letterhead	2			Insert the file w05D_Marketing	4	
Insert today's date	1			Bold the first two title lines	2	
Add address block, subject line, and greeting	2			Correct spelling of "Marketting"	2	
Add two-paragraph body of letter	2			Correct spelling of "geners"	2	
Add closing, name, and title	2			Correct all misspellings of "allready"	2	
In subject line, capitalize "receipt"	1			Correct grammar error "are" to "is"	2	
Change "standards" to "guidelines"	1			Insert the Piano image	4	
Insert "quite"	1			Correct/add footer as instructed	2	
Insert "all"	1			Circled information is incorrect or formatted incorrectly		
Change the first line of text to Arial Black 20 pt. font	2					
Bold the first line of text	1					
Change the 2nd through 4th lines to Arial 10 pt.	1					
Italicize the 2nd through 4th lines of text	1					
Correct/add footer as instructed	2					
Circled information is incorrect or formatted incorrectly						
Total Points	**20**	**0**		**Total Points**	**20**	**0**

Music School Records

2620 Vine Street
Los Angeles, CA 90028
323-555-0028

[20 point Arial Black, bold and underline]

[10 point Arial, italic]

September 12, 2009

Mr. William Hawken
123 Eighth Street
Harrisville, MI 48740

[Text vertically centered on page]

[Body of document changed to Cambria font, 11 point]

Dear William:

Subject: Your Application to Music School Records

Thank you for submitting your application to Music School Records. Our talent scout for Northern Michigan, Catherine McDonald, is very enthusiastic about your music, and the demo CD you submitted certainly confirms her opinion.

[Word "really" deleted]

We discuss our applications from potential clients during the first week of each month. We will have a decision for you by the second week of October.

Yours Truly,

[Words "try to" deleted]

Lucy Burroughs

Point-Counted Production Tests (PCPTs)

A cumulative exam for each **project**, **chapter**, and **application**. Easy to score using the provided checklist with suggested points for each task.

GO! with Microsoft® Office 2007 Introductory

Point-Counted Production Test—Project
for GO! with Microsoft® Office 2007 Introductory
Project 5A

Instructor Name: _____

Course Information: _____

1. Start Word 2007 to begin a new blank document. Save your document as 5A_Cover_Letter_Firstname_Lastname Remember to save your file frequently as you work.

2. If necessary, display the formatting marks. With the insertion point blinking in the upper left corner of the document to the left of the default first paragraph mark, type the current date (you can use AutoComplete).

3. Press Enter three times and type the inside address:

    Music School Records

    2620 Vine Street

    Los Angeles, CA 90028

4. Press Enter three times, and type Dear Ms. Burroughs:

    Press Enter twice, and type Subject: Application to Music School Records

    Press Enter twice, and type the following text (skipping one line between paragraphs):

    I read about Music School Records in Con Brio magazine and I would like to inquire about the possibility of being represented by your company.

    I am very interested in a career in jazz and am planning to relocate to the Los Angeles area in the very near future. I would be interested in learning more about the company and about available opportunities.

    I was a member of my high school jazz band for three years. In addition, I have been playing in the local coffee shop for the last two years. My demo CD, which is enclosed, contains three of my most requested songs.

    I would appreciate the opportunity to speak with you. Thank you for your time and consideration. I look forward to speaking with you about this exciting opportunity.

5. Press Enter three times, and type the closing Sincerely, Press enter four times, and type your name.

6. Insert a footer that contains the file name.

7. Delete the first instance of the word *very* in the second body paragraph, and insert the word modern in front of *jazz*.

Copyright © 2008 Pearson Prentice Hall

Page 1 of 1

Test Bank

Available as TestGen Software or as a Word document for customization.

Chapter 5: Creating Documents with Microsoft Word 2007

Multiple Choice:

1. With word processing programs, how are documents stored?

    A. On a network

    B. On the computer

    C. Electronically

    D. On the floppy disk

    Answer: C **Reference:** Objective 1: Create and Save a New Document **Difficulty:** Moderate

2. Because you will see the document as it will print, _____ view is the ideal view to use when learning Microsoft Word 2007.

    A. Reading

    B. Normal

    C. Print Layout

    D. Outline

    Answer: C **Reference:** Objective 1: Create and Save a New Document **Difficulty:** Moderate

3. The blinking vertical line where text or graphics will be inserted is called the:

    A. cursor.

    B. insertion point.

    C. blinking line.

    D. I-beam.

    Answer: B **Reference:** Objective 1: Create and Save a New Document **Difficulty:** Easy

Solution Files–Application and PDF format

♫ Music School Records

Music School Records discovers, launches, and develops the careers of young artists in classical, jazz, and contemporary music. Our philosophy is to not only shape, distribute, and sell a music product, but to help artists create a career that can last a lifetime. Too often in the music industry, artists are forced to fit their music to a trend that is short-lived. Music School Records does not just follow trends, we take a long-term view of the music industry and help our artists develop a style and repertoire that is fluid and flexible and that will appeal to audiences for years and even decades.

The music industry is constantly changing, but over the last decade, the changes have been enormous. New forms of entertainment such as DVDs, video games, and the Internet mean there is more competition for the leisure dollar in the market. New technologies give consumers more options for buying and listening to music, and they are demanding high quality recordings. Young consumers are comfortable with technology and want the music they love when and where they want it, no matter where they are or what they are doing.

Music School Records embraces new technologies and the sophisticated market of young music lovers. We believe that providing high quality recordings of truly talented artists make for more discerning listeners who will cherish the gift of music for the rest of their lives. The expertise of Music School Records includes:

- Insight into our target market and the ability to reach the desired audience
- The ability to access all current sources of music income
- A management team with years of experience in music commerce
- Innovative business strategies and artist development plans
- Investment in technology infrastructure for high quality recordings and business services

pagexxxix_top.docx

Online Assessment and Training

my**it**lab is Prentice Hall's new performance-based solution that allows you to easily deliver outcomes-based courses on Microsoft Office 2007, with customized training and defensible assessment. Key features of my**it**lab include:

A *true* "system" approach: my**it**lab content is the same as in your textbook.

Project-based *and* skills-based: Students complete real-life assignments.

Advanced reporting *and* gradebook: These include student click stream data.

***No* installation required:** my**it**lab is completely Web-based. You just need an Internet connection, small plug-in, and Adobe Flash Player.

Ask your Prentice Hall sales representative for a demonstration or visit:

www.prenhall.com/myitlab

1 chapterone

Getting Started with Access Databases and Tables

OBJECTIVES

At the end of this chapter you will be able to:

OUTCOMES

Mastering these objectives will enable you to:

1. Start Access and Create a New Blank Database

2. Add Records to a Table

3. Rename Table Fields in Datasheet View

4. Modify the Design of a Table

5. Add a Second Table to a Database

6. Print a Table

7. Create and Use a Query

8. Create and Use a Form

9. Create and Print a Report

10. Close and Save a Database

PROJECT 1A
Create a New Blank Database

11. Create a Database Using a Template

12. Organize Database Objects in the Navigation Pane

13. Create a New Table in a Database Created with a Template

14. View a Report and Print a Table in a Database Created with a Template

15. Use the Access Help System

PROJECT 1B
Create a Database from a Template

Texas Lakes Medical Center

Texas Lakes Medical Center is an urban hospital serving the city of Austin and surrounding Travis County, an area with a population of over 1 million people. Texas Lakes is renowned for its cardiac care unit, which is rated among the top 10 in Texas. The hospital also offers state-of-the-art maternity and diagnostic services, a children's center, a Level II trauma center, and a number of specialized outpatient services. Physicians, nurses, scientists, and researchers from around the world come together at Texas Lakes to provide the highest quality patient care.

Getting Started with Access Databases and Tables

Do you have a collection of belongings that you like, such as a coin or stamp collection, a box of favorite recipes, or a stack of music CDs? Do you have an address book with the names, addresses, and phone numbers of your friends, business associates, and family members? If you collect something, chances are you have made an attempt to keep track of and organize the items in your collection. If you have an address book, you have probably wished it was better organized. A program like Microsoft Office Access can help you organize and keep track of information.

Microsoft Office Access 2007 is a program to organize a collection of related information about a particular topic, such as an inventory list, a list of people in an organization, or the students who are enrolled in classes in a college. Whether you use Access for personal or business purposes, it is a powerful program that helps you organize, search, sort, retrieve, and present information about a particular subject in an organized manner.

Project 1A Doctor and Patient Contact Information

In Activities 1.1 through 1.14, you will assist June Liu, Chief Administrative Officer at Texas Lakes Medical Center, in creating a new database for tracking the contact information for doctors and patients. June has a list of doctors and their contact information and a list of patients and their contact information. Using June's lists, you will create an Access database to track this information and use it to prepare a report. Your results will look similar to Figure 1.1.

For Project 1A, you will need the following file:

New blank Access database

You will save your database as
1A_Contact_Information_Firstname_Lastname

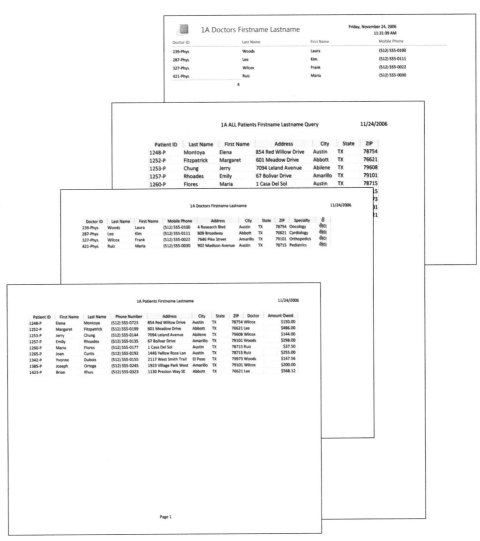

Figure 1.1
Project 1A—Contact Information

Objective 1
Start Access and Create a New Blank Database

A *database* collects and organizes *data*—facts about people, events, things, or ideas—related to a particular topic or purpose. Data that has been organized in a useful manner is referred to as *information*.

Many databases start as a simple list on paper, in a Word document, or in an Excel spreadsheet. As the list grows bigger and the data becomes more difficult to keep track of, it is a good idea to transfer the data to a database management system (*DBMS*) such as Access.

Examples of data that could be in a database include the titles and artists of all the CDs in a collection or the names and addresses of all the doctors and patients at a medical facility. A database includes not only the data, but also the tools for organizing the data in a way that is useful to you.

The first step in creating a new database from data that you already have is to plan your database on paper. Determine what information you want to track, and then ask yourself, *What questions should this database be able to answer for me?*

For example, in the Contact Information database for the Texas Lakes Medical Center, the questions to be answered may include:

- How many doctors and patients are there at the Texas Lakes Medical Center?

- Which and how many patients live in Austin?

- Is any doctor or patient listed twice?

- Which and how many patients have a balance owed?

Activity 1.1 Starting Access, Creating and Naming a Folder, and Creating a Database from a New Blank Database

There are two methods to create a new Access database: create a new database using a *template*—a preformatted database designed for a specific purpose—or create a new *blank database*. A blank database has no data and has no database tools; you create the data and the tools as you need them. In this activity, you will create a new blank database.

Regardless of which method you use, you must name and save the database before you can create any *objects* in the database. Objects are the basic parts of a database; you will create objects to store your data and work with your data. Think of an Access database as a container for the database objects that you will create.

1 On the left side of the Windows taskbar, click the **Start** button

start , determine where the **Access** program is located, point to **Microsoft Office Access 2007**, and then click one time to open the program. Take a moment to compare your screen with Figure 1.2 and study the parts of the Microsoft Access window described in the table in Figure 1.3.

From this Access starting point, you can open an existing database, start a new blank database, or begin a new database from one of the available database templates.

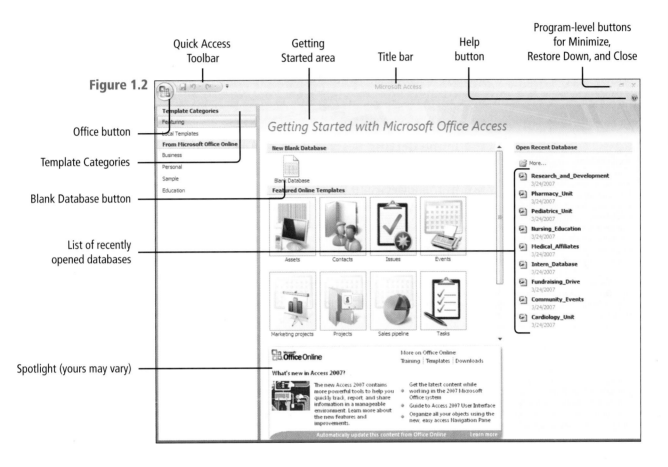

Figure 1.2

The Access Getting Started Screen

Window Part	Description
Blank Database button	Starts a new blank database.
Getting Started area	Contains the starting point to begin a New Blank Database or view new information from Microsoft Office Online.
Help button	Displays the Access Help window.
Open Recent Database	Displays a list of the most recently opened databases on the computer at which you are working.
Office button	Displays a menu of commands related to things you can do *with* a database, such as opening, saving, printing, or managing.
Program-level buttons for Minimize, Restore Down, and Close	Minimizes, restores, or closes the Access program.

(Continued)

(Continued)

Window Part	Description
Quick Access Toolbar	Displays buttons to perform frequently used commands with a single click. Frequently used commands in Access include Save, Undo, and Redo. You can add commands that you use frequently to the Quick Access Toolbar.
Spotlight	Displays the latest online content, such as new templates, articles about Access, and tips from Microsoft's Web site.
Template Categories	Displays a list of available database templates.
Title bar	Displays the program name and the program-level buttons.

Figure 1.3

2 In the **Getting Started with Microsoft Office Access** area, under **New Blank Database**, click **Blank Database**.

3 In the lower right portion of the screen, to the right of the **File Name** box, point to the **open file folder icon** to display the words *Browse for a location to put your database*, and then click the file folder icon.

4 In the displayed **File New Database *dialog box*—**a window containing commands or that asks you to make a decision—click the **Save in arrow**. From the displayed list, navigate to the drive where you are storing your projects for this chapter, for example, *Removable Disk (J:) drive.* Be sure the drive name and letter display in the **Save in** box, and then compare your screen with Figure 1.4.

File New Database dialog box   Create New Folder button

Figure 1.4

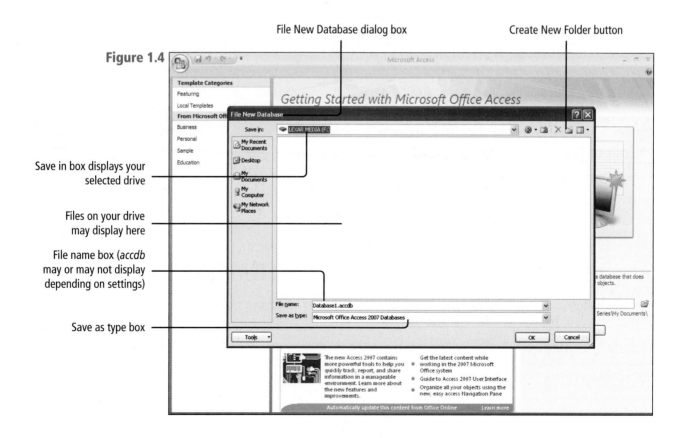

Save in box displays your selected drive

Files on your drive may display here

File name box (*accdb* may or may not display depending on settings)

Save as type box

5 In the upper right corner of the **File New Database** dialog box, click the **Create New Folder** button ▣. In the displayed **New Folder** dialog box, type **Access Chapter 1** and then click **OK**. At the bottom of the dialog box, in the **File name** box, select the existing text, and then type **1A_Contact_Information_Firstname_Lastname** Press Enter, and then compare your screen with Figure 1.5.

Text that you select is replaced by new text that you type. The Microsoft Windows operating system recognizes file names with spaces. However, some Internet file transfer programs do not. To facilitate sending your files over the Internet, in this textbook you will save files using an underscore rather than a space. On most keyboards, the underscore key is the shift of the hyphen key, which is to the right of the zero key.

Figure 1.5

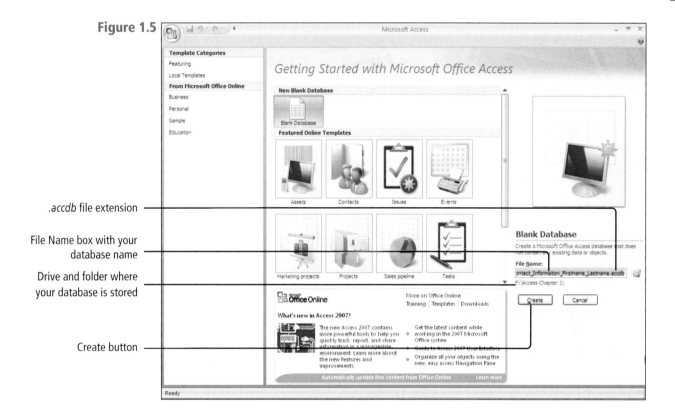

.accdb file extension

File Name box with your database name

Drive and folder where your database is stored

Create button

6 In the lower right corner, click the **Create** button, compare your screen with Figure 1.6, and then take a moment to study the screen elements described in the table in Figure 1.7.

Access creates the new database and opens a *table* named *Table1*. A table is the Access object that stores your data organized in an arrangement of columns and rows. Recall that *object* is the term used to refer to the parts of an Access database that you will use to store and work with your data.

Table objects are the foundation of your Access database because tables store the actual data.

Note — Comparing Your Screen with the Figures in This Textbook

Your screen will match the figures shown in this textbook if you set your screen resolution to 1024 × 768. At other resolutions, your screen will closely resemble, but not match, the figures shown. To view your screen's resolution, on the Windows desktop, right-click in a blank area, click Properties, and then click the Settings tab.

Figure 1.6

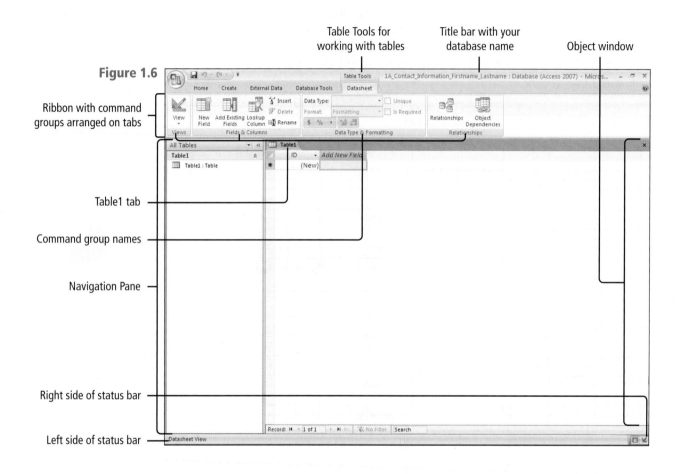

Table Tools for working with tables

Title bar with your database name

Object window

Ribbon with command groups arranged on tabs

Table1 tab

Command group names

Navigation Pane

Right side of status bar

Left side of status bar

Parts of the Access Window

Window Part	Description
Command group names	Contains groups of related command buttons associated with the selected command tab.
Left side of status bar	Indicates the active view and the status of actions occurring within the database.
Navigation Pane	Displays the database objects; from here you open the database objects to display in the object window at the right.
Object window	Displays the open table object.
Ribbon with command groups arranged on tabs	Groups the commands for performing related database tasks on tabs.
Right side of status bar	Provides buttons to switch between Datasheet View and Design View.
Table Tools for working with tables	Provides tools for working with a table object; Table Tools display only when a table is displayed.
Table1 tab	Enables you to select the table object.
Title bar with your database name	Displays the name of your database.

Figure 1.7

7 Leave your database open for the next activity.

Objective 2
Add Records to a Table

After you have saved and named the database, the next step is to plan and create the tables in which to record your data. Recall that tables are the foundation of your database because the actual data is stored there.

Limit the data in each table to one subject. For example, think of all the data at your college; there is likely one table for student information, another table for course information, another table for classroom information, and so on.

Within each table, create columns that are broken down into the smallest usable part. For example, instead of a complete address, break the address down into a part for the street address, a part for the city, a part for the state, and a part for the postal code. With small usable parts, you can, for example, find all of the people who live in a particular city or state or postal code.

To answer all the questions you want your database to answer, in this project you will create a database with two tables. One table will list the names and contact information for patients at Texas Lakes Medical Center and the other table will list the names and contact information for doctors at Texas Lakes Medical Center.

Activity 1.2 Adding Records to a Table

In a table object, each column contains a category of data called a **field**. Fields are categories that describe each piece of data stored in the table. You can add the field names, which display at the top of each column of the table, before or while you are entering your data. Each row in a table contains a **record**—all of the categories of data pertaining to one person, place, thing, event, or idea. Your **table design** refers to the number of fields, the names of fields, and the type of content within a field, for example numbers or text.

There are two ways to view a table—in **Datasheet view** or in **Design view**. Datasheet view displays the table data organized in a format of columns and rows similar to an Excel spreadsheet. Design view displays the underlying structure of the table object.

When you buy a new address book, it is not very useful until you fill it with names, addresses, and phone numbers. Likewise, a new database is not useful until you **populate**, or fill, a table with data. You can populate a table with records by typing data directly into the table.

In this activity, you will populate a table in Datasheet view that will list contact information for patients at Texas Lakes Medical Center.

1 Look at your screen and notice that the Datasheet view for a table displays. Then, take a moment to study the elements of the table object window as shown in Figure 1.8.

When you create a new blank database, only one object—a new blank table—is created. You will create the remaining database objects as you need them.

Because you have not yet named this table, the Table tab indicates the default name *Table1*. Access creates the first field and names it *ID*. In the ID field, Access will assign a unique sequential number— each number incremented by one—to each record as you type it into the table.

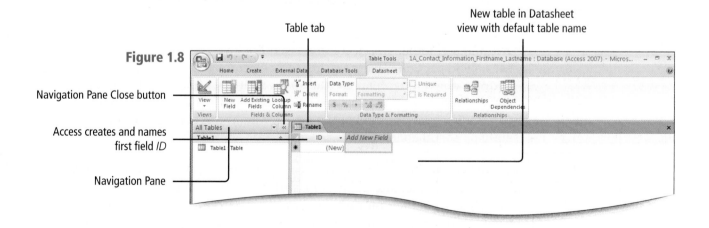

Figure 1.8

New table in Datasheet view with default table name

Table tab

Navigation Pane Close button

Access creates and names first field *ID*

Navigation Pane

2 In the **Navigation Pane**, click the **Open/Close** button ⎡«⎤ to collapse the **Navigation Pane** into a narrow bar at the left side of your screen.

Collapsing the Navigation Pane in this manner gives you more screen space in which to work with your database.

3 In the second column, click in the *cell*—the box formed by the intersection of a row and a column—under *Add New Field*, type **Elena** and then press ⎡Tab⎤ or ⎡Enter⎤. Click in the **ID** field. On the **Datasheet tab**, in the **Data Type & Formatting group**, click the **Data Type arrow**, and then click **Text**. Type **1248-P** and then to the right of *Elena*, click in the **Add New Field** cell, and type **L** Press ⎡Tab⎤. Compare your screen with Figure 1.9.

As soon as information is entered, Access assigns the name *Field1* to the field and enters an AutoNumber of 1 in the ID field. The ID field is automatically created by Access. By default, Access creates this field for all new tables and sets the data type for the field to *AutoNumber*, which sequentially numbers each entry. Changing the ID field data type from *AutoNumber* to *Text* lets you enter a custom patient number. As you enter data, Access assigns Field names as *Field1*, *Field2*, and so on; you can rename the fields when it is convenient for you to do so.

The pencil icon in the *record selector box*—the small box at the left of a record in Datasheet view which, when clicked, selects the entire record—indicates that a new record is being entered.

Field named *Field1*

Figure 1.9

Pencil icon indicates a new record is being entered

Record selector box

First patient ID is *1248-P*

First name of first patient entered

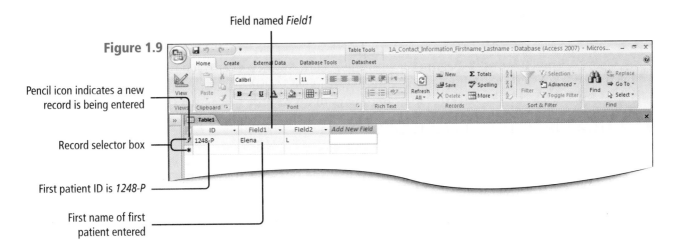

4 With the insertion point positioned in the fourth column, in the cell under *Add New Field*, type **Montoya** and then press ⎡Tab⎤ or ⎡Enter⎤.

5 Type **(512) 555-0723** and then press ⎡Enter⎤. Type **854 Red Willow Drive** and then press ⎡Enter⎤ to form *Field5*.

Do not be concerned if the data does not completely display in the column. As you progress in your study of Access, you will adjust the column widths so that you can view the data.

6 Type **Austin** and then press ⎡Enter⎤ to form *Field6*. Type **TX** and then press ⎡Enter⎤ to form *Field7*.

7 Type **78754** and then press ⏎ to form *Field8*. Type **Wilcox** and then press ⏎ to form *Field9*. Type **150** and then press ⏎ two times. Compare your screen with Figure 1.10.

To move across the row, you can press Tab or ⏎. Pressing ⏎ two times moves the insertion point to the next row to begin a new record. As soon as you move to the next row, the record is saved— you do not have to take any specific action to save the record.

First record entered

Figure 1.10

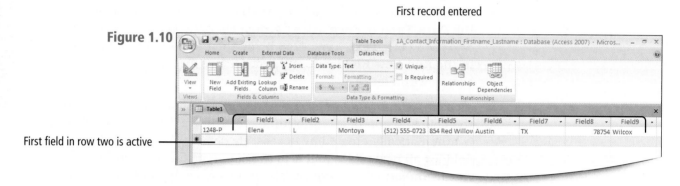

First field in row two is active

Note — Correct Typing Errors by Using Techniques Similar to Documents and Worksheets

If you make a mistake while entering data, you can correct the error by using ←Bksp to remove characters to the left, Delete to remove characters to the right, or select the text you want to replace and type the correct information. You can also press Esc to exit out of a new record.

8 Beginning with the record for *Margaret E Fitzpatrick*, and using the technique you just practiced, enter the contact information for three additional patients, pressing ⏎ as necessary after entering the information in *Field10*. Then compare your screen with Figure 1.11.

ID	Field1	Field2	Field3	Field4	Field5	Field6	Field7	Field8	Field9	Field10
1248-P	Elena	L	Montoya	(512) 555-0723	854 Red Willow Drive	Austin	TX	78754	Wilcox	150
1252-P	Margaret	E	Fitzpatrick	(512) 555-0199	601 Meadow Drive	Abbott	TX	76621	Lee	486
1253-P	Jerry	R	Chung	(512) 555-0144	7094 Leland Avenue	Abilene	TX	79608	Wilcox	144
1257-P	Emily	A	Rhoades	(512) 555-0135	67 Bolivar Drive	Amarillo	TX	79101	Woods	298

Field 10 out of view (your screen may
vary in how many columns are shown)

Figure 1.11

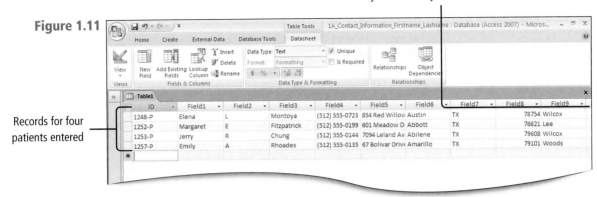

Records for four
patients entered

More Knowledge

Format for Typing Telephone Numbers in Access

Access does not require any specific format for entering telephone numbers
in a database. The examples in this project use the format used in Microsoft
Outlook. Using such a format facilitates easy transfer of Outlook information
to and from Access.

Objective 3
Rename Table Fields in Datasheet View

Recall that each column in a table contains a category of data called a
field, and that field names display at the top of each column of the table.
Recall also that each row contains a *record*—all of the data pertaining to
one person, place, thing, event, or idea—and that each record is broken
up into small parts—the *fields*.

Activity 1.3 Renaming the Fields In a Table in Datasheet View

In this activity, you will rename fields in your table to give the fields more
meaningful names.

1 At the top of the second column, point to the text *Field1* to display

the ⬇ pointer and click. Compare your screen with Figure 1.12.

Figure 1.12

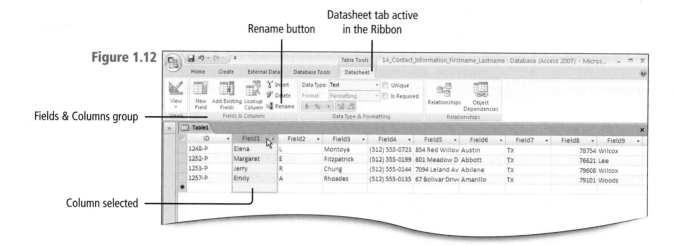

Fields & Columns group

Column selected

2 On the Ribbon, notice that **Table Tools** display above the **Datasheet tab**. In the **Fields & Columns group**, click the **Rename** button, and notice that the text *Field1* is selected.

3 Type **First Name** as the field name, and then press Enter. Point to the text *Field2*, click to select the column, and then in the **Fields & Columns group**, click the **Rename** button. Type **Middle Initial** and then press Enter.

4 Point to the text *Field3* and *double-click* to select the text. With the text selected, type **Last Name** and then press Enter. Point to the text *Field4* and right-click. From the displayed shortcut menu, click **Rename Column**, and then type **Phone Number** and press Enter.

5 Using any of the techniques you just practiced, rename the remaining fields as follows, and then compare your screen with Figure 1.13.

Field5	**Address**
Field6	**City**
Field7	**State/Province**
Field8	**ZIP/Postal Code**
Field9	**Doctor**
Field10	**Amount Owed**

Fields renamed

Figure 1.13

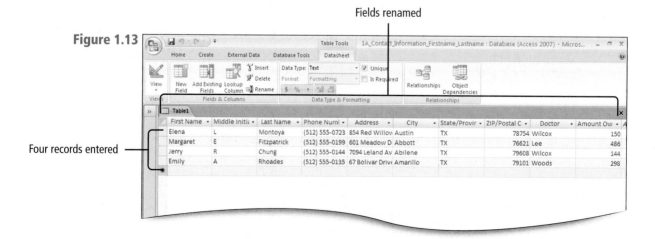

Four records entered

Activity 1.4 Changing the Data Type of a Field in Datasheet View

Data type is the characteristic that defines the kind of data that can be entered into a field, such as numbers, text, or dates. A field in a table can have only one data type. Based on the data you type into a field, Access assigns a data type, but you can change the data type if another type more accurately describes your data. In this activity, you will change the data type of fields.

1 In any of the four records that you have entered, click in the **ID field**. On the Ribbon, on the **Datasheet tab**, in the **Data Type & Formatting group**, notice that in the **Data Type** box, *Text* displays. Compare your screen with Figure 1.14.

Recall that the ID field has been changed from *AutoNumber*, which sequentially numbers each entry to *Text* so that a custom ID number for patients can be assigned.

Text indicated as Data Type

Datasheet tab is active

Figure 1.14

Data Type box

ID field

Data Type & Formatting group

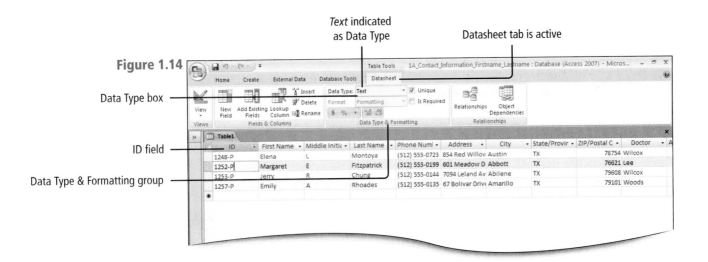

2 In any record, click in the **Last Name** field, and then on the **Datasheet tab**, notice that the **Data Type** indicates *Text*. Click the **Data Type arrow** to display a list of data types as shown in Figure 1.15 and take a moment to study the table in Figure 1.16 that describes the different data types.

Data Type arrow

Figure 1.15

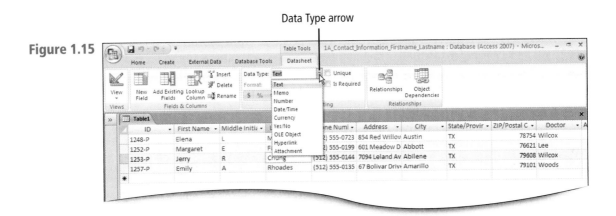

Data Type	Description	Example
AutoNumber	Available in Design view. A unique sequential or random number assigned by Access as each record is entered and that cannot be updated.	An inventory item number, such as 1, 2, 3 or a randomly assigned employee number, such as 3852788.
Text	Text or combinations of text and numbers; also numbers that are not used in calculations. Limited to 255 characters or length set on field, whichever is less. Access does not reserve space for unused portions of the text field. This is the default data type.	An inventory item such as a computer, or a phone number or postal code that is not used in calculations, and which may contain characters other than numbers.
Memo	Lengthy text or combinations of text and numbers up to 65,535 characters or limitations of database size.	Description of a product or information pertaining to a patient.
Number	Numeric data used in mathematical calculations with varying field sizes.	A quantity, such as 500.
Date/Time	Date and time values for the years 100 through 9999.	An order date, such as 11/10/2009 3:30 P.M.
Currency	Monetary values and numeric data that can be used in mathematical calculations involving data with one to four decimal places. Accurate to 15 digits on the left side of the decimal separator and to 4 digits on the right side. Use this data type to store financial data and when you do not want Access to round values.	An item price, such as $8.50.
Yes/No	Contains only one of two values—Yes/No, True/False, or On/Off. Access assigns -1 for all Yes values and 0 for all No values.	Whether an item was ordered—Yes or No.
OLE Object	An object created by programs other than Access that is linked to or embedded in the table. *OLE* is an abbreviation for *object linking and embedding*, a technology for transferring and sharing information among programs.	A graphics file, such as a picture of a product, a sound file, a Word document, or an Excel spreadsheet stored as a bitmap image.
Hyperlink	Web or email addresses.	An email address, such as dwalker@txlakemed.org or a Web page, such as *www.txlakemed.org*.
Attachment	Any supported type of file—images, spreadsheet files, documents, charts. Similar to email attachments.	A graphics file, such as a picture of a product, a sound file, a Word document, or an Excel spreadsheet stored as a bitmap image—same as OLE Object.
Lookup Wizard	Available in Design view. Not a data type, but will display on data type menu. Links to fields in other tables to display a list of data instead of having to manually type in the data.	Link to another field in another table.

Figure 1.16

3 Click the **Data Type arrow** again to close the list without changing the data type. In any record, click in the **Address** field, and notice that the **Data Type** box indicates *Text*.

As described in the table in Figure 1.16, Access assigns a data type of *Text* to combinations of letters and numbers.

4 Scroll to the right as necessary, in any record click in the **Amount Owed** field, and then in the **Data Type** box, notice that Access assigned the data type of *Number*. Click the **Data Type arrow** to the right of *Number*, and then from the displayed list, click **Currency**.

Based on your typing, Access determined this data type to be *Number*. However, Amount Owed refers to a monetary value, so the data type must be defined as *Currency*. When you click the Currency data type, Access automatically adds a U.S. dollar sign ($) and two decimal places to all the fields in the column. Compare your screen with Figure 1.17.

Data Type box indicates *Currency*

Amount Owed field data type changed to *Currency*

Figure 1.17

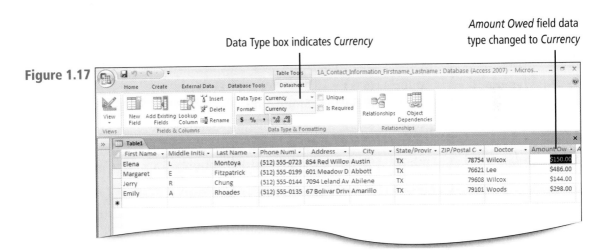

5 Scroll to the left as necessary, and in any record, click in the **ID** field.

In a database, each record should, in some way, be different from all the other records. What is important is that the number is unique; no other record in the table will be assigned this number.

You are probably familiar with unique numbers. For example, at your college, no two students have the same Student ID number, although they could have the same name, such as *David Michaels*.

When records in a database have *no* unique number, for example the CDs in your personal collection probably have no unique number, the AutoNumber data type is a useful way to automatically create a unique number so that you have a way to ensure that every record is unique.

6 Change the name of the **ID** field to **Patient ID**. In the new record row, which is indicated by an asterisk (*) in the record selector box on the left, click in the **Patient ID** field, and then type the records shown in the following list. When you are finished, compare your screen with Figure 1.18.

Recall that you need not be concerned if the data does not completely display in the column. Also, as soon as you move to the next row, the record is saved—you do not have to take any specific action to save the record. Correct typing mistakes using ordinary methods you have practiced in this and other programs.

Patient ID	First Name	Middle Initial	Last Name	Phone Number	Address	City	State/ Province	ZIP/ Postal Code	Doctor Name	Amount Owed
1260-P	Maria	S	Flores	(512) 555-0177	1 Casa Del Sol	Austin	TX	78715	Ruiz	37.50
1265-P	Joan	M	Curtis	(512) 555-0192	1446 Yellow Rose Lane	Austin	TX	78715	Ruiz	255
1342-P	Yvonne	L	Dubois	(512) 555-0155	2117 West Smith Trail	El Paso	TX	79973	Woods	147.56
1385-P	Joseph	C	Ortega	(512) 555-0245	1923 Village Park West	Amarillo	TX	79101	Wilcox	200
1423-P	Brian	K	Khuu	(512) 555-0323	1130 Preston Way SE	Abbott	TX	76621	Lee	568.12

Figure 1.18

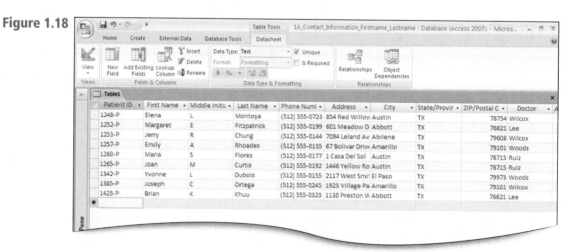

7 On the **Quick Access Toolbar**, click the **Save** button 🖫.

The Save As dialog box displays. Recall that an individual record is saved as soon as you move to another row in the table. However, because you have changed the table *design* by changing field names and data types, Access will prompt you to save the design changes made to the table.

Here you can also give the table a more meaningful name if you want to do so. In the Table Name box, a suggested name of *Table1* displays and is selected—yours may differ depending on the number of tables you have attempted to create in this database.

You will likely want to give your table a name that describes the information it contains. You can use up to 64 characters (letters or numbers), including spaces, to name a table.

8 In the **Save As** dialog box, in the **Table Name** box and using your first and last name, type **1A Patients Firstname Lastname** and then click **OK**. Compare your screen with Figure 1.19.

The table tab displays the new table name.

When you save objects within a database, it is not necessary to use underscores. Your name is included as part of the object name so that you and your instructor will be able to identify your printouts and electronic files.

Table name

Figure 1.19

Patient ID	First Name	Middle Initi	Last Name	Phone Numl	Address	City	State/Provir	ZIP/Postal C	Doctor
1248-P	Elena	L	Montoya	(512) 555-0723	854 Red Willov	Austin	TX	78754	Wilcox
1252-P	Margaret	E	Fitzpatrick	(512) 555-0199	601 Meadow D	Abbott	TX	76621	Lee
1253-P	Jerry	R	Chung	(512) 555-0144	7094 Leland Av	Abilene	TX	79608	Wilcox
1257-P	Emily	A	Rhoades	(512) 555-0135	67 Bolivar Driv	Amarillo	TX	79101	Woods
1260-P	Maria	S	Flores	(512) 555-0177	1 Casa Del Sol	Austin	TX	78715	Ruiz
1265-P	Joan	M	Curtis	(512) 555-0192	1446 Yellow Ro	Austin	TX	78715	Ruiz
1342-P	Yvonne	L	Dubois	(512) 555-0155	2117 West Smi	El Paso	TX	79973	Woods
1385-P	Joseph	C	Ortega	(512) 555-0245	1923 Village Pa	Amarillo	TX	79101	Wilcox
1423-P	Brian	K	Khuu	(512) 555-0323	1130 Preston V	Abbott	TX	76621	Lee

More Knowledge

Changing the Table Name

If you type the table name incorrectly or need to change the name of a table, click the Close button ⊠ in the upper right corner of the object window to close the table. Open the Navigation Pane, right-click the table name, and then from the displayed shortcut menu, click Rename. The table name will display in edit mode so that you can type the new name or edit it as you would any selected text.

Objective 4
Modify the Design of a Table

When you create and populate a new table in Datasheet view, the data that you type for the first record determines the number and content of the fields in the table. Recall that the number and names of the fields and the data type of each field is referred to as the *table design*. After you have created a table, you may find that you need to make changes to the design of the table by adding or deleting fields, or changing the order of the fields within a table. You can modify a table in Datasheet view, but you may prefer to modify the table in Design view where you have additional options.

Activity 1.5 Deleting a Field in Design View

June Liu has decided that a field for the patient's middle initial is not necessary for the Patients table. In this activity, you will delete the Middle Initial field in Design view.

1 On the **Datasheet tab**, in the **Views group**, click the **View button arrow**.

There are four common views in Access, but two that you will use often are Datasheet view and Design view. On the displayed list, Design view is represented by a picture of a pencil, a ruler, and a protractor. Datasheet view is represented by a small table of rows and columns. When you see these icons on the View button, you will know that clicking the button will take you to the view represented by the icon.

2 From the displayed list, click **Design View**, and then take a moment to study Figure 1.20.

Design view displays the underlying structure of your table. Each field name is listed, along with its data type. A column to add a Description—information about the data in the field—is provided. At the bottom of the Design view window, you can make numerous other decisions about how each individual field will look and behave. For example, you can set a specific field size.

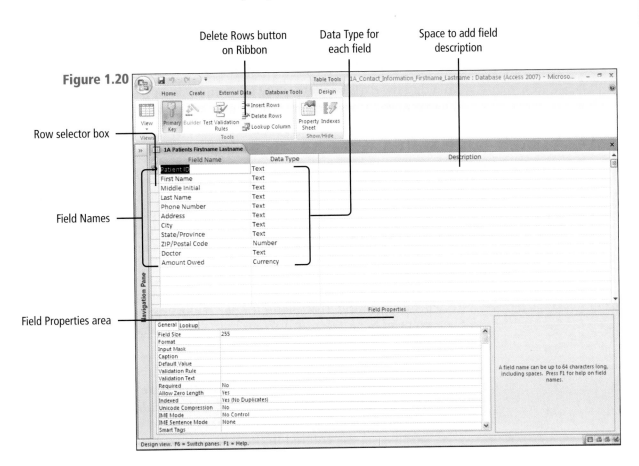

Figure 1.20

Delete Rows button on Ribbon

Data Type for each field

Space to add field description

Row selector box

Field Names

Field Properties area

3 In the **Field Name** column, to the left of **Middle Initial**, point to the row selector box to display the ➡ pointer, and then click to select—outline in orange—the entire row. Then, on the **Design tab**, in the **Tools group**, click the **Delete Rows** button, read the message in the displayed dialog box, and then click **Yes**.

If the field is deleted, both the field and its data will be deleted; you cannot undo this action. If you change your mind after deleting the field, you will have to add the field back into the table and then reenter the data for that field in each record.

More Knowledge

Choosing the Proper View To Make Changes

You can make design changes in Datasheet view or Design view. Design view provides more flexibility in the types of design changes you can make, and you will become familiar with these as you progress in your study of Access.

Activity 1.6 Modifying a Field Size and Description in Design View

In a database, there is typically more than one person entering data. For example, at your college there are likely numerous Registration Assistants who enter and modify student and course information every day.

When you design your database, there are things you can do to help yourself and others to always enter accurate data. Two ways to ensure accuracy are to restrict what can be typed in a field and to communicate information within the database itself. In this activity, you will modify fields to control the data entry process to ensure greater accuracy.

1 With your table still displayed in **Design view**, in the **Field Name** column, click anywhere in the **State/Province** field name. In the lower portion of the screen, under **Field Properties**, click in the **Field Size** box, select the text *255*, and then type **2** Compare your screen with Figure 1.21.

This action limits the size of the State/Province field to no more than two characters—the size of the two-letter state abbreviations provided by the United States Postal Service. *Field properties* are characteristics of a field that control how the field will display and how the data can be entered in the field. Using this portion of the Design view screen, you can define properties for each field.

The default field size for a text field is 255. By limiting the field size property to 2, you ensure that only two characters can be entered for each state. A primary goal of any database is to ensure the accuracy of the data that is entered. Setting the proper data type for the field and limiting the field size are two ways to help to reduce errors.

Figure 1.21

Field Properties Field Size changed to 2

State/Province field selected —

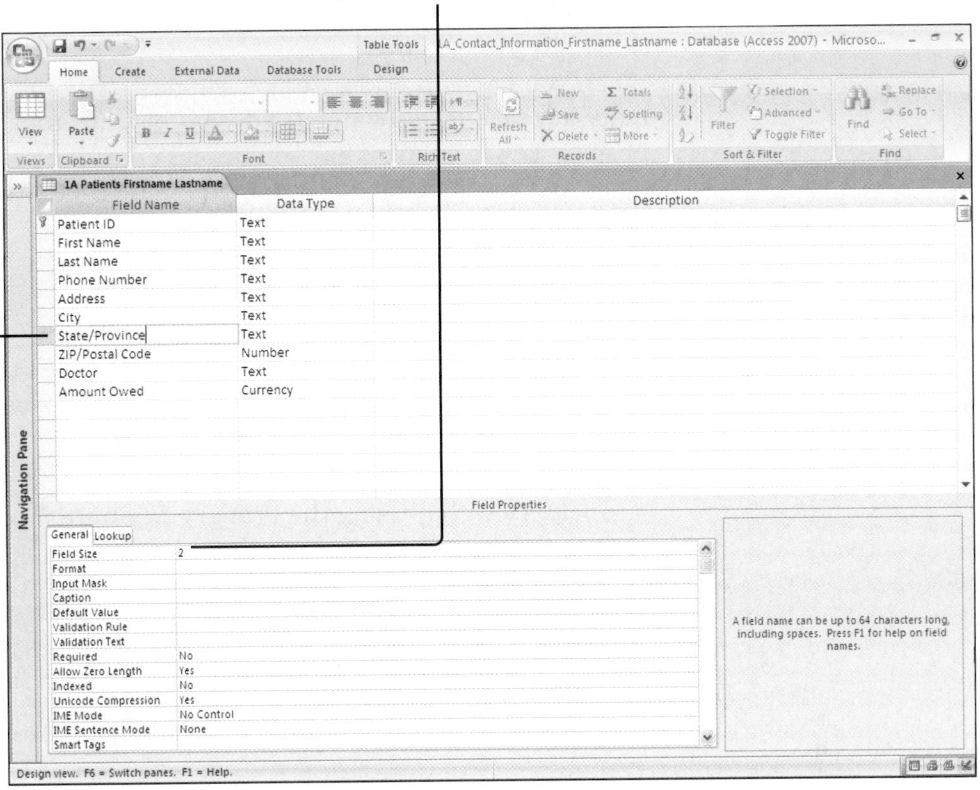

2 In the **State/Province** field name row, click in the **Description** column, and then type **Two-character state abbreviation**

Descriptions for fields in a table are not required. Include a description if the field name does not provide an obvious description of the field. Information typed in the description area displays in the status bar of the Datasheet view when the field is active. In this manner, the description communicates additional information to individuals who are entering data.

3 For the **Amount Owed** field name, click in the **Description** column, and then type **Outstanding balance**

4 On the **Quick Access Toolbar**, click the **Save** button [icon], and then click **Yes** when the warning dialog box appears. Leave your table in Design view for the next activity.

The changes you have made to the fields and their properties will help to ensure accurate data entry and provide communication to users of the database. The warning indicates that if more than two characters are currently present in the State/Province field, the data could be lost because the field was not previously restricted to two characters.

Activity 1.7 Setting a Primary Key and Saving a Table

A *primary key* is the field that uniquely identifies a record in a table. For example, in a college registration system, your Student ID number uniquely identifies you—no other student at the college has your exact student number. In your 1A Patients table, the Patient ID uniquely identifies each patient.

When you create a table, Access will designate the first field as the primary key field. Good database design dictates that you establish a primary key to ensure that you do not enter the same record more than once. You can imagine the confusion if another student at your college had the exact same Student ID number as you do. The function of a primary key is to prevent duplicate records within the same table.

1 With your table still displayed in **Design view**, in the **Field Name** column, click to place your insertion point in the **Patient ID** box. To the left of the box, notice the small icon of a key as shown in Figure 1.22.

Access automatically designates the first field as the primary key field. However, using the Primary Key button on the Ribbon, you can set any field as the primary key.

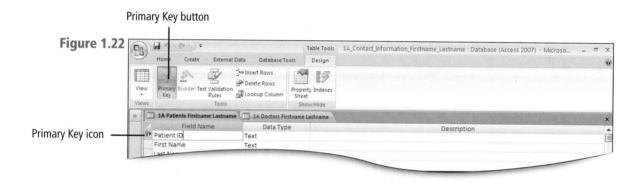

Figure 1.22

Primary Key button

Primary Key icon

2 On the **Design tab**, in the **Views group**, notice that the **View** button contains a picture of a Datasheet, indicating that clicking the button will return you to Datasheet view. Click the **View** button; if prompted, click **Yes** to save the changes you have made to the design of your table.

Objective 5
Add a Second Table to a Database

Access includes a ***table template***—a pre-built table format for common topics such as contacts, issues, and tasks. You can use the table template as it is or customize it to suit your needs. Using a table template is a fast way to add an additional table to your database.

Activity 1.8 Adding a Second Table to a Database

In this activity, you will add a second table in your database. The table will contain contact information for the doctors at the medical center. You will create the table using a table template specifically designed for contact information.

1 With your **1A Patients** table displayed in Datasheet view, on the Ribbon, click the **Create tab**. In the **Tables group**, click **Table Templates**, and then from the displayed list, click **Contacts**. Compare your screen with Figure 1.23.

A new table with predefined fields displays in the object window. Your 1A Patients table is still open—its tab is visible—but is behind the new table. The Contacts Table Template most closely matches the business need to track doctor information.

New Table1 added

Table Templates button   with predefined fields

Figure 1.23

1A Patients table still open

2 On the Ribbon, click the **Datasheet tab** to display the groups of Datasheet commands. In the second column, point to the **Company** field name, click to select the field, and then on the **Datasheet tab**, in the **Fields & Columns group**, click **Delete**. Alternatively, right-click on the selected field name, and from the displayed shortcut menu, click Delete Column.

You can delete fields in Design view, in the manner you did in a previous activity, or you can delete fields directly in Datasheet view as you have done here.

3 Point to the **E-mail Address** field, and then with your ⬇ pointer displayed, drag to the right to select both the **E-mail Address** field and the **Job Title** field. Right-click over the selected field names, and then from the displayed shortcut menu, click **Delete Column**.

4 Using the techniques you have just practiced, delete the following fields: **Business Phone**, **Home Phone**, **Fax Number**, **Country/Region**, **Web Page**, and **Notes**.

The field that displays a paperclip is the *Attachments* field. Recall that an attachment field can contain a graphics file such as a picture, a sound file, a Word document, or an Excel spreadsheet. In the future, June may attach a picture and a biography of each doctor to this field, so do not delete it.

5 On the **Datasheet tab**, in the **Views group**, click the **View** button to switch to **Design view**. In the **Save As** dialog box, in the **Table Name** box, type **1A Doctors Firstname Lastname** and then click **OK**.

This action will save the changes you have made to the design of the table—deleting fields—and provide a more meaningful table name. Your table displays in Design view, where you can see the names of each field and the data types assigned to the fields.

6 In the **Field Name** column, click anywhere in the **Attachments** box, and then on the **Design tab**, in the **Tools group**, click **Insert Rows**. In the newly inserted field name box, type **Specialty** In the **Description** box, type **Medical field specialty** and then compare your screen with Figure 1.24.

Description for new field

Figure 1.24

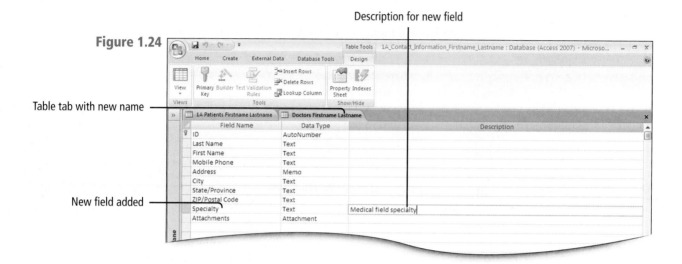

Table tab with new name

New field added

7 In the **Field Name** column, click in the **ID** box, and then replace the text with **Doctor ID** Press [Tab] to move to the **Data Type** column, click the arrow, and then from the displayed list, click **Text**. Press [Tab] to move to the **Description** column, and then type **Physician ID Number**

Because the medical center assigns a unique ID number to each doctor, you will use that number as the Primary Key instead of the AutoNumber generated by Access. Recall that AutoNumber is useful only when no other unique number for a record is available.

8 Click in the **State/Province** box, and then in the lower portion of the screen, under **Field Properties**, change the **Field Size** to **2** Compare your screen with Figure 1.25.

Figure 1.25

Description for Doctor ID

Doctor ID Data Type set to *Text*

Doctor ID field name

Descriptions added for two fields

State/Province Field Size changed to 2

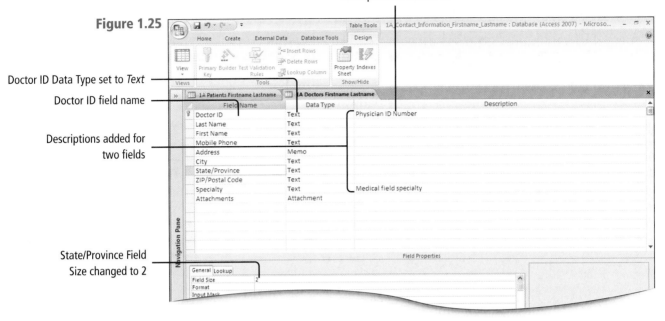

9 On the **Design tab**, in the **Views group**, click the **View** button to switch to Datasheet view—the picture of a datasheet reminds you that clicking the button will switch you to Datasheet view. Click **Yes** to save the changes you have made to the design of your table.

Activity 1.9 Adding Records to a Second Table

In this Activity, you will add the records for the doctors' contact information.

1 With your **1A Doctors** table displayed in Datasheet view, beginning in the first row under **Doctor ID**, use the techniques you have practiced to enter the following four records, and then compare your screen with Figure 1.26.

As you type in the Doctor ID field, *Physician ID Number* displays in the status bar. As you type in the Specialty field, *Medical field specialty* displays in the status bar.

Doctor ID	Last Name	First Name	Mobile Phone	Address	City	State/ Province	ZIP/Postal Code	Specialty
239-Phys	Woods	Laura	(512) 555-0100	4 Research Blvd	Austin	TX	78754	Oncology
287-Phys	Lee	Kim	(512) 555-0111	809 Broadway	Abbott	TX	76621	Cardiology
327-Phys	Wilcox	Frank	(512) 555-0022	7646 Pike Street	Amarillo	TX	79101	Orthopedics
421-Phys	Ruiz	Maria	(512) 555-0030	902 Madison Avenue	Austin	TX	78715	Pediatrics

Figure 1.26

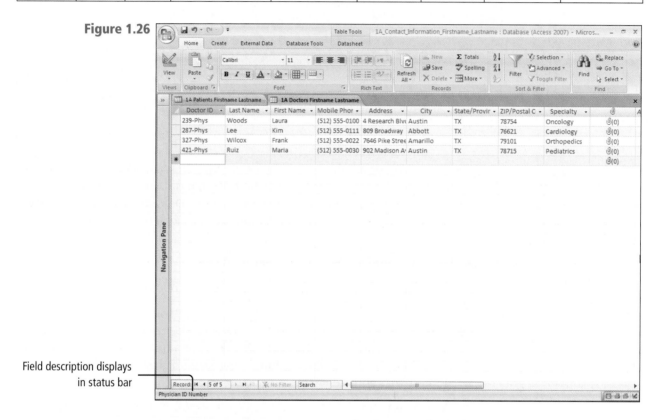

Field description displays in status bar

Objective 6
Print a Table

A printed table is not as professional looking as a formal report, but there are times when you may want to print your table in this manner as a quick reference or to proofread the data you have entered.

Activity 1.10 Adjusting Column Widths and Printing a Table

1 In the object window, click the tab for your **1A Patients** table.

By clicking the tabs along the top of the object window, you can display open objects so that you can work with them.

In the table, you can see that all of the columns are the same width regardless of the amount of data that is entered in the field or the field size that was set. If you print the table as currently displayed, some of the fields in some records may not fully display. Thus, it is recommended that you adjust the column widths.

2 Change the field name of the **State/Province** field to **State** and change the name of the **ZIP/Postal Code** field to **ZIP**

3 In the row of field names, point to the right boundary of the **Address** field to display the ⟨+|+⟩ pointer, and then compare your screen with Figure 1.27.

Pointer positioned on right boundary of Address field

Figure 1.27

Field name changed to *State*
Field name changed to *ZIP*

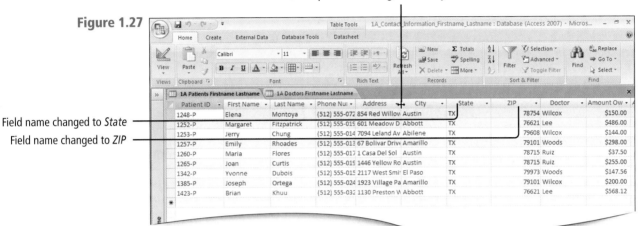

4 With your ⟨+|+⟩ pointer positioned as shown in Figure 1.27, double-click the right boundary of the **Address** field.

The column width of the Address field widens to fully display the field name and the longest entry in the column. In this manner, the width of a column can be increased or decreased to fit its contents.

5 In the field headings row, point to the right border of the **City** field, and then with the ⟨+|+⟩ pointer, hold down the left mouse button and drag to the left to visually narrow the column width to accommodate only the widest entry in that column.

Adjusting the width of columns does not change the data contained in the table's records. It changes only your view of the data.

Another Way ── **To Adjust Column Widths**

You can select multiple columns, and then in the heading area, double-click the right boundary of any selected column to adjust all widths, in a manner similar to an Excel spreadsheet. Or, you can select one or more columns, right-click over the selection, from the displayed menu click Column Width, and then in the Column Width dialog box, click Best Fit.

6 Using any of the techniques you have practiced or described above, adjust all the column widths, and then compare your screen with Figure 1.28.

All column widths adjusted to fit longest entry in the column

Figure 1.28

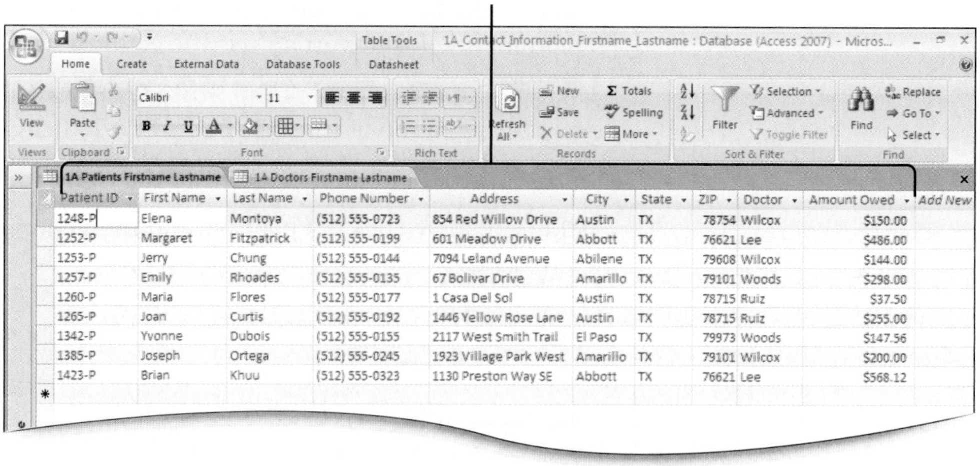

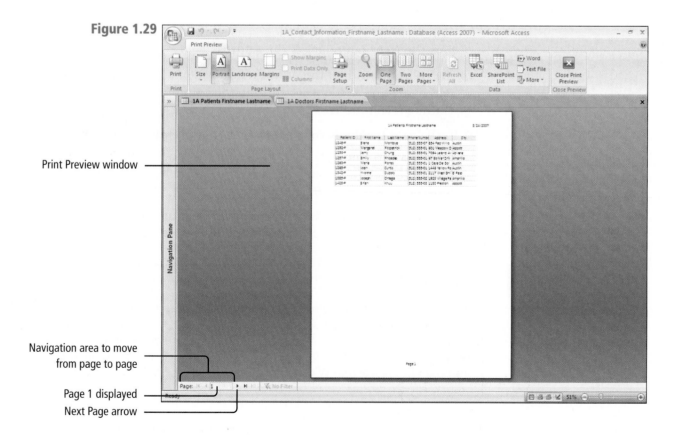

7 On the **Quick Access Toolbar**, click **Save** to save the changes you have made to the table's design—changing the column widths.

If you forget to save the table, Access will remind you to save when you close the table.

8 In the upper left corner of your screen, click the **Office** button. From the displayed menu, point to the **Print** button, click **Print Preview**, and then compare your screen with Figure 1.29.

Figure 1.29

Print Preview window

Navigation area to move from page to page

Page 1 displayed

Next Page arrow

9 In the navigation area in the lower left of your screen, click the **Next Page arrow**, point to the displayed data at the top of the page to display the 🔍 pointer, click one time to zoom in, and then compare your screen with Figure 1.30.

The second page of the table displays the last four field columns.

Figure 1.30

Last four fields display on a second page

Previous Page arrow

Page 2

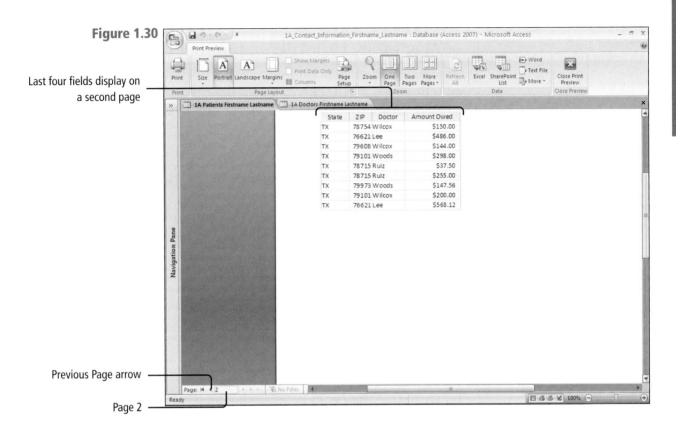

10 On the Ribbon, in the **Zoom group**, click the **Zoom** button to zoom back to Fit to Window view. In the **Page Layout group**, click the **Margins** button. In the displayed **Margins gallery**, point to **Wide**, and then compare your screen with Figure 1.31.

Wide gallery choice

Figure 1.31

Margins button

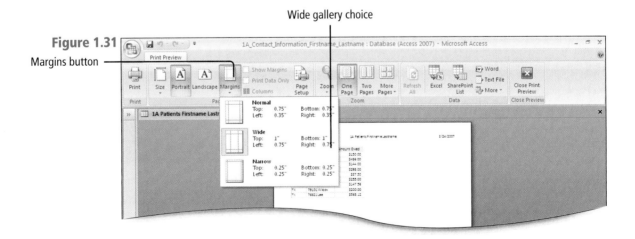

11 Click **Wide**. Then, in the **Page Layout group**, click the **Landscape** button.

The orientation of the printout changes, and the navigation arrows are inactive because all of the fields and all of the records display on one page. Additionally, the table name and current date display at the top of the page, and the page number displays at the bottom.

By default, Access prints in *portrait orientation*—the printed page is taller than it is wide. An alternate orientation is *landscape orientation*—the printed page is wider than it is tall.

The change in orientation from portrait to landscape is not saved with the table. Each time you want to print, you must check the margins, page orientation, and other print parameters to ensure that the data will print as you intend.

Note — Headers and Footers in Access Objects

The headers and footers in Access tables and queries are controlled by default settings; you cannot add additional information or edit the information. The object name displays in the center of the header area with the date on the right—that is why adding your own name to the object name is helpful to identify your paper or electronic results. The page number displays in the center of the footer area. The headers and footers in Access reports and forms, however, are more flexible; you can add to and edit the information.

12 On the right side of the status bar, just to the right of the **View** buttons, drag the **Zoom** slider to the right—or click the **Zoom In** button—until you have zoomed to approximately **120%**, as shown in Figure 1.32.

To *zoom* means to increase or to decrease the viewing area of the screen. You can zoom in to look closely at a particular section of a document, and then zoom out to see a whole page on the screen. You can also zoom to view multiple pages on the screen.

Zoom In button

Figure 1.32

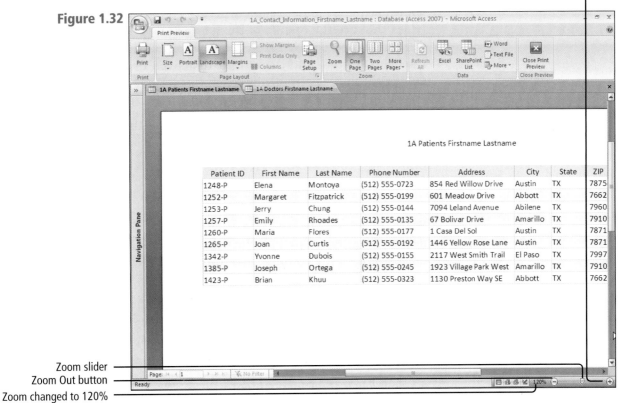

Zoom slider
Zoom Out button
Zoom changed to 120%

13 Drag the **Zoom** slider to the left—or click the **Zoom Out** button—until you have zoomed to approximately **50%**, as shown in Figure 1.33.

Figure 1.33

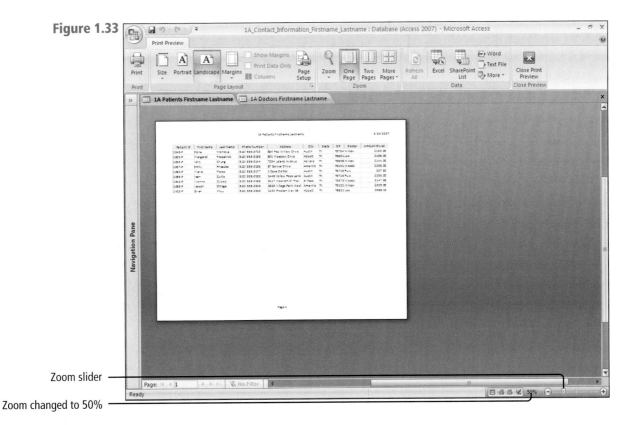

Zoom slider

Zoom changed to 50%

14 Check your *Chapter Assignment Sheet* or *Course Syllabus*, or consult your instructor, to determine whether you are to submit the printed pages that are the results of this project. If you are submitting your work on paper, on the **Print Preview tab**, in the **Print group**, click the **Print** button, and then in the displayed **Print** dialog box, click **OK**. To submit electronically, click Close Print Preview, and then follow the directions provided by your instructor.

15 In the **Close Preview group**, click the **Close Print Preview** button. At the far right edge of the object window, click the **Close Object** button ⊠ to close your **1A Patients** table. If prompted to do so, click Yes to save any unsaved design changes.

16 With your **1A Doctors** table displayed, change the name of the **State/Province** field to **State** and the name of the **ZIP/Postal Code** field to **ZIP** Then, adjust all the column widths to accommodate the longest line in the column, including the **Attachments** column, which displays a paperclip icon.

17 Display the table in **Print Preview**. Change the **Margins** to **Wide** and the orientation to **Landscape**. Print if you are directed to do so, or submit your work electronically.

18 Click **Close Print Preview**, and then at the far right of the object window, click the **Close Object** button ⊠. Click **Yes** to save the changes you made to the layout—changing the column widths.

All of your database objects—the 1A Patients table and the 1A Doctors table—are closed, and the object window is empty.

Objective 7
Create and Use a Query

A *query* is a database object that retrieves specific data from one or more tables and then, in a single datasheet, displays only the data you specified. Because the word *query* means *to ask a question*, you can think of a query as a question formed in a manner that Access can interpret.

One type of query in Access is a *select query*. A select query, also called a *simple select query*, retrieves (selects) data from one or more tables and makes it available for use in the format of a datasheet. A select query is used to create subsets of data that you can use to answer specific questions; for example, *Which patients live in Austin, TX?*

Activity 1.11 Using the Simple Query Wizard To Create a Query

The table or tables from which a query gets its data are referred to as the query's *data source*. In the following activity, you will create a simple select query using a *wizard*. A wizard is a feature in Microsoft Office programs that walks you step by step through a process.

The process involves choosing the data source, and then indicating the fields you want to include in the query result. The query—the question that you want to ask—is *What is the name, complete mailing address, and Patient ID of every patient in the database?*

1 On the Ribbon, click the **Create tab**, and then in the **Other group**, click the **Query Wizard** button. In the **New Query** dialog box, click **Simple Query Wizard**, and then click **OK**. Compare your screen with Figure 1.34.

Figure 1.34

Simple Query Wizard dialog box

Tables/Queries arrow

Add Field button

No database objects display in object window; all are closed

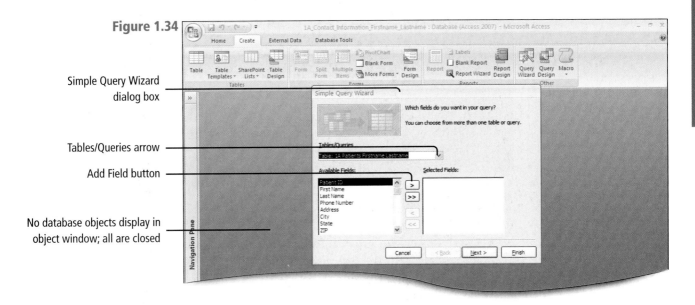

2 Click the **Tables/Queries arrow**, and then click your **Table: 1A Patients**.

To create a query, first choose the data source—the tables or queries from which you will select the data you want. To find the name and complete mailing address of every patient, you will need the 1A Patients table.

3 Under **Available Fields**, click **Patient ID**, and then click the **Add Field** button to move the field to the **Selected Fields** list on the right. Using the same technique, add the **Last Name** field to the list. Alternatively, double-click the field name to move it to the Selected Fields list. Compare your screen with Figure 1.35.

Recall that the second step is to choose the fields that you want to include in your resulting query.

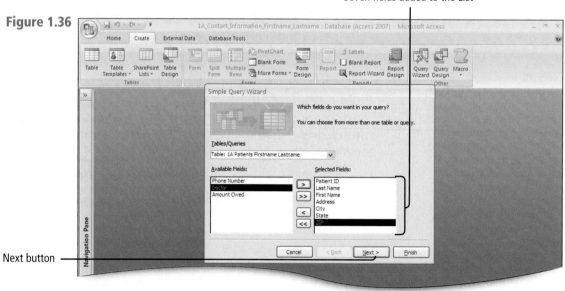

Figure 1.35

Two fields added to Selected Fields list

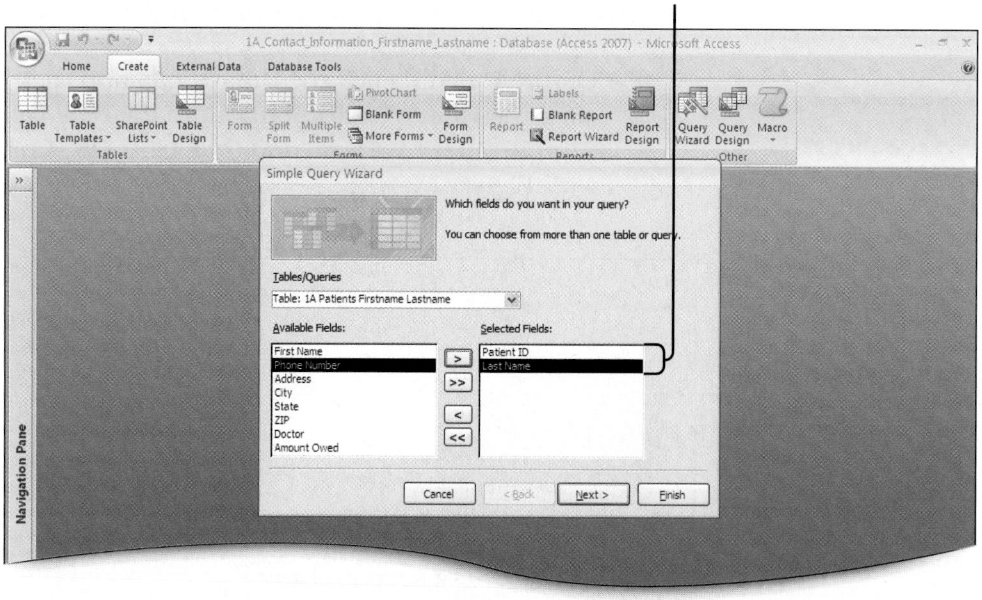

4 Using either the **Add Field** button [>] or double-click, add the following fields to the **Selected Fields** list: **First Name**, **Address**, **City**, **State**, **ZIP**. Compare your screen with Figure 1.36.

Choosing these seven fields will give you the query result that you want—it will answer the question, *What is the name, address, and Patient ID of every patient in the database?*

Seven fields added to the List

Figure 1.36

Next button

5 In the lower right corner, click the **Next** button. Be sure that the option for **Detail (shows every field of every record)** is selected, and then in the lower right corner, click the **Next** button. Click in the **What title do you want for your query?** box, and then edit as necessary so that the query name, using your own first and last name, is **1A ALL Patients Firstname Lastname Query** Compare your screen with Figure 1.37.

Name of query

Figure 1.37

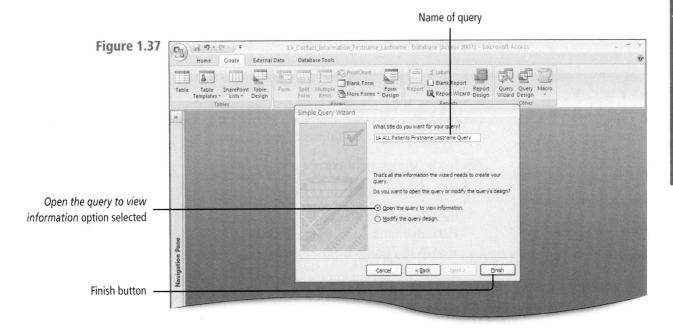

Open the query to view information option selected

Finish button

6 Click **Finish**.

Access *runs* the query—performs the actions indicated in your query design by searching the table of records included in the query, finding the records that match the criteria, and then displaying the records in a datasheet—so that you can see the results. In this manner, a select query *selects*—pulls out and displays—*only* the information from the table that you requested.

In the object window, Access displays every patient record in Datasheet view, but displays only the seven fields that you included in the Selected Fields list in the query wizard.

7 Display the query in **Print Preview**, and then print or submit electronically as directed. Click **Close Print Preview**; leave the query object open.

Objective 8
Create and Use a Form

A **form** is an Access object with which you can enter data, edit data, or display data from a table or a query. Think of a form as a window through which you and others can view and work with the data. In a form, the fields are laid out in a visually attractive format on the screen, which makes working with the database more pleasant and more efficient.

One type of Access form displays only one record in the database at a time. Such a form is useful not only to the individual who performs the data entry—typing in the actual records—but also to anyone who has the job of viewing information in a database.

For example, when you visit the Records office at your college to obtain a transcript, someone displays your record on a screen. For the viewer, it is much easier to look at one record at a time, using a form, than to look at all the student records in the database table.

Activity 1.12 Creating a Form

The Form command on the Ribbon creates a form that displays all the fields from the underlying data source (table) on the form, and does so one record at a time. You can use this new form immediately, or you can modify it. Records that you edit or create by using a form automatically update the underlying table or tables.

1 In the upper right corner of the object window, click the **Close Object** button ☒ to close your query. Then, at the top of the **Navigation Pane**, click the **Open** button ⟩⟩. Point to your **1A Patients** table, and then right-click to display a shortcut menu as shown in Figure 1.38.

In the Navigation Pane, a table displays a datasheet icon and a query displays an icon of two overlapping datasheets.

Navigation Pane Close button   Shortcut menu

Figure 1.38

1A Patients table
Table icon
Query icon

Navigation Pane expanded

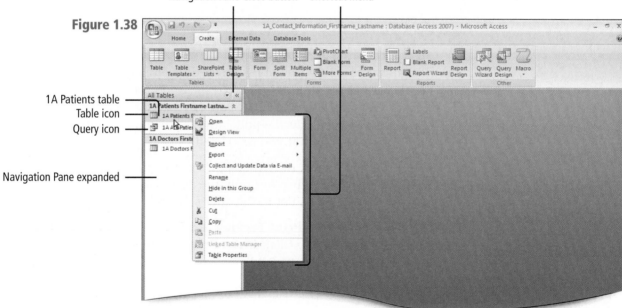

2 From the displayed menu, click **Open** to display the table in the object window, and then in the upper right corner of the **Navigation Pane**, click the **Close** button ⟨⟨ to maximize your screen space.

3 Notice that there are 10 fields in your table. On the Ribbon, click the **Create tab**, and then in the **Forms group**, click the **Form** button. Compare your screen with Figure 1.39.

Access creates a form based on the currently selected object—your 1A Patients table. Access creates the form in a simple top-to-bottom format, with all the fields in the table lined up in a single column.

The form displays in Layout view, which means you can make modifications to the form on this screen. The data for the first record in the table—for *Elena Montoya*—displays in each field.

Figure 1.39

Form object tab displays red form icon

Layout View button active

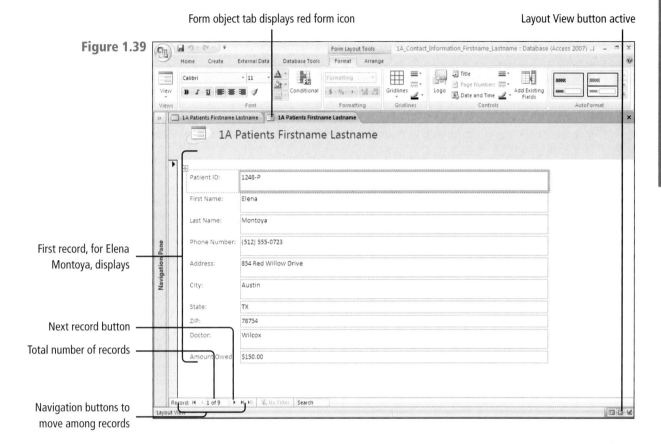

First record, for Elena Montoya, displays

Next record button

Total number of records

Navigation buttons to move among records

4 In the lower right corner of the screen, at the right edge of the status bar, notice that the **Layout View** button 🔲 is active, indicating the form is displayed in Layout view.

5 At the right edge of the status bar, click the **Form View** button 🔲. Alternatively, on the Home tab, in the Views group, click the View button, which displays an icon of a form indicating the Form view.

In this view, you can view the records, but you cannot change the layout of the form.

6 In the navigation area, click the **Next record** button ▶ three times.

The fourth record—for *Emily Rhoades*—displays. The navigation buttons are useful to scroll among the records to select any single record you need to display.

7 On the **Quick Access Toolbar**, click the **Save** button 🔲. In the displayed **Save As** dialog box, accept the default name for the form—

1A Patients Firstname Lastname—by clicking **OK**. **Close** ✕ the form object.

Your 1A Patients Firstname Lastname table remains open in the object window.

Objective 9
Create and Print a Report

A *report* is a database object that displays the fields and records from a table or a query in an easy-to-read format suitable for printing. Create reports to summarize information in a database in a professional-looking manner.

Activity 1.13 Creating and Printing a Report

In this activity, you will create a report that lists mobile phone contact information for doctors at Texas Lakes Medical Center.

1 **Open** ⏩ the **Navigation Pane**, and then open your **1A Doctors** table by double-clicking the table name or by right-clicking and clicking Open from the shortcut menu.

Your 1A Doctors table displays in Datasheet view in the object window.

2 **Close** ⏪ the **Navigation Pane**. Click the **Create tab**, and then in the **Reports group**, click **Report**. Compare your screen with Figure 1.40.

A report displays each of the fields in the table laid out in a report format suitable for printing. The report displays in Layout view, which means you can make quick changes to the design of the report on this screen.

Dotted lines indicate how the report would be broken across pages if you print in the current layout.

Report Layout Tools available

Figure 1.40

Report object tab displays a Report icon

Dotted line indicates page break if printed in current layout

Layout View button active

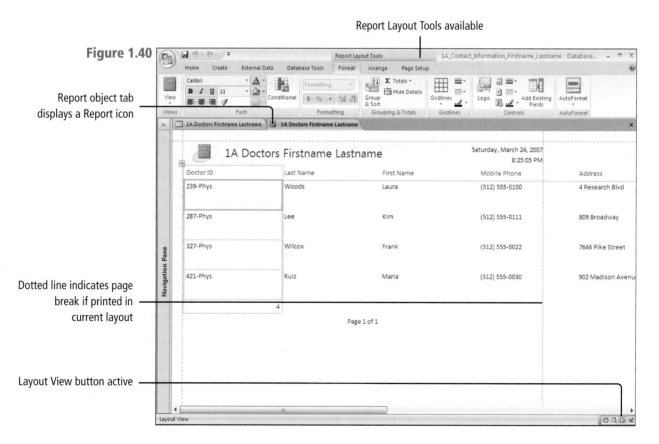

3 Scroll to the right as necessary, point to the **Address** field, right-click, and then from the displayed shortcut menu, click **Delete**.

The Address field and data are deleted and the report readjusts to accommodate the deletion.

4 Use the same technique to delete the following fields on the report layout: **City**, **State**, **ZIP**, **Specialty**, and **Attachments**.

This report will provide June with a quick list of each doctor and his or her ID and mobile phone number.

5 Click the **Page Setup tab**, and then in the **Page Layout group**, click **Landscape**. Scroll to the left, and then compare your screen with Figure 1.41.

Figure 1.41

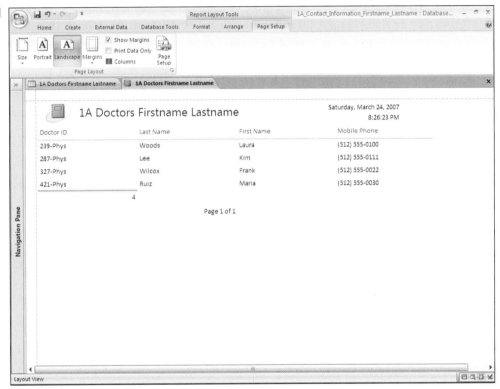

6 If you are submitting your results from this Project on paper, from the **Office** menu 📋, point to the **Print** button, click **Print Preview**, and then in the **Print group**, click **Print**. To submit electronically, follow the directions provided by your instructor.

7 Click the **Close Print Preview** button. Click the **Close Object** button ⊠ to close the report. In the **Microsoft Office Access** dialog box, click **Yes** to save the report. In the **Save As** dialog box, click **OK** to accept the report name.

8 **Close** ⊠ all the open objects so that there are no objects displayed in the object window.

Objective 10
Close and Save a Database

When you close an Access table, any changes made to the records are saved automatically. If you have changed the design of the table, or have changed the layout of the Datasheet view, such as adjusting the column widths, you will be prompted to save your changes. At the end of your Access session, close your database, and then close Access.

Activity 1.14 Closing and Saving a Database

1 Be sure all objects are closed.

2 From the **Office** menu 🔲, click **Close Database**, and then at the right edge of the Access title bar, click the **Close** button ⊠ to close the Access program. Alternatively, from the Office menu, click Exit Access.

End **You have completed Project 1A** ————————

Project 1B **Health Seminars**

In Activities 1.15 through 1.21, you will assist June Liu, Chief Administrative Officer, in creating a database to store information about community health seminars presented by Texas Lakes Medical Center. You will use a database template that tracks event information. You will add seminar information to the database and print a page displaying the results. Your printout will look similar to Figure 1.42.

For Project 1B, you will need the following file:

New Access database using the Events template

You will save your database as
1B_Health_Seminars_Firstname_Lastname

1B Seminar Locations Firstname Lastname				11/24/2006
Location	**On Site/Off Site**	**Seating Capacity**	**Room Arrangement**	**Visual Equipment**
Dogwood Room	On Site	50	Classroom	Computer Projector
Jefferson High School	Off Site	150	Theater	Computer Projector
Sandbox Preschool	Off Site	20	Classroom	White Board
Yellow Rose Room	On Site	20	U-Shape Table	Computer Projector

Page 1

Figure 1.42
Project 1B—Health Seminars

Objective 11
Create a Database Using a Template

A database template contains pre-built tables, queries, forms, and reports to perform a specific task, such as tracking a large number of events. For example, your college probably holds a large number of events, such as athletic contests, plays, lectures, concerts, and club meetings. Using a predefined template, your college Activities Director could quickly establish a database to manage such events.

The advantage of using a template to start a new database is that you do not have to create the objects—all you need to do is enter your data and modify the pre-built objects to suit your needs.

The purpose of the database in this project is to track the health seminars offered by Texas Lakes Medical Center. The questions to be answered may include:

- *What seminars will be offered and when will they be offered?*

- *In what Medical Center rooms or community locations will the seminars be held?*

- *Which seminar rooms have a computer projector for PowerPoint presentations?*

Activity 1.15 Creating a New Database Using a Template

In this activity, you will create a new database using the Events template.

1 **Start** Access. On the left side of the screen, under **Template Categories**, click **Local Templates**. Compare your screen with Figure 1.43.

Available Local Templates

Figure 1.43

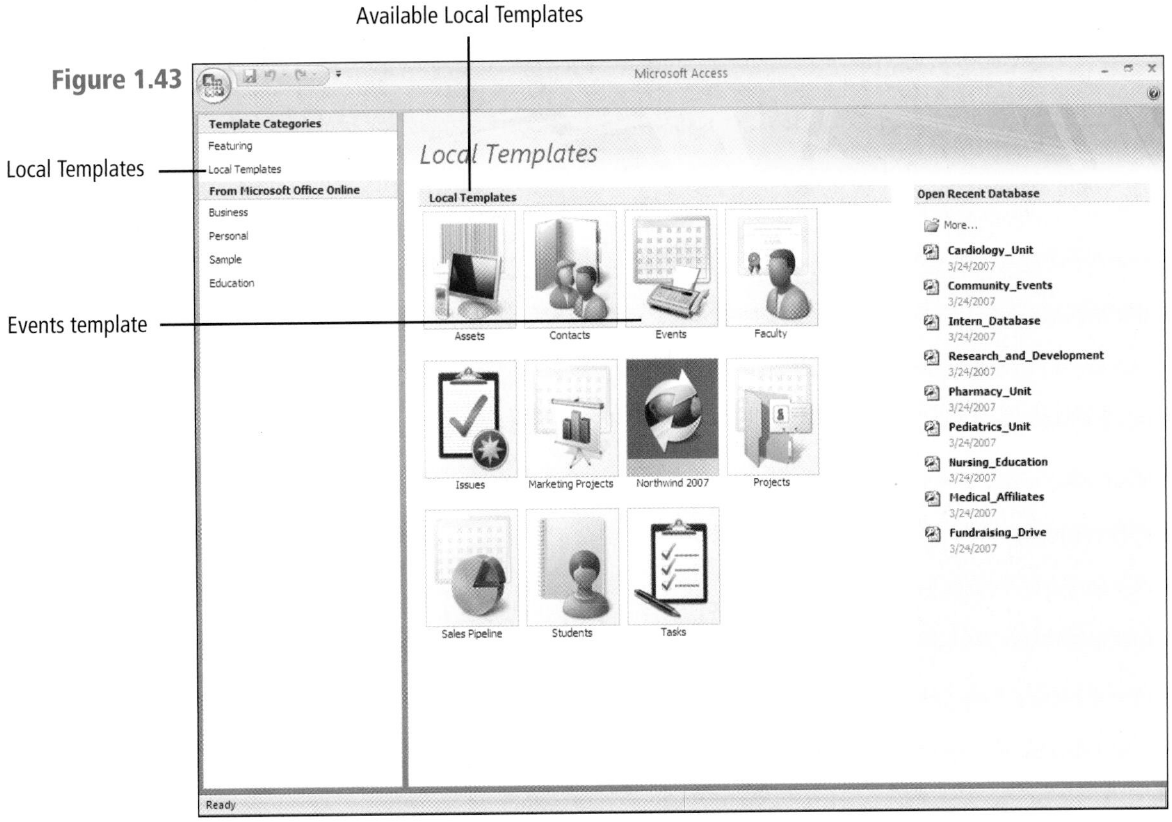

Local Templates —

Events template —

2 Under **Local Templates**, click **Events**. In the lower right portion of your screen, to the right of the **File Name** box, click the **file folder icon**, and then navigate to your **Access Chapter 1** folder that you created in Project 1A.

3 At the bottom of the **File New Database** dialog box, delete any text in the **File name** box, and then, using your own information, type **1B_Health_Seminars_Firstname_Lastname** and press Enter.

4 In the lower right corner of your screen, click the **Create** button.

Your 1B Health Seminars database is created, and the name displays in the title bar.

5 Directly below the Ribbon, on the **Message Bar**, check to see if a **Security Warning** displays.

Note

If no Security Warning displays, skip the next step and move to Activity 1.16.

6 On the **Message Bar**, click the **Options** button. In the displayed **Microsoft Office Security Options** dialog box, click the **Enable this content** option button, and then click **OK** or press Enter. Compare your screen with Figure 1.44.

Databases provided by Microsoft are safe to use on your computer.

Figure 1.44

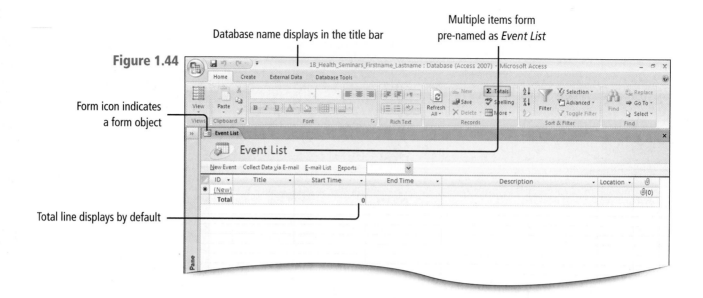

Database name displays in the title bar

Multiple items form
pre-named as *Event List*

Form icon indicates
a form object

Total line displays by default

Activity 1.16 Building a Table by Entering Records in a Multiple Items Form

The purpose of a form is to simplify the entry of data into a table—either for you or for others who enter data. In Project 1A, you created a simple form, in which you can display or enter records in a table one record at a time.

The Events template creates a ***multiple items form***, a form in which you can display or enter *multiple* records in a table, but still with an easier and more simplified screen than typing directly into the table itself.

1 Click in the first empty **Title** field. Type **Repetitive Stress Injuries** and then press Tab. In the **Start Time** field, type **3/9/09 7p** and then press Tab.

Access formats the date and time. As you enter dates and times, a small calendar displays to the right of the field, which you can click to select a date instead of typing.

2 In the **End Time** field, type **3/9/09 9p** and then press Tab. In the **Description** field, type **Workplace Health** and then press Tab. In the **Location** field, type **Yellow Rose Room** and then press Tab three times to move to the new record row. Compare your screen with Figure 1.45.

Because the seminars have no unique number, the AutoNumber feature of Access is useful to assign a unique number to each seminar.

First record entered

Figure 1.45

Access formats date and time

Link bar

AutoNumber creates a unique number

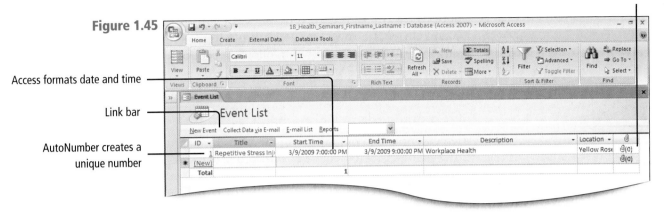

3 In the **Link bar**, just above the field names, click **New Event**.

A single-record form displays, similar to the simple form you created in Project 1A.

4 Using Tab to move from field to field, enter the following record—press Tab three times to move from the **End Time** field to the **Description** field. Compare your screen with Figure 1.46.

Title	Location	Start Time	End Time	Description
First Aid for Teens	**Jefferson High School**	**3/10/09 4p**	**3/10/09 6p**	**Teen Health**

Single-record form

Close button

Figure 1.46

Save and New button

New Event button on Link bar

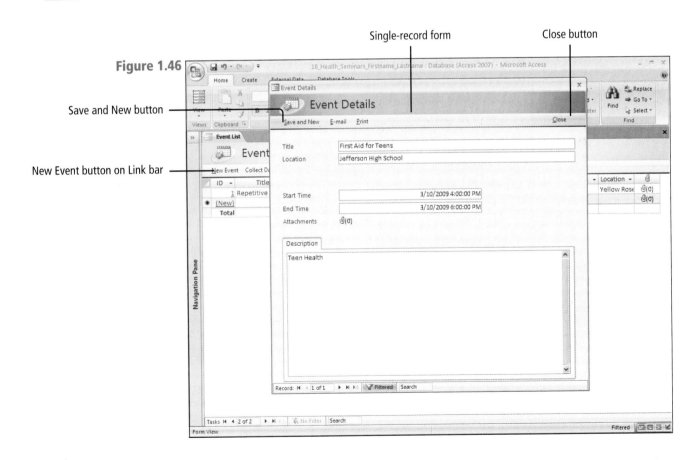

5 In the upper right corner of the single-record form, click **Close**, and notice that the new record displays in your Multiple Items form. Using either the rows on the Multiple Items form or the New Event single-record form, enter the following records, and then compare your screen with Figure 1.47:

Alert!

Does a single record form open?

When entering records in the multiple items form, pressing [Enter] three times at the end of a row to begin a new record may display the single-record New Event form. If you prefer to use the multiple items form, close the single record form and continue entering records, using the [Tab] key to move from field to field.

ID	Title	Start Time	End Time	Description	Location
3	Safety on the Job	3/18/09 2p	3/18/09 4p	Workplace Health	Yellow Rose Room
4	Nutrition for Toddlers	3/19/09 1p	3/19/09 3p	Child Health and Development	Sandbox Preschool
5	Stay Healthy While You Travel	4/6/09 9a	4/6/09 11a	Life Style and Health	Dogwood Room
6	Work Smart at Your Computer	4/8/09 11a	4/8/09 12:30p	Workplace Health	Dogwood Room
7	Be Heart Smart	4/14/09 7p	4/14/09 9p	Life Style and Health	Yellow Rose Room

Figure 1.47

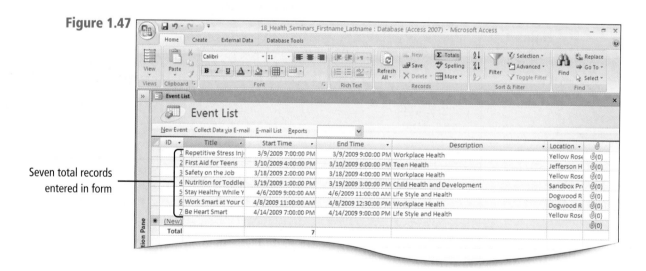

Seven total records entered in form

Objective 12
Organize Database Objects in the Navigation Pane

Use the Navigation Pane to organize your database objects, to open them for use, and to perform common tasks like renaming an object. So far, your databases have had only a few objects, but databases can have a large number of tables and other objects. Thus, the Navigation Pane will become your tool for organizing your database objects.

Activity 1.17 Organizing Database Objects in the Navigation Pane

The Navigation Pane groups and displays your database objects, and can do so in predefined arrangements. In this activity, you will group your database objects using the **Tables and Views category**, an arrangement that groups objects by the table to which they are related. Because all of your data must be stored in one or more tables, this is a useful arrangement.

1 Open ⟩⟩ the **Navigation Pane**. At the top of the **Navigation Pane**, click the **Navigation arrow** ⌄ , and then from the displayed list, in the **Navigate To Category** section, click **Tables and Related Views**.

Click the **Navigation arrow** ⌄ to display the list again, and then in the **Filter By Group** section, point to **All Tables**. Compare your screen with Figure 1.48.

Figure 1.48

All Tables displays

Tables and Related Views selected

All Tables selected

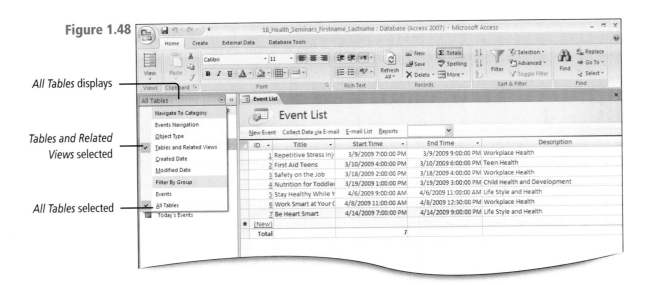

2 Click **All Tables** to close the list, and then confirm that *Events* displays in the blue bar at the top of the **Navigation Pane**. Compare your screen with Figure 1.49.

The icons to the left of the objects listed in the Navigation Pane indicate that the Events template created a number of objects for you—among them, one table titled *Events*, five reports, two forms, and one query. The Event List Multiple Items form, which is currently displayed in the object window, is included in the list.

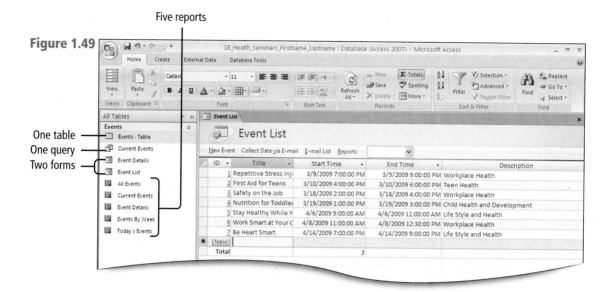

Figure 1.49

Five reports

One table

One query

Two forms

3 In the **Navigation Pane**, point to the **Events** *table*, and then right-click to display a shortcut menu. On the shortcut menu, click **Open**. Alternatively, double-click the table name to open it in the object window.

The Events table becomes the active object in the object window. Use the Navigation Pane to open objects for use.

The seven records that you entered using the Multiple Items *form* display in the *table*. Recall that the purpose of a form is to make it easy to get records into a table. Tables are the foundation of your database because your data must be stored in a table. You can enter records directly into a table in the manner you did in Project 1A, or you can use a simple form or a Multiple Items form to enter records.

4 In the object window, click the **Event List** form tab to bring it into view and make it the active object.

Recall that a form presents a more user-friendly screen with which to enter records into a table.

5 In the **Navigation Pane**, right-click the report named **Current Events**, and then click **Open**. Alternatively, double-click the report name to open it. Compare your screen with Figure 1.50.

An advantage of using a template to begin a database is that many objects, such as attractively formatted reports, are already designed for you.

Current Events report preformatted
and designed by the template

Figure 1.50

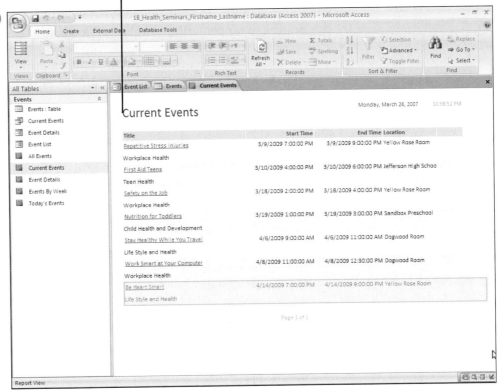

6 In the object window, **Close** ☒ the **Current Events** report.

7 From the **Navigation Pane**, open the **Events By Week** report.

In this predesigned report, the events are displayed by week. These are among the reports that are predesigned and come with the template. After you enter your records, these preformatted reports are instantly available to you.

8 In the object window, **Close** ☒ the **Events By Week** report. Then **Close** ☒ the remaining two open objects. Leave the **Navigation Pane** fully displayed.

There are no open objects in your object window.

Objective 13
Create a New Table in a Database Created with a Template

The Events template created only one table—the *Events* table. Although the database was started from a template and contains many necessary objects, you can add additional objects as you need them.

Create a new table in a database when you begin to see repeated information. Repeated information is a good indication that an additional table is needed. For example, in the Events database, both the Yellow Rose Room and the Dogwood Room are listed more than one time.

Activity 1.18 Creating a New Table and Changing Its Design

June has information about the various locations where seminars are held. For example, for the Yellow Rose Room, she has information about the seating arrangements, number of seats, and audio-visual equipment.

In your database, three seminars are currently scheduled in the Yellow Rose Room and two are scheduled in the Dogwood Room. It would not make sense to store information about the rooms multiple times in the same table. It is *not* considered good database design to have duplicate information in a table.

When data in a table becomes redundant in this manner, it is usually a signal to create a new table to contain the information about the topic. In this activity, you will create a table to track the seminar locations and the equipment and seating arrangements in each location.

1 **Close** ≪ the **Navigation Pane** to maximize your screen space. On the Ribbon, click the **Create tab**, and then in the **Tables group**, click the **Table** button.

2 Click in the cell under **Add New Field**, type **Yellow Rose Room** and then press Tab. Type **On Site** and then press Tab. Type **20** and then press Tab. Type **U-Shape Table** and then press Tab. Type **Computer Projector** and then press Tab three times. Compare your screen with Figure 1.51.

Access will assign an AutoNumber in the ID field.

Figure 1.51

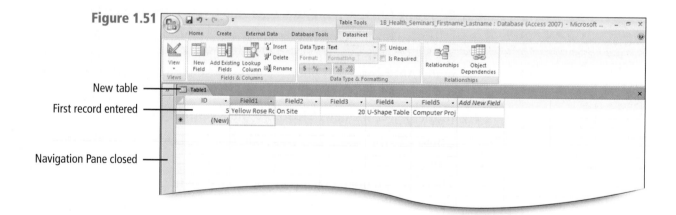

New table

First record entered

Navigation Pane closed

3 Point to the text *Field1*, right-click, and then from the displayed shortcut menu, click **Rename Column**. Type **Location** Point to the text *Field2*, double-click, and then type **On Site/Off Site** Point to and click *Field3*, click the **Datasheet tab**, and then in the **Fields & Columns group**, click **Rename**. Type **Seating Capacity** Using any of the techniques you have practiced, change *Field4* to **Room Arrangement** and *Field5* to **Visual Equipment**

4 In the **Views group**, click the **View** button to switch to **Design view**. **Save** the table as **1B Seminar Locations Firstname Lastname** and then click **OK**.

5 In **Design view**, in the **Field Name** column, click in the **Location** box. Then on the **Design tab**, in the **Tools group**, click the **Primary Key** button.

The key icon moves to the left of the Location field. Recall that the Primary Key is the field that contains a unique identifier for the record. In the Seminar Locations table, the Location name is unique; no other record will have the same Location name.

6 Point to the **row selector box** for the **ID** field to display the ➡ pointer, and then click to select the entire row. On the **Design tab**, in the **Tools group**, click the **Delete Rows** button, and then click **Yes** in the warning box.

Because the Location name will serve as the primary key field, the ID field is not necessary.

7 On the Ribbon, in the **Views group**, click the **View** button, which by its icon indicates that you will return to the Datasheet view of the table. Click **Yes** to save the changes you have made to the table design.

8 Enter the remaining records in the table:

Location	On Site/ Off Site	Seating Capacity	Room Arrangement	Visual Equipment
Jefferson High School	Off Site	150	Theater	Computer Projector
Dogwood Room	On Site	50	Classroom	Computer Projector
Sandbox Preschool	Off Site	20	Classroom	White Board

9 Point to the field name *Location* to display the ⬇ pointer, hold down the left mouse button, and then drag across to select all of the columns, as shown in Figure 1.52.

All the columns selected

Figure 1.52

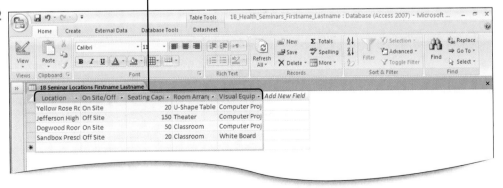

10 Point to any of the selected field names in the top row, right-click, and then from the displayed shortcut menu, click **Column Width**. In the displayed **Column Width** dialog box, click **Best Fit**. Alternatively, with the columns selected, in the field heading row, point to the right boundary of any of the selected rows to display the ⊞ pointer, and then double-click to apply Best Fit to all of the selected columns.

All of the columns widths are adjusted to accommodate the longest entry in the column.

11 Click in any record to cancel the selection of the columns. **Open** ⟩⟩ the **Navigation Pane**, locate the name of your new table, and then compare your screen with Figure 1.53.

Recall that as it is currently arranged, the Navigation Pane organizes the objects by table name. The Events table is listed first, followed by its associated objects, and then the Seminar Locations table is listed. Currently, there are no other objects associated with the Seminar Locations table.

New table listed in Navigation Pane

No additional objects currently associated with Seminar Locations table

Figure 1.53

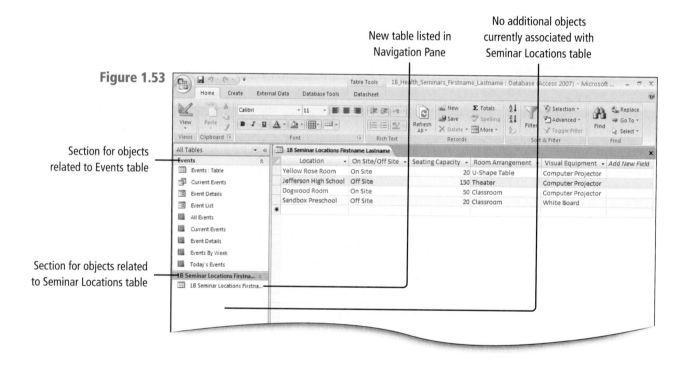

Section for objects related to Events table

Section for objects related to Seminar Locations table

12 In the object window, **Close** ☒ your **1B Seminar Locations** table, and then click **Yes** to save the layout changes you made to the column widths. Leave the **Navigation Pane** open.

Objective 14
View a Report and Print a Table in a Database Created with a Template

Recall that an advantage to starting a new database with a template is that many report objects are already created for you.

Activity 1.19 Viewing a Report

1 From the **Navigation Pane**, open the **All Events** report. Compare your screen with Figure 1.54.

The All Events report displays in an attractively arranged pre-built report.

All Events report

Figure 1.54

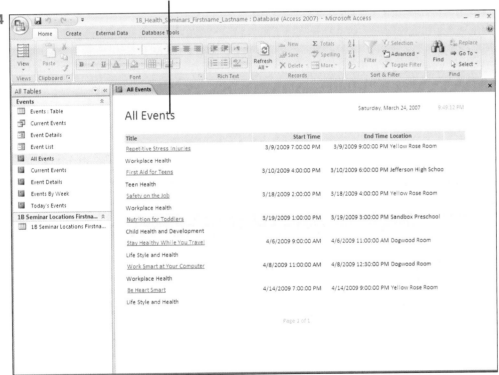

2 **Close** ☒ the **All Events** report.

3 Open the **Event Details** report and compare your screen with Figure 1.55.

The Event Details report displays in a pre-built report. Each report displays the records in the table in different useful formats.

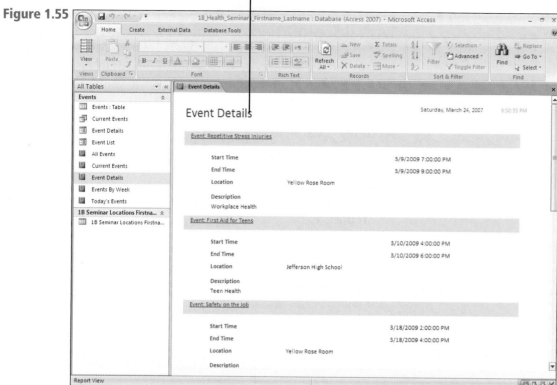

Event Details report

Figure 1.55

---

4 Close ⊠ the **Event Details** report.

Activity 1.20 Printing a Table

Use the Print Preview command to determine if a table will print on one page, or if you need to adjust column widths, margins, or the direction the data displays on the page.

Recall that there will be occasions when you want to print your table for a quick reference or for proofreading. For more formal-looking information, print a report.

1 From the **Navigation Pane**, open your **1B Seminar Locations** table. Display the **Office** menu 🔲 , point to the **Print** button, and then click **Print Preview**.

The table displays in the Print Preview window so you can see how it will look when it is printed. The name of the table displays at the top of the page. The navigation area at the bottom of the window displays *1* in the Pages box, and the right-pointing arrow—the Next arrow—is active. Recall that when you are in the Print Preview window, the navigation arrows are used to navigate from one page to the next, rather than from one record to the next.

2 In the navigation area, click the **Next Page** arrow.

The second page of the table displays the last field column. Whenever possible, try to print all of the fields horizontally on one page. Of course, if you have many records you may need more than one page to print all of the records.

3 On the **Print Preview tab**, in the **Page Layout group**, click **Margins**, and then click **Wide**. Then, click the **Landscape** button and compare your screen with Figure 1.56.

Table in landscape orientation

Figure 1.56
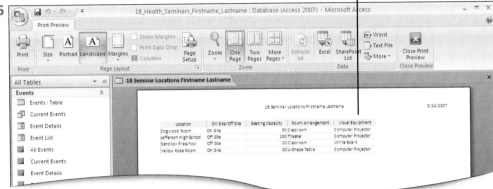

4 Check your *Chapter Assignment Sheet* or *Course Syllabus*, or consult your instructor, to determine whether you are to submit the printed pages that are the results of this project. To submit your work on paper, on the **Print Preview tab**, in the **Print group**, click the **Print** button. To submit electronically, close the Print Preview and follow the directions provided by your instructor.

5 On the **Print Preview tab**, click **Close Print Preview. Close** ⊠ your **1B Seminar Locations** table.

6 Close any open objects, and then **Close** ⊠ the **Navigation Pane**. From the **Office** menu 🔲, click **Close Database**. From the **Getting Started** screen, display the **Office** menu 🔲, and then click **Exit Access**.

Objective 15
Use the Access Help System

Access has a Help feature to assist you when performing a task in Access or to get more information about a particular topic in Access. You can activate the Help feature by clicking the Help button or by pressing ⌑F1⌑.

Activity 1.21 Using the Access Help System

1 **Start** Access. In the upper right corner of the Access window, click the **Help** button 🔘. In the **Access Help** window, click the **Search arrow**, and then under **Content from this computer**, click **Access Help**.

2 Click in the **Search** box, type **database design** and then press Enter. In the list that displays, click **Database design basics**.

This information is an informative overview of how to design a database from the beginning—from the stage where you are just writing your ideas on paper. If desired, print this information by clicking the Print button.

3 In the upper right corner of the Help window, click the **Close** button ⊠ to close the Help window.

End You have completed Project 1B ─────────────

There's More You Can Do!

From My Computer, navigate to the student files that accompany this textbook. In the folder **02_theres_more_you_can_do_pg1_36**, locate and open the folder for this chapter. Open and print the instructions for this project, which are provided to you in Adobe PDF format.

Try IT! 1—Convert a Database to a Different Format

In this Try IT! exercise, you will convert an Access 2007 database to a database that others can view and edit in Access 2002 or Access 2003.

Content-Based Assessments

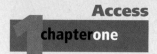

Summary

Microsoft Office Access is a database management system that uses various objects—tables, forms, queries, reports—to organize a database. Data is stored in tables in which you establish fields, set the data type and field size, and create a primary key. Data from a database can be reported and printed.

Key Terms

The ⓘ symbol represents Key Terms found on the Student CD in the 02_theres_more_you_can_do folder for this chapter.

Content-Based Assessments

Matching

Match each term in the second column with its correct definition in the first column. Write the letter of the term on the blank line in front of the correct definition.

____ **1.** An organized collection of facts about people, events, things, or ideas related to a particular topic or purpose.

____ **2.** Facts about people, events, things, or ideas.

____ **3.** Data that is organized in a useful manner.

____ **4.** The basic parts of a database, which include tables, forms, queries, reports, and macros.

____ **5.** The Access object that stores your data organized in an arrangement of columns and rows.

____ **6.** The area of the Access window that displays and organizes the names of the objects in a database, and from where you open objects for use.

____ **7.** The portion of the Access window that displays open objects.

____ **8.** A category that describes each piece of data stored in a table.

____ **9.** All of the categories of data pertaining to one person, place, thing, event, or idea.

____ **10.** The number of fields, and the type of content within each field, in an Access table.

____ **11.** The Access view that displays an object organized in a format of columns and rows similar to an Excel spreadsheet.

____ **12.** The Access view that displays the underlying structure of an object.

____ **13.** The action of filling a database table with records.

____ **14.** The characteristic that defines the kind of data that can be entered into a field, such as numbers, text, or dates.

____ **15.** An Access feature that sequentially numbers entered records creating a unique number for each field and which is useful for data that has no distinct field that is unique.

A AutoNumber

B Data

C Data type

D Database

E Datasheet view

F Design view

G Field

H Information

I Navigation Pane

J Object window

K Objects

L Populate

M Record

N Table

O Table design

Content-Based Assessments

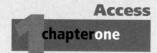

Fill in the Blank

Write the correct word in the space provided.

1. DBMS is an acronym for _____ _____ _____.

2. A preformatted database designed for a specific purpose is a database _____.

3. A database that has no data and has no database tools, in which you create the data and the tools as you need them, is referred to as a _____ database.

4. Characteristics of a field that control how the field will display and how data can be entered in a field are known as the _____ _____.

5. The field that uniquely identifies a record in a table is the _____ _____.

6. A pre-built table format for common topics such as contacts, issues, and tasks is a _____ _____.

7. A database object that retrieves specific data from one or more tables, and then displays the specified data in Datasheet view is a _____.

8. A type of query that retrieves data from one or more tables and makes it available for use in the format of a datasheet is a _____ query.

9. The table or tables from which a query gets its data is the _____ _____.

10. A feature in Microsoft Office programs that walks you step by step through a process is a _____.

11. The process in which Access searches a table of records included in a query, finds the records that match the criteria, and then displays the records in a datasheet is called _____.

12. An Access object with which you can enter new records into a table, edit existing records in a table, or display existing records from a table is a _____.

13. The Access object that displays data in a formatted manner for printing and publication is a _____.

14. The Access form object in which multiple records can be entered into or displayed from a table is a _____ _____ form.

15. An arrangement of objects in the Navigation Pane in which the objects are grouped by the table to which they are related is the _____ _____ _____ category.

Content-Based Assessments

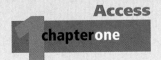

Project 1C—Medical Center Departments

In this project, you will apply the skills you practiced from the Objectives in Project 1A.

Objectives: 1. *Start Access and Create a New Blank Database;* **2.** *Add Records to a Table;* **3.** *Rename Table Fields in Datasheet View;* **4.** *Modify the Design of a Table;* **5.** *Add a Second Table to a Database;* **6.** *Print a Table;* **7.** *Create and Use a Query;* **8.** *Create and Use a Form;* **9.** *Create and Print a Report;* **10.** *Close and Save a Database.*

In the following Skills Review, you will assist Kendall Walker, the CEO of Texas Lakes Medical Center, in creating a database to store information about the Departments and Department Directors at Texas Lakes Medical Center. Your printed results will look similar to those in Figure 1.57.

For Project 1C, you will need the following file:

New blank Access database

You will save your database as
1C_Departments_Firstname_Lastname

Figure 1.57

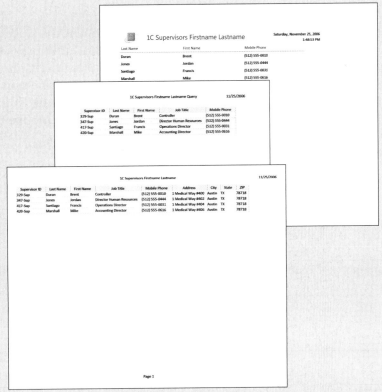

(Project 1C—Medical Center Departments continues on the next page)

Content-Based Assessments

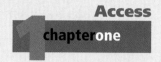
(Project 1C–Medical Center Departments continued)

1. **Start** Access and create a new **Blank Database**. In the lower right portion of the screen, click the **file folder icon**, navigate to your Access Chapter 1 folder, and then save the database as **1C_Departments_Firstname_Lastname** Press Enter. In the lower right corner, click the **Create** button.

2. In the **Navigation Pane**, click the **Close** button to collapse the **Navigation Pane** and maximize your screen space. Click in the first **Add New Field** box, type **Accounting** and then click in the **ID** field. To assign custom Department IDs, on the **Datasheet tab**, in the **Data Type & Formatting group**, click the **Data Type arrow**, and then click **Text**. Type **1212-D** and then click in the next **Add New Field** box to the right of *Accounting*, and complete the entry of this record and the next record as follows.

ID	Field1	Field2	Field3	Field4	Field5	Field6	Field7	Field8	Field9	Field10
1212-D	Accounting	Jennifer	R	Lee	(512) 555-0987	1 Medical Way #216	Austin	TX	78718	Duran
1233-D	Employee Benefits	Mike	M	Hernandez	(512) 555-0344	1 Medical Way #214	Austin	TX	78718	Duran

3. Point to the text *ID*, and then click to select the column. On the **Datasheet tab**, in the **Fields & Columns group**, click the **Rename** button, type **Dept ID** and press Enter. Point to the text *Field1*, right-click, and from the displayed menu, click **Rename Column**. Type **Department** and press Enter. Point to the text *Field2* and double-click. With the text selected, type **Director First Name** and press Enter. Using any of these techniques, rename *Field3* as **Director Middle Initial** Rename *Field4* as **Director Last Name** Rename *Field5* as **Mobile Phone** Rename *Field6* as **Address** Rename *Field7* as **City** Rename *Field8* as **State** Rename *Field9* as **ZIP** Rename *Field10* as **Supervisor**

4. Enter the following additional records:

Dept ID	Department	Director First Name	Director Middle Initial	Director Last Name	Mobile Phone	Address	City	State	ZIP	Supervisor
1259-D	Emergency Room	Paul	S	Roberts	(512) 555-0234	1 Medical Way #212	Austin	TX	78718	Marshall
1265-D	Nursing Services	Andrea	T	McMillan	(512) 555-0233	1 Medical Way #302	Austin	TX	78718	Jones

(Project 1C–Medical Center Departments continues on the next page)

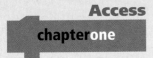
(Project 1C–Medical Center Departments continued)

1313-D	Finance	Beth	N	Crosby	(512) 555-0266	1 Medical Way #301	Austin	TX	78718	Duran
1355-D	Physician Services	Laura	O	Klein	(512) 555-0277	1 Medical Way #146	Austin	TX	78718	Jones
1459-D	Facilities	Mario	B	Bartello	(512) 555-0211	1 Medical Way #236	Austin	TX	78718	Santiago

5. On the **Datasheet tab**, in the **Views group**, click the **View button arrow**. From the displayed list, click **Design View**. To save the changes you made to the field names and data types, and to give the table a more meaningful name, save the table, using your own first and last name, as **1C Departments Firstname Lastname** and then click **OK**.

6. In the **Field Name** column, click the row selector box to the left of the **Director Middle Initial** field name to select the entire row. Then, on the **Design tab**, in the **Tools group**, click the **Delete Rows** button, read the message in the displayed dialog box, and then click **Yes**. For this table, Kendall decides that having the Director's middle initial is not necessary.

7. With your table still displayed in Design view, in the **Field Name** column, click in the **Dept ID** box. To the left of the box, notice the small icon of a key representing the primary key. Recall that the primary key is the field that uniquely identifies each individual record—no two records in the database will have the same Dept ID.

8. In the **Field Name** column, click in the **State** field, and then in the **Field Properties** area, set the **Field Size** to 2 In the **Description** column, click in the **Address** row, and then type **Include the Room number** Recall that descriptions entered here will display in the status bar when entering records using a form. This will communicate additional information to the person entering data about how to enter data in the field.

9. Click the **View** button to return to Datasheet view, and then click **Yes** two times to save the changes you have made to the design of your table—deleting a field, adding a description, and changing a field property.

10. With your **1C Departments** table displayed in Datasheet view, notice that in the **Supervisor** field, several names are repeated. Thus, it would not make sense to include information about these individuals multiple times in the same table. Recall that when you see repeated information, it is likely that an additional table should be added to your database. On the Ribbon, click the **Create tab**. In the **Tables group**, click **Table Templates**, and then from the displayed list, click **Contacts**.

11. Click the **Datasheet tab** to display the groups of Datasheet commands. In the second column, point to the text *Company*, click to select the field, and then on the **Datasheet tab**, in the **Fields & Columns group**, click **Delete**.

(Project 1C–Medical Center Departments continues on the next page)

Content-Based Assessments

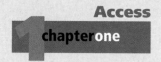
(Project 1C–Medical Center Departments continued)

12. Delete the **E-mail Address** field. With your mouse, drag to the right to select the **Business Phone** field and **Home Phone** field. Right-click over the field names, and then from the displayed shortcut menu, click **Delete Column**. Delete the **Fax Number** field. Then, delete the fields **Country/Region**, **Web Page**, **Notes**, and **Attachments** (the field with the paper clip icon).

13. On the **Datasheet tab**, in the **Views group**, click the **View** button to switch to **Design view**. To save the changes you made to the field arrangement and to give the table a more meaningful name, save the table, using your own first and last name, as **1C Supervisors Firstname Lastname** and then click **OK**.

14. In the **Field Name** column, click the **ID** box, delete the text, and then type **Supervisor ID** Click in the **Data Type** box, click the **Data Type arrow**, and then from the displayed list, click **Text**. Click in the **Description** column, and type **Supervisor's ID number** The medical center assigns a unique ID number to each Supervisor, which you will use as the primary key instead of the AutoNumber.

15. In the **Field Name** column, click in the **State/Province** field, and then in the **Field Properties** area, set the **Field Size** to **2** Click the **View** button to switch to Datasheet view, and then click **Yes** to save the changes you have made to the design of your table—changing a field name, adding a description, and changing a field property.

16. With your **1C Supervisors** table displayed in Datasheet view, in the new record row which is indicated by an asterisk (*) in the record selector box on the left, click in the **Supervisor ID** field, and then add the following records:

Supervisor ID	Last Name	First Name	Job Title	Mobile Phone	Address	City	State/ Province	ZIP/Postal Code
329-Sup	Duran	Brent	Controller	(512) 555-0010	1 Medical Way #400	Austin	TX	78718
347-Sup	Jones	Jordan	Director Human Resources	(512) 555-0444	1 Medical Way #402	Austin	TX	78718
417-Sup	Santiago	Francis	Operations Director	(512) 555-0031	1 Medical Way #404	Austin	TX	78718
420-Sup	Marshall	Mike	Accounting Director	(512) 555-0616	1 Medical Way #406	Austin	TX	78718

17. Change the field name **State/Province** to **State** and **ZIP/Postal Code** to **ZIP** Select all of the columns, and then apply **Best Fit** either by double-clicking the right border of any selected column or by displaying the shortcut menu, clicking Column Width, and then clicking Best Fit. On the **Quick Access Toolbar**, click **Save** to save the changes you have made to the layout of the table.

(Project 1C–Medical Center Departments continues on the next page)

Content-Based Assessments

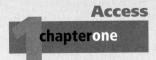
(Project 1C–Medical Center Departments continued)

18. From the **Office** menu, point to the **Print** button, and then click **Print Preview**. In the **Page Layout group**, click the **Margins** button, and then click **Normal**. Click the **Landscape** button. If you are submitting paper results, click the **Print** button, and in the displayed **Print** dialog box, click **OK**. To submit electronically, follow the directions provided by your instructor. Click **Close Print Preview**.

19. **Close** your **1C Supervisors** table and **Close** your **1C Departments** table. Click the **Create tab**, and then in the **Other group**, click **Query Wizard**. In the **New Query** dialog box, click **Simple Query Wizard**, and then click **OK**. Click the **Tables/Queries arrow**, and then click your **Table: 1C Supervisors**. Under **Available Fields**, click **Supervisor ID**, and then click the **Add Field** button to move the field to the **Selected Fields** list on the right. Add the **Last Name**, **First Name**, **Job Title**, and **Mobile Phone** fields to the **Selected Fields** list. Recall that you can also double-click a field name to move it.

This query will answer the question *What is the Supervisor ID, name, job title, and mobile phone number of every Supervisor in the database?* Click the **Next** button. Be sure that the option **Open the query to view information** is selected. Click **Finish**. Display the query in Print Preview, use the default margins and orientation, and then print or submit electronically. Close the Print Preview.

20. **Close** your query. **Open** the **Navigation Pane**, click to select your **1C Supervisors** table. You need not open the table, just select it. **Close** the **Navigation Pane**. On the Ribbon, click the **Create tab**, and then in the **Forms group**, click **Form**. The form displays in Layout view, in which you can make changes to the layout of the form. Because no changes are necessary, on the **Home tab**, in the **Views group**, click the **View button arrow**, and then from the displayed list, click **Form View**. From the **Office** menu, click **Save** to save your newly designed form, and then click **OK** to accept the default name. **Close** the form object. Recall that you typically create forms to make data entry easier for the individuals who enter new records into your database.

21. **Open** the **Navigation Pane**, locate your **1C Supervisors** table—recall that a table displays a small icon of a datasheet, a query displays a small icon of two datasheets, and a form displays a red form icon. Open the table either by double-clicking the table name or right-clicking and clicking Open from the shortcut menu. **Close** the **Navigation Pane**. On the **Create tab**, in the **Reports group**, click **Report**.

22. Point to the **Supervisor ID** column heading, right-click, and then click **Delete**. Delete the **Job Title**, **Address**, **City**, **State**, and **ZIP** fields from the report layout. From the **Office** menu, display **Print Preview**. In the **Page Layout group**, click the **Margins** button, and then click **Wide**. Click the **Landscape** button. If you are submitting paper results, click the **Print** button. To submit electronically, follow the instructions provided by your instructor. Click **Close Print Preview**.

23. **Close** your **1C Supervisors** report, and then click **Yes** to save the design changes. In the **Save As** dialog box, click **OK** to save the report with the default name. If necessary, close any remaining objects and close the Navigation Pane. From the **Office** menu, click **Exit Access**.

 End **You have completed Project 1C**

Content-Based Assessments

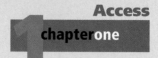
Skills Review

Project 1D—Benefits Fair

In this project, you will apply the skills you practiced from the Objectives in Project 1B.

Objectives: 11. *Create a Database Using a Template;* **12.** *Organize Database Objects in the Navigation Pane;* **13.** *Create a New Table in a Database Created with a Template;* **14.** *View a Report and Print a Table in a Database Created with a Template.*

In the following Skills Review, you will assist Sharon Fitzgerald, the Human Resources Director at Texas Lakes Medical Center, in creating a database to store information about the Employee Benefits Fair at Texas Lakes Medical Center. Your printed result will look similar to Figure 1.58.

For Project 1D, you will need the following file:

New Access database using the Events Template

You will save your database as
1D_Benefits_Fair_Firstname_Lastname

Figure 1.58

(Project 1D–Benefits Fair continues on the next page)

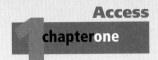

(Project 1D–Benefits Fair continued)

1. **Start** Access, under **Template Categories**, click **Local Templates**, and then click **Events**. In the lower right portion of the screen, click the **file folder icon**, navigate to your Access Chapter 1 folder, and then save the database as **1D_Benefits_Fair_Firstname_Lastname** Press Enter. In the lower right corner, click the **Create** button. If necessary, to the right of the **Security Warning**, click **Options**, click **Enable this content**, and then click **OK**.

2. Recall that a template opens with a pre-built Multiple Items form into which you can enter records to build a table. In the Event List Multiple Items form, enter the following records, pressing Tab to move across the row:

ID	Title	Start Time	End Time	Description	Location
1	**Medical Plan**	**5/1/09 8a**	**5/1/09 5p**	**Health Benefits**	**Lone Star Room**
2	**Eye Care Plan**	**5/1/09 9a**	**5/1/09 3p**	**Health Benefits**	**Red River Room**
3	**Prescription Plan**	**5/1/09 8a**	**5/1/09 8p**	**Health Benefits**	**Lone Star Room**
4	**Pension Plan**	**5/1/09 10a**	**5/1/09 7:30p**	**Retirement Benefits**	**Capitol Room**
5	**Life Insurance Plan**	**5/1/09 1p**	**5/1/09 5p**	**Life Insurance Benefits**	**Blue Bird Room**
6	**Deferred Compensation Plan**	**5/1/09 10a**	**5/1/09 3p**	**Compensation Benefits**	**Red River Room**

3. In the **Link bar**, just above the Field names, click **New Event**, and then enter the following record using the single record form. Recall that you can also use this form to enter records into a table:

Title	Location	Start Time	End Time	Description
Dental Plan	**Blue Bird Room**	**5/1/09 8a**	**5/1/09 5p**	**Health Benefits**

4. **Close** the single record form. **Close** the **Event List** form. **Open** the **Navigation Pane**. At the top of the **Navigation Pane**, click the **Navigation arrow**. In the **Navigate To Category** section, click **Tables and Related Views**. Click the **Navigation arrow** again, and then in the **Filter By Group** section, notice that **All Tables** is selected. Recall that this arrangement organizes the database objects by the table to which they are related.

5. From the **Navigation Pane**, right-click the **Events** table, and then click **Open**—or double-click the table name to open it. This is the table that was built from the records you entered into the form. Rather than enter information about the Locations multiple times in this table, you will create another table for the Location information. **Close** the **Events** table, and then **Close** the **Navigation Pane**.

(Project 1D–Benefits Fair continues on the next page)

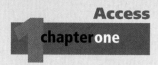
(Project 1D–Benefits Fair continued)

6. On the Ribbon, click the **Create tab**, and then in the **Tables group**, click **Table**. Enter the following records, pressing (Tab) or (Enter) to move across the row. Recall that Access will assign unique numbers; your assigned numbers may vary.

ID	Field1	Field2	Field3	Field4
4	Blue Bird Room	30	U-Shape Table	Computer Projector
5	Red River Room	20	Classroom	Computer Projector
6	Capitol Room	30	Classroom	Computer Projector

7. Point to the text *Field1* and click to select the column. On the **Datasheet tab**, in the **Fields & Columns group**, click **Rename**, and then type **Location** Point to the text *Field2*, right-click, and then from the displayed menu, click **Rename Column**. Type **Seating Capacity** Point to the text *Field3* and double-click. With the text selected, type **Room Arrangement** Using any of these techniques, rename *Field4* as **Visual Equipment**

8. Enter one additional record as follows:

ID	Location	Seating Capacity	Room Arrangement	Visual Equipment
7	Lone Star Room	50	Theater	Computer Projector

9. On the **Home tab**, in the **Views group**, click the **View button arrow**, and then click **Design View**. **Save** the table as **1D Room Locations Firstname Lastname** and then click **OK**.

10. In the **Field Name** column, click in the **Location** box, and then on the **Design tab**, click the **Primary Key** button. Point to the row selector box for the **ID** field, and then click to select the entire row. On the **Design tab**, click **Delete Rows**, and then click **Yes**. The Location name will serve as the primary key for this table. In the **Views group**, click the **View** button, and then click **Yes** to save the changes you made to the table design.

11. On the field name row, drag across to select all of the columns. Right-click over any column heading, click **Column Width**, and then in the displayed **Column Width** dialog box, click **Best Fit**.

12. **Close** the **1D Room Locations** table, and then click **Yes** to save the layout changes you made to the column widths. From the **Navigation Pane**, open the **All Events** report. Open the **Event Details** report. The pre-built reports are arranged in various useful formats. **Close** both reports.

13. From the **Navigation Pane**, open your **1D Room Locations** table. From the **Office** menu, point to the **Print** button, and then click **Print Preview**. Check your *Chapter Assignment Sheet* or *Course Syllabus*, or consult your instructor, to determine whether you are to submit the

(Project 1D–Benefits Fair continues on the next page)

Content-Based Assessments

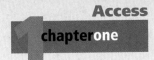
(Project 1D–Benefits Fair continued)

printed page. If you are submitting your work on paper, on the **Print Preview tab**, in the **Print group**, click **Print**. To submit electronically, follow the directions provided by your instructor.

14. **Close Print Preview**, and then **Close** your **1D Room Locations** table. **Close** the **Navigation Pane**. Be sure all database objects are closed. From the **Office** menu, click **Exit Access**.

 You have completed Project 1D ————————————————————————

Content-Based Assessments

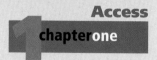

Mastering Access

Project 1E—Orthopedic Supplies

In this project, you will apply the skills you practiced from the Objectives in Project 1A.

Objectives: 1. *Start Access and Create a New Blank Database;* **2.** *Add Records to a Table;* **3.** *Rename Table Fields in Datasheet View;* **4.** *Modify the Design of a Table;* **5.** *Add a Second Table to a Database;* **6.** *Print a Table;* **7.** *Create and Use a Query;* **8.** *Create and Use a Form;* **9.** *Create and Print a Report;* **10.** *Close and Save a Database.*

In the following Mastering Access assessment, you will assist Kelley Martin, the Orthopedics Director of Texas Lakes Medical Center, in creating a database to store information about medical suppliers and supplies. Your printed results will look similar to those shown in Figure 1.59.

For Project 1E, you will need the following file:

New blank Access database

You will save your database as
1E_Orthopedic_Supplies_Firstname_Lastname

Figure 1.59

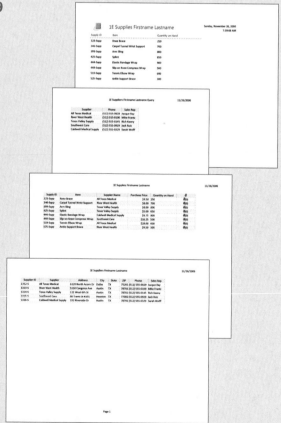

(Project 1E–Orthopedic Supplies continues on the next page)

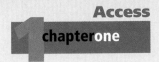

(Project 1E–Orthopedic Supplies continued)

1. **Start** Access, create a new **Blank Database**, use the **open folder icon** to navigate to your chapter folder, and then name the new database **1E_Orthopedic_Supplies_Firstname_Lastname** Close the **Navigation Pane**, and then beginning in the first new field, add the following records:

ID	Field1	Field2	Field3	Field4	Field5	Field6	Field7	Field8	Field9
9	1312-S	All Texas Medical	6120 North Acorn Dr	Dallas	TX	75201	(512) 555-0929	Jacque Ray	14-O
10	1313-S	River West Health	5150 Congress Ave	Austin	TX	78701	(512) 555-0100	Mike Frantz	16-R

2. Rename *Field1* as **Supplier ID** Rename *Field2* as **Supplier** Rename *Field3* as **Address** Rename *Field4* as **City** Rename *Field5* as **State** Rename *Field6* as **ZIP** Rename *Field7* as **Phone** Rename *Field8* as **Sales Rep** Rename *Field9* as **Sales Code**

3. Click **View** to open the table in **Design view**. Name the table **1E Suppliers Firstname Lastname** Set the **Supplier ID** field as the **Primary Key**, and then delete the **ID** field. Set the **Field Size** for the **State** field to **2** Return to **Datasheet view**, save the changes, and then, beginning with *Supplier ID 1314-S*, enter the following records:

Supplier ID	Supplier	Address	City	State	ZIP	Phone	Sales Rep	Sales Code
1312-S	All Texas Medical	6120 North Acorn Dr	Dallas	TX	75201	(512) 555-0929	Jacque Ray	14-O
1313-S	River West Health	5150 Congress Ave	Austin	TX	78701	(512) 555-0100	Mike Frantz	16-R
1314-S	Texas Valley Supply	121 West 6th St	Austin	TX	78701	(512) 555-0145	Rich Keeny	12-R
1315-S	Southwest Care	80 Travis St #101	Houston	TX	77002	(512) 555-0929	Jack Ruiz	14-O
1316-S	Caldwell Medical Supply	192 Riverside Dr	Austin	TX	78701	(512) 555-0329	Sarah Wolff	16-O

4. **Delete** the **Sales Code** field. Apply **Best Fit** to all of the columns to accommodate their data and column headings. If you are submitting printed pages, display the **Print Preview**, change the margins to **Wide**, change the orientation to **Landscape**, and then print the table. For electronic submissions, follow your instructor's directions. **Close Print Preview**, and then on the **Quick Access Toolbar**, **Save** the changes you have made to your table.

(Project 1E–Orthopedic Supplies continues on the next page)

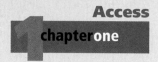

(Project 1E–Orthopedic Supplies continued)

5. Close your **1E Suppliers** table. Create a second table using the **Table Templates Assets** template to record the information about the orthopedic supplies that have been purchased by the medical center. Delete the following fields from the template: **Category, Condition, Acquired Date, Current Value, Location, Manufacturer, Model, Comments,** and **Retired Date.**

6. Rename the **Description** field as **Supplier Name** and then rename the **ID** field as **Supply ID** From the **Datasheet tab**, set the **Data Type** for the **Supply ID** field to **Text.** From the **Home tab,** switch to **Design view,** save the table as **1E Supplies Firstname Lastname** and then in the **Field Name** column, insert a new row above **Attachments.** Name the new field **Quantity on Hand** Click the **Supply ID** field, and then change its **Field Size** to 8 Return to **Datasheet view,** save your changes, and then add the following records:

Supply ID	Item	Supplier Name	Purchase Price Each	Quantity on Hand
323-Supp	Knee Brace	All Texas Medical	9.50	250
346-Supp	Carpal Tunnel Wrist Support	River West Health	8	700
399-Supp	Arm Sling	Texas Valley Supply	8	800
425-Supp	Splint	Texas Valley Supply	5	650
444-Supp	Elastic Bandage Wrap	Caldwell Medical Supply	9.75	900
449-Supp	Slip-on Knee Compress Wrap	Southwest Care	16.25	500
519-Supp	Tennis Elbow Wrap	All Texas Medical	28	600
525-Supp	Ankle Support Brace	River West Health	9.50	300

7. Select all the columns, and then apply **Best Fit.** Display the table in **Print Preview,** and then select **Wide** margins and **Landscape** orientation. If you are submitting printed pages, print the table. To submit electronically, follow the directions provided by your instructor.

8. **Close Print Preview, Close** the **1E Supplies** table, and then save the changes. On the **Create tab,** use the **Query Wizard** to create a **Simple Query** based on the **1E Suppliers** table. The query will answer the question *What is the name of every supplier, their phone number, and their Sale Rep's name?* Add the **Supplier** field, **Phone** field, and **Sales Rep** field. Title the query as **1E Suppliers Firstname Lastname Query** Print and then close the query.

9. From the **Navigation Pane,** select your **1E Supplies** table—you do not need to open the table, just be sure that it is selected. **Create** a **Form** based on the table, click the **View button arrow**

(Project 1E–Orthopedic Supplies continues on the next page)

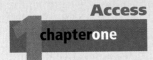

(Project 1E–Orthopedic Supplies continued)

and then click **Form View**. When needed, the form can be used to enter or view records one record at a time.

10. **Close** the form, and then save it with the default name. **Create** a **Report** based on your **1E Supplies** table. Delete the **Supplier Name** field, the **Purchase Price** field, and the **Attachments** field from the report. In **Print Preview**, set the **Margins** to **Wide** and the orientation to **Landscape**. If you are submitting printed pages, print the table. To submit electronically, follow the directions provided by your instructor.

11. **Close Print Preview**, close and save the report with the default name. Close any open objects, close the **Navigation Pane**, and then from the **Office** menu, click **Exit Access**.

 End **You have completed Project 1E**

Content-Based Assessments

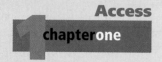
Project 1F—Fundraisers

In this project, you will apply the skills you practiced from the Objectives in Project 1B.

Objectives: 11. *Create a Database Using a Template;* **12.** *Organize Database Objects in the Navigation Pane;* **13.** *Create a New Table in a Database Created with a Template;* **14.** *View a Report and Print a Table in a Database Created with a Template.*

In the following Mastering Access project, you will assist Kirk Shaw, the Development Director for Texas Lakes Medical Center, in creating a database to store information about the various fundraising events held throughout the year. Your printed results will look similar to those shown in Figure 1.60.

For Project 1F, you will need the following file:

New Access database using the Events Template

You will save your database as
1F_Fundraisers_Firstname_Lastname

Figure 1.60

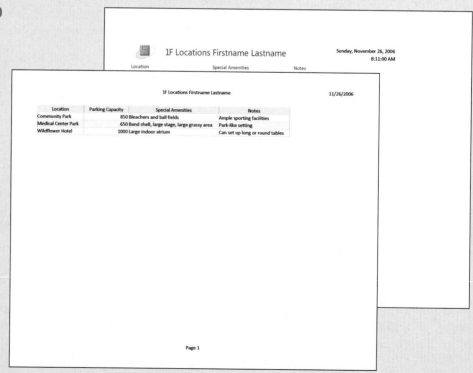

(Project 1F–Fundraisers continues on the next page)

Content-Based Assessments

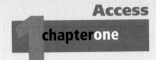

(Project 1F—Fundraisers continued)

1. **Start** Access, and then from **Local Templates**, create a new database using the **Events** database template. In the lower right portion of the screen, click the **file folder icon**, navigate to your Access Chapter 1 folder, and then name the new database **1F_Fundraisers_Firstname_ Lastname** In the lower right corner, click the **Create** button. If necessary, to the right of the **Security Warning**, click **Options**, click **Enable this content**, and then click **OK**.

2. To build the Event List table, enter the following records using either the displayed Multiple Items form or the single record form, which is available by clicking New Event in the Link bar:

ID	Title	Start Time	End Time	Description	Location
1	Heart Ball	2/14/09 6p	2/14/09 11p	Gala Ball	Wildflower Hotel
2	Auto Raffle	3/30/09 4p	3/30/09 6p	Raffle	Medical Center Park
3	Spring Book Sale	4/5/09 8a	4/5/09 8p	New and Used Book Sale	Wildflower Hotel
4	Softball Contest	6/10/09 11a	6/10/09 6p	Softball games	Community Park
5	Taste of Texas	8/28/09 11a	8/28/09 11p	Food and music festival	Community Park
6	Holiday Kids Fair	12/15/09 1p	12/15/09 7p	Children's Rides and Games	Medical Center Park

3. **Close** the **Event List** form. **Open** the **Navigation Pane**, and then using the **Navigation arrow**, arrange the **Navigation Pane** by **Tables and Related Views**. From the **Navigation Pane**, open the **Events** table that you created by entering records in the form. Select all the columns in the table, apply **Best Fit**, and then **Close** the table and save the changes to the layout. **Close** the **Navigation Pane**, and then **Create** a second **Table**. Enter the following records. Recall that Access will assign unique ID numbers; yours may vary.

ID	Field1	Field2	Field3	Field4
4	Wildflower Hotel	1000	Large indoor atrium	Can set up long or round tables
5	Community Park	850	Bleachers and ball fields	Ample sporting facilities
6	Medical Center Park	650	Band shell, large stage, large grassy area	Park-like setting

4. Rename *Field1* as **Location** Rename *Field2* as **Parking Capacity** Rename *Field3* as **Special Amenities** Rename *Field4* as **Notes** Display the table in **Design view**, and then name it **1F Locations Firstname Lastname** Set the **Location** field as the **Primary Key**—no two locations will have the same name. Delete the **ID** field row.

5. Return to Datasheet view, save the design changes, select all the table columns, and then apply **Best Fit**. Display the table in **Print Preview**; select **Wide** margins and **Landscape**

(Project 1F—Fundraisers continues on the next page)

Content-Based Assessments

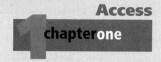

(Project 1F—Fundraisers continued)

orientation. If you are submitting printed pages, print the table. To submit electronically, follow the directions provided by your instructor. **Close** the table and save the changes to the layout.

6. Be sure your **1F Locations** table is still active, **Create** a **Report** based on the table. In the report, delete the **Parking Capacity** field, and then display the report in **Print Preview**. Select **Landscape** orientation, **Wide** margins, and then **Print** the report. To submit electronically, follow the directions provided by your instructor.

7. **Close Print Preview**, **Close** the report, save the changes to the design, and then accept the default report name. Close and save any open objects, and then **Exit** Access.

 End **You have completed Project 1F**

Content-Based Assessments

Access

chapterone

Mastering Access

Project 1G — Gift Shop

In this project, you will apply skills you practiced from the Objectives in Projects 1A and 1B.

Objectives: 1. *Start Access and Create a New Blank Database;* **2.** *Add Records to a Table;* **3.** *Rename Table Fields in Datasheet View;* **4.** *Modify the Design of a Table;* **5.** *Add a Second Table to a Database;* **6.** *Print a Table;* **7.** *Create and Use a Query;* **8.** *Create and Use a Form;* **9.** *Create and Print a Report;* **10.** *Close and Save a Database;* **12.** *Organize Database Objects in the Navigation Pane.*

In the following Mastering Access project, you will assist Scott Williams, the Gift Shop Manager of Texas Lakes Medical Center, in creating a database to store information about gift items in the shop's inventory. Your printed results will look similar to those shown in Figure 1.61.

For Project 1G, you will need the following file:

New Access database

You will save your database as
1G_Gift_Shop_Firstname_Lastname

Figure 1.61

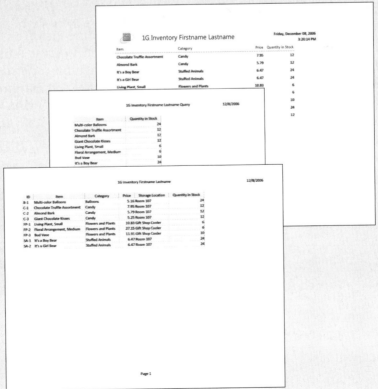

(Project 1G—Gift Shop continues on the next page)

Project 1G: Gift Shop | **Access** 79

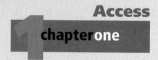
(Project 1G—Gift Shop continued)

1. **Start** Access, create a new **Blank Database**, and then store it in your Access Chapter 1 folder as **1G_Gift_Shop_Firstname_Lastname**

2. **Close** the **Navigation Pane**. Change the **ID** field **Data Type** to **Text**. Enter the following records:

ID	Field1	Field2	Field3	Field4	Field5
C-1	Chocolate Truffle Assortment	Candy	7.95	Room 107	12
C-2	Almond Bark	Candy	5.79	Room 107	12
SA-1	It's a Boy Bear	Stuffed Animals	6.47	Room 107	24
SA-2	It's a Girl Bear	Stuffed Animals	6.47	Room 107	24
FP-1	Living Plant, Small	Flowers and Plants	10.83	Gift Shop Cooler	6
FP-2	Floral Arrangement, Medium	Flowers and Plants	27.15	Gift Shop Cooler	6
FP-3	Bud Vase	Flowers and Plants	11.91	Gift Shop Cooler	10
B-1	Multi-color Balloons	Balloons	5.16	Room 107	24
C-3	Giant Chocolate Kisses	Candy	5.25	Room 107	12

3. Rename *Field1* as **Item** Rename *Field2* as **Category** Rename *Field3* as **Price** Rename *Field4* as **Storage Location** Rename *Field5* as **Quantity in Stock** Select all the table columns, and then apply **Best Fit**. On the **Quick Access Toolbar**, **Save** the table, and name it **1G Inventory Firstname Lastname** Display the table in **Print Preview**, set the margins to **Wide** and the orientation to **Landscape**. If you are submitting printed pages, click **Print**; or submit electronically as directed by your instructor. **Close Print Preview**; close the table and save any changes.

4. **Create** a second **Table** to record the information about the storage of inventory categories. Add the following records to the new table. Recall that Access will assign unique ID numbers; yours may vary.

ID	Field1	Field2	Field3
3	Candy	Room 107	North Zone 1
4	Stuffed Animals	Room 107	South Zone 2
5	Flowers and Plants	Gift Shop Coolers	Cooler 1
6	Balloons	Room 107	East Zone 3

(Project 1G–Gift Shop continues on the next page)

Content-Based Assessments

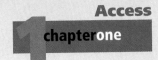
(Project 1G–Gift Shop continued)

5. Rename *Field1* as **Category** Rename *Field2* as **Storage Location** Rename *Field3* as **Location Detail** Switch to Design view, name the table **1G Categories Firstname Lastname** Set the **Category** field as the **Primary Key**—each category of inventory items is unique. Delete the **ID** field. Switch back to Datasheet view and save the changes. Select all the columns, and then apply **Best Fit. Close** your **1G Categories** table, and then save the changes to the layout.

6. **Create**, using the **Query Wizard**, a **Simple Query** based on your **1G Inventory** table. Include only the **Item** and **Quantity in Stock** fields in the query result. The query will answer the question *How many of each item do we currently have in stock?* Accept the default name, and then print and close the query.

7. **Create** a **Report** based on your **1G Inventory** table. Delete the **ID** field and the **Storage Location** field. Display the report in **Print Preview**, set the margins to **Wide** and the orientation to **Landscape**. If you are submitting printed pages, print the table. To submit electronically, follow the directions provided by your instructor. Close the report, save the design changes, and then accept the default name. **Close** any open objects and close the **Navigation Pane**. From the **Office** menu, **Exit Access**.

End **You have completed Project 1G**

Content-Based Assessments

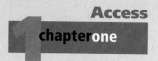
Mastering Access

Project 1H — Recruiting Events

In this project, you will apply skills you practiced from the Objectives in Projects 1A and 1B.

Objectives: 2. *Add Records to a Table;* **6.** *Print a Table;* **7.** *Create and Use a Query;* **10.** *Close and Save a Database;* **11.** *Create a Database Using a Template;* **12.** *Organize Database Objects in the Navigation Pane;* **13.** *Create a New Table in a Database Created with a Template;* **14.** *View a Report and Print a Table in a Database Created with a Template.*

In the following Mastering Access project, you will assist Serge Juco, Vice President of Human Resources, in creating a database to track recruiting events that are scheduled to attract new employees to careers at the medical center. Your printed results will look similar to those shown in Figure 1.62.

For Project 1H, you will need the following file:

New Access database using the Events Template

You will save your database as
1H_Recruiting_Events_Firstname_Lastname

Figure 1.62

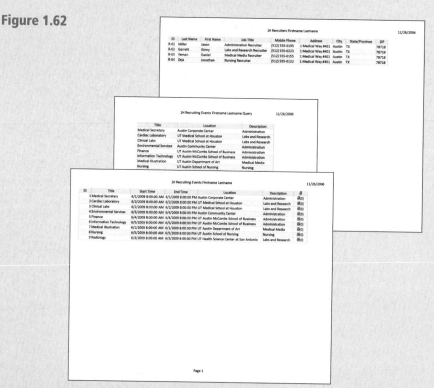

(Project 1H–Recruiting Events continues on the next page)

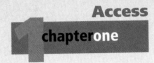
(Project 1H–Recruiting Events continued)

1. **Start** Access and then from **Local Templates**, create a new database based on the **Events** template. In your Access Chapter 1 folder, name the new database **1H_Recruiting_Events_ Firstname_Lastname** In the lower right corner, click the **Create** button. If necessary, to the right of the **Security Warning**, click **Options**, click **Enable this content**, and then click **OK**.

2. In the **Multiple Items** form, enter the following records to build the Event List table; if you prefer, use the New Event single record form available on the Link bar:

ID	Title	Start Time	End Time	Description	Location
1	Medical Secretary	6/1/09 8a	6/1/09 8p	Administration	Austin Corporate Center
2	Cardiac Laboratory	6/2/09 8a	6/2/09 8p	Labs and Research	UT Medical School at Houston
3	Clinical Labs	6/2/09 8a	6/2/09 8p	Labs and Research	UT Medical School at Houston
4	Environmental Services	6/3/09 8a	6/4/09 8p	Administration	Austin Community Center
5	Finance	6/4/09 8a	6/4/09 8p	Administration	UT Austin McCombs School of Business
6	Information Technology	6/5/09 8a	6/5/09 8p	Administration	UT Austin McCombs School of Business
7	Medical Illustration	6/1/09 8a	6/1/09 8p	Medical Media	UT Austin Department of Art
8	Nursing	6/5/09 8a	6/5/09 8p	Nursing	UT Austin School of Nursing
9	Radiology	6/3/09 8a	6/3/09 8p	Labs and Research	UT Health Science Center at San Antonio

3. **Close** the form, and then display the **Navigation Pane**. Using the **Navigation arrow**, organize the objects by **Tables and Related Views**. Point to the **Events** table, right-click, click **Rename**, and then type **1H Recruiting Events Firstname Lastname** and press [Enter] to rename the table.

4. **Open** the table; recall that the table was built by typing records into the Multiple Items form. Leave the Attachments field because Serge may decide to attach job description brochures for each event. The AutoNumber ID will serve as the primary key—the unique identifier for each record. **Close** the **Navigation Pane**. Select all the columns and apply **Best Fit**. Display the table in **Print Preview**, set the margins to **Normal** and the orientation to **Landscape**. Print if

(Project 1H–Recruiting Events continues on the next page)

Content-Based Assessments

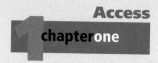
Mastering Access

(Project 1H–Recruiting Events continued)

you are submitting paper results; or, follow your instructor's directions for electronic submission. **Close Print Preview**, and then **Close** the table, saving the changes to the layout.

5. **Create** a new table using the **Contacts Table Template**. Delete the **Company** field. Delete the **E-mail Address** field. Delete the **Business Phone** and **Home Phone** fields. Delete the **Fax Number** field. Delete the **Country/Region**, **Web Page**, **Notes**, and **Attachments** fields. Click in the first **ID** field, from the **Datasheet tab**, change the **Data Type** of the ID field to **Text**, and then enter the following records:

ID	Last Name	First Name	Job Title	Mobile Phone	Address	City	State/ Province	ZIP/ Postal Code
R-01	Miller	Jason	Administration Recruiter	(512) 555-0195	1 Medical Way #401	Austin	TX	78718
R-02	Garrett	Ginny	Labs and Research Recruiter	(512) 555-0223	1 Medical Way #401	Austin	TX	78718
R-03	Yeman	Daniel	Medical Media Recruiter	(512) 555-0155	1 Medical Way #401	Austin	TX	78718
R-04	Zeja	Jonathan	Nursing Recruiter	(512) 555-0122	1 Medical Way #401	Austin	TX	78718

6. **Close** the table, save the changes, and then name the table **1H Recruiters Firstname Lastname Create**, using the **Query Wizard**, a **Simple Query** based on your **1H Recruiting Events** table. Add the appropriate fields to the query to answer the question *What is the title, location, and description of all the recruiting events?* Accept the default name for the query. Print and then close the query.

7. From the **Navigation Pane**, open your **1H Recruiters** table. Change the name of the **ZIP/Postal Code** field to **ZIP** Select all the columns in the table and apply **Best Fit**. Display the table in **Print Preview**, set the margins to **Normal** and the orientation to **Landscape** and then either print or submit electronically.

8. **Close Print Preview**, and then **Close** the table, saving the layout changes. From the **Navigation Pane**, open the **All Events** report. Then, open the **Events By Week** report. Recall that one advantage of starting a database from a database template is that many objects, such as attractively arranged reports, are provided.

9. **Close** the reports and any other open objects. **Close** the **Navigation Pane**. From the **Office** menu, **Exit Access**.

 You have completed Project 1H ————————————

Content-Based Assessments

Mastering Access

Project 1I—Facility Expansion

In this project, you will apply all the skills you practiced from the Objectives in Projects 1A and 1B.

Objectives: 1. *Start Access and Create a New Blank Database;* **2.** *Add Records to a Table;* **3.** *Rename Table Fields in Datasheet View;* **4.** *Modify the Design of a Table;* **5.** *Add a Second Table to a Database;* **6.** *Print a Table;* **7.** *Create and Use a Query;* **8.** *Create and Use a Form;* **9.** *Create and Print a Report;* **10.** *Close and Save a Database;* **11.** *Create a Database Using a Template;* **12.** *Organize Database Objects in the Navigation Pane;* **13.** *Create a New Table in a Database Created with a Template;* **14.** *View a Report and Print a Table in a Database Created with a Template.*

In the following Mastering Access project, you will assist Jerry Lopez, the Budget Director, in creating a database to store information about the facility expansion at Texas Lakes Medical Center and in creating a separate database to store information about public events related to the expansion. Your printed results will look similar to the ones shown in Figure 1.63.

For Project 1I, you will need the following files:

New Access database
New Events database

You will save your databases as
1I_Facility_Expansion_Firstname_Lastname
1I_Public_Events_Firstname_Lastname

Figure 1.63

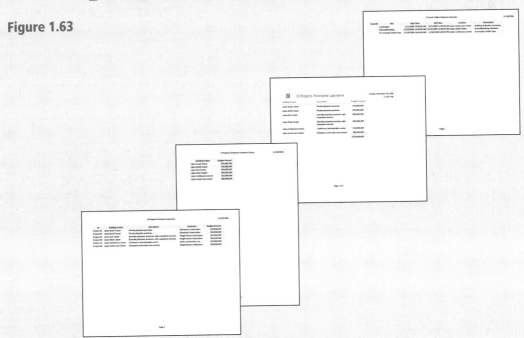

(Project 1I—Facility Expansion continues on the next page)

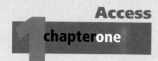

Mastering Access

(Project 1I—Facility Expansion continued)

1. **Start** Access, create a new **Blank Database**, and store it in your Access Chapter 1 folder as 1I_Facility_Expansion_Firstname_Lastname

2. **Close** the **Navigation Pane**. Change the **ID** field **Data Type** to **Text**. Enter the following records:

ID	Field1	Field2	Field3	Field4
Project-01	Lakes South Tower	Private physician practices	Glenmore Construction	30,000,000
Project-02	Lakes North Tower	Private physician practices	Glenmore Construction	30,000,000
Project-03	Lakes East Center	Specialty physician practices with outpatient services	Wright Rosen Contractors	60,000,000
Project-04	Lakes West Center	Specialty physician practices with outpatient services	Wright Rosen Contractors	60,000,000
Project-05	Lakes Conference Center	Conference and education center	Wells Construction, Inc.	10,000,000
Project-06	Lakes Acute Care Center	Emergency and acute care services	Wright Rosen Contractors	80,000,000

3. Rename *Field1* as **Building Project** Rename *Field2* as **Description** Rename *Field3* as **Contractor** Rename *Field4* as **Budget Amount** Change the **Data Type** of the **Budget Amount** field to **Currency**. Apply **Best Fit** to all the columns in the table. **Save** the table as **1I Projects Firstname Lastname** In **Print Preview**, set the margins to **Wide** and the orientation to **Landscape**. If you are submitting printed pages, click **Print**; or submit electronically as directed by your instructor. **Close Print Preview** and then close your **1I Projects** table.

4. **Create** a second **Table** to record the information about the contractors for the facility expansion. Add the following records to the new table. Recall that Access will assign unique ID numbers; your numbers may vary.

ID	Field1	Field2	Field3
3	Glenmore Construction	Bob Ballard	(512) 555-0900
4	Wright Rosen Contractors	Lisa Li	(512) 555-0707
5	Wells Construction, Inc.	Frank Levin	(512) 555-0444

(Project 1I—Facility Expansion continues on the next page)

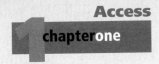
(Project 1I—Facility Expansion continued)

5. Rename *Field1* as **Contractor** Rename *Field2* as **Project Manager** Rename *Field3* as **Phone Number** Switch to **Design view**, name the table **1I Contractors Firstname Lastname** Set the **Contractor** field as the **Primary Key**—each contractor name is unique. Delete the **ID** field. Switch back to **Datasheet view** and save the changes. Apply **Best Fit** to all the columns. **Close** your **1I Contractors** table and save the changes to the layout—the column widths.

6. **Create**, using the **Query Wizard**, a **Simple Query** based on your **1I Projects** table. Include only the appropriate fields to answer the question *For each Building Project, what is the Budget Amount?* Accept the default name, display the query in **Print Preview**, and then print or submit electronically. **Close Print Preview**, and then close the query.

7. In the **Navigation Pane**, select your **1I Projects** table. **Create** a **Form**, close the **Navigation Pane**, view and then **Close** the form. Save and accept the default name.

8. **Open** your **1I Projects** table from the **Navigation Pane**. With the table open, **Create** a **Report**. Delete the **ID** field and the **Contractor** field. Display the report in **Print Preview**, set the margins to **Wide** and the orientation to **Landscape**. If you are submitting printed pages, print the report. To submit electronically, follow the directions provided by your instructor. **Close Print Preview**, close the report, save the changes, and accept the default name. **Close** any open objects and close the **Navigation Pane**. From the **Office** menu, click **Close Database**.

9. From the **Local Templates**, create a new database using the **Events template**. Create the database in your chapter folder and name it **1I_Public_Events_Firstname_Lastname** If necessary, enable the content.

10. To build the Events table, enter the following records using either the displayed Multiple Items Event List form or the single record form, which is available by clicking New Event in the Link bar:

Title	Start Time	End Time	Description	Location
Dedication	12/1/09 10a	12/1/09 11a	Building dedication ceremony	Lakes Acute Care Center
Groundbreaking	11/15/09 10a	11/15/09 11a	Groundbreaking ceremony	Lakes South Tower
Community Health Expo	11/30/09 10a	11/30/09 9p	Community Health Expo	Lakes Conference Center

11. **Close** the **Event List** form. **Open** the **Navigation Pane**, and then using the **navigation arrow**, arrange the **Navigation Pane** by **Tables and Related Views**. From the **Navigation Pane**, point to the **Events** table and right-click. From the shortcut menu, click **Rename**, type **1I Events Table Firstname Lastname** and then press Enter. Then open the table. Recall that the table was created by entering records in the form. Change the field name **ID** to **Event ID** Delete the **Attachments** field. Select all the columns in the table, apply **Best Fit**, and then display the table in **Print Preview**. Set the margins to **Normal** and the orientation to **Landscape**. Print or submit electronically, **Close Print Preview**, and then close the table and save the changes to the layout.

12. If necessary, close the Navigation Pane and close any open objects. Close the database and exit Access.

 End **You have completed Project 1I**

Content-Based Assessments

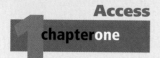

Business Running Case

Project 1J — Business Running Case

In this project, you will apply the skills you practiced in Projects 1A and 1B.

From My Computer, navigate to the student files that accompany this textbook. In the folder **03_business_running_case_pg37_86**, locate and open the folder for this chapter. Open and print the instructions for this project, which are provided to you in Adobe PDF format. Follow the instructions and use the skills you have gained thus far to assist Jennifer Nelson in meeting the challenges of owning and running her business.

 End **You have completed Project 1J** _____

Outcomes-Based Assessments

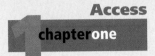

Rubric

The following outcomes-based assessments are *open-ended assessments*. That is, there is no specific correct result; your result will depend on your approach to the information provided. Make *Professional Quality* your goal. Use the following scoring rubric to guide you in *how* to approach the problem and then to evaluate *how well* your approach solves the problem.

The *criteria*—Software Mastery, Content, Format and Layout, and Process—represent the knowledge and skills you have gained that you can apply to solving the problem. The *levels of performance*—Professional Quality, Approaching Professional Quality, or Needs Quality Improvements—help you and your instructor evaluate your result.

	Your completed project is of Professional Quality if you:	Your completed project is Approaching Professional Quality if you:	Your completed project Needs Quality Improvements if you:
1-Software Mastery	Choose and apply the most appropriate skills, tools, and features and identify efficient methods to solve the problem.	Choose and apply some appropriate skills, tools, and features, but not in the most efficient manner.	Choose inappropriate skills, tools, or features, or are inefficient in solving the problem.
2-Content	Construct a solution that is clear and well organized, contains content that is accurate, appropriate to the audience and purpose, and is complete. Provide a solution that contains no errors of spelling, grammar, or style.	Construct a solution in which some components are unclear, poorly organized, inconsistent, or incomplete. Misjudge the needs of the audience. Have some errors in spelling, grammar, or style, but the errors do not detract from comprehension.	Construct a solution that is unclear, incomplete, or poorly organized, containing some inaccurate or inappropriate content; and contains many errors of spelling, grammar, or style. Do not solve the problem.
3-Format and Layout	Format and arrange all elements to communicate information and ideas, clarify function, illustrate relationships, and indicate relative importance.	Apply appropriate format and layout features to some elements, but not others. Overuse features, causing minor distraction.	Apply format and layout that does not communicate information or ideas clearly. Do not use format and layout features to clarify function, illustrate relationships, or indicate relative importance. Use available features excessively, causing distraction.
4-Process	Use an organized approach that integrates planning, development, self-assessment, revision, and reflection.	Demonstrate an organized approach in some areas, but not others; or, use an insufficient process of organization throughout.	Do not use an organized approach to solve the problem.

Outcomes-Based Assessments

Problem Solving

Project 1K—Public Seminars

In this project, you will construct a solution by applying any combination of the skills you practiced from the Objectives in Projects 1A and 1B.

For Project 1K, you will need the following files:

New Access database
a1K_Public_Seminars (Word document)

**You will save your database as
1K_Public_Seminars_Firstname_Lastname**

Texas Lakes Medical Center has developed a series of public health seminars. The information about the seminars is located in your student files, in the Word document **a1K_Public_Seminars**. Using the data in the Word document and a new database created from the Events database template, enter the data into the Multiple Items form. Each seminar will begin at 7 p.m. and end at 9 p.m. After entering the records, in the Navigation Pane, point to the name of the table that was created as a result of entering the records into the Multiple Items form, click Rename, and then name the table **1K Seminars Firstname Lastname** Open the table, apply Best Fit to the table's columns, and then display and modify the Print Preview so that that all the columns fully display on a single sheet. Print the table or submit electronically. Close the database.

End **You have completed Project 1K** ——————

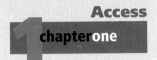

Problem Solving

Project 1L — Media Contacts

In this project, you will construct a solution by applying any combination of the skills you practiced from the Objectives in Projects 1A and 1B.

For Project 1L, you will need the following files:

New Access database
a1L_Media_Contacts (Word document)

**You will save your database as
1L_Media_Contacts_Firstname_Lastname**

The Public Relations Department at Texas Lakes Medical Center maintains a list of media contacts who receive e-mail notification when press releases regarding the Medical Center are issued. The information about the media contacts is located in your student files, in the Word document **a1L_Media_Contacts**. Create a new blank database, and then close the default Table1. Create a new table using the Contacts table template, and then use the data in the Word document to enter the records. Delete the unneeded fields from the table. As necessary, rename fields to match those in the Word document. Change the data type of the ID field to Text, and use the IDs provided. Close the table, and save it as **1L Media Contacts Firstname Lastname** Create a report and delete the Media ID column. In Page Setup or Print Preview, use narrow margins and landscape orientation to arrange the report. Print or submit the report electronically. Close the database.

 End **You have completed Project 1L** _____

Outcomes-Based Assessments

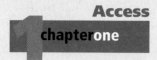
Problem Solving

Project 1M — Billing Rates

In this project, you will construct a solution by applying any combination of the skills you practiced from the Objectives in Projects 1A and 1B.

> **For Project 1M, you will need the following files:**
>
> New Access database
> a1M_Billing_Rates (Word document)

You will save your database as
1M_Billing_Rates_Firstname_Lastname

Physicians at Texas Lakes Medical Center have varying billing rates. The information about the physician names and billing rates is located in your student files, in the Word document **a1M_Billing_Rates**. Create a new blank database. Create a table with the Physician IDs and billing rates. For the rates, change data type to Currency. Apply Best Fit to the columns, save and name the table **1M Rates Firstname Lastname** and then print the table, or submit electronically as directed. From the table, create a query indicating only the Physician ID and the rate, and print or submit the query electronically. Create a second table using the Contacts table template, enter the names and phone numbers of the physicians, and delete unneeded columns. Apply Best Fit to the columns, save and name the table **1M Physicians Firstname Lastname** Print the table or submit electronically. Close the database.

End **You have completed Project 1M** ——————

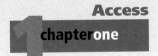

Problem Solving

Project 1N — Training

In this project, you will construct a solution by applying any combination of the skills you practiced from the Objectives in Projects 1A and 1B.

For Project 1N, you will need the following files:

New Access database
a1N_Training (Word document)

You will save your database as
1N_Training_Firstname_Lastname

Texas Lakes Medical Center has developed a series of training seminars to increase the skills of staff members in making public presentations and in dealing with the media. The information about the seminars is located in your student files, in the Word document **a1N_Training**. Using the data in the Word document and a new database created from the Events database template, enter the data into the Multiple Items form. Each seminar will begin at 8:30 a.m. and end at 11:30 a.m. After entering the records, in the Navigation Pane, point to the name of the table that was created as a result of entering the records into the Multiple Items form, click Rename, and then name the table **1N Training Firstname Lastname** Open the table, apply Best Fit to the table's columns, and then display and modify the Print Preview so that that all the columns fully display on a single sheet. Print the table or submit electronically. Close the database.

End **You have completed Project 1N**

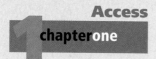

Problem Solving

Project 10 — Nurses

In this project, you will construct a solution by applying any combination of the skills you practiced from the Objectives in Projects 1A and 1B.

For Project 10, you will need the following files:

New Access database
a10_Nurses (Word document)

**You will save your database as
10_Nurses_Firstname_Lastname**

The Nursing Supervisor at Texas Lakes Medical Center maintains a list of nurses and the departments to which they are assigned. The information about the nurses is located in your student files, in the Word document **a10_Nurses**. Create a new blank database, and then close the default Table1. Create a new table using the Contacts table template, and then use the data in the Word document to enter the records. Use the Department data for the Company field, and change the field name accordingly. Delete the unneeded fields from the table. Change the ID field name to Emp#, and use the Employee numbers provided. Close the table, and save it as **10 Nurses Firstname Lastname** Based on the table, create a report and print it or submit the report electronically. Close the database.

 End **You have completed Project 10** —————

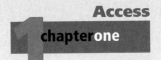

Access

chapter one

You and *GO!*

Project 1P — You and *GO!*

In this project, you will construct a solution by applying any combination of the skills you practiced from the Objectives in Projects 1A and 1B.

From My Computer, navigate to the student files that accompany this textbook. In the folder **04_you_and_go_pg87_102**, locate and open the folder for this chapter. Open and print the instructions for this project, which are provided to you in Adobe PDF format. Follow the instructions to create a personal inventory database for insurance purposes.

End **You have completed Project 1P** ——————

GO! with Help

Project 1Q — *GO!* with Help

1 **Start** Access and in the upper right corner, click the **Help** button . Click the **Search arrow**, and then under **Content from this computer**, click **Access Help**. In the **Search** box, type **Help** and then press Enter.

2 From the displayed list, scroll down as necessary, and then locate and click **What's new in Microsoft Office Access 2007?** Maximize the displayed window. Scroll through and read all the various features of Microsoft Access 2007.

3 If you want to do so, print a copy of the information by clicking the printer button at the top of the Access Help window. **Close** ☒ the Help window, and then exit Access.

End **You have completed Project 1Q** ——————

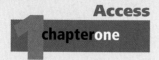

Group Business Running Case

Project 1R—Group Business Running Case

In this project, you will apply the skills you practiced from the Objectives in Projects 1A and 1B.

Your instructor may assign this group case project to your class. If your instructor assigns this project, he or she will provide you with information and instructions to work as part of a group. The group will apply the skills gained thus far to help the Bell Orchid Hotel Group achieve its business goals.

 End **You have completed Project 1R** ————————————

2 chaptertwo

Sort and Query a Database

OBJECTIVES

At the end of this chapter you will be able to:

1. Open an Existing Database
2. Create Table Relationships
3. Sort Records in a Table
4. Create a Query in Design View
5. Create a New Query from an Existing Query
6. Sort Query Results
7. Specify Criteria in a Query

8. Create a New Table by Importing an Excel Spreadsheet
9. Specify Numeric Criteria in a Query
10. Use Compound Criteria
11. Create a Query Based on More Than One Table
12. Use Wildcards in a Query
13. Use Calculated Fields in a Query
14. Group Data and Calculate Statistics in a Query

OUTCOMES

Mastering these objectives will enable you to:

PROJECT 2A
Sort and Query a Database

PROJECT 2B
Create a Database Table from an Excel Spreadsheet and Create Complex Queries

Florida Port Community College

Florida Port Community College is located in St. Petersburg, Florida, a coastal port city located near the Florida High Tech Corridor. With 60 percent of Florida's high tech companies and a third of the state's manufacturing companies located in the St. Petersburg and Tampa Bay areas, the college partners with businesses to play a vital role in providing a skilled workforce. The curriculum covers many areas including medical technology, computer science, electronics, aviation and aerospace, and simulation and modeling. The college also serves the community through cultural, athletic, and diversity programs, and provides adult basic education.

Sort and Query a Database

To convert data into meaningful information, you must manipulate the data in a way that you can answer questions. For example, you might ask the question, *What are the names and addresses of students who are enrolled in the Business Information Technology program and who has a grade point average of 3.0 or higher?* With such information, you could send the selected students information about scholarships that might be available to them.

Questions concerning the data in database tables can be answered by sorting the data or by creating a query. Access queries enable you to isolate specific data in database tables by limiting the fields that display and by setting conditions that limit the records to those that match specified conditions. You can also use a query to create calculations. In this chapter, you will sort Access database tables. You will also create and modify queries in an Access database.

Project 2A **Instructors and Courses**

Port Florida Community College uses sorting techniques and queries to locate information about data in their databases. In Activities 2.1 through 2.13, you will assist Lydia Barwari, Dean, in locating information about the records in the Instructors and Courses database in the Business Information Technology Department. Your completed queries and report will look similar to those in Figure 2.1.

For Project 2A, you will need the following file:

a2A_Instructors_and_Courses

You will save your database as
2A_Instructors_and_Courses_Firstname_Lastname

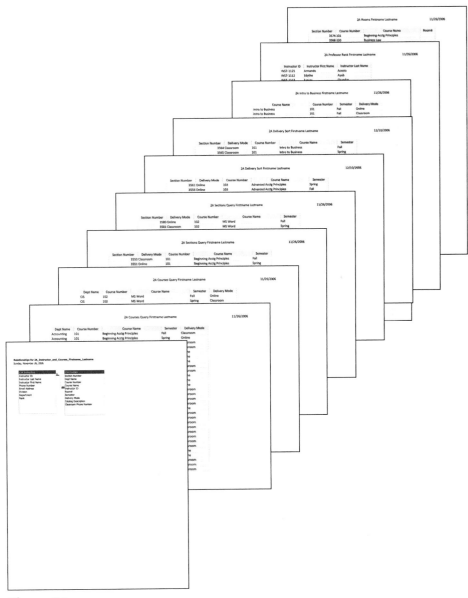

Figure 2.1
Project 2A—Instructors and Courses

Objective 1
Open an Existing Database

In other Microsoft Office 2007 applications, when you open a file, your computer loads the program and the file into random access memory (RAM). When you save and close, the file is transferred to a permanent storage location that you designate, such as a removable USB flash drive or your hard disk drive.

Because database files are typically very large, the entire database file is *not* loaded to RAM; rather, you work with the file from its permanent storage location. For this reason, Access does not have a Save As command with which you can save an entire database file with a new name. Thus, to work with the student files that accompany this textbook, you will use commands within your Windows operating system to copy the file to your chapter folder, and then rename the file before opening it.

Activity 2.1 Renaming and Opening an Existing Database

In this activity, you will use My Computer to copy a database file to a new storage location and then rename the database.

1 On the left side of the Windows taskbar, click **Start** `start`, and then click **My Computer**. Navigate to the location where you are storing your projects for this chapter.

2 On the menu bar, click **File**, point to **New**, and then click **Folder**.

A new folder is created, the words *New Folder* display highlighted in the folder's name box, and the insertion point is blinking. Recall that within Windows, highlighted text will be replaced by your typing.

3 Type **Access Chapter 2** and press Enter to rename the folder.

4 Navigate to the location where the student files that accompany this textbook are located, and then click one time to select the file **a2A_Instructors_and_Courses**. Point to the selected file name, and then right-click to display a shortcut menu. On the displayed shortcut menu, click **Copy**.

5 Navigate to and open the Access Chapter 2 folder you created in Step 3. In an open area, right-click to display a shortcut menu, and then click **Paste**.

The database file is copied to your folder and is selected.

6 Right-click the selected file name, and then from the displayed shortcut menu, click **Rename**. As shown in Figure 2.2, and using your own first and last name, type **2A_Instructors_and_Courses_ Firstname_Lastname**

Access Chapter 2
indicated in the title bar

Figure 2.2

Your folder name

Your name here

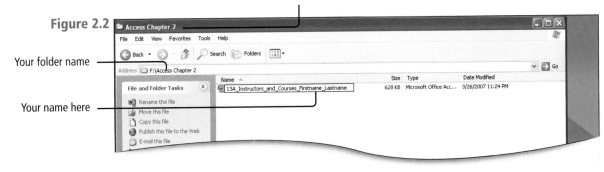

7 Press Enter to save the file with the new name. On the title bar, click the **Close** button ☒ to close the **My Computer** window.

Activity 2.2 Opening an Existing Database and Resolving Security Alerts

The **Message Bar** is the area directly below the Ribbon that displays information such as security alerts when there is potentially unsafe, active content in an Office 2007 document that you open. Settings that determine which alerts display on your Message Bar are set in the Access **Trust Center**. The Trust Center is an area of the Access program where you can view the security and privacy settings for your Access installation.

You may or may not be able to change the settings in the Trust Center, depending upon decisions made within your organization's computing environment. To display the Trust Center, from the Office menu, in the lower right corner click Access Options, and then click Trust Center.

1 **Start** Access. From the **Office** menu 🗐, click **Open**. In the displayed **Open** dialog box, click the **Look in arrow**, and then navigate to your Access Chapter 2 folder.

2️⃣ Locate the database file that you saved and renamed with your name in Activity 2.1. Click your **2A_Instructors_and_Courses_Firstname_Lastname** database file one time to select it, and then, in the lower right corner, click the **Open** button. Alternatively, double-click the name of the database to open it.

The database window opens, and the database name displays in the title bar.

3️⃣ Directly below the Ribbon, on the **Message Bar**, check to see if a **Security Warning**, similar to the one shown in Figure 2.3, displays.

Database name in title bar

Figure 2.3

Security Warning message

Message Bar

Options button

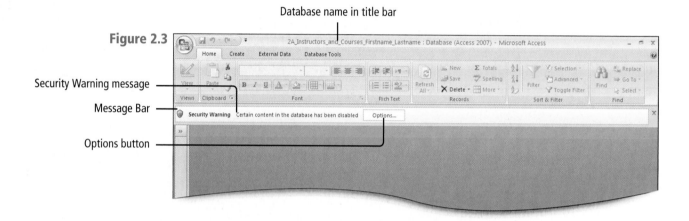

4️⃣ On the **Message Bar**, click the **Options** button. In the displayed **Microsoft Office Security Options** dialog box, click the **Enable this content** option button, and then click **OK** or press Enter.

When working with the student files that accompany this textbook, repeat these actions each time you see this security warning. Databases provided with this textbook are safe to use on your computer.

Objective 2
Create Table Relationships

Access databases are *relational databases* because the tables in the database can relate—actually *connect*—to other tables through *common fields*. Common fields are fields that contain the same data in more than one table.

After you have set up a table for each different subject in your database, you must provide a way to bring that data back together again when you need to create meaningful information. To do this, place common fields in tables that are related and then define table *relationships*. A relationship is an association that you establish between two tables based on common fields. After the relationship is established, you can create a query, a form, or a report that displays information from more than one table.

Activity 2.3 Creating Table Relationships and Enforcing Referential Integrity

In this activity, you will connect a field in one table with a field in another table to create a relationship. The common field between the two tables is Instructor ID; that is, Instructor ID is the field that appears in both tables. By connecting this information, you could identify the name, and not just the Instructor ID, of an instructor for a course section.

1 **Open** ⏩ the **Navigation Pane**. At the top of the **Navigation Pane**, click the **Navigation Pane menu arrow** ▾, and then look at the displayed menu to verify that the objects are organized by **Tables and Related Views**. Click outside the menu to close it, and then compare your screen with Figure 2.4.

Two objects, the *2A Instructors* table and the *2A Courses* table, display in the Navigation Pane.

No objects open in the object window

Figure 2.4

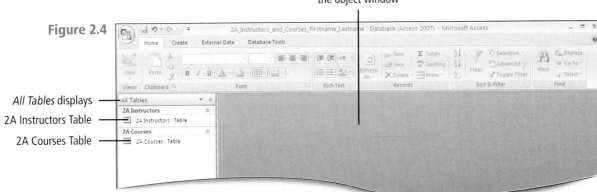

All Tables displays

2A Instructors Table

2A Courses Table

2 By right-clicking and clicking **Open**, or by double-clicking, open the **2A Instructors** table and take a moment to examine its contents. Then, open the **2A Courses** table and examine its contents.

In the 2A Instructors table, Instructor ID is the primary key field, which ensures that each individual instructor will appear in the table only one time. In the 2A Courses table, Section Number is the primary key. Each course's record includes the Instructor ID of the instructor who teaches the course.

Because *one* instructor can teach *many* different courses, *one* instructor's Instructor ID number can appear *many* times in the 2A Courses table. Thus, the relationship between each instructor and the courses is referred to as a ***one-to-many relationship***. This is the most common type of relationship in Access.

3 **Close** ✖ both tables so that the object window is empty; leave the **Navigation Pane** displayed. On the Ribbon, click the **Database Tools tab**. In the **Show/Hide group**, click the **Relationships** button to open the Relationships window and display the **Relationship Tools** on the Ribbon.

4 On the **Design tab**, in the **Relationships group**, click the **Show Table** button to display the **Show Table** dialog box. In the **Show Table** dialog box, in the list of table objects, click **2A Courses**, and then at the bottom of the dialog box, click **Add**.

5 In the **Show Table** dialog box, point to the **2A Instructors** table, double-click to add the table to the **Relationships** window, and then click **Close** to close the **Show Table** dialog box.

Use either technique to add a table to the Relationships window. A *field list*—a list of the field names in a table—for each of the two table objects displays and each table's primary key is identified. Although this database currently has only two tables, larger databases can have many tables.

6 In the **2A Courses** field list, position your mouse pointer over the lower right corner of the field list to display the ⬉ pointer, and then drag downward and to the right as necessary to display the names of each field completely.

Because you can now view the entire list, the scroll bar on the right is removed. Expanding the field list in this manner enables you to see all of the available fields.

7 Using the same technique, use the ⬉ pointer to resize the **2A Instructors** field list as necessary so that all of the field names are completely visible. Then, by pointing to the title bar of each field list and dragging, position the expanded field lists approximately as shown in Figure 2.5.

Recall that *one* instructor can teach *many* courses. By arranging the tables in this manner on your screen, the *one table* is on the left and the *many table* is on the right.

Recall that the primary key in each table is the field that uniquely identifies the record in each table. For example, in the Instructors table, each instructor is uniquely identified by the Instructor ID. In the Courses table, each course section offered is uniquely identified by the Section Number.

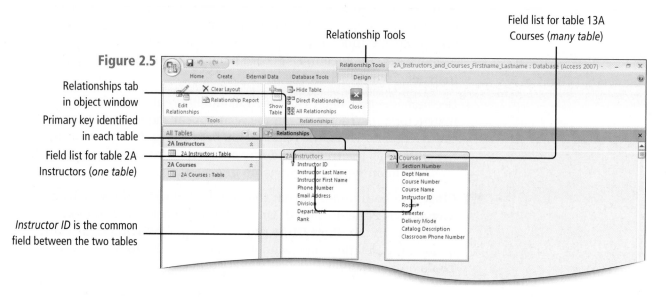

Figure 2.5

Relationships tab in object window
Primary key identified in each table
Field list for table 2A Instructors (*one table*)

Instructor ID is the common field between the two tables

Relationship Tools

Field list for table 13A Courses (*many table*)

Note — Highlighted Field Does Not Matter

As you rearrange the two field lists in the Relationships window, the high-lighted field indicates which field list and which field is active. This is of no consequence for completing the activity. It simply indicates which of the field lists you moved last.

8 In the **2A Instructors** field list, point to **Instructor ID**, hold down the left mouse button, and then drag to the right to the **2A Courses** field list until your mouse pointer is on top of **Instructor ID** as shown in Figure 2.6. Then release the mouse button.

As you drag, a small graphic displays to indicate that you are drag-ging the Instructor ID primary key from the Instructors table to the Instructor ID field in the Courses table. The Edit Relationships dialog box displays.

A table relationship works by matching data in two fields—typically two fields with the same name in both tables.

Icon indicates you are dragging the
primary key field to another table

Figure 2.6

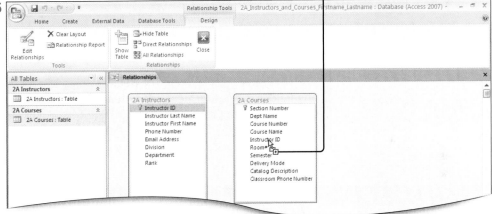

9 Point to the title bar of the **Edit Relationships** dialog box, and then drag the dialog box below the two field lists as shown in Figure 2.7.

Both tables include the Instructor ID field—that is the common field between the two tables. By dragging, you created the one-to-many relationship. In the Instructors table, Instructor ID is the primary key. In the Courses table, Instructor ID is referred to as the *foreign key* field. The foreign key is the field that is included in the related table so the field can be joined with the primary key in another table.

The field on the *one* side of the relationship is typically the primary key. Recall that *one* instructor can teach *many* courses. Thus, *one* instructor record in the Instructors table can be related to *many* course records in the Courses table.

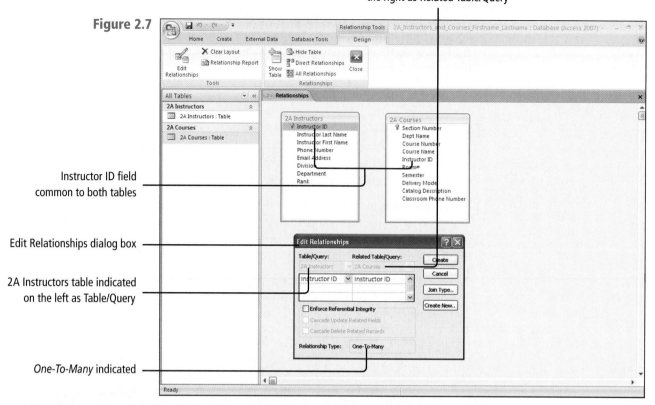

Figure 2.7

2A Courses table indicated on the right as Related Table/Query

Instructor ID field common to both tables

Edit Relationships dialog box

2A Instructors table indicated on the left as Table/Query

One-To-Many indicated

Another Way ── **To Create a Table Relationship**

With the tables displayed in the Relationships window, rather than dragging one field into another field list, instead, click the Edit Relationships button on the Ribbon, click Create New, and then in the Create New dialog box, designate the Left and Right tables and fields that will create the relationship.

10 In the **Edit Relationships** dialog box, click to select the **Enforce Referential Integrity** check box—as you progress in your study of Access, you will use the Cascade options.

Referential integrity is a set of rules that Access uses to ensure that the data between related tables is valid. Enforcing referential integrity ensures that a course cannot be added to the 2A Courses table with the name of an instructor who is *not* included in the 2A Instructors table. In this manner, you ensure that you do not have courses listed in the 2A Courses table with no corresponding instructor in the 2A Instructors table. Similarly, you will not be able to delete an Instructor from the 2A Instructors table if there is a course listed for that instructor in the 2A Courses table.

11 In the upper right corner of the **Edit Relationships** dialog box, click the **Create** button, and then compare your screen with Figure 2.8.

A *join line*—the line joining two tables—displays between the two tables. On the line, *1* indicates the *one* side of the relationship, and the infinity symbol (∞) indicates the *many* side of the relationship. These symbols display when referential integrity has been enforced.

Common field in both tables

Figure 2.8

Join line connects the
two common fields

Line indicates relationship
and 1 and ∞ indicate referential
integrity established

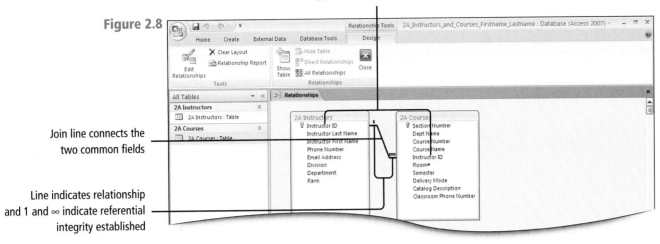

More Knowledge

Fields in a Relationship

To create a relationship, the two connected fields must have the same data type and the same field size, but they need not have the exact same field name.

Activity 2.4 Printing a Relationship Report

Table relationships provide a map of how your database is organized, and you can print this information as a report. In this activity, you will print your relationship report.

1 With the **Relationships** window open, on the **Design tab**, in the **Tools group**, click **Relationship Report** to create the report and display it in Print Preview. On the displayed **Print Preview tab**, in the **Page Layout group**, click **Margins**, and then click **Normal**. Compare your screen with Figure 2.9.

Print Preview tab

Figure 2.9

Database name

Current date (yours will differ)

Field list boxes with join line

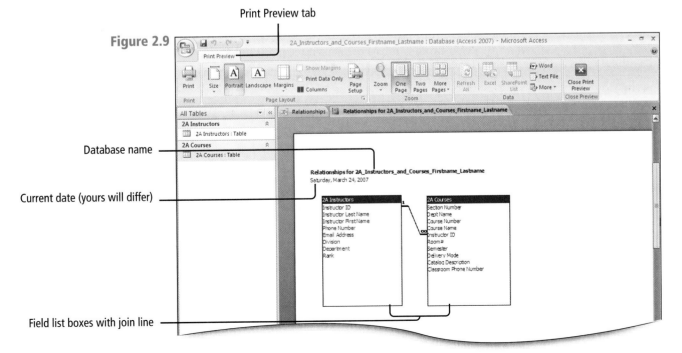

2 Check your *Chapter Assignment Sheet* or *Course Syllabus*, or consult your instructor, to determine whether you are to submit the printed pages that are the results of this project. To print, on the **Print Preview tab**, in the **Print group**, click the **Print** button, and then click **OK**. To submit electronically, follow the directions provided by your instructor.

3 On the **Quick Access Toolbar**, click the **Save** button [icon] to save the report, and then in the displayed **Save As** dialog box, click **OK** to accept the default name.

The report name displays in the Navigation Pane under *Unrelated Objects*. Because the report is just a map of the relationships, and not a report containing actual records, it is not associated with either of the tables.

4 Click **Close Print Preview**. In the object window, **Close** [X] the **Relationships** report, and then **Close** [X] the **Relationships** window.

Note

The report may briefly display in the Design view (with dotted grid lines) as you close the report.

5 In the **Navigation Pane**, open your **2A Instructors** table. On the left side of the table, in the first record, point to the **plus sign**, and then click one time. Compare your screen with Figure 2.10.

Plus signs to the left of a record in a table indicate that related records exist in a *related* table. In the first record for *Julie Adeeb*, you can see that related records exist in the Courses table. The relationship displays because you created a relationship between the two tables using the Instructor ID field.

Figure 2.10

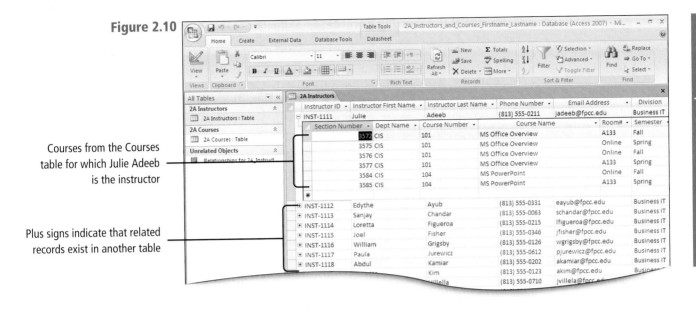

Courses from the Courses table for which Julie Adeeb is the instructor

Plus signs indicate that related records exist in another table

6 **Close** ☒ the **2A Instructors** table.

More Knowledge

Other Types of Relationships: One-to-One and Multiple One-to-Many

There are other relationships that can be created using the same process in the Relationships window. The type of relationship is determined by the placement of the primary key field. A one-to-one relationship exists between two tables when a record in one table is related to a single record in a second table. In this case, both tables use the same field as the primary key. This is most often used when data is placed in a separate table because access to the information is restricted. You can also create multiple one-to-many relationships between tables in a database simply by adding more tables to the Relationships window and creating a join line between the tables based on their common field. A primary key field from one table can be joined to the same field in more than one table.

Objective 3
Sort Records in a Table

Sorting is the process of arranging data in a specific order based on the value in each field. For example, you could sort the names in your address book alphabetically by each person's last name, or you could sort your CD collection by the date of purchase.

Initially, records in an Access table display in the order in which they are entered into the table. After a primary key is established, the records are displayed in order based on the primary key field.

Activity 2.5 Sorting Records in a Table in Ascending or Descending Order

In the following activity, you will sort records in the Courses table to determine which courses in the Business IT Division will be offered each semester. You can sort data in either ***ascending order*** or ***descending order***. Ascending order sorts text alphabetically (A to Z) and sorts numbers from the lowest number to the highest number. Descending order sorts text in reverse alphabetical order (Z to A) and sorts numbers from the highest number to the lowest number.

1 From the **Navigation Pane**, open the **2A Courses** table, and then **Close** ⟪ ⟫ the **Navigation Pane** to maximize your screen space.

The records are sorted in ascending order by Section Number, which is the primary key field. Recall that the primary key is the field whose value uniquely identifies each record in a table—each section of a course that is offered has a unique section number.

2 At the top of the **Dept Name** column, click the **Dept Name arrow**. In the displayed list, click **Sort A to Z**, and then compare your screen with Figure 2.11.

To sort records in a table, click the arrow to the right of the field name in the column on which you want to sort, and then choose the sort order you prefer. After a field is sorted in ascending or descending order, a small arrow in the field name indicates its sort order.

The records display in alphabetical order by Dept Name. Because like names are now grouped together, you can quickly scroll the length of the table and see how many courses are offered by each department.

Ascending button selected

Figure 2.11

Small arrow indicates order in which field is sorted

Records sorted alphabetically by Dept Name

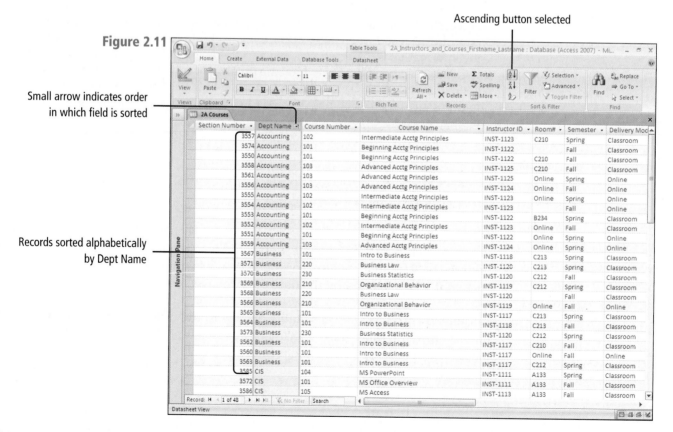

3 In the **Sort & Filter group**, click the **Clear All Sorts** button 🔲 to clear all the sorts and return the records to the default sort order, which is by the primary key field—*Section Number*. Scroll to the right if necessary, click the **Semester arrow**, and then click **Sort Z to A**.

The records in the table are sorted by semester in reverse alphabetical order; thus *Spring* courses are listed before *Fall* courses. The small arrow in the Field name points downward indicating a descending sort, and in the Ribbon, the Descending button is selected.

Activity 2.6 Sorting Records in a Table on Multiple Fields

To sort a table on two or more fields, first identify the fields that will act as the **outermost sort field** and the **innermost sort field**. The outermost sort field is the first level of sorting, and the innermost sort field is the second level of sorting. After you identify your outermost and innermost sort fields, sort the innermost field first, and then sort the outermost field.

Lydia Barwari, the Dean, would like to view the course names in alphabetical order by delivery mode, with online classes listed first. Access enables you to sort on two or more fields in a table in this manner.

1 Click the **Clear All Sorts** button 🔲 to clear any sorts from the previous activity. In the **Delivery Mode** column, click any record. In the

Sort & Filter group, click the **Descending** button 🔲.

The records are sorted in descending alphabetical order by Delivery Mode, with Online courses listed before Classroom courses.

2 Point anywhere in the **Course Name** column, and then right-click. From the displayed shortcut menu, click **Sort A to Z**. Notice the first four records in the **Course Name** column, for *Advanced Acctg Principles*, and then compare your screen with Figure 2.12.

The records are sorted first by Course Name—the *outermost* sort field—and then within a specific Course Name grouping, the sort continues in descending alphabetical order by Delivery Mode—the *innermost* sort field.

In this manner, you can perform a sort on multiple fields using both ascending and descending order.

Figure 2.12

Within each *Course Name,*
Online and *Classroom* sorted
in descending order

Small arrows indicate sort
order in each column

Course Name column
sorted in ascending order

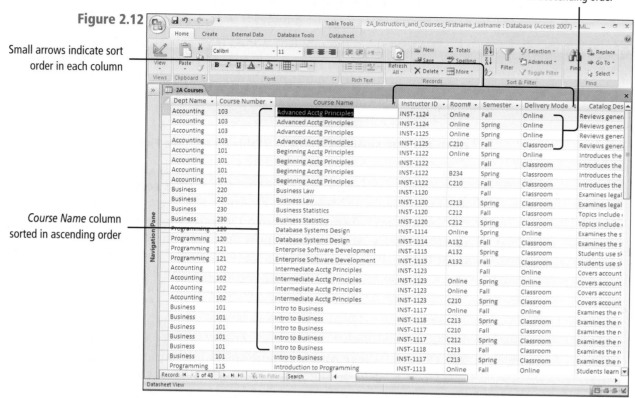

3 In the **Sort & Filter group**, click the **Clear All Sorts** button. In
the object window, **Close** the table, and then click **No**; you need
not save any changes made to the design.

Objective 4
Create a Query in Design View

Recall that a ***select query*** is a database object that retrieves (selects)
specific data from one or more tables and then displays the specified
data in datasheet view. A query answers a question such as *Which
instructors are teaching CIS courses in the Fall semester?* Unless a query
has already been set up to ask this question, you must create a new
query.

Individuals who use databases rarely need to see all of the records in all
of the tables. That is why a query is so useful; it creates a subset of
records according to your specifications and then displays only those
records—and does so in a useful manner.

Activity 2.7 Creating a New Select Query in Design View

Previously, you practiced creating a query using the Query Wizard. In
this chapter, you will create queries in Design view, in which you can

create queries that are more complex. Recall that the table or tables from which a query selects its data is referred to as the *data source*.

1 On the Ribbon, click the **Create tab**, and then in the **Other group**, click the **Query Design** button. Compare your screen with Figure 2.13.

A new query opens in Design view and the Show Table dialog box displays. The Show Table dialog box lists all of the tables in the database.

Available tables

Figure 2.13

Query1 tab

Show Table dialog box

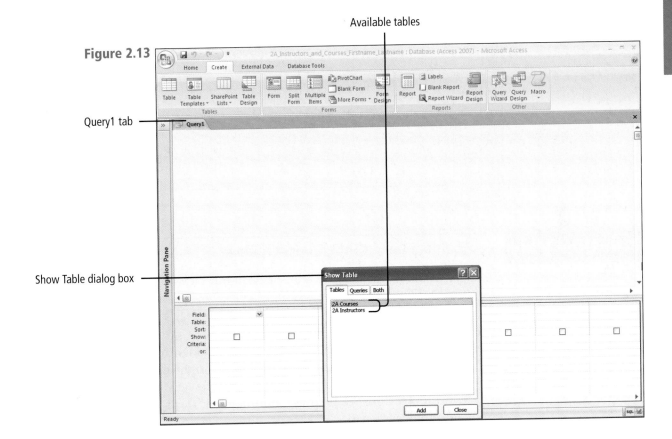

2 In the **Show Table** dialog box, click **2A Courses**, click the **Add** button, and then **Close** the **Show Table** dialog box. Compare your screen with Figure 2.14.

A field list for the 2A Courses table displays in the upper pane of the Query window. The Section Number field is indicated as the primary key field in this table. The Query window has two parts: the *table area* (upper pane) displays the field lists for tables that are used in the query, and the *design grid* (lower pane) displays the design of the query.

Figure 2.14

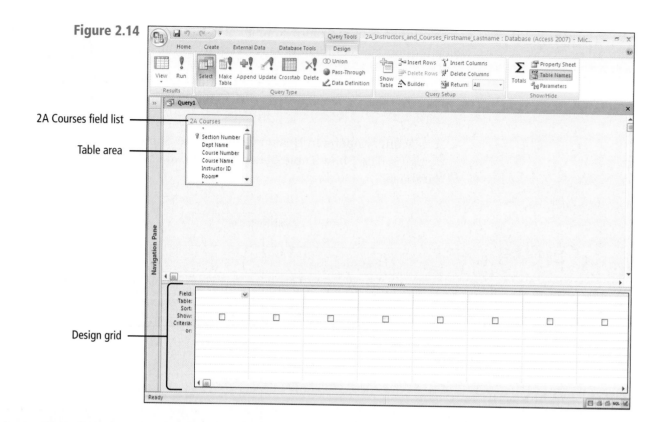

2A Courses field list

Table area

Design grid

Another Way **To Add a Table to the Query Window**

You can also double-click a table name in the Show Table dialog box to add it to the Query window.

---

3 Point to the lower right corner of the field list to display the ⬉ pointer, and then drag down and to the right to expand the height and width of the field list as necessary to view all of the field names. In the **2A Courses** field list, double-click **Dept Name**, and then look at the design grid.

The Dept Name field displays in the design grid in the Field row. By designing a query in Design view, you can limit the fields that display in the result by placing only the fields you want in the design grid.

4 In the **2A Courses** field list, point to **Course Number**, hold down the left mouse button, and then drag down into the design grid until you are pointing to the **Field** row in the next available column. Release the mouse button, and then compare your screen with Figure 2.15.

This is another way to add field names to the design grid. As you drag the field, a small rectangular shape attaches to the mouse pointer. When you release the mouse button, the field name displays in the Field row.

Figure 2.15

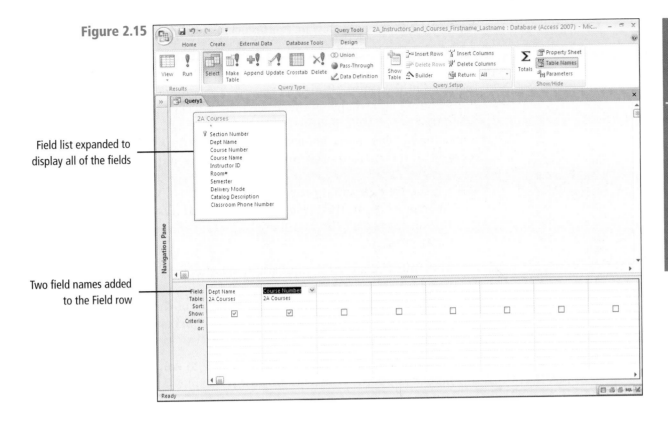

Field list expanded to display all of the fields

Two field names added to the Field row

> **5** In the **Field** row of the design grid, click in the third column, and then click the **arrow** that displays. From the displayed list, click **Course Name** to add this field to the design grid, which is another way to add a field to the design of the query.

> **6** Using one of the methods you just practiced, add the **Semester** field as the fourth column in the design grid, and then add the **Delivery Mode** field as the fifth column in the design grid. Compare your screen with Figure 2.16.

Figure 2.16

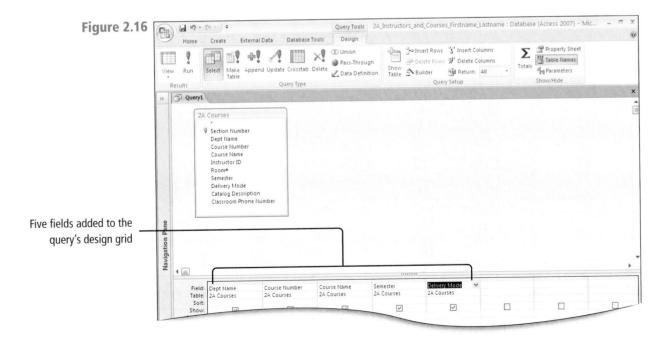

Five fields added to the query's design grid

Activity 2.8 Running, Saving, Printing, and Closing a Query

After you create a query, you *run* it to see the results. When you run a query, Access looks at the records in the table (or tables) you have included in the query, finds the records that match the specified conditions (if any), and displays those records in a datasheet view. Only the fields that have been included in the query design are displayed in the query result. The query is always run against the current table of records, and therefore presents the most up-to-date information.

1 On the **Design tab**, in the **Results group**, click the **Run** button. Alternatively, on the Design tab, in the Results group, click the View button to display the results of a query. Compare your screen with Figure 2.17.

This query answers the question, *What is the Dept Name, Course Number, Course Name, Semester, and Delivery Mode of all the courses in the table?* Think of a query as a subset of the records in one or more tables, arranged in datasheet view, according to the conditions that you specify.

The five fields that you specified display in columns, the records display in rows, and navigation buttons display at the bottom of the window in the same manner as in a table.

Five fields specified in
query design display

Figure 2.17

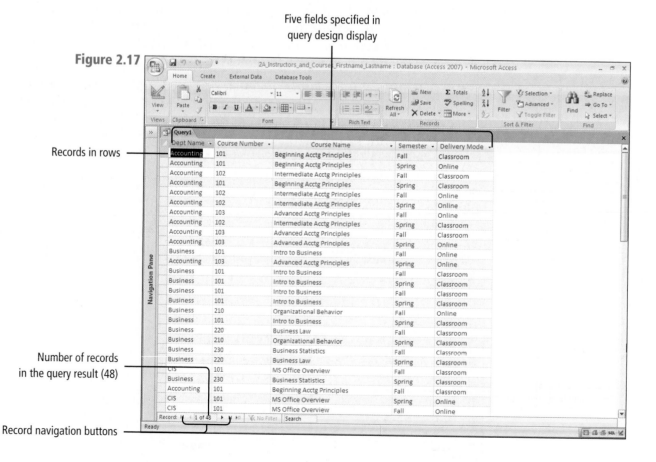

Records in rows

Number of records
in the query result (48)

Record navigation buttons

2 On the **Quick Access Toolbar**, click the **Save** button 🖫 to display the **Save As** dialog box. Type **2A Courses Query Firstname Lastname** and then click **OK**.

It is not necessary to save all queries, but save your queries if it is likely that you will need to ask the same question again. Doing so will save you the effort of creating the query again to answer the same question.

3 From the **Office** menu 🗔, point to the **Print** button, and then click **Print Preview**. In the **Page Layout group**, click the **Landscape** button. In the **Zoom group**, click the **Two Pages** button to see how your query will print on two pages. If you are printing your assignments on paper, click the **Print** button, and then in the displayed **Print** dialog box, click **OK**. To submit electronically, follow the directions provided by your instructor.

Two pages will print. Queries are created to answer questions and to create information from the data contained in the tables. Queries are typically created as a basis for a report. As you have just done here, however, the actual query result can be printed in a manner similar to tables and other database objects.

4 Click the **Close Print Preview** button. In the object window, **Close** ⊠ the query. **Open** ⧽ the **Navigation Pane**, and then compare your screen with Figure 2.18.

The query is saved and closed. The new query name displays in the Navigation Pane under the table with which it is associated—the *Courses* table. When you save a query, only the design of the query is saved. The records still reside in the table object. Each time you open the query, Access runs it again and displays the results based on the data stored in the associated table(s). Thus, the results of a query always reflect the latest information in the associated tables.

Figure 2.18

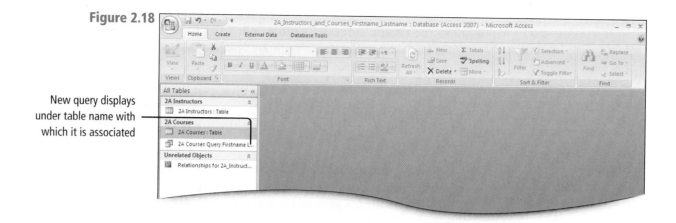

New query displays
under table name with
which it is associated

Objective 5
Create a New Query from an Existing Query

In this activity, you will begin with an existing query, save it with a new name, and then create a new query from the existing one.

Activity 2.9 Creating a New Query from an Existing Query

1 From the **Navigation Pane**, open your **2A Courses Query** by either double-clicking the name or right-clicking and clicking Open.

The query opens in the Datasheet view, which is the view used to display the records in a query result.

2 From the **Office** menu, click **Save As**, which will save the current database object—a query—as a new object. In the **Save As** dialog box, edit as necessary to name the new query **2A Sections Query Firstname Lastname** and then click **OK**. On the **Home tab**, in the **Views group**, click the **View** button to switch to Design view. Compare your screen with Figure 2.19.

A new query, based on a copy of your 2A Courses Query, is created and displays in the object window and is added to the Navigation Pane. Your query displays in Design view.

Figure 2.19

New *2A Sections* query in object window

New query *2A Sections* displays in Navigation Pane

Selection bar in design grid

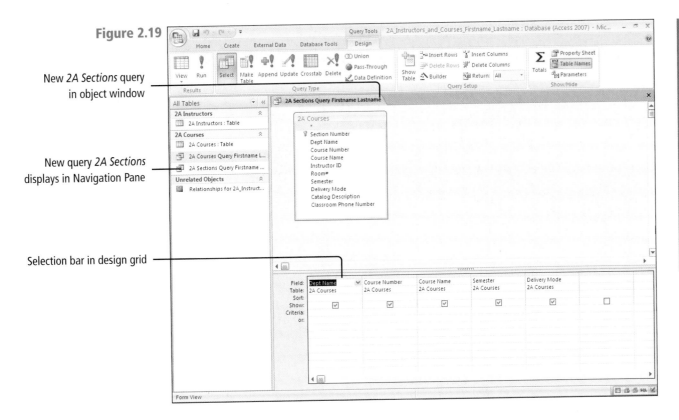

3 **Close** the **Navigation Pane**. In the design grid, point to the thin gray selection bar above the **Dept Name** field until the ⬇ pointer displays. Click to select the **Dept Name** column, and then press Delete.

The Dept Name field is removed from the design grid and the Delivery Mode field moves to the fourth column in the design grid. This action deletes the field from the query design only—it has no effect on the underlying 2A Courses table.

4 Using a similar technique, from the gray selection bar, select the **Delivery Mode** column. Then, point to the **selection bar** at the top of the selected column to display the ⬚ pointer, and drag to the left to position **Delivery Mode** in the first column.

To rearrange fields in the query design, first select the field you want to move, and then drag it to a new position in the design grid.

5 From the field list, add the **Section Number** field as the fifth column in the design grid. Then using the technique you just practiced, select and move the **Section Number** field to the first column in the design grid. Compare your screen with Figure 2.20.

Figure 2.20

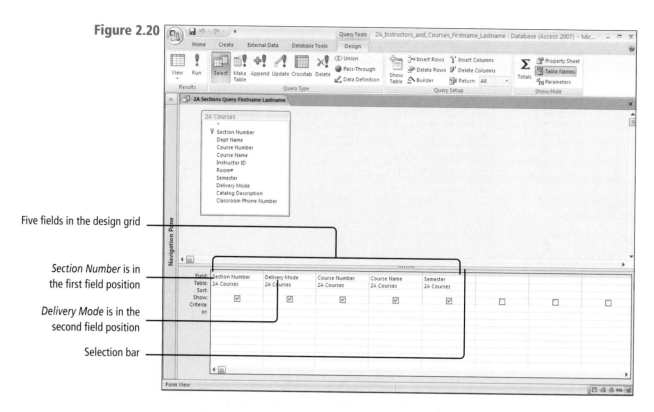

Five fields in the design grid

Section Number is in
the first field position

Delivery Mode is in the
second field position

Selection bar

6 On the **Query Tools Design tab**, in the **Results group**, click the **Run** button. The result of the query displays five fields in the new arrangement. Compare your screen with Figure 2.21.

This query answers the question, *What is the Section Number, Delivery Mode, Course Number, Course Name, and Semester of every course?* Recall that you can think of a query as a subset of the records in one or more tables, arranged in datasheet view, according to the conditions that you specify.

Figure 2.21

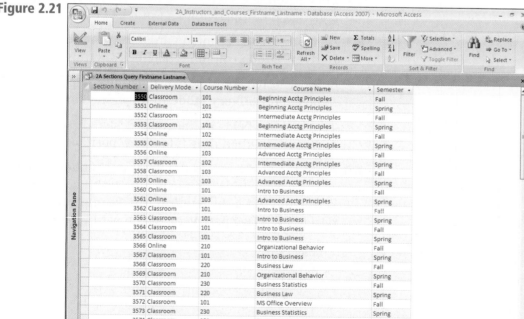

7 From the **Office** menu 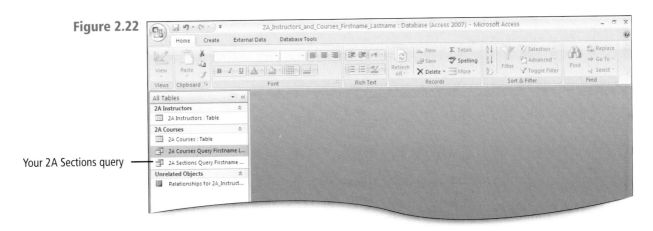, point to the **Print** button, and then click **Print Preview**. On the **Print Preview tab**, in the **Page Layout group**, click **Landscape**. In the **Zoom group**, click the **Two Pages** button to view how your query will print on two pages. If you are printing on paper, in the **Print group**, click the **Print** button. In the displayed **Print** dialog box, click **OK**. To submit electronically, follow your instructor's directions.

8 Click the **Close Print Preview** button. In the object window, **Close** ❌ the query, and then click **Yes** to save the changes to the design.

Open ⏩ the **Navigation Pane**, and then compare your screen with Figure 2.22.

The query is saved and closed. The new query name displays in the Navigation Pane under the table with which it is associated. Recall that when you save a query, only the design of the query is saved. The records still reside in the respective table objects.

Each time you open the query, Access runs it again and displays the results based on the records stored in the associated table(s).

Figure 2.22

Your 2A Sections query

Objective 6
Sort Query Results

You can sort the results of a query. Because the results of a query are formatted like a table in Datasheet view, the process for sorting is similar to sorting in a table. Records can be sorted in ascending or descending order. Data in a query can be sorted from the Datasheet view or from the Design view.

Activity 2.10 Sorting Query Results

In this activity, you will open an existing query, save it with a new name, and then sort the query results in a new arrangement.

1 From the **Navigation Pane**, open your **2A Sections Query**. From the **Office** menu , click **Save As**. In the **Save As** dialog box, edit as necessary to name the query **2A Delivery Sort Firstname Lastname** and then click **OK**.

Access creates a new query, based on a copy of your 2A Sections Query.

2 **Close** the **Navigation Pane**, and then in the **Views group**, click the **View** button to switch to Design view. In the design grid, in the **Sort** row, click in the **Delivery Mode** field to place the insertion point there and display an arrow. Click the **Sort arrow**, and then in the displayed list, click **Descending**. Compare your screen with Figure 2.23.

Figure 2.23

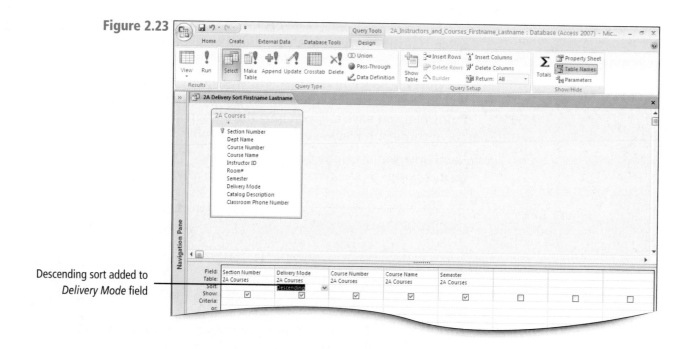

Descending sort added to
Delivery Mode field

3 In the **Sort** row, under **Course Name**, click to display the **Sort arrow**, click the arrow, and then click **Ascending**.

4 On the **Design tab**, in the **Results group**, click the **Run** button, and then compare your screen with Figure 2.24.

Fields that have a Sort designation are sorted from left to right. That is, the sorted field on the left becomes the outermost sort field, and the sorted field on the right becomes the innermost sort field. Thus, the records are sorted first in descending alphabetical order by the Delivery Mode field—the leftmost indicated sort field. Then in the Course Name field, within the Online records, the Course Names are sorted in ascending alphabetical order.

Figure 2.24

Within Course Name, records sorted in ascending order

Within Delivery Mode, records sorted in descending order

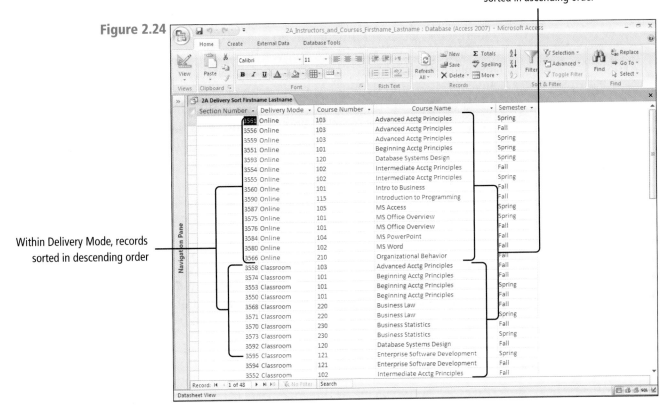

5 From the **Office** menu, point to the **Print** button, and then click **Print Preview**. On the **Print Preview tab**, in the **Page Layout group**, click **Landscape**. In the **Zoom group**, click the **Two Pages** button to view the layout of the pages. If you are printing on paper, in the **Print group**, click the **Print** button. In the displayed **Print** dialog box, click **OK**. To submit electronically, follow your instructor's directions.

6 Click the **Close Print Preview** button. **Close** ✕ the query, and then click **Yes** to save the changes to this query's design.

More Knowledge

Sorting

If you add a sort order to the *design* of a query, it remains as a permanent part of the query design. If you use the sort buttons in the Datasheet view, it will override the sort order of the query design, and can be saved as part of the query. A sort order designated directly in datasheet view will not display in the Sort row of the query design grid.

Objective 7
Specify Criteria in a Query

Queries can locate information in an Access database based on **criteria** that you specify as part of the query. Criteria are conditions that identify the specific records you are looking for. Criteria enable you to ask a more specific question, and therefore you will get a more specific result. For example, if you want to find out how many *Business Law* courses will be offered in the Fall and Spring semesters, you can limit the results to a specific course name, and only records that match the specified course name will display.

Activity 2.11 Specifying Text Criteria in a Query

In this activity, you will assist Lydia in creating a query to answer the question *How many sections of Intro to Business will be offered in the Fall and Spring semesters?*

1 Be sure that all objects are closed and that the **Navigation Pane** is closed. Click the **Create tab**, and then in the **Other group**, click the **Query Design** button. In the **Show Table** dialog box, **Add** the **2A Courses** table to the table area, and then **Close** the **Show Table** dialog box.

2 Use the ⬉ pointer to expand the lower right corner of the field list to view all the field names. Using any technique, add the following fields to the design grid in the order listed: **Course Name**, **Course Number**, **Semester**, and **Delivery Mode**.

3 In the **Criteria** row of the design grid, click in the **Course Name** field, type **Intro to Business** and then press Enter. Compare your screen with Figure 2.25.

Access places quote marks around your criteria. Use the Criteria row to specify the criteria that will limit the results of the query to your exact specifications. Access adds quote marks to text criteria in this manner to indicate that this is a **text string**—a sequence of characters—that must be matched.

Figure 2.25

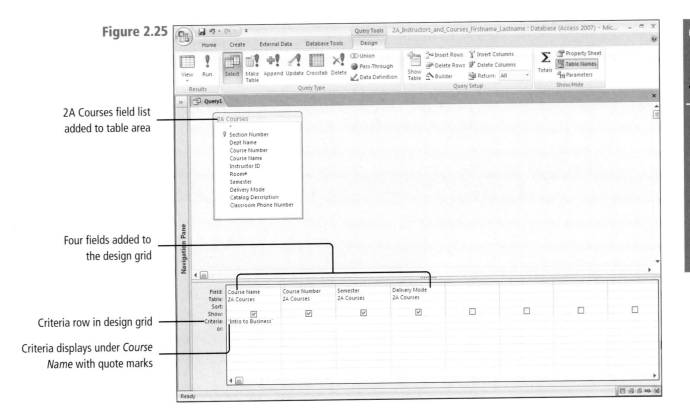

2A Courses field list added to table area

Four fields added to the design grid

Criteria row in design grid

Criteria displays under *Course Name* with quote marks

---

4 **Run** the query, and then compare your screen with Figure 2.26.

Six records display that meet the specified criteria—records that have *Intro to Business* in the Course Name field.

Figure 2.26

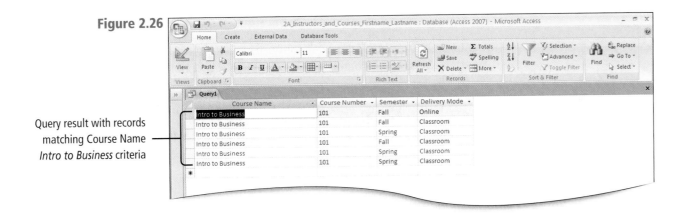

Query result with records matching Course Name *Intro to Business* criteria

---

5 On the **Quick Access Toolbar**, click the **Save** button, and then in the **Save As** dialog box, type **2A Intro to Business Firstname Lastname** and then click **OK**.

6 From the **Office** menu, point to the **Print** button, and then click **Print Preview**. If you are printing your assignments on paper, in the **Print group**, click the **Print** button. In the displayed **Print** dialog box, click **OK**. Or, submit electronically as directed.

7 Click the **Close Print Preview** button. **Close** ☒ the query, **Open** ⟫ the **Navigation Pane**, and then compare your screen with Figure 2.27.

Recall that queries in the Navigation Pane display a distinctive icon— that of two overlapping tables.

Figure 2.27

Queries display a distinctive icon of two tables overlapping

Four queries created based on 2A Courses table

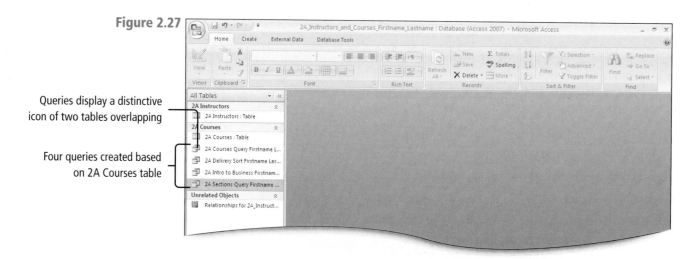

Activity 2.12 Specifying Criteria Using a Field Not Displayed in the Query Result

So far, all of the fields that you included in the query design have also been included in the query result. It is not required to have every field in the query actually display in the result. In fact, there will be times when you will want to prevent some fields from displaying in the result.

In this activity, you will assist Lydia in creating a query to answer the question, *Which instructors have a rank of Professor?*

1 **Close** ⟪ the **Navigation Pane**. Click the **Create tab**, and then in the **Other group,** click **Query Design**.

2 From the **Show Table** dialog box, **Add** the **2A Instructors** table to the table area, and then **Close** the dialog box. Use the ⬉ pointer to expand the height and width of the field list as necessary.

3 Using any of the techniques you have practiced—double-clicking, dragging, or displaying the arrow, and then selecting in the list—add the following fields, in the order listed, to the design grid: **Instructor ID, Instructor First Name, Instructor Last Name**, and **Rank**.

4 In the **Sort** row, click in the **Instructor Last Name** field, click the **arrow**, and then click **Ascending**.

5 In the **Criteria** row, click in the **Rank** field, type **Professor** and then press [Enter]. Compare your screen with Figure 2.28.

When you press [Enter], the insertion point moves to the next criteria box and quote marks are added around the text you entered. Recall that Access adds quote marks to text criteria to indicate that this is a text string—a sequence of characters—that must be matched.

Figure 2.28

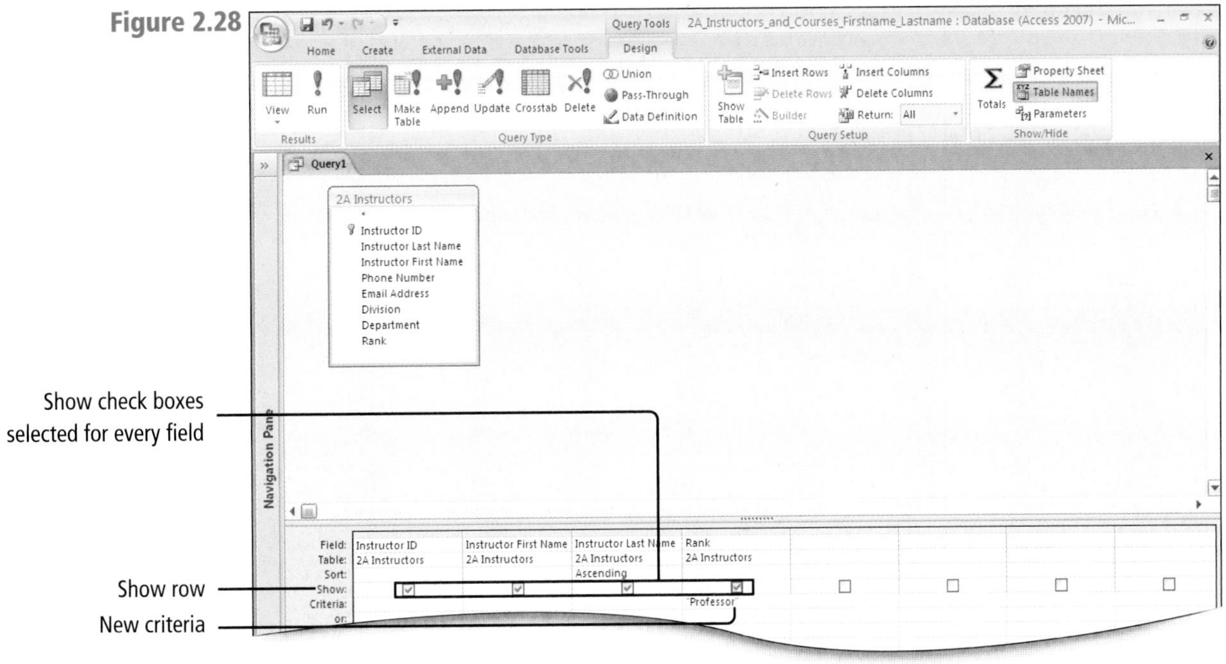

Show check boxes
selected for every field

Show row

New criteria

6 In the design grid, in the **Show** row, notice that the check box is selected for every field. **Run** the query to view the result of the query.

Six records meet the criteria, and each of the six records displays *Professor* in the Rank column.

Alert!

Do your query results differ?

If you mistype the criteria, enter it under the wrong field, or make some other error, the result will display no records. This indicates that there are no records in the table that match the criteria as you entered it. If this occurs, return to the Design view and reexamine the query design. Verify that the criteria are typed on the Criteria row, under the correct field, and that it is spelled correctly. Then rerun the query.

7 On the **Home tab**, in the **Views group**, click the **View** button to return to Design view. In the design grid, under **Rank**, in the **Show** row, click to clear the check box, and then compare your screen with Figure 2.29.

Because it is repetitive and not particularly useful to have *Professor* display for each record in the query result, you can clear this check box so that the field does not display.

Figure 2.29

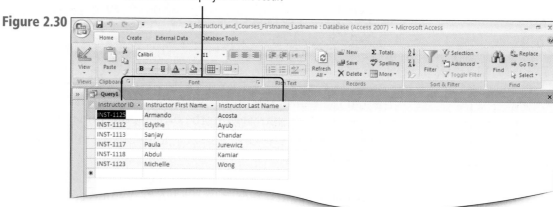

Show check box cleared for the Rank field

8 **Run** the query again, and then compare your screen with Figure 2.30.

The query results display the same six records, but the *Rank* field does not display. Although the Rank field was still included in the query criteria for the purpose of identifying specific records, it is not necessary to display the field in the result.

Clear the Show check box when necessary to avoid cluttering the query results with redundant data.

Rank field not displayed in the result

Figure 2.30

9 On the **Quick Access Toolbar**, click the **Save** button [icon], and then in the **Save As** dialog box, type **2A Professor Rank Firstname Lastname** Click **OK**.

10 From the **Office** menu [icon], point to the **Print** button, and then click **Print Preview**. If you are printing your assignments on paper, in the

Print group, click the **Print** button. In the displayed **Print** dialog box, click **OK**. To submit electronically, follow your instructor's directions.

[11] Click the **Close Print Preview** button. **Close** [×] the query, **Open**

[»] the **Navigation Pane**, and then notice the query listed under the table with which it is associated—the 2A Instructors table.

Activity 2.13 Using Is Null Criteria To Find Empty Fields

Sometimes you must locate records where specific data is missing. You can locate such records by using *is null*—empty—as a criteria in a field. Additionally, you can display only the records where a value *has* been entered in a field by using *is not null* as a criteria, which will exclude records where the specified field is empty.

In this activity, you will help Lydia run a query to find out *Which course sections have not yet had a classroom assigned?*

[1] **Close** [«] the **Navigation Pane**. Click the **Create tab**, and then in the **Other group**, click the **Query Design** button to begin a new query. **Add** the **2A Courses** table, and then **Close** the **Show Table** dialog box. Use the [↖] pointer as necessary to expand the height and width of the field list.

[2] Using any of the techniques you have practiced, add the following fields to the design grid in the order given: **Section Number**, **Course Number**, **Course Name**, and **Room#**.

[3] On the **Criteria** row, click in the **Room#** field, type **Is Null** and press [Enter]. Alternatively, type *is null* and Access will change the criteria to display with capital letters. Compare your screen with Figure 2.31.

The criteria *Is Null* examines the field and looks for records that do *not* have any values entered in the Room# field. In this manner, you can determine which courses still need to have a classroom assigned.

Figure 2.31

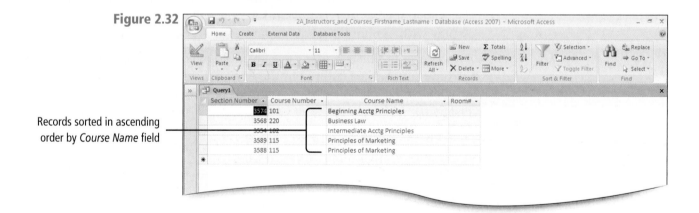

Is Null criteria added to the Room# field

---

4 On the **Sort** row, click in the **Course Name** field, click the **Sort arrow**, and then click **Ascending**. **Run** the query to see the results, and then compare your screen with Figure 2.32.

Five course sections do not have a Room# assigned—the Room# field is empty for these course sections. The course names are sorted in ascending (alphabetical) order.

Figure 2.32

Records sorted in ascending order by *Course Name* field

Section Number	Course Number	Course Name	Room#
3574	101	Beginning Acctg Principles	
3568	220	Business Law	
3554	102	Intermediate Acctg Principles	
3589	115	Principles of Marketing	
3588	115	Principles of Marketing	

5 **Save** your query, and then in the **Save As** dialog box, type **2A Rooms Firstname Lastname** Click **OK**.

6 From the **Office** menu, point to the **Print** button, and then click **Print Preview**. If you are printing your assignments on paper, in the **Print group**, click the **Print** button. In the displayed **Print** dialog box, click **OK**. To submit electronically, follow your instructor's directions.

7 Click the **Close Print Preview** button, and then **Close** [×] the query. **Open** [»] the **Navigation Pane**, and then compare your screen with Figure 2.33.

Each query that you created displays under the table with which it is associated. The objects display in alphabetical order.

Figure 2.33

Query objects display, in alphabetical order, with table on which they are based

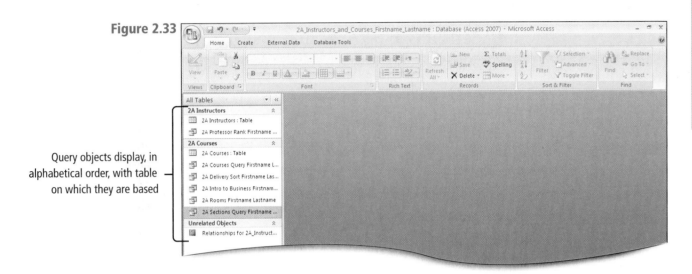

8 **Close** [«] the **Navigation Pane** and be sure all objects are closed.

9 From the **Office** menu, click **Close Database**, and then at the right edge of the Access title bar, click the **Close** button [×] to close the Access program. Alternatively, from the Office menu, click Exit Access.

End **You have completed Project 2A** ——————————

Project 2B **Athletes and Scholarships**

In Activities 2.14 through 2.25, you will assist Marcus Simmons, Athletic Director for Florida Port Community College, in developing and querying his Athletes and Scholarships database. In this database, Mr. Simmons tracks the scholarships awarded to student athletes. Your completed Relationships report and queries will look similar to those in Figure 2.34.

For Project 2B, you will need the following files:

a2B_Athletes_and_Scholarships
a2B_Athletes (Excel file)

You will save your database as
2B_Athletes_and_Scholarships_Firstname_Lastname

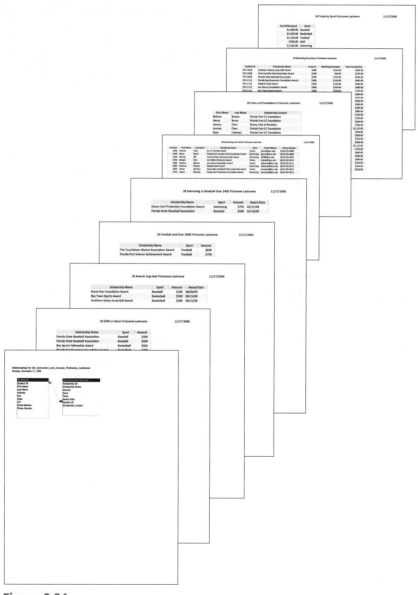

Figure 2.34
Project 2B—Athletes and Scholarships

Objective 8
Create a New Table by Importing an Excel Spreadsheet

Many users of Microsoft Office track their data in an Excel spreadsheet. The sorting and filtering capabilities of Excel are useful enough for a simple database where all the information can reside in one large table, which is the Excel spreadsheet itself.

Excel is limited as a database management program because it cannot support multiple tables nor can it *relate* the information so that you can retrieve information from multiple spreadsheets using a query. However, data in an Excel spreadsheet can easily become an Access table by importing the spreadsheet, because Excel's format of columns and rows is similar to that of an Access table.

Activity 2.14 Opening an Existing Database and Preparing To Import an Excel Spreadsheet

In this activity, you will open, rename, and save an existing database, and then examine an Excel spreadsheet that Mr. Simmons wants to bring into Access as a new table.

1 On the left side of the Windows taskbar, click **Start** 🔲 *start*, and then click **My Computer**. Navigate to the location where the student files that accompany this textbook are stored, and then click one time to select the file **a2B_Athletes_and_Scholarships**.

2 Point to the selected file name, right-click to display a shortcut menu, and then click **Copy**. Navigate to and open the Access Chapter 2 folder you created in Project 2A. In an open area, right-click to display a shortcut menu, and then click **Paste**.

3 Right-click the selected file name, click **Rename**, and then using your own first and last name type **2B_Athletes_and_Scholarships_Firstname_Lastname** Press ⏎ to save the new file name. On the title bar, **Close** 🔲 the **My Computer** window.

4 **Start** Access. From the **Office** menu 🔲, click **Open**. In the displayed **Open** dialog box, click the **Look in arrow**, navigate to your Access Chapter 2 folder, and then open your **2B_Athletes_and_Scholarships** database file.

5 If necessary, on the **Message Bar**, click the **Options** button, and then in the **Microsoft Office Security Options** dialog box, click the **Enable this content** options button. Click **OK**.

6 **Open** 🔲 the **Navigation Pane**, open the **2B Scholarships Awarded** table, **Close** 🔲 the **Navigation Pane**, and then take a moment to examine the data in the table. Compare your screen with Figure 2.35.

In this table, Mr. Simmons tracks the name and amount of scholarships awarded to student athletes. In the table, the students are identified only by their Student ID numbers; the table's primary key is the Scholarship ID field.

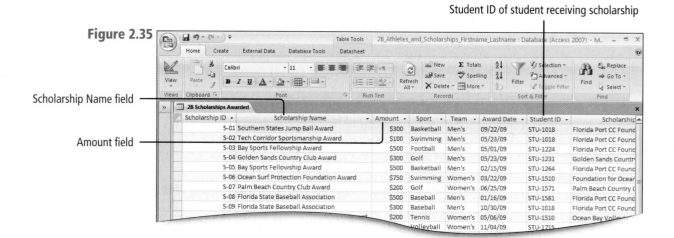

Figure 2.35

Scholarship Name field

Amount field

Student ID of student receiving scholarship

7 **Close** ☒ the table. From the Windows taskbar, click **Start** ▐ start ▌, and then locate and open **Microsoft Office Excel 2007**.

In Excel, from the **Office** menu 🔘, click **Open**, navigate to the location where the student files for this textbook are stored, and then open the file **a2B_Athletes**. Compare your screen with Figure 2.36.

Mr. Simmons created an Excel spreadsheet to store the names, addresses, and other information of all the student athletes. Because *one* athlete can receive *many* scholarships, Mr. Simmons can see that using Access, rather than Excel, and having two *related* tables of information, will enable him to track and query this information more efficiently.

Excel spreadsheet containing student information

Figure 2.36

Student ID field

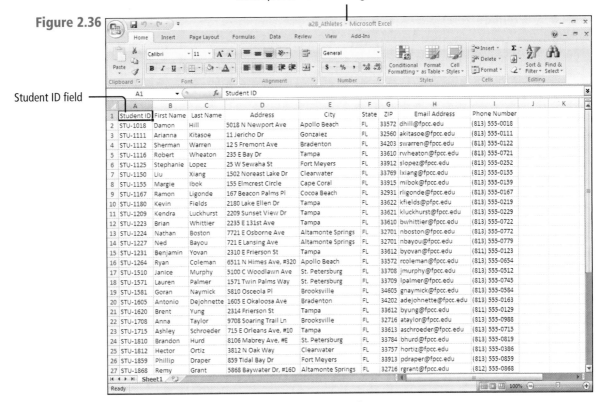

8 In the Excel spreadsheet, notice that in **row 1**, the column titles are similar to the field names in an Access table, and that each row contains the information for one student in a manner similar to a record in Access. Then, display the **Office** menu, and in the lower right corner of the menu, click **Exit Excel**.

Activity 2.15 Creating a New Table by Importing an Excel Spreadsheet

In this activity, you will create a new Access table by importing the Excel spreadsheet containing the names and addresses of the student athletes, create a one-to-many relationship between the new table and the 2A Scholarships Awarded table, enforce referential integrity, and then print a Relationship report.

1 **Open** the **Navigation Pane**. On the Ribbon, click the **External Data tab**, and then in the **Import group**, click **Excel**. In the displayed **Get External Data – Excel Spreadsheet** dialog box, to the right of the **File name** box, click the **Browse** button.

2 In the displayed **File Open** dialog box, click the **Look in arrow**, navigate to the location where the student files for this textbook are stored, and then click the Excel file **a2B_Athletes**. In the lower right corner, click **Open**, and then compare your screen with Figure 2.37.

Figure 2.37

Browse button

Get External Data – Excel Spreadsheet dialog box

Location of Excel file displays here (yours may vary)

Option button selected

OK button

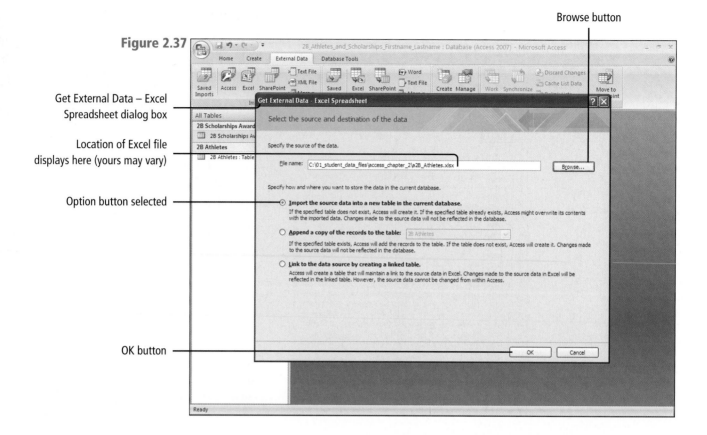

3 Be sure the **Import the source data into a new table in the current database** option button is selected, and then in the lower right corner, click **OK**.

The Import Spreadsheet Wizard opens and displays the worksheet data.

4 In the upper portion of the **Import Spreadsheet Wizard**, click to select the **First Row Contains Column Headings** check box.

The Excel data in the lower portion of the dialog box is framed so that the first row of Excel column titles can become the Access table field names, and the remaining rows can become the individual records for the new Access table.

5 In the lower right corner, click **Next**. Notice that the first column is selected, and in the upper portion of the dialog box, the **Field Name** is indicated and the **Data Type** is indicated. Click anywhere in the **First Name** column, and then compare your screen with Figure 2.38.

Here you can review and change the field properties of each field (column).

Figure 2.38

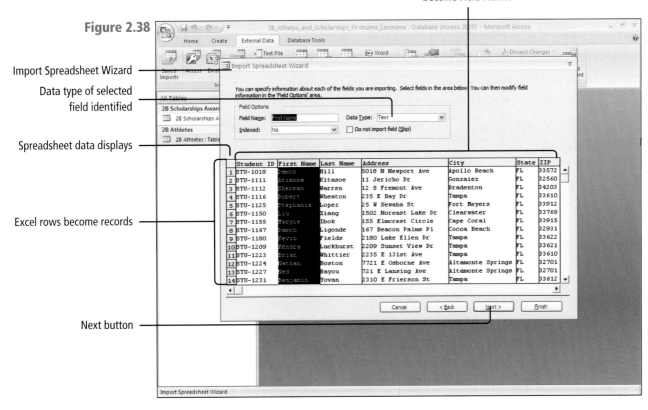

Excel column titles become Field Names

Import Spreadsheet Wizard

Data type of selected field identified

Spreadsheet data displays

Excel rows become records

Next button

6 Under **Field Options**, make no changes for any of the fields, and then in the lower right corner, click **Next**. In the upper portion of the dialog box, click the **Choose my own primary key** option button, and then be sure that **Student ID** displays.

In the new table, Student ID will be the primary key. No two students will have the same Student ID. By default, Access selects the first field as the primary key.

7 In the lower right corner, click **Next**. In the **Import to Table** box, type **2B Athletes** and then click **Finish**. In the lower right corner of the **Get External Data – Excel Spreadsheet** dialog box, click **Close**.

That is all the information the Wizard needs to import your data. In the Navigation Pane, your new table displays.

8 On the Ribbon, click the **Database Tools tab**, and then in the **Show/Hide group**, click the **Relationships** button. On the **Design tab**, in the **Relationships group**, click **Show Table**. In the **Show Table** dialog box, **Add** the **2B Athletes** table, and then **Add** the **2B Scholarships Awarded** table. **Close** the **Show Table** dialog box.

9 Use the ⬉ pointer as necessary to expand the height and width of the field lists, position the field lists as necessary so that the **2B Athletes** table is on the left, and allow approximately 1 inch of space between the two field lists. Compare your screen with Figure 2.39.

Positioning the field lists in this manner is not required, but while studying Access, it makes it easier for you to view while creating the relationships.

Figure 2.39

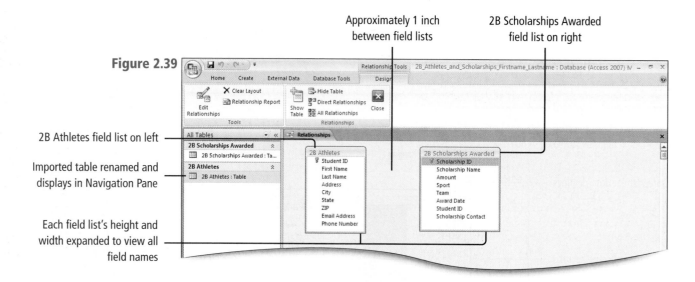

Approximately 1 inch
between field lists

2B Scholarships Awarded
field list on right

2B Athletes field list on left

Imported table renamed and
displays in Navigation Pane

Each field list's height and
width expanded to view all
field names

10 In the **2B Athletes** field list, point to the **Student ID** field, hold down the left mouse button, drag into the **2B Scholarships Awarded** field list, and then position the mouse pointer on top of the **Student ID** field near the bottom of the list. Release the mouse button.

11 Point to the title bar of the **Edit Relationships** dialog box, and then drag it below the two field lists. In the **Edit Relationships** dialog box, be sure that the **2B Athletes** table is indicated on the left, that the **2B Scholarships Awarded** table is indicated on the right, and that **Student ID** is indicated as the field for both the *Table* and the *Related Table.*

The two tables are related in a one-to-many relationship—*one* athlete can be awarded *many* scholarships. The common field between the two tables is the Student ID field. In the 2B Athletes table, Student ID is the primary key. In the 2B Scholarships Awarded table, Student ID is the foreign key.

12 In the **Edit Relationships** dialog box, select the **Enforce Referential Integrity** check box, click the **Create** button, and then compare your screen with Figure 2.40.

The one-to-many relationship is established, and the *1* and ∞ indicate that referential integrity is enforced. Enforcing referential integrity ensures that a scholarship cannot be awarded to a student whose name does not appear in the 2B Athletes table. Similarly, you will not be able to delete a student athlete from the 2B Athletes table if there is a scholarship listed for that student in the 2B Scholarships Awarded table.

Figure 2.40

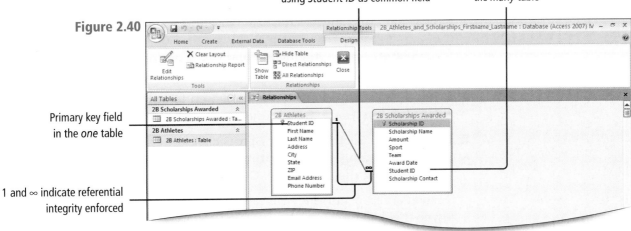

Join line indicates relationship established using *Student ID* as common field

Foreign key field in the *many* table

Primary key field in the *one* table

1 and ∞ indicate referential integrity enforced

13 On the **Design tab**, in the **Tools group**, click **Relationship Report**. On the displayed **Print Preview tab**, in the **Page Layout group**, click **Margins**, and then click **Normal**. Submit electronically as directed, or, if you are printing your assignments on paper, click the **Print** button, and then click **OK**. Click **Close Print Preview**. On the **Quick Access Toolbar**, click the **Save** button to save the report. With the text in the **Save As** dialog box highlighted, type **2B Relationships Firstname Lastname** and then click **OK**.

14 Close the report and the Relationships window. From the **Navigation Pane**, open the **2B Athletes** table. On the left side of the table, in the first record, point to the **plus sign**, and then click one time.

In the first record—for *Damon Hill*—you can see that three related records exist in the 2B Scholarships Awarded table. The relationship displays because you created a relationship between the two tables using the Student ID field as the common field.

15 Close the **2B Athletes** table, and then Close the **Navigation Pane**.

Objective 9
Specify Numeric Criteria in a Query

Criteria can be set for fields that contain numeric data. When you design your table, set the appropriate data type for fields that will contain numbers, currency, or dates so that mathematical calculations can be performed.

Activity 2.16 Specifying Numeric Criteria in a Query

Mr. Simmons wants to know *Which scholarships, and for which sport, are in the amount of $300?* In this activity, you will specify criteria in the query so that only the records of scholarships in the amount of $300 will display.

1 On the **Create tab**, in the **Other group**, click the **Query Design** button. In the **Show Table** dialog box, **Add** the **2B Scholarships Awarded** table, and then **Close** the **Show Table** dialog box. With the

pointer, adjust the height and width of the field list so that all of the fields display.

2 Add the following fields to the design grid in the order given: **Scholarship Name**, **Sport**, and **Amount**.

3 Click in the **Sort** row under **Sport**, click the **Sort arrow**, and then click **Ascending**. On the **Criteria** row, click in the **Amount** field, type **300** and then press Enter. Compare your screen with Figure 2.41.

When entering currency values as criteria in the design grid, do not type the dollar sign, and include a decimal point only if you are looking for a specific amount that includes cents—for example 300.50.

Figure 2.41

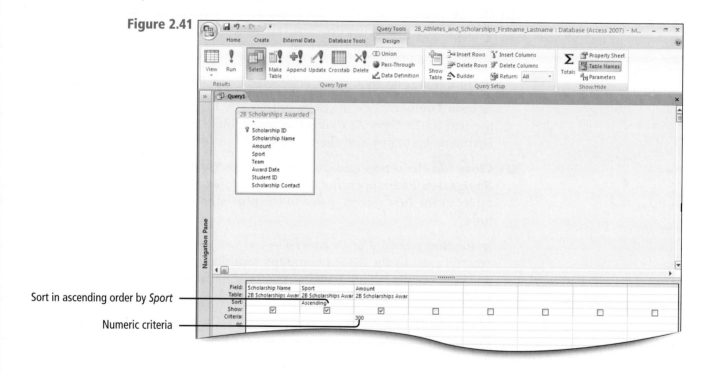

Sort in ascending order by *Sport*

Numeric criteria

4 On the **Design tab**, in the **Results group**, click the **Run** button to view the results. Alternatively, click the View button.

Five scholarships awarded were in the exact amount of $300. At the bottom of the datasheet, *1 of 5* displays to indicate the number of records that match the criteria.

5 On the **Home tab**, in the **Views group**, click the **View** button to return to Design view. Leave the query open in Design view for the next activity.

Activity 2.17 Using Comparison Operators

Comparison operators are symbols that evaluate each field value to determine if it is the same (=), greater than (>), less than (<), or in between a range of values as specified by the criteria.

If no comparison operator is specified, equal (=) is assumed. For example, in the previous activity, you created a query to display only records where the *Amount* was 300. The comparison operator of = was assumed, and Access displayed only records that had entries equal to 300.

In this activity, you will specify criteria in the query to display records from the 2B Scholarships Awarded table that have scholarships that are *greater* than $300 and then to display scholarships that are *less* than $300.

1 Be sure your query from the last activity is displayed in Design view. On the **Criteria** row, click in the **Amount** field, delete the existing criteria, type **>300** and then press Enter. Compare your screen with Figure 2.42.

Unlike a field with a data type of *Text*, Access does not add quote marks around criteria entered in a field that has a data type of *Number* or *Currency*.

Figure 2.42

Criteria with *greater than* comparison operator

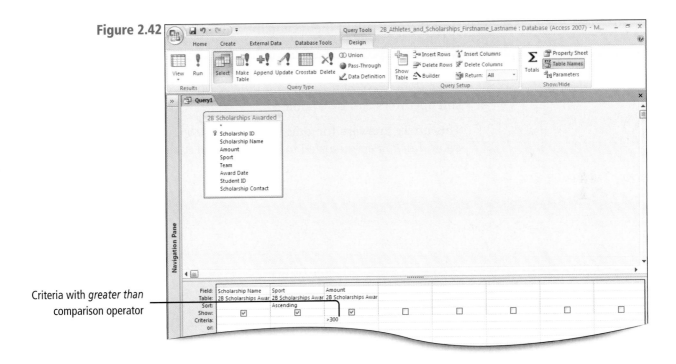

2 Click the **Design tab**, and then in the **Results group**, click the **Run** button.

Fourteen records match the criteria for an Amount that is greater than $300. The results show the records for which the Amount is *greater than* $300, but not *equal* to $300.

3 Click the **View** button to return to Design view. On the **Criteria** row, under **Amount**, delete the existing criteria, type **<300** Press (Enter), and then on the **Design tab**, in the **Results group**, click the **Run** button.

Eleven records display and each has an Amount less than $300. The results show the records for which the Amount is *less than* $300, but not *equal to* $300.

4 Switch to Design view. On the **Criteria** row, click in the **Amount** field, delete the existing criteria, type **>=300** and then press (Enter).

Note — Pressing Enter After Criteria Is Added

If you press (Enter) or click in another column or row in the query design grid after you have added your criteria, you can see how Access alters the criteria so it can interpret what you have typed. Sometimes, there is no change, such as when a number is added to a number or currency field. Other times, Access may capitalize a letter or add quote marks or other symbols to clarify the criteria. Whether or not you press (Enter) after criteria is added does not affect the query results. It is used in this text to help you see how the program behaves.

---

5 **Run** the query, and then compare your screen with Figure 2.43.

Nineteen records display, including the records for scholarships in the exact amount of $300. Thus, the displayed records include scholarships *equal to* or *greater than* $300. In this manner, comparison operators can be combined.

This query answers the question, *Which scholarships, and for which sport, have been awarded in the amount of $300 or more?*

Figure 2.43

Records with a scholarship amount of $300 or more

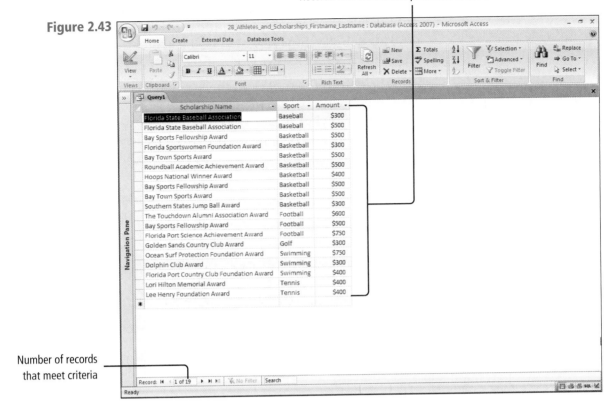

Number of records
that meet criteria

6 On the **Quick Access Toolbar**, click the **Save** button ![save button], and then in the **Save As** dialog box, type **2B $300 or More Firstname Lastname** Click **OK**.

7 From the **Office** menu ![office menu], point to the **Print** button, and then click **Print Preview**. If you are printing your assignments on paper, in the **Print group**, click the **Print** button. In the displayed **Print** dialog box, click **OK**. To submit electronically, follow your instructor's directions.

8 Click the **Close Print Preview** button, and then **Close** ![x] the query.

Open ![>>] the **Navigation Pane**, and notice that your new query displays under the table from which it retrieved the records.

Activity 2.18 Using the Between. . . And Comparison Operator

The **Between. . . And** operator is a comparison operator that looks for values within a range. It is particularly useful when you need to locate records that are within a range of dates, for example, scholarships awarded between August 1 and September 30. In this activity, you will create a new query from an existing query, and then add criteria to look for values within a range of dates. The query will answer the question *Which scholarships were awarded between August 1 and September 30?*

1 From the **Navigation Pane**, open your **2B $300 or More** query.

From the **Office** menu ![office menu], click **Save As**. In the **Save As** dialog box, type **2B Awards Aug-Sept Firstname Lastname** and then click **OK**.

2 **Close** 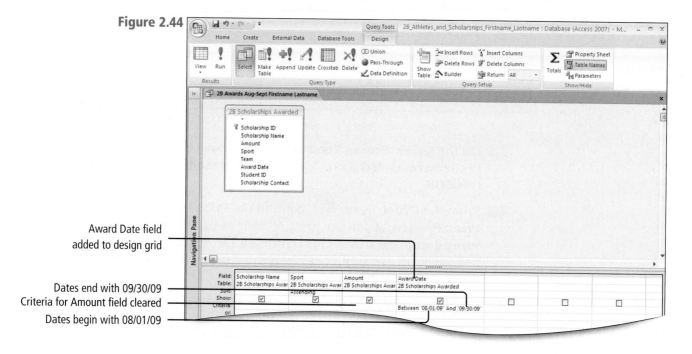 the **Navigation Pane**, and then on the **Home tab**, in the **Views group**, click the **View** button to switch to Design view. From the **2B Scholarships Awarded** field list, add the **Award Date** as the fourth field in the design grid.

3 On the **Criteria** row, click in the **Amount** field, and then delete the existing criteria so that the query is not restricted by amount. On the **Criteria** row, click in the **Award Date** field, type **Between 08/01/09 And 09/30/09** and then press Enter. Access places quote marks around the dates. Compare your screen with Figure 2.44, where the column has been widened to fully display the criteria.

This criteria instructs Access to look for values in the Award Date field that begin with 08/01/09 and end with 09/30/09. Both the beginning and ending dates will be included in the query results. If you type the operators *Between. . . And*, using lowercase letters, Access will capitalize the first letter of each operator.

Figure 2.44

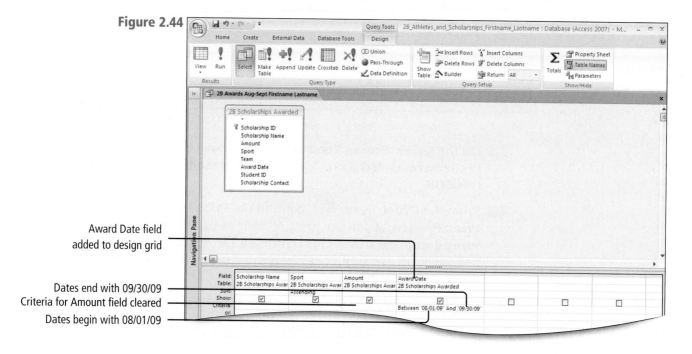

Award Date field added to design grid

Dates end with 09/30/09
Criteria for Amount field cleared
Dates begin with 08/01/09

4 **Run** the query and notice that three scholarships were awarded between the dates you specified in your criteria.

5 From the **Office** menu, point to the **Print** button, and then click **Print Preview**. If you are printing your assignments on paper, in the **Print group**, click the **Print** button. In the displayed **Print** dialog box, click **OK**. To submit electronically, follow your instructor's directions.

6 Click the **Close Print Preview** button. In the object window, **Close** the query, and then click **Yes** to save the changes to the design.

Open the **Navigation Pane**, and notice that your new query displays under the table from which it retrieved records.

Note — Widening Columns in the Query Grid

For a better view of your criteria, you can widen a column in the design grid using the same techniques that are used in a table. In the selection bar at the top of the column, point to the right border and double-click to expand the column to fully display the contents on the criteria row. You can also drag the right border to the width you want.

Objective 10
Use Compound Criteria

You can specify more than one condition—criteria—in a query; this is called *compound criteria*. Compound criteria enable you to create queries that are quite specific. Two types of compound criteria used in queries are AND and OR, which are *logical operators*. Logical operators allow you to enter criteria for the same field or different fields.

Activity 2.19 Using AND Criteria in a Query

Compound criteria that create an AND condition will display the records in the query result that meet *both* parts of the specified criteria. In this activity, you will help Mr. Simmons answer the question *Which scholarships over $500 were awarded for Football?* The results will match the criteria >$500 *and* Football.

1 **Close** `«` the **Navigation Pane**, and then from the **Create tab**, open a new query in Design view. **Add** the **2B Scholarships Awarded** table to the table area, **Close** the **Show Table** dialog box, and then adjust the height and width of the field list with the `↖` pointer.

2 Add the following fields to the design grid in the order given: **Scholarship Name**, **Sport**, and **Amount**.

3 On the **Criteria** row, click in the **Sport** field, type **Football** and then press `Tab`. On the **Criteria** row, in the **Amount** field, type **>500** press `Enter`, and then compare your screen with Figure 2.45.

The AND condition is created by placing the criteria for both fields on the same line in the Criteria row. The results will display records that contain *Football* and an amount greater than *$500*.

Figure 2.45

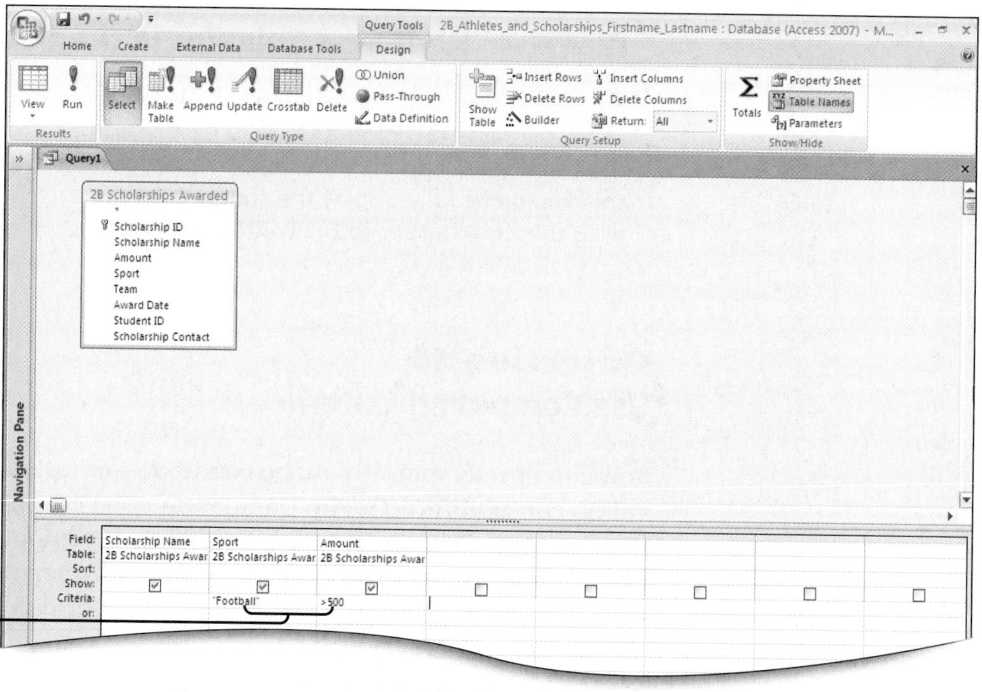

Criteria specified for
Sport and Amount

4 On the **Design tab**, in the **Results group**, click the **Run** button.

Two records display that match both conditions—Football in the Sport field and greater than $500 in the Amount field.

5 **Close** [×] the query, click **Yes** to save changes to the query, and then in the **Save As** dialog box, type **2B Football and Over $500 Firstname Lastname** as the query name. Click **OK** or press Enter.

6 **Open** [»] the **Navigation Pane**, click one time to select the query you just named and saved, and then from the **Office** menu [icon], point to the **Print** button and click **Print Preview**. If you are printing your assignments on paper, in the **Print group**, click the **Print** button. In the displayed **Print** dialog box, click **OK**. To submit electronically, follow your instructor's directions.

7 Click the **Close Print Preview** button, and then **Close** [«] the **Navigation Pane**.

You can print any selected object from the Navigation Pane in this manner—the object does not have to be displayed on your screen to print.

Activity 2.20 Using OR Criteria in a Query

Use the OR condition to specify multiple criteria for a single field, or multiple criteria on different fields when you want the records that meet either condition to display in the results. In this activity, you will help Mr. Simmons answer the question *Which scholarships over $400 were awarded in the sports of Baseball or Swimming?*

1 From the **Create tab**, open a new query in Design view. **Add** the **2B Scholarships Awarded** table, **Close** the dialog box, expand the field list, and then add the following four fields to the design grid in the order given: **Scholarship Name**, **Sport**, **Amount**, and **Award Date**.

2 On the **Criteria** row, click in the **Sport** field, and then type **Baseball**

3 In the design grid, locate the **or** row. On the **or** row, click in the **Sport** field, type **Swimming** and then press Enter. **Run** the query.

The query results display seven scholarship records whose Sport is either Baseball *or* Swimming. Use the OR condition in this manner to specify multiple criteria for a single field.

4 Return to Design view. Under **Sport**, on the **or** row, delete the text. Under **Sport**, click in the **Criteria** row, delete the existing text, and then type **Swimming Or Baseball** On the **Criteria** row, under **Amount**, type **>400** press Enter, and then compare your screen with Figure 2.46.

This is an alternative way to use the OR compound operator. Because criteria has been entered for two different fields, Access will return the records that are Baseball *or* Swimming and that have a scholarship awarded in an amount greater than $400.

In this manner, you can type multiple criteria for the same field on the Criteria row.

Figure 2.46

OR condition for two
criteria in the same field

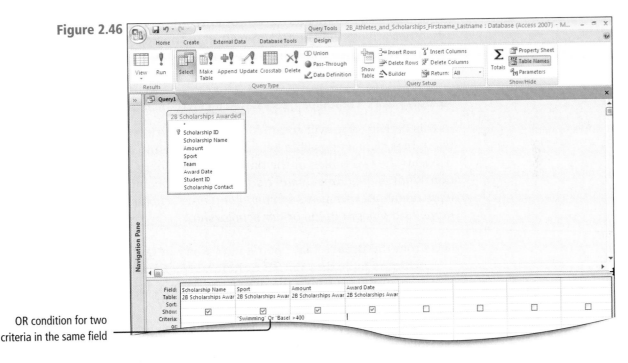

5 **Run** the query to display the two records that match the conditions.

6 **Close** [×] the query, click **Yes** to save changes to the query, and then in the **Save As** dialog box, type **2B Swimming or Baseball Over $400 Firstname Lastname** as the query name. Click **OK** or press Enter.

7 **Open** `»` the **Navigation Pane**, click one time to select the query you just named and saved, and then from the **Office** menu `[icon]`, display the **Print Preview**. If you are printing your assignments on paper, in the **Print group**, click the **Print** button, and then click **OK**. To submit electronically, follow your instructor's directions.

8 Click the **Close Print Preview** button, and then **Close** `«` the **Navigation Pane**.

Objective 11
Create a Query Based on More Than One Table

In a relational database, you can retrieve information from more than one table. Recall that each table in a relational database contains all of the records about a single topic. Tables are joined by relating the primary key field in one table to a foreign key field in another table. This common field creates a relationship, which enables you to include data from more than one table in a query.

For example, the Athletes table contains all of the information about the student athletes—name, address, and so on. The Scholarships Awarded table includes the scholarship name, amount, award date, and so on. When an athlete receives a scholarship, only the Student ID field is included with the scholarship to identify who received the scholarship. It is not necessary to include, and would result in repeated information, if any other athlete information appeared in the Scholarships Awarded table, because the athlete information is contained in the Athletes table.

Activity 2.21 Creating a Query Based on More Than One Table

In this activity, you will create a query that retrieves information from two tables. This is possible because a relationship has been established between the two tables in the database. The query will answer the question *What is the name, email address, and phone number of student athletes who have received swimming or tennis scholarships, and what is the name and amount of his or her scholarship?*

1 From the **Create tab**, open a new query in Design view. **Add** the **2B Athletes** table and the **2B Scholarships Awarded** table to the table area, and then **Close** the dialog box. Expand the two tables, and then compare your screen with Figure 2.47.

The join line indicates the one-to-many relationship—one athlete can have many scholarships. Student ID is the common field in the two tables. Notice that Student ID is designated by a key in the Athletes table where it is the primary key field, but it is not designated by a key in the Scholarships Awarded table where it is the foreign key field.

Join line

Figure 2.47

Student ID is common field

Field lists expanded

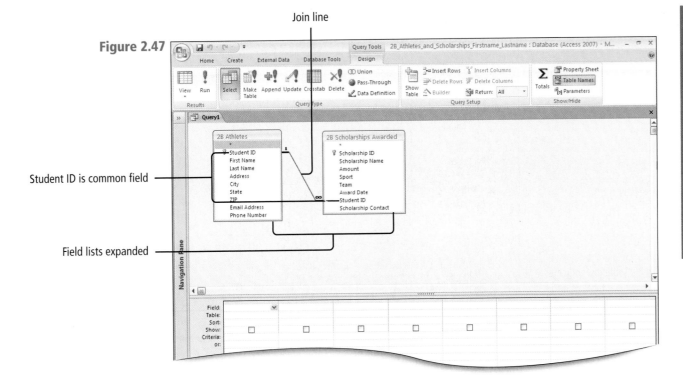

2 From the **2B Athletes** field list, add the following fields in the order given: **First Name**, **Last Name**, **Address**, **City**, **State**, and **ZIP**. On the **Sort** row, under **Last Name**, click to select **Ascending** to sort the records in alphabetical order by last name.

3 From the **2B Scholarships Awarded** field list, add **Scholarship Name**, **Sport**, and **Amount** to the design grid. On the **Criteria** row, under **Sport**, type **Swimming** On the **or** row, under **Sport**, type **Tennis** and then press Enter.

4 In the design grid, locate the second row—the **Table** row, and notice that for each field, the table from which the field was added is indicated. Compare your screen with Figure 2.48.

When using multiple tables in a query, this information is helpful, especially when some tables may include the same field names, such as address, but different data, such as a student's address or a coach's address.

Figure 2.48

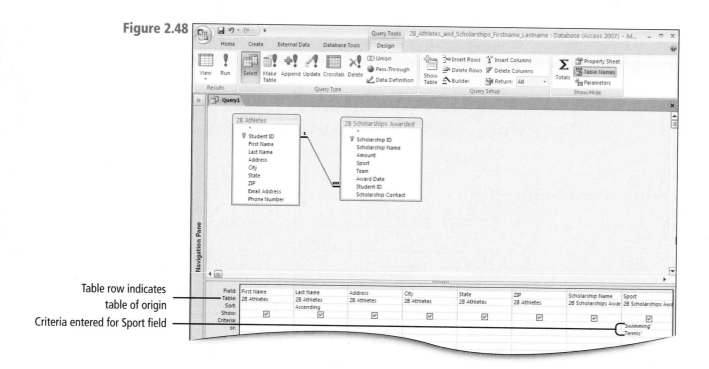

Table row indicates table of origin

Criteria entered for Sport field

5 **Run** the query.

The names and addresses of eight student athletes display. Notice that the First Name and Last Name is included in the query results even though the common field—Student ID—was *not* included in the query design. Because Student ID is included in both tables, and a one-to-many relationship was created between the tables, you can display data from both tables in one query.

Two students—*Arianna Kitasoe* and *Janice Murphy*—received scholarships in both Swimming and Tennis. Recall that *one* student athlete can have *many* scholarships.

6 Return to Design view. From the **Athletes** field list, add **Phone Number** to the design grid. Point to **Email Address**, drag it to the design grid on top of **Amount**, and then release the mouse button.

When you release the mouse button, Email Address is inserted to the left of the Amount field.

7 In the design grid, select, by dragging in the gray selection bar, the **Address**, **City**, **State**, and **ZIP** fields, and then press Delete. In the design grid, select the **Amount** field, and then drag it to the first field position in the grid. Click outside of the grid to cancel the selection, and then compare your screen with Figure 2.49.

Phone Number is added as the last field in the design grid. The Address, City, State, and ZIP fields are deleted. The amount field is in the first position. In this manner, you can modify your query design.

Figure 2.49

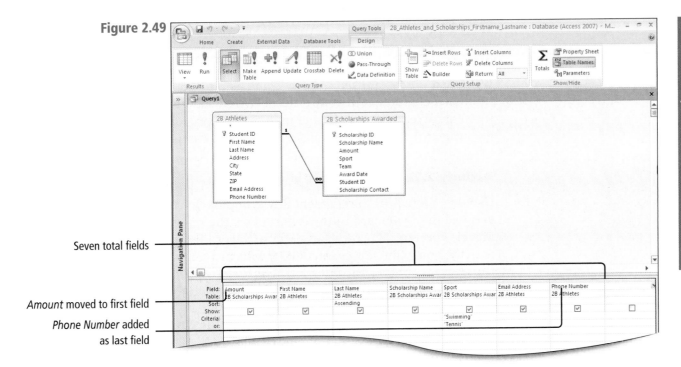

Seven total fields

Amount moved to first field

Phone Number added as last field

8 **Run** the query again. Using techniques similar to that of a table, select all the columns in the query and apply **Best Fit** (with the columns selected, in the field heading row, point to the right boundary of any of the selected rows to display the ⊕ pointer, and then double-click to apply Best Fit to all of the selected columns).

9 On the **Quick Access Toolbar,** click the **Save** button 🖫 , type **2B Swimming and Tennis Firstname Lastname** and then click **OK**. Display the query in **Print Preview**, set the **Margins** to **Normal**, and then change the orientation to **Landscape**. Print or submit electronically as directed.

10 **Close** the print preview, close the query, open the **Navigation Pane**, and notice that your new query displays under *both* tables from which it retrieved records.

In the Tables and Related Views arrangement of the Navigation Pane, any object that references a table will display with that table.

More Knowledge

Add a Table to the Table Area

To add another table to the table area, in the Query Setup group, click Show Table; or, right-click in the table area, and from the shortcut menu, click Show Table.

Objective 12
Use Wildcards in a Query

Wildcard characters in a query serve as a placeholder for one or more unknown characters in your criteria. When you are unsure of the particular character or set of characters to include in your criteria, you can use wildcard characters in place of the characters in the criteria.

Activity 2.22 Using a Wildcard in a Query

Use the asterisk (*) to represent any group of characters. For example, if you use the * wildcard in the criteria Fo*, the results would return Foster, Forrester, Forrest, Fossil, or any word beginning with *Fo*. In this activity, you will use the asterisk (*) wildcard and specify the criteria in the query to answer the question *Which student athletes received scholarships from local Rotary Clubs, country clubs, and foundations?*

1 **Close** 〈〈 the **Navigation Pane**. From the **Create tab**, start a new query in Design view, add both tables to the table area, and then expand the field lists to view all the field names. Add the following fields to the design grid: **First Name** and **Last Name** from the **2B Athletes** table, and **Scholarship Contact** from the **2B Scholarships Awarded** table. On the **Sort** row, sort the query results in **Ascending** order by **Last Name**.

2 On the **Criteria** row, under **Scholarship Contact**, type **Rotary*** and then press Enter.

The wildcard character * is used as a placeholder to match any number of characters. When you press Enter, *Like* is added by Access at the beginning of the criteria. This is used to compare a sequence of characters and test whether or not the text matches a pattern.

Access will automatically insert expressions similar to this when creating queries.

3 **Run** the query to display the three student athletes who received scholarships from Rotary Clubs.

4 Return to the Design view. On the **or** row, under **Scholarship Contact**, type ***Country Club** and then press Enter.

The * can be used at the beginning or end of the criteria. The position of the wildcard determines the location of the unknown characters. Here you will search for records that end in *Country Club*.

5 **Run** the query to display a total of six records.

6 Return to Design view. In the next available row under **Scholarship Contact**, type ***Foundation*** press Enter, and then compare your screen with Figure 2.50.

In this manner, the query will return records that have the word *Foundation* anywhere—beginning, middle, or end—in the field. You can also see that you can combine many *or* criteria in a query.

Figure 2.50

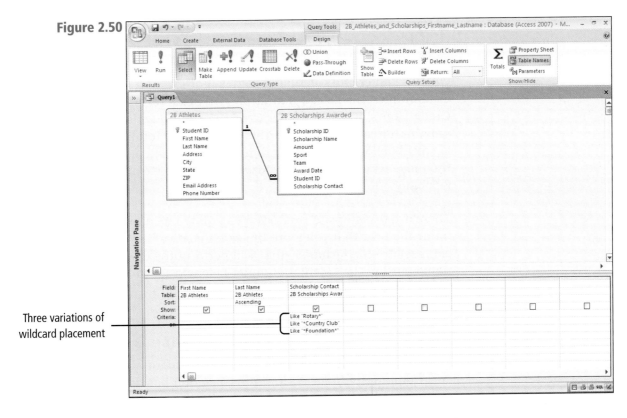

Three variations of wildcard placement

7 **Run** the query to display a total of 28 records.

Twenty-eight scholarships were awarded from either a Country Club, a Rotary club, or a Foundation.

8 On the **Quick Access Toolbar**, click the **Save** button, and name the query **2B Clubs and Foundations Firstname Lastname** Display the **Print Preview**, and print your result if you are submitting paper assignments, or submit electronically as directed. **Close Print Preview**, **Close** the query ☒, and then **Open** ⟫ the **Navigation Pane**.

Because the query retrieved data from two tables, the query displays below each table's name.

More Knowledge

Search for a Single Unknown Character by Using the ? Wildcard

The question mark (?) is another wildcard that is used to search for unknown single characters. For each question mark included in a criteria, any character can be inserted. For example, if you used *b?d* as a criteria, the query could locate bid, bud, bed or any three-character word beginning with *b* and ending with *d*. If *b??d* is entered as the criteria, the results could include bind, bend, bard or any four-character word beginning with *b* and ending with *d*.

Objective 13
Use Calculated Fields in a Query

Queries can create calculated values. For example, Florida Port Community College could multiply two fields together, such as Total Credit Hours and Tuition per Credit Hour and get a Total Tuition Due amount for each student. In this manner, the total amount of tuition due is calculated without having to include a specific field for this amount in the table, which reduces the size of the database and provides more flexibility.

There are two steps to produce a calculated field in a query. First, name the field that will store the calculated values. Second, write the expression—the formula—that will perform the calculation. Each field name used in the calculation must be enclosed within its own pair of square brackets.

Activity 2.23 Using Calculated Fields in a Query

For each scholarship received by college student athletes, the Florida Port Community College Alumni Association has agreed to donate an amount equal to 50 percent of each scholarship. In this activity, you will create a calculated field to determine the additional amount each scholarship is worth. The query will answer the question *What will the value of each scholarship be if the Alumni Association makes a matching 50% donation?*

1 **Close** `«` the **Navigation Pane**. From the **Create tab**, start a new query in Design view. **Add** the **2B Scholarships Awarded** table and expand the field list. Add the following fields to the design grid: **Student ID**, **Scholarship Name**, and **Amount**.

2 Click in the **Sort** row under **Student ID**, click the **Sort arrow**, and then click **Ascending**. In the **Field** row, right-click in the first empty column to display a shortcut menu, and then click **Zoom**.

The Zoom dialog box that displays gives you working space so that you can see the calculation as you type it. The calculation can also be typed directly in the empty Field box in the column.

3 In the **Zoom** dialog box, type **Matching Donation: [Amount]*0.5** and then compare your screen with Figure 2.51.

The first element, *Matching Donation*, is the new field name where the calculated amounts will display. Following that is a colon (:). A colon in a calculated field separates the new field name from the expression. *Amount* is in square brackets because it is an existing field name from the 2B Scholarships Awarded table. It contains the information on which the calculation will be performed. Following the square brackets is an asterisk (*), which in math calculations signifies multiplication. Finally, the percentage (50% or 0.5) is indicated.

Calculated value

Figure 2.51

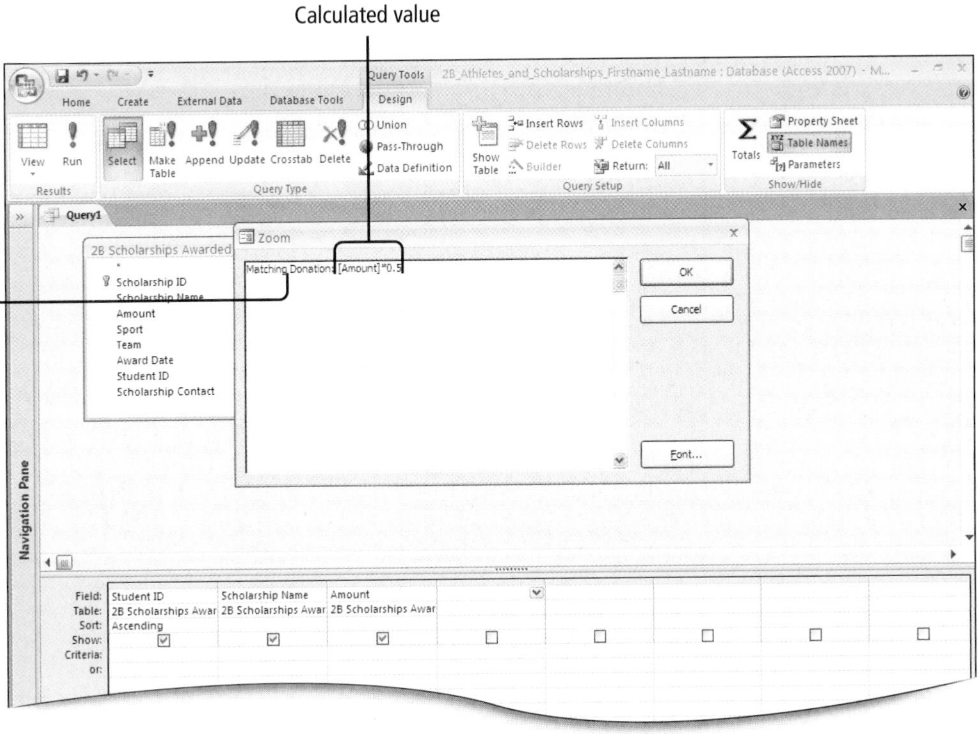

New field name

Access | chapter 2

Alert!

Does your screen differ?

If your calculations in a query do not work, carefully check the expression you typed. Spelling or syntax errors will prevent calculated fields from working properly.

---

[4] In the **Zoom** dialog box, click **OK**, and then **Run** the query. Select all the columns and apply **Best Fit**. Compare your screen with Figure 2.52.

The query results display the three fields from the 2B Scholarships Awarded table plus a fourth field—Matching Donation—in which a calculated amount displays. Each calculated amount equals the amount in the Amount field multiplied by 0.5.

Figure 2.52

New calculated field
created (50% of Amount)

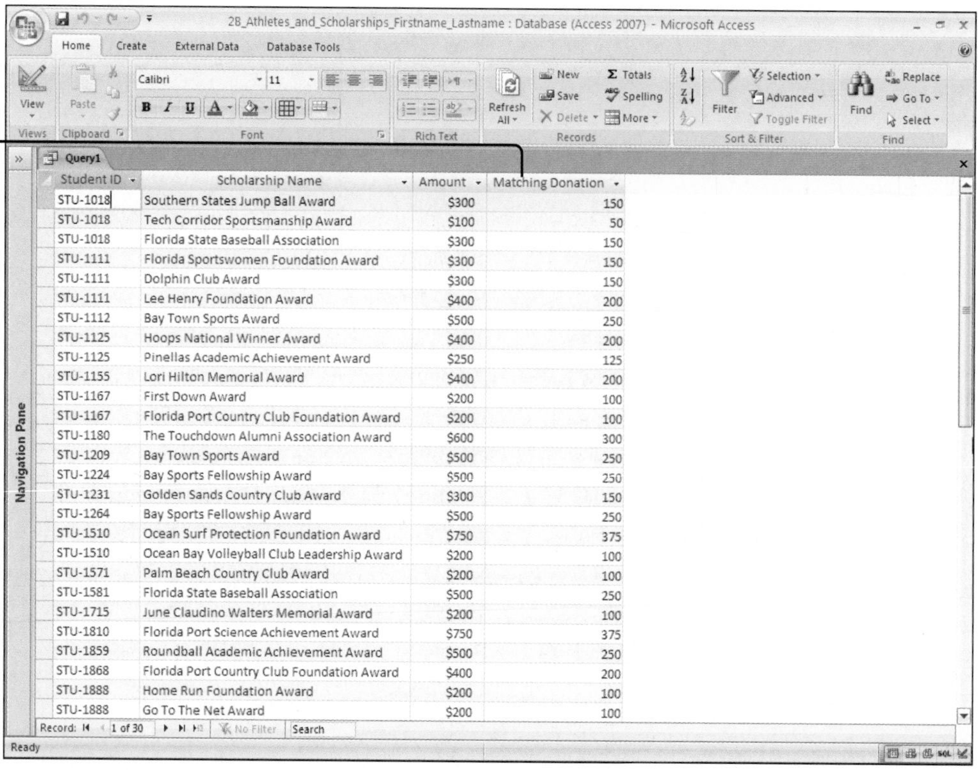

5 Notice the formatting of the **Matching Donation** field—there are no dollar signs, commas, or decimal places; you will adjust this formatting later. Return to Design view. On the **Field** row, in the first empty column, right-click, and then click **Zoom**.

6 In the **Zoom** dialog box, type **Total Scholarship: [Amount]+[Matching Donation]** and then click **OK**. **Run** the query to view the results. Apply **Best Fit** to the new column.

Total Scholarship is calculated by adding together the Amount field and the Matching Donation field. The Total Scholarship column includes dollar signs, commas, and decimal points, which carried over from the Amount field.

7 Return to Design view. On the **Field** row, click in the **Matching Donation** field. On the **Design tab**, in the **Show/Hide group**, click the **Property Sheet** button. Alternatively, right-click the Matching Donation field, and then click Properties.

The Property Sheet task pane displays on the right side of your screen. Here you can customize fields in a query, for example, the format of numbers in the field.

8 In the **Property Sheet** task pane, on the **General tab**, click the text *Format*, and then click the **arrow** that displays. Compare your screen with Figure 2.53.

A list of possible formats for this field displays.

Figure 2.53

Property Sheet

Format arrow

List of possible formats

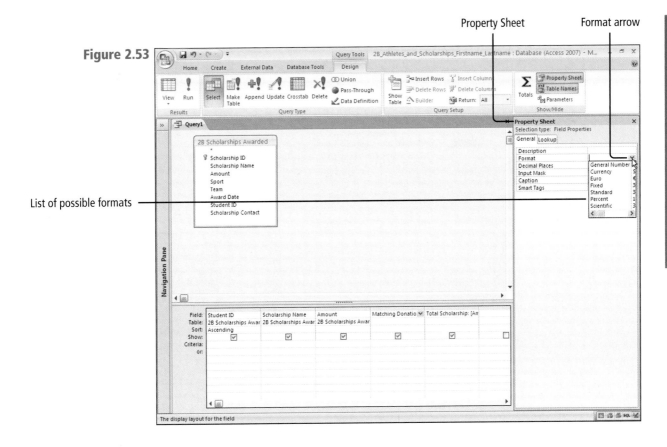

9 In the list of formats, click **Currency**, and then **Close** ☒ the **Property Sheet** task pane.

10 **Run** the query to view the results. If necessary, select all the columns, and apply **Best Fit**. Click in any record to cancel the selection, and then compare your screen with Figure 2.54.

The Matching Donation column displays with currency formatting—a dollar sign, thousands comma separators, and two decimal places.

Figure 2.54

Currency format applied to all columns

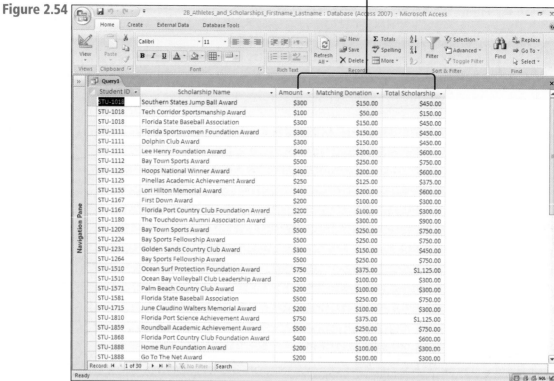

11 On the **Quick Access Toolbar**, click the **Save** button, and then name the query **2B Matching Donations Firstname Lastname** Display the **Print Preview**, change the **Orientation** to **Landscape**, and then print or submit electronically as directed. **Close Print Preview**, and then **Close** the query.

Objective 14
Group Data and Calculate Statistics in a Query

In Access queries, you can perform statistical calculations on a group of records. Calculations that are performed on a group of records are called *aggregate functions*. In the activities that follow, you will use AVG, SUM, MAX, and MIN functions. As you progress in your study of Access, you will use other functions.

Activity 2.24 Using the MIN, MAX, AVG and SUM Functions in a Query

In this activity, you will use the average, sum, maximum, and minimum functions in a query to examine the amounts of scholarships awarded. The last query will answer the question *What is the total amount of scholarships awarded?*

1 From the **Create tab**, create a new query in Design view. **Add** the **2B Scholarships Awarded** table, and then expand the field list. Add **Amount** to the design grid.

When you want to summarize a field, include only the field you want to summarize in the query, so that the aggregate function (sum, average, minimum, maximum, and so forth) is applied to that single field.

2 On the **Design tab**, in the **Show/Hide group**, click the **Totals** button to add a **Total** row as the third row in the design grid. Notice that in the design grid, on the **Total** row, under **Amount**, *Group By* displays.

Here you select the function—such as Avg, Sum, Min, or Max—that you want to use for this field.

3 In the **Total** row, under **Amount**, click in the **Group By** box, and then click the **arrow** to display the list of functions. Access supports the aggregate functions summarized in the table shown in Figure 2.55. Take a moment to review this table, and then compare your screen with Figure 2.56.

Aggregate Functions

Function Name	What It Does
Sum	Totals the values in a field.
Avg	Averages the values in a field.
Min	Locates the smallest value in a field.
Max	Locates the largest value in a field.
Count	Counts the number of records in a field.
StDev	Calculates the Standard Deviation on the values in a field.
Var	Calculates the Variance on the values in a field.
First	Displays the First value in a field.
Last	Displays the Last value in a field.
Expression	Creates a calculated field that includes an aggregate function.
Where	Limits records displayed to those that match a condition specified on the Criteria row.

Figure 2.55

List of aggregate functions

Totals button in the Show/Hide group

Figure 2.56

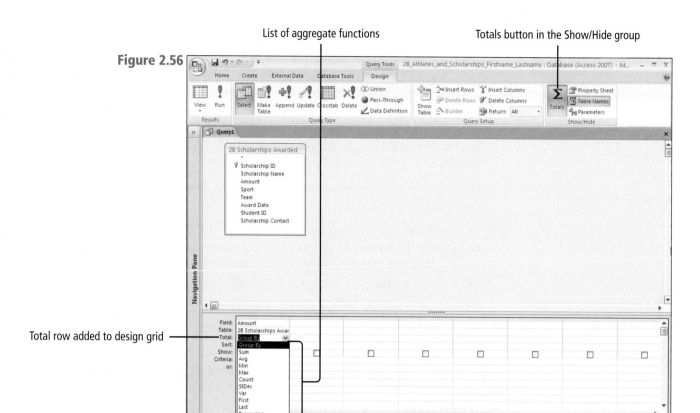

Total row added to design grid

4 From the list of functions, click **Min**, and then **Run** the query. Double-click the right boundary of the column heading to widen the column.

Access calculates the minimum (smallest) scholarship award—$100.00. The field name, *MinOfAmount* displays for the calculation. This query answers the question, *What is the minimum (smallest) scholarship amount awarded?*

5 Return to Design view. Using the technique you just practiced, select the **Max** function, and then **Run** the query.

The maximum (largest) scholarship amount is $750.00.

6 Switch to Design view, select the **Avg** function, and then **Run** the query.

The average scholarship amount awarded is $358.33.

7 Return to Design view. Select the **Sum** function. **Run** the query.

Access sums the Amount field for all records and displays a result of *$10,750.00*. The field name, SumOfAmount, displays. This query answers the question, *What is the total of all the scholarships awarded?*

Activity 2.25 Grouping Data in a Query

The aggregate functions can also be used to calculate totals by groups of data. For example, if you wanted to group (summarize) the amount of scholarships awarded to each student, you would include the Student ID field, in addition to the Amount field, and then group all of the records for each student together to calculate a total awarded to each student. Similarly, you could calculate how much money was awarded to each sport.

1 Switch to Design view. Add the **Student ID** field to the design grid.

On the Total row, under Student ID, *Group By* displays by default. The design of this query will group—summarize—the records by StudentID and calculate a total Amount for each student.

2 **Run** the query to display the results, apply **Best Fit** to the columns, click any record to deselect, and then compare your screen with Figure 2.57.

The query calculates totals for each student.

Figure 2.57

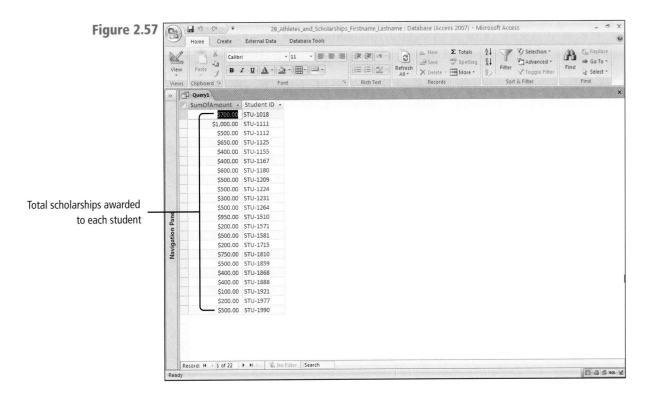

Total scholarships awarded to each student

3 Switch to Design view. In the design grid, select and delete the **Student ID** field, and then add the **Sport** field to the design grid. **Run** the query to see the results. Compare your screen with Figure 2.58.

Access summarizes the data by each sport. You can see that Basketball received the largest total Amount—$3,500.00.

Figure 2.58

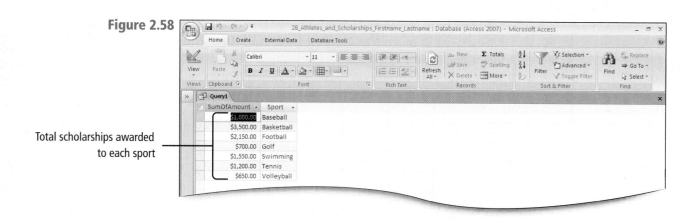

Total scholarships awarded
to each sport

4 On the **Quick Access Toolbar**, click the **Save** button, and then name the query **2B Totals by Sport Firstname Lastname** Display the **Print Preview**, and print your result if you are submitting paper assignments. **Close Print Preview**, close the query, and then

Open ⟫ the **Navigation Pane** to view the queries you have created.

5 **Close** ⟪ the **Navigation Pane**, close your **2B_Athletes_ Scholarships** database, and then **Close** Access.

End **You have completed Project 2B**

There's More You Can Do!

From My Computer, navigate to the student files that accompany this textbook. In the folder **02_theres_more_you_can_do_pg1_36**, locate and open the folder for this chapter. Open and print the instructions for this project, which are provided to you in Adobe PDF format.

Try IT! 1— Password Protect Your Database

In this Try IT! exercise, you will encrypt and password protect your database to conceal data and prevent unwanted users from opening your database.

Content-Based Assessments

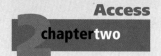

Summary

Importing an Excel spreadsheet is an efficient way to create new tables in an Access database. Sorting data in a table reorders the records based on one or more fields and is a quick way to alphabetize records or to find the highest or lowest amount in a numeric, currency, or date field. Use queries to ask complex questions about the data in a database in a manner that Access can interpret. Save queries so they can be run as needed against current records. By using queries, you can limit the fields that display, add criteria to restrict the number of records in the query result, create calculated values, and include data from more than one table.

Key Terms

Content-Based Assessments

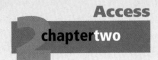
Matching

Match each term in the second column with its correct definition in the first column. Write the letter of the term on the blank line in front of the correct definition.

_____ **1.** The area directly below the Ribbon that displays information such as security alerts when there is potentially unsafe, active content in an Office 2007 document that you open.

_____ **2.** An area of the Access program where you can view the security and privacy settings for your Access installation.

_____ **3.** A type of database in which the tables in the database can relate or connect to other tables through common fields.

_____ **4.** Fields that contain the same data in more than one table.

_____ **5.** An association that is established between two tables using common fields.

_____ **6.** A relationship between two tables where one record in the first table corresponds to many records in the second table—the most common type of relationship in Access.

_____ **7.** A list of the field names in a table.

_____ **8.** The field that is included in the related table so that it can be joined to the primary key in another table for the purpose of creating a relationship.

_____ **9.** A set of rules that Access uses to ensure that the data between related tables is valid.

_____ **10.** In the Relationships window, the line joining two tables that visually indicates the related field and the type of relationship.

_____ **11.** The process of arranging data in a specific order based on the value in each field.

_____ **12.** A sorting order that arranges text in alphabetical order (A to Z) or numbers from the lowest to highest number.

_____ **13.** A database object that retrieves (selects) specific data from one or more tables and then displays the specified data in datasheet view.

_____ **14.** When sorting on multiple fields in datasheet view, the field that will be used for the first level of sorting.

_____ **15.** The table or tables from which a query selects its data.

A Ascending

B Common fields

C Data source

D Field list

E Foreign key

F Join line

G Message Bar

H One-to-many

I Outermost sort field

J Referential integrity

K Relational

L Relationship

M Select Query

N Sorting

O Trust Center

Content-Based Assessments

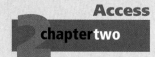

Fill in the Blank

Write the correct word in the space provided.

1. The upper pane of the Query window, which displays the field lists for tables that are used in the query is the _____.

2. The lower pane of the Query window, which displays the design of the query is the _____.

3. The process in which Access searches the records in the table(s) included in a query design, finds the records that match the specified criteria, and then displays those records in a datasheet is called _____.

4. Conditions that identify the specific records you are looking for are called _____.

5. Each time you open a saved query, Access _____ the query again and displays the results based on the data stored in the associated tables; thus, the results always reflect the latest information in the tables.

6. A sequence of characters, which when used in query criteria, must be matched, is referred to as a _____.

7. A criteria that searches for fields that are empty is called _____.

8. A criteria that searches for fields that are *not* empty is called _____.

9. Symbols that evaluate each field value to determine if it is the same (=), greater than (>), less than (<), or in between a range of values as specified by the criteria are referred to as _____.

10. In a(n) _____ condition, both parts of the query must be met.

11. In a(n) _____ condition, either part of the query must be met.

12. Multiple conditions in a query or filter are called _____.

13. In a query, a character that serves as a placeholder for one or more unknown characters is a _____.

14. Calculations that are performed on a group of records are called _____.

15. To locate the largest value in a group of records, use the _____ function.

Content-Based Assessments

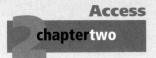
Skills Review

Project 2C — Music Department

In this project, you will apply the skills you practiced from the Objectives in Project 2A.

Objectives: 1. *Open an Existing Database;* **2.** *Create Table Relationships;* **3.** *Sort Records in a Table;* **4.** *Create a Query in Design View;* **5.** *Create a New Query from an Existing Query;* **6.** *Sort Query Results;* **7.** *Specify Criteria in a Query.*

In the following Skills Review, you will assist Pascal Sanchez, Florida Port Community College Music Director, in using his database to answer various questions about the instruments in the Music Department's inventory. Your query results will look similar to those shown in Figure 2.59.

For Project 2C, you will need the following file:

a2C_Music_Department

**You will save your database as
2C_Music_Department_Firstname_Lastname**

Figure 2.59

(Project 2C–Music Department continues on the next page)

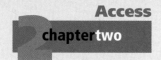
(Project 2C–Music Department continued)

1. From the student files that accompany this textbook, locate the file **a2C_Music_ Department**. Copy and then paste the file to your Access Chapter 2 folder. Rename the file **2C_Music_Department_Firstname_ Lastname Start** Access, open your database, and then enable the content.

2. Click the **Database Tools tab**. In the **Show/Hide group**, click the **Relationships** button. On the **Design tab**, in the **Relationships group**, click the **Show Table** button. Click the **2C Student Musicians** table, and then at the bottom of the dialog box, click **Add**. Point to the **2C Instruments Inventory** table, and then double-click to add the table to the Relationships window. **Close** the **Show Table** dialog box. In each table, use the pointer to resize the field list as necessary to display the table name and all the field names completely.

3. In your **2C Student Musicians** field list, point to **Student ID**, hold down the left mouse button, and then drag to the right to the **2C Instruments Inventory** field list until your mouse pointer is on top of **Student ID**. Release the mouse button, and then drag the **Edit Relationships** dialog box below the two field lists. The relationship between the two tables is a one-to-many relationship; *one* student can play *many* instruments. The common field is Student ID.

4. Click to select the **Enforce Referential Integrity** check box, and then click the **Create** button. With the **Relationships** window open, on the **Design tab**, in the **Tools group**, click **Relationship Report**. To print, on the **Print Preview tab**, in the **Print group**, click the **Print** button, and then click **OK**, or submit electronically as directed. Click **Close Print Preview**. On the **Quick Access Toolbar**, click the **Save** button, and then in the displayed **Save As** dialog box, click **OK** to accept the default name. Close all open objects.

5. **Open** the **2C Instruments Inventory** table, and then **Close** the **Navigation Pane**. In the **Condition** field, click any record. In the **Sort & Filter group**, click the **Descending** button to sort the records from *Poor* to *Excellent*. Point anywhere in the **Category** field, and then right-click. From the displayed shortcut menu, click **Sort A to Z**. The records are sorted first by **Category**, the outermost sort field, and then within categories, by **Condition**, the innermost sort field. In the **Sort & Filter group**, click the **Clear All Sorts** button. **Close** the table, and then click **No**; you need not save the changes to the design after viewing a sort.

6. Click the **Create tab**, and then in the **Other group**, click the **Query Design** button. From the **Show Table** dialog box, **Add** the **2C Instruments Inventory** table, and then **Close** the **Show Table** dialog box. Use the pointer to adjust the height and width of the field list as necessary.

7. In the **2C Instruments Inventory** field list, double-click **Instrument ID** to add it to the design grid. In the **2C Instruments Inventory** field list, point to **Category**, hold down the left mouse button, and then drag down into the design grid until you are pointing to the **Field** row in the next available column. Release the mouse button. In the **Field** row of the design grid, click in the third column, and then click the **arrow** that displays. From the dis-

(Project 2C–Music Department continues on the next page)

Content-Based Assessments

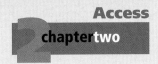

(Project 2C–Music Department continued)

played list, click **Instrument** to add this field to the design grid.

8. Using any technique, add the **Student ID** and **Condition** fields as the fourth and fifth field in the design grid. On the **Query Tools Design tab**, in the **Results group**, click the **Run** button. This query answers the question, *What is the Instrument ID, Category, Instrument, Student ID, and Condition of all the instruments in the inventory?* On the **Quick Access Toolbar**, click the **Save** button to display the **Save As** dialog box. Type **2C All Instruments Query Firstname Lastname** and then click **OK**.

9. From the **Office** menu, point to the **Print** button, and then click **Print Preview**. Click the **Print** button; or, submit electronically as directed. Click the **Close Print Preview** button. Leave the query open. From the **Office** menu, click **Save As**. In the **Save As** dialog box, type **2C Condition Query Firstname Lastname** and then click **OK**. Recall that you can create a new query based on an existing query in this manner.

10. On the **Home tab**, in the **Views group**, click the **View** button to switch to Design view. In the design grid, point to the thin gray selection bar above the **Student ID** field until the ⬇ pointer displays. Click to select the **Student ID** column, and then press ⌨Delete. From the gray selection bar, select the **Instrument ID** column. Then, point to the selection bar at the top of the selected column to display the ⬚ pointer, and drag to the right to position **Instrument ID** as the fourth (last) column.

11. **Run** the query. The results of the query display four fields in the new arrangement. This query answers the question, *What is*

the Category, Instrument, Condition, and Instrument ID of every instrument in the inventory?* **Close** the query, and then click **Yes**. Open the **Navigation Pane**, select the query name, display the **Print Preview**, and then print or submit electronically as directed. Close the print preview.

12. **Open** your **2C All Instruments Query**, and then save it as **2C Instrument Sort Firstname Lastname** Switch to Design view. In the design grid, delete the **Student ID** field. In the **Category** field, click in the **Sort** row, click the **Sort arrow**, and then click **Descending**. Under **Condition**, click to display the **Sort arrow**, and then click **Ascending**. **Run** the query. This query answers the question *Within each category (with Category in descending alphabetical order), what instruments are in the inventory and what is the instrument's condition (with the condition listed in ascending alphabetic order)?* Print the query or submit electronically as directed. **Close** the query, and then click **Yes** to save the changes.

13. Close any open objects and close the **Navigation Pane**. **Create** a new query in Design view, and then **Add** the **2C Instruments Inventory** table. Add the following fields to the design grid: **Instrument ID**, **Category**, **Instrument**, and **Condition**. On the **Criteria** row of the design grid, under **Condition**, type **Fair** and then press ⌨Enter. **Run** the query. This query answers the question, *What is the Instrument ID, Category, and Instrument type of instruments that are in Fair condition?* Click the **Save** button, and then name the query **2C Fair Condition Firstname Lastname** Print or submit the query electronically, and then close the query.

(Project 2C–Music Department continues on the next page)

Content-Based Assessments

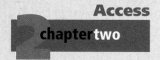

(Project 2C–Music Department continued)

14. Create a new query in Design view, **Add** the **2C Instruments Inventory** table, and then add the following fields to the design grid: **Category**, **Instrument**, and **Condition**. On the **Criteria** row, under **Category**, type Woodwinds and then press Enter. Under **Category**, click to clear the **Show** check box, and then **Run** the query. This query answers the question, *What is the condition of the woodwind instruments in the inventory?* Recall that if all results are of the same criteria, it is not necessary to display the field name of the criteria. **Save** the query with the name 2C **Woodwinds Condition Firstname Lastname** Print or submit electronically as directed, and then close the query.

15. Create a new query in Design view, **Add** the **2C Student Musicians** table, and then add the following fields to the design grid

in the order listed: **First Name**, **Last Name**, **Email Address**, and **Phone Number**. On the **Criteria** row, under the **Phone Number** field, type **Is Null** and then press Enter. On the **Sort** row, click in the **Last Name** field, click the **Sort arrow**, and then click **Ascending**. **Run** the query. This query answers the question, *For which student musicians are phone numbers missing?* **Save** the query as 2C **Missing Phone Numbers Firstname Lastname** Print or submit electronically as directed, and then close the query.

16. If necessary, close any open objects and close the **Navigation Pane**. From the **Office** menu, click **Close Database**, and then at the right end of the Access title bar, click the **Close** button to close the Access program. Alternatively, from the Office menu, click **Exit Access.**

 End **You have completed Project 2C** ―――――――――――――――

Skills Review

Project 2D — Concerts and Sponsors

In this project, you will apply the skills you practiced from the Objectives in Project 2B.

Objectives: 8. *Create a New Table by Importing an Excel Spreadsheet;* **9.** *Specify Numeric Criteria in a Query;* **10.** *Use Compound Criteria;* **11.** *Create a Query Based on More Than One Table;* **12.** *Use Wildcards in a Query;* **13.** *Use Calculated Fields in a Query;* **14.** *Group Data and Calculate Statistics in a Query.*

In the following Skills Review, you will assist Pascal Sanchez, College Music Director, in answering questions about concerts, sponsors, box office receipts, dates, and concert locations. Your query results will look similar to those shown in Figure 2.60.

For Project 2D, you will need the following files:

a2D_Concerts_Sponsors
a2D_Sponsors (Excel file)

**You will save your database as
2D_Concerts_Sponsors_Firstname_Lastname**

Figure 2.60

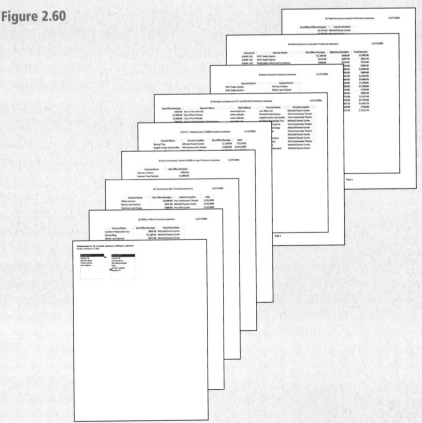

(Project 2D–Concerts and Sponsors continues on the next page)

Content-Based Assessments

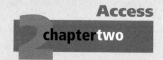
(Project 2D–Concerts and Sponsors continued)

1. From the student files that accompany this textbook, locate the file **a2D_Concerts_Sponsors**. Copy and paste the file to your Access Chapter 2 folder. Rename the file **2D_Concerts_Sponsors_Firstname_Lastname** Start Access, open your database, and then enable the content.

2. **Open** the **Navigation Pane**. On the Ribbon, click the **External Data tab**, and then in the **Import group**, click the **Excel** button. In the displayed **Get External Data – Excel Spreadsheet** dialog box, to the right of the **File name** box, click the **Browse** button. Navigate to the location where the student files for this textbook are stored, and then click the Excel file **a2D_Sponsors**. In the lower right corner, click **Open**. Be sure the **Import the source data into a new table in the current database** option button is selected, and then in the lower right corner, click **OK**.

3. In the upper portion of the **Import Spreadsheet Wizard**, click to select the **First Row Contains Column Headings** check box. In the lower right corner, click **Next**. Under **Field Options**, make no changes for any of the fields, and then in the lower right corner, click **Next**. In the upper portion of the dialog box, click the **Choose my own primary key** option button, and then be sure that **Sponsor ID** displays. Click **Next**. In the **Import to Table** box, type **2D Sponsors** and then in the lower right corner, click **Finish**. In the displayed dialog box, in the lower right corner, click **Close**. The imported Excel spreadsheet becomes the second table in the database.

4. Click the **Database Tools tab**, and then in the **Show/Hide group**, click the

Relationships button. On the **Design tab**, in the **Relationships group**, click **Show Table**. **Add** the **2D Concerts** table, and then **Add** the **2D Sponsors** table. Expand the height and width of the field lists and position the field lists as necessary so that the **2D Sponsors** table is on the left. In the **2D Sponsors** field list, point to the **Sponsor ID** field, hold down the left mouse button, drag into the **2D Concerts** field list, position the mouse pointer on top of the **Sponsor ID** field, and then release the mouse button. Click to select the **Enforce Referential Integrity** check box, and then click the **Create** button. A one-to-many relationship is established; *one* sponsor organization can sponsor *many* concerts.

5. On the **Design tab**, in the **Tools group**, click the **Relationship Report** button. On the displayed **Print Preview tab**, click **Print**; or, submit electronically as directed. Click the **Save** button, and then click **OK** to accept the default name. **Close Print Preview**, close all open objects, and then close the **Navigation Pane**.

6. On the **Create tab**, in the **Other group**, click the **Query Design** button. **Add** the **2D Concerts** table, and then add the following fields to the design grid in the order given: **Concert Name**, **Box Office Receipts**, and **Concert Location**. Click in the **Sort** row under **Concert Location**, click the **arrow**, and then click **Ascending**. On the **Criteria** row, under **Box Office Receipts**, type **800** and then press Enter. **Run** the query. Only one concert—*Southern Hospitality Tour*—had Box Office Receipts of exactly $800.

7. On the **Home tab**, in the **Views group**, click the **View** button to return to Design view. On the **Criteria** row, under **Box**

(Project 2D–Concerts and Sponsors continues on the next page)

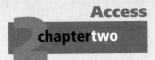
(Project 2D–Concerts and Sponsors continued)

Office Receipts, delete the existing criteria, type **>800** and then press Enter. **Run** the query again. Eight concerts had Box Office Receipts greater than $800. Return to Design view, change the **Box Office Receipts** criteria to **<800** and then run the query. Eight concerts had Box Office Receipts less than $800. Return to Design view, change **Box Office Receipts** criteria to **>=800** and then run the query. Nine records meet the criteria. This query answers the question, *Which concerts had Box Office Receipts of $800 or more, what was the amount of the Box Office Receipts, and where was each concert held?* **Save** the query as **2D $800 or More Firstname Lastname** Print or submit electronically as directed. Leave the query open. From the **Office** menu, click **Save As**, and then type **2D Concerts Jan-Apr Firstname Lastname** and click **OK**.

8. Return to Design view. From the **2D Concerts** field list, add the **Date** as the fourth field in the design grid. On the **Criteria** row, under **Box Office Receipts**, delete the existing criteria so that the query is not restricted by receipts. Under **Concert Location**, in the **Sort** row, click the arrow, and then click **(not sorted)**. Under **Date**, in the **Sort** row, click the arrow, and then click **Ascending**. Under **Date**, in the **Criteria** row, type **Between 01/01/2009 And 04/30/2009** and then press Enter. **Run** the query; five records meet the criteria. This query answers the question, *What is the name, box office receipts, location, and date, in chronological order, of concerts held between January 1, 2009 and April 30, 2009?* Print or submit electronically as directed. **Close** the query, and click **Yes** to save the changes to the design.

9. Create a new query in Design view. From the **2D Concerts** table, add the following fields to the design grid in the order given: **Concert Name**, **Concert Location**, and **Box Office Receipts**. In the **Criteria** row, under **Concert Location**, type **Port Community Theater** and then press Tab. In the **Criteria** row under **Box Office Receipts**, type **<=1000** and then press Enter. **Run** the query; two records display. This query answers the question, *Which concerts that were held at the Port Community Theater had Box Office Receipts of $1,000 or less?* Return to Design view, and then in the **Concert Location** field, clear the **Show** check box. **Run** the query. Recall that if all the records have the same criteria in one of the fields, it is not necessary to display that field in the query results. **Save** the query and name it **2D Port Community Theater $1000 or Less Firstname Lastname** Print or submit electronically, and then close the query.

10. Create a new query in Design view. From the **2D Concerts** table, add the following four fields to the design grid in the order given: **Concert Name**, **Concert Location**, **Box Office Receipts**, and **Date**. On the **Criteria** row, under **Concert Location**, type **Port Community Theater** In the design grid, locate the **or** row. On the **or** row, under **Concert Location**, type **Mitchell Events Center** and then press Enter. **Run** the query. This query answers the question, *How many concerts were held at either the Port Community Theater or the Mitchell Events Center?* Twelve records meet the criteria. Return to Design view.

11. Under **Concert Location**, on the **or** row, delete the text. Under **Concert Location**, click in the **Criteria** row, delete the existing text, and then type **Port Community**

(Project 2D–Concerts and Sponsors continues on the next page)

Content-Based Assessments

(Project 2D–Concerts and Sponsors continued)

Theater Or Mitchell Events Center On the **Criteria** row, under **Box Office Receipts**, type **>1000** and then press Enter. **Run** the query. Four records display. This query answers the question, *Which concerts held at either the Mitchell Events Center or the Port Community Theater had Box Office Receipts of more than $1,000 and on what dates were the concerts held?* **Save** the query as **2D PCT or Mitchell Over $1000 Firstname Lastname** Print or submit the query electronically as directed. Close the query.

12. Create a new query in Design view and add both tables. From the **2D Sponsors** field list, add the following fields: **Sponsor ID**, **Sponsor Name**, and **Phone Number**. On the **Sort** row, under **Sponsor Name**, click to select **Ascending** to sort the results in alphabetical order by Sponsor Name. From the **2D Concerts** field list, add **Concert Name**, **Concert Location**, **Box Office Receipts**, and **Date** to the design grid.

13. On the **Criteria** row, under **Concert Location**, type **Port Community Theater** On the **or** row, under **Concert Location**, type **Mitchell Events Center** and then press Enter. **Run** the query. Twelve records display. Return to the Design view. From the **Sponsors** field list, drag **Web Address** to the design grid on top of **Phone Number** and release the mouse button to insert the new field to the right of **Sponsor Name**. Select the **Sponsor ID** field and delete it.

14. In the design grid, select the **Box Office Receipts** field, and then drag it to the first field position in the grid. Delete the **Phone Number** and **Date** fields. **Run** the query. This query answers the question, *What were the box office receipts, sponsor name, sponsor Web address, concert name, and*

concert location of all concerts held at either the Port Community Theater or the Mitchell Events center, sorted alphabetically by sponsor name? Using techniques similar to that of a table, select all the columns in the query, and then apply **Best Fit**.

15. **Save** the query and name it **2D Receipts and Sponsors PCT and Mitchell Firstname Lastname** In **Print Preview**, change the orientation to **Landscape**, change the **Margins** to **Normal**, and then print the query or submit electronically as directed. Close the Print Preview and close the query. **Open** the **Navigation Pane** and notice that your new query displays under *both* tables from which it retrieved records. **Close** the **Navigation Pane**.

16. Create a new query in Design view, add both tables, and then add the following fields to the design grid: From the **2D Sponsors** table, add the **Sponsor Name** field. From the **2D Concerts** table, add the **Concert Name** field. On the **Criteria** row, under **Sponsor Name**, type **Florida*** and then press Enter. **Run** the query and widen the **Sponsor Name** column to view all of the data. Three sponsors have names that begin with *Florida*.

17. Return to Design view. On the **Criteria** row, under **Sponsor Name**, delete the text. On the **Criteria** row, under **Concert Name**, type ***Festival** and then press Enter. **Run** the query; five Concert Names end with the word *Festival*. Return to Design view. On the **Criteria** row, under **Sponsor Name**, type ***Radio*** and then press Enter. **Run** the query; two records have the word *Radio* somewhere in the Sponsor Name and the word *Festival* at the end of the Concert Name. This query answers the question, *Which radio stations are sponsor-*

(Project 2D–Concerts and Sponsors continues on the next page)

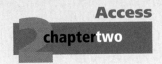

(Project 2D–Concerts and Sponsors continued)

ing Festival-type concerts? **Save** the query and name it **2D Radio Festivals Firstname Lastname** Print or submit the query electronically as directed, and then close the query.

18. Create a new query in Design view, add both tables, and then add the following fields to the design grid: **Concert ID**, **Sponsor Name**, and **Box Office Receipts**. Click in the **Sort** row under **Concert ID**, click the **Sort arrow**, and then click **Ascending**. Sponsors have indicated that they will donate an additional amount to the Music Department based on 50 % of the **Box Office Receipts**. On the **Field** row, right-click in the first empty column to display a shortcut menu, and then click **Zoom**. In the **Zoom** dialog box, type **Matching Donation: [Box Office Receipts]*0.5** In the **Zoom** dialog box, click **OK**, and then **Run** the query to view the new field— *Matching Donation.* Return to Design view.

19. In the **Field** row, in the first empty column, right-click, and then click **Zoom**. In the **Zoom** dialog box, type **Total Receipts: [Box Office Receipts]+[Matching Donation]** and then click **OK**. In the **Field** row, click in the **Matching Donation** field (fourth column), and then in the **Show/Hide group**, click the **Property Sheet** button. In the **Property Sheet** task pane, click in the white text box next to **Format**, click the **arrow** that displays, and then from the displayed list of formats, click **Currency**. **Close** the **Property Sheet** task pane.

20. **Run** the query to view the results. This query answers the question, *In ascending order by Concert ID, assuming each sponsor makes a matching 50% donation based on each concert's Box Office Receipts, what is the Sponsor Name, Box Office Receipts, Matching Donation, and Total Receipts for*

each concert? Select all the columns, and then apply **Best Fit**. **Save** the query and name it **2D Matching Sponsor Donation Firstname Lastname** In **Print Preview**, change the orientation to **Landscape**, and then print or submit the query electronically. Close the Print Preview and then close the query.

21. Create a new query in Design view, **Add** the **2D Concerts** table, and then add the **Box Office Receipts** field to the design grid. On the **Design tab**, in the **Show/Hide group**, click the **Totals** button to add a **Total** row as the third row in the design grid. On the **Total** row, under **Box Office Receipts**, click in the **Group By** box, and then click the **arrow** to display the list of functions. In the list of functions, click **Min**, and then **Run** the query. The lowest amount of Box Office Receipts for any concert was *$400.00.*

22. Return to Design view. Using the technique you just practiced, select the **Max** function, and then **Run** the query. The highest amount of Box Office Receipts for any concert was *$2,500.00.* Switch to **Design** view, select the **Avg** function, and then **Run** the query. The average Box Office Receipts for each concert was *$1,027.94.* Using the same technique, select the **Sum** function and **Run** the query. The total Box Office Receipts for all the concerts was *$17,475.00.*

23. Apply **Best Fit** to the **SumOfBox Office Receipts** column. Switch to Design view. Add the **Sponsor ID** field to the design grid. **Run** the query; concerts sponsored by SPONSOR-101 had the largest amount of Box Office Receipts—*$4,975.00.*

24. Switch to Design view. In the design grid, select and delete the **Sponsor ID** field from

(Project 2D–Concerts and Sponsors continues on the next page)

Content-Based Assessments

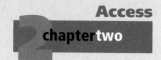
Skills Review

(Project 2D—Concerts and Sponsors continued)

the query design, and then add the **Concert Location** field to the design grid. **Run** the query. This query answers the question *What are the total Box Office Receipts for each concert location?* **Save** the query and name it **2D Totals by Concert Location Firstname Lastname** Print or sub-

mit the query electronically. **Close** the query. From the **Office** menu, click **Close Database**, and then at the right end of the Access title bar, click the **Close** button to close the Access program. Alternatively, from the Office menu, click **Exit Access.**

 End **You have completed Project 2D**

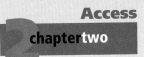

Mastering Access

Project 2E—Lab Administrators

In this project, you will apply the skills you practiced from the Objectives in Project 2A.

Objectives: 1. *Open an Existing Database;* **2.** *Create Table Relationships;* **3.** *Sort Records in a Table;* **4.** *Create a Query in Design View;* **5.** *Create a New Query from an Existing Query;* **6.** *Sort Query Results;* **7.** *Specify Criteria in a Query.*

In the following Mastering Access project, you will assist Stephanie Cannon, Computing Services Director at the college, in querying the database to answer questions about computer lab administrators and their skill specialties. Your query results will look similar to those shown in Figure 2.61.

For Project 2E, you will need the following file:

a2E_Lab_Administrators

You will save your database as
2E_Lab_Administrators_Firstname_Lastname

Figure 2.61

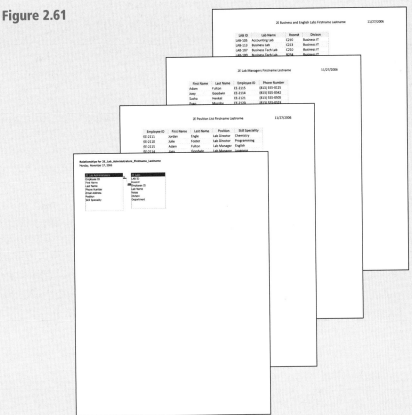

(Project 2E–Lab Administrators continues on the next page)

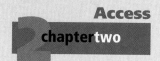
(Project 2E–Lab Administrators continued)

1. From the student files that accompany this textbook, locate the file **a2E_Lab_Administrators**. Copy and paste the file to your Access Chapter 2 folder. Rename the file **2E_Lab_Administrators_Firstname_Lastname** Start Access, open your database, and then enable the content.

2. Open the database tables and examine their fields and records to become familiar with the data; then close the tables. Create a one-to-many relationship between the **2E Lab Administrators** table and the **2E Labs** table based on the **Employee ID** field and enforce referential integrity; *one* Lab Administrator can be responsible for *many* Labs. Create the **Relationship Report** and save it with the default name. Print the report, or submit electronically as directed, and then close all open objects.

3. Display the **2E_Lab_Administrators** table; close the **Navigation Pane**. Notice the + signs that indicate the relationships you created. Perform a multiple-field sort on the table as follows, and remember to sort *first* by the innermost sort field: sort the table in **Ascending** order by **Last Name** (*innermost* sort field) and then sort in **Descending** order by **Position** (*outermost* sort field). The result is that your table is sorted by Position, with Lab Managers listed first, Lab Directors second, and Lab Assistants third, and within each Position, the names are alphabetized by Last Name. After examining the organization of the data, **Clear All Sorts**, close the table, and do not save the changes.

4. Create a new query in Design view and add the **2E Lab Administrators** table. Add fields to the design grid so that your query will answer the question, *What is the Employee ID, First Name, and Last Name of each Lab Administrator in alphabetical order by Last Name, and what is each Lab Administrator's Position and Skill Specialty if any?* **Run** the query, save it with the name **2E Position List Firstname Lastname** Print or submit the query electronically as directed. Leave the query open.

5. From the previous query, create a new query and name it **2E Lab Managers Firstname Lastname** Switch to Design view, and then edit the design so that the query will answer the question, *What is the First Name, Last Name, Employee ID, and Phone Number of those who have the Position of Lab Manager, sorted alphabetically by Last Name?* Display the fields in the order listed in the question, display *only* the fields listed in the question, and do *not* show the **Position** field in the query result. Six employees have the position of Lab Manager. Print or submit the query electronically; close the query, and then save any changes to the design.

6. Create a new query in Design view based on the **2E Labs** table to answer the question, *What is the LAB ID, Lab Name, and Room# of every lab in the Business IT Division and the English Division, sorted alphabetically by Lab Name?* Display the fields in the order listed in the question. Eight records meet the criteria. Save the query with the name **2E Business and English Labs Firstname Lastname** Print or submit electronically, and then close the query. Close the database, and then close Access.

End **You have completed Project 2E** _____

Content-Based Assessments

Mastering Access

Project 2F — Bookstore Inventory

In this project, you will apply the skills you practiced from the Objectives in Project 2B.

Objectives: 8. *Create a New Table by Importing an Excel Spreadsheet;* **9.** *Specify Numeric Criteria in a Query;* **10.** *Use Compound Criteria;* **11.** *Create a Query Based on More Than One Table;* **12.** *Use Wildcards in a Query;* **13.** *Use Calculated Fields in a Query;* **14.** *Group Data and Calculate Statistics in a Query.*

In the following Mastering Access project, you will assist Nancy Pelo, College Bookstore Manager, in using her database to answer questions about the bookstore inventory. Your query results will look similar to those shown in Figure 2.62.

For Project 2F, you will need the following files:

a2F_Bookstore_Inventory
a2F_Vendors (Excel file)

You will save your database as
2F_Bookstore_Inventory_Firstname_Lastname

Figure 2.62

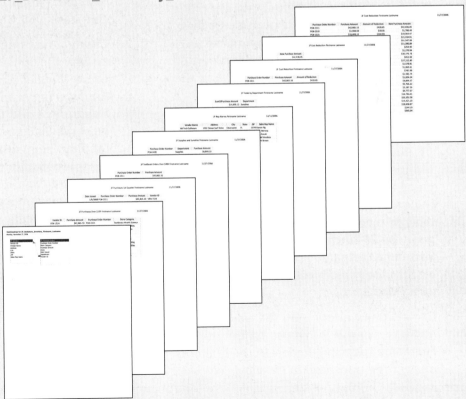

(Project 2F–Bookstore Inventory continues on the next page)

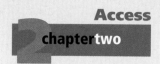
(Project 2F—Bookstore Inventory continued)

1. From the student files that accompany this textbook, locate the file **a2F_Bookstore_Inventory**. Copy and paste the file to your Access Chapter 2 folder. Rename the file **2F_Bookstore_Inventory_Firstname_Lastname Start** Access, open your database, and then enable the content.

2. From the student files that accompany this textbook, import the Excel spreadsheet **a2F_Vendors**. Use the first row of the spreadsheet as the column headings, and choose the **Vendor ID** column as the primary key. Name the table **2F Vendors**

3. Open the database tables and examine their fields and records to become familiar with the data; then close the tables. Create a one-to-many relationship between the **2F Vendors** table and the **2F Purchase Orders** table based on the **Vendor ID** field, and then enforce referential integrity; *one* Vendor can have *many* Purchase Orders. Create the **Relationship Report**, saving it with the default name. Print the report or submit electronically as directed, and then close all open objects.

4. Create a new query in Design view to answer the question, *What is the Vendor ID, Purchase Amount, Purchase Order Number, and Store Category for purchases greater than $10,000?* Display the fields in the order listed in the question. Eleven records meet the criteria. Save the query as **2F Purchases Over $10K Firstname Lastname** Print or submit electronically as directed; leave the query open.

5. Create a new query from the existing query and save it as **2F Purchases 1st Quarter Firstname Lastname** Redesign the query to answer the question, *In chronological order by Date Issued, which Purchase Order Numbers were issued between 01/01/2009 and 03/31/2009, for what amount, and to which Vendor ID?* Display the fields in the order listed in the question, display *only* the fields listed in the question, and do not restrict the purchase amount. Seventeen records meet the criteria. Print or submit electronically as directed; close the query and save the design changes.

6. Create a new query in Design view to answer the question, *Which Purchase Order Numbers issued for the Textbooks department had a Purchase Amount greater than $30,000 and for what amount?* Do *not* show the **Dept** field in the result. Two records meet the criteria. Save the query as **2F Textbook Orders Over $30K Firstname Lastname** Print or submit electronically as directed; close the query and save any changes.

7. Create a new query in Design view to answer the question, *Which Purchase Order Numbers were issued for either the Supplies Department or the Sundries Department and for what amount, with the amounts listed in descending order?* Display the results in the order listed in the question. Fourteen records meet the criteria. Save the query as **2F Supplies and Sundries Firstname Lastname** Print or submit electronically as directed; close the query and save any changes.

8. By using both tables, create a new query to answer the question, *Which Purchase Order Numbers were issued for either the Textbooks or Technology Department, sorted in Ascending order by Department name, and what is the Vendor Name and amount of each purchase order?* Apply **Best**

(Project 2F—Bookstore Inventory continues on the next page)

Content-Based Assessments

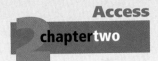

(Project 2F–Bookstore Inventory continued)

Fit to the columns in the query result. Twelve records meet the criteria. Save the query as **2F Textbooks and Technology Firstname Lastname** Print or submit electronically as directed; close the query and save any changes.

9. Create a new query in Design view, and then by using a wildcard in the format of *C**, answer the following question: *What is the Vendor Name, Address, City, State, and Zip of all vendors in the cities of Clearwater, Cape Coral or Cocoa Beach, and who is their Sales Rep?* Five records meet the criteria. Apply **Best Fit** to the columns in the query result, and then save the query as **2F Rep Names Firstname Lastname** Print or submit electronically as directed; close the query and save any changes.

10. Create a new query in Design view, and then by using the **Sum** aggregate function, answer the question, *What are the total Purchase Order Amounts for each Department?* Apply **Best Fit** to the columns in the result, and then save the query as **2F Totals by Department Firstname**

Lastname Print or submit electronically as directed; close the query and save any changes.

11. The state government announced a reduction in the tax rate applied to college bookstore purchases of 1%. Create a query to answer the question, *For each Purchase Order Number, assuming the state reduces each Purchase Amount by 1%, what will be the Amount of Reduction and the New Purchase Amount?* (Hint: First compute the amount of the reduction, naming the new field **Amount of Reduction** Then calculate the new purchase amount, naming the new field **New Purchase Amount**) As necessary, change the properties of all the new fields so that the **Format** is **Currency** and the **Decimal Places** are set to **2**. Apply **Best Fit** to the columns in the query result. **Save** the query as **2F Cost Reduction Firstname Lastname** In **Print Preview**, set the orientation to **Landscape**. Print or submit electronically as directed; close the query and save any changes. Close the database and **Close** Access.

End **You have completed Project 2F**

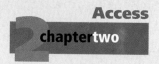

Project 2G — Grants and Organizations

In this project, you will apply the skills you practiced from the Objectives in Projects 2A and 2B.

Objectives: 1. *Open an Existing Database;* **2.** *Create Table Relationships;* **3.** *Sort Records in a Table;* **4.** *Create a Query in Design View;* **5.** *Create a new Query from an Existing Query;* **6.** *Sort Query Results;* **7.** *Specify Criteria in a Query;* **8.** *Create a New Table by Importing an Excel Spreadsheet;* **9.** *Specify Numeric Criteria in a Query;* **10.** *Use Compound Criteria;* **11.** *Create a Query Based on More Than One Table;* **12.** *Use Wildcards in a Query;* **13.** *Use Calculated Fields in a Query;* **14.** *Group Data and Calculate Statistics in a Query.*

In the following Mastering Access project, you will assist Peter Donahue, Director of Grants for the college, in using his database to answer questions about public and private grants awarded to college departments. Your query results will look similar to those shown in Figure 2.63.

For Project 2G, you will need the following files:

a2G_Grants_Organizations
a2G_Organizations (Excel file)

**You will save your database as
2G_Grants_Organizations_Firstname_Lastname**

Figure 2.63

(Project 2G–Grants and Organizations continues on the next page)

Content-Based Assessments

(Project 2G–Grants and Organizations continued)

1. From the student files that accompany this textbook, locate the file **a2G_Grants_Organizations**. Copy and paste the file to your Access Chapter 2 folder. Rename the file **2G_Grants_Organizations_Firstname_Lastname Start** Access, open your database, and then enable the content.

2. From the student files that accompany this textbook, import the Excel spreadsheet **a2G_Organizations**. Use the first row of the spreadsheet as the column headings, and then choose the **Organization ID** column as the primary key. Name the table **2G Organizations**

3. Open the database tables, and then examine their fields and records to become familiar with the data; then close the tables. Create a one-to-many relationship between the **2G Organizations** table and the **2G Grants Awarded** table based on the **Organization ID** field and enforce referential integrity; *one* Organization can give *many* Grants. Create the **Relationship Report**, saving it with the default name. Print the report or submit electronically as directed, and then close all open objects.

4. Create a new query in Design view to answer the question, *What is the Organization ID and Award Amount for grants greater than $10,000 and, in alphabetical order, to what Departments were the grants awarded?* Display the fields in the order listed in the question. Twelve records meet the criteria. Save the query as **2G Grants Over $10K Firstname Lastname** Print or submit electronically as directed; leave the query open.

5. Create a new query from the existing query and save it as **2G Grants 1st Quarter Firstname Lastname** Redesign the query to

answer the question, *In chronological order by Award Date, which Grants were awarded between 01/01/2009 and 03/31/2009, from which Organization ID, for what amount, and to which Department?* Display the fields in the order listed in the question, display *only* the fields listed in the question, sort *only* on one field, and do *not* restrict the amount. Seven records meet the criteria. Apply **Best Fit** to the columns in the query result. In **Print Preview**, set the print to **Landscape**, and then print or submit electronically as directed; close the Print Preview, close the query, and then save any design changes.

6. Create a new query in Design view to answer the question, *What are the names of privately funded grants awarded to either the Humanities or Social Science department, on what date were they awarded, and with the largest grants listed first, for what amount?* Display the results in the order listed in the question, and do not show the type of grant in the query result. Nine records meet the criteria. Save the query as **2G Private HMN and SS Grants Firstname Lastname** In **Print Preview**, set the print to **Landscape**, and then print or submit electronically as directed. Close the Print Preview; close the query, and then save any changes.

7. Create a new query in Design view using both tables to answer the question, *Which grants were awarded to either the Science or Health Technology department, for what amount, and, in alphabetical order, from which Organization Name?* Seven records meet the criteria. Apply **Best Fit** to the columns in the result. Save the query as **2G Science and Health Tech Firstname Lastname** In **Print Preview**, set the print to

(Project 2G–Grants and Organizations continues on the next page)

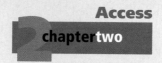

(Project 2G–Grants and Organizations continued)

Landscape, and then print or submit electronically as directed. Close the Print Preview, close the query, and then save any changes.

8. Using both tables, create a new query to answer the question, *Which grants were awarded from organizations that are Foundations, what is the name of the organization, what is the amount of the grant listed in descending order by amount, and what is the name and phone number of the organization contact?* Hint: Use a wildcard in the format of *Foundation* to find organization names containing the word *Foundation*. Fourteen records meet the criteria. Apply **Best Fit** to the columns in the result, and then save the query as **2G**

Foundation Grants Firstname Lastname Change the orientation to **Landscape**, set the **Margins** to **Normal**, and then print or submit electronically as directed; close the query, and then save any changes.

9. Create a new query in Design view, and then by using the **SUM** aggregate function, answer the question, *Listed from the largest amounts to the smallest, what are the total Award Amounts for each Department?* Apply **Best Fit** to the columns in the result, and then save the query as **2G Totals by Department Firstname Lastname** Print or submit electronically as directed; close the query, and then save any changes. Close the database, and then **Close** Access.

 End **You have completed Project 2G**

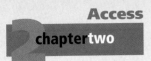

Project 2H—Events and Clients

In this project, you will apply skills you practiced from the Objectives in Projects 2A and 2B.

Objectives: 1. *Open an Existing Database;* **2.** *Create Table Relationships;* **4.** *Create a Query in Design View;* **5.** *Create a New Query from an Existing Query;* **7.** *Specify Criteria in a Query;* **8.** *Create a New Table by Importing an Excel Spreadsheet;* **9.** *Specify Numeric Criteria in a Query;* **10.** *Use Compound Criteria;* **11.** *Create a Query Based on More Than One Table;* **12.** *Use Wildcards in a Query;* **13.** *Use Calculated Fields in a Query;* **14.** *Group Data and Calculate Statistics in a Query*

In the following Mastering Access project, you will assist Peter Steinmetz, Facilities Manager at the college, in using his database to answer questions about facilities that the college rents to community and private organizations. Renting the facilities at times when they are not in use for college activities provides additional funding to maintain and staff the facilities. Your query results will look similar to those shown in Figure 2.64.

For Project 2H, you will need the following files:

a2H_Events_Clients

a2H_Rental_Clients (Excel file)

**You will save your database as
2H_Events_Clients_Firstname_Lastname**

Figure 2.64

(Project 2H–Events and Clients continues on the next page)

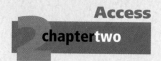
(Project 2H–Events and Clients continued)

1. From the student files that accompany this textbook, locate the file **a2H_Events_Clients**. Copy and paste the file to your Access Chapter 2 folder. Rename the file **2H_Events_Clients_Firstname_Lastname Start** Access, open your database, and then enable the content.

2. From the student files that accompany this textbook, import the Excel spreadsheet **a2H_Rental_Clients**. Use the first row of the spreadsheet as the column headings, and then choose the **Rental Client ID** column as the primary key. Name the table **2H Rental Clients**

3. Open the database tables, and then examine their fields and records to become familiar with the data; then close the tables. Create a one-to-many relationship between the **2H Rental Clients** table and the **2H Events** table based on the **Rental Client ID** field and enforce referential integrity; *one* Rental Client can have *many* Events. Create the **Relationship Report**, print or submit electronically as directed, and then save it with the default name. Close all open objects.

4. Create a new query in Design view to answer the question, *What is the Event Name, Rental Client ID, and Rental Fee for events with fees greater than or equal to $500, in ascending order by Rental Client ID, and in which Facility was the event held?* Display the fields in the order listed in the question. Eleven records meet the criteria. Save the query as **2H Fees $500 or More Firstname Lastname** Print or submit electronically as directed; leave the query open.

5. Create a new query from the existing query, and save it as **2H Afternoon Events**

Firstname Lastname Redesign the query to answer the question, *Which Events were held in the Afternoon between 07/01/2009 and 08/31/2009, in chronological order by date, what was the Rental Fee, and what was the Event ID?* Display the fields in the order listed in the question, but do *not* display the **Time** field in the result. Do *not* restrict the result by Rental Fee. Four records meet the criteria. Print or submit electronically as directed; close the query, and then save the design changes.

6. Create a new query in Design view to answer the question, *Which Events and Event Types were held in either the White Sands Music Hall or the Theater that had Rental Fees greater than $500?* Three records meet the criteria. Apply **Best Fit** to the columns, save the query as **2H White Sands and Theater Over $500 Firstname Lastname** Print or submit electronically as directed; close the query and save any changes.

7. Using both tables, create a new query in Design view to answer the question *Which Events were held on one of the sports Fields, for which Renter Name, and what was the Rental Fee in order of lowest fee to highest fee?* Hint: Use a wildcard with the word *Field*. Five records meet the criteria. Apply **Best Fit** to the columns in the result. Save the query as **2H Field Usage Firstname Lastname** Print or submit electronically as directed; close the query, and then save any changes.

8. Create a new query in Design view, and then by using the **Sum** aggregate function, answer the question *In descending order by total, what are the total Rental Fees for each Event Type?* As necessary, change the properties of all appropriate fields to

(Project 2H–Events and Clients continues on the next page)

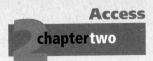
(Project 2H–Events and Clients continued)

display in **Currency** format with **0** decimal places. Apply **Best Fit** to the columns in the result, and then save the query as **2H Totals by Event Type Firstname Lastname** Print or submit electronically as directed; close the query, and then save any changes.

9. The college Alumni Association will donate money to the Building Fund in an amount based on 10% of total facility rental fees. Create a query to answer the question, *In ascending order by Event ID, what will the total of each Rental Fee be if the Alumni*

Association donates an additional 10% of each fee? Hint: First compute the amount of the donation and name the new field **Amount of Donation** Then calculate the new rental fee and name the new field **New Rental Fee Amount** As necessary, change the properties of the all appropriate fields to display in **Currency** format with **0** decimal places. Apply **Best Fit** to the columns in the query result. Save the query as **2H Alumni Donation Firstname Lastname** Print or submit electronically as directed; close the query, and then save any changes. Close the database, and then close Access.

End **You have completed Project 2H**

Content-Based Assessments

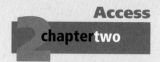
Project 2I — Students and Scholarships

In this project, you will apply the skills you practiced from all the Objectives in Projects 2A and 2B.

Objectives: 1. *Open an Existing Database;* **2.** *Create Table Relationships;* **3.** *Sort Records in a Table;* **4.** *Create a Query in Design View;* **5.** *Create a New Query From an Existing Query;* **6.** *Sort Query Results;* **7.** *Specify Criteria in a Query;* **8.** *Create a New Table by Importing an Excel Spreadsheet;* **9.** *Specify Numeric Criteria in a Query;* **10.** *Use Compound Criteria;* **11.** *Create a Query Based on More Than One Table;* **12.** *Use Wildcards in a Query;* **13.** *Use Calculated Fields in a Query;* **14.** *Group Data and Calculate Statistics in a Query.*

In the following Mastering Access project, you will assist Diane Nguyen, Director of Academic Scholarships, in using her database to answer questions about academic scholarships awarded to students. Your query results will look similar to those shown in Figure 2.65.

For Project 2I, you will need the following files:

a2I_Students_Scholarships
a2I_Students (Excel file)

You will save your database as
2I_Students_Scholarships_Firstname_Lastname

Figure 2.65

(Project 2I–Students and Scholarships continues on the next page)

(Project 2I–Students and Scholarships continued)

1. From the student files that accompany this textbook, locate the file **a2I_Students_Scholarships**. Copy and paste the file to your Access Chapter 2 folder. Rename the file **2I_Students_Scholarships_Firstname_Lastname Start** Access, open your database, and then enable the content.

2. From the student files that accompany this textbook, import the Excel spreadsheet **a2I_Students**. Use the first row of the spreadsheet as the column headings, and then choose the **Student ID** column as the primary key. Name the table **2I Students**

3. Open the database tables and examine their fields and records to become familiar with the data; then close the tables. Create a one-to-many relationship between the **2I Students** table and the **2I Scholarships** table based on the **Student ID** field and enforce referential integrity; *one* student can have *many* scholarships. Create the **Relationship Report**, print or submit electronically as directed, and then save it with the default name. Close all open objects.

4. Display the **2I Students** table; notice the + signs that indicate the relationships you created. Perform a multiple-field sort on the table to sort students in alphabetic order by Last Name within groups of cities, and sort the City names in alphabetical order. Remember to sort *first* by the innermost sort field. After examining the sorted table, **Clear All Sorts**, close the table, and do not save the changes.

5. Create a new query in Design view, based on the **2I Scholarships Awarded** table, to answer the question, *In alphabetical order by Scholarship Name, what is the*

Scholarship Name, Amount, and Major for scholarships greater than or equal to $500? Display the fields in the order listed in the question. Ten records meet the criteria. Save the query as **2I Scholarships $500 or More Firstname Lastname** Print or submit electronically as directed; leave the query open.

6. Create a new query from the existing query, and then save it as **2I Scholarships 1st Quarter Firstname Lastname** Add the **2I Students** table to the table area, and then redesign the query to answer the question, *In chronological order by Award Date, which scholarships were awarded between 01/01/2009 and 03/31/2009, for what amount, and what was the name of the student?* Be sure the fields display in the order listed in the question, display *only* the fields listed in the question, do not restrict the amount, and sort only by date. Eight records meet the criteria. In **Print Preview**, set **Wide** margins and **Landscape** orientation. Print or submit electronically as directed; close the query, and then save the design changes.

7. Create a new query in Design view to answer the question, *Which scholarships were awarded for either CIS or Nursing majors for amounts greater than $100, listed in descending order by amount?* Four records meet the criteria. Save the query as **2I Nursing and CIS $100 and Over Firstname Lastname** Print or submit electronically as directed; close the query, and then save any changes.

8. Create a new query in Design view using only the 2I Students table, and then by using a wildcard, answer the question, *In alphabetical order by Last Name, what is the Student ID, First Name, Last Name, and*

(Project 2I–Students and Scholarships continues on the next page)

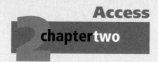
(Project 2I–Students and Scholarships continued)

City of all students in cities that begin with the letter B? Five records meet the criteria. Save the query as **2I Cities Firstname Lastname** Print or submit electronically as directed; close the query, and then save any changes.

9. Create a new query in Design view based on the **2I Students** table, and that includes all the table's fields, to answer the question *For which students is the Address missing?* Three students are missing addresses. Apply **Best Fit** to the columns, and save the query as **2I Missing Addresses Firstname Lastname** Print or submit electronically as directed; close the query, and then save any changes.

10. Create a new query in Design view, and then by using the **Sum** aggregate function, answer the question, *In descending order by amount, what are the total scholarship amounts for each Major?* Use the Property Sheet as necessary to display the sums with **0** decimal places. Apply **Best Fit** to the columns in the result, and then save the query as **2I Totals by Major Firstname Lastname** Print or submit electronically as

directed; close the query, and then save any changes.

11. For each academic scholarship received by students, the Board of Trustees of the college will donate an amount equal to 50% of each scholarship. By using a calculated field and both tables, answer the question, *In alphabetical order by scholarship name, and including the first and last name of the scholarship recipient, what will the value of each scholarship be if the Board of Trustees makes a matching 50% donation?* Hint: First compute the amount of the donation, and then name the new field **Donation** Then calculate the new scholarship value and name the new field **New Value** As necessary, change the properties of all the fields to display in **Currency** format with **0** decimal places. Apply **Best Fit** to the columns in the query result. Save the query as **2I Trustee Donation Firstname Lastname** Print in **Landscape** or submit electronically as directed. Close the query, and then save any changes. Close the database, and then close Access.

End You have completed Project 2I

Content-Based Assessments

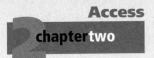

Business Running Case

Project 2J — Business Running Case

In this project, you will apply the skills you practiced in Projects 2A and 2B.

From My Computer, navigate to the student files that accompany this textbook. In the folder **03_business_running_case_pg37_86**, locate and open the folder for this chapter. Open and print the instructions for this project, which are provided to you in Adobe PDF format. Follow the instructions and use the skills you have gained thus far to assist Jennifer Nelson in meeting the challenges of owning and running her business.

End **You have completed Project 2J** ————————————

Outcomes-Based Assessments

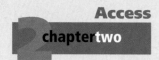
Rubric

The following outcomes-based assessments are *open-ended assessments*. That is, there is no specific correct result; your result will depend on your approach to the information provided. Make *Professional Quality* your goal. Use the following scoring rubric to guide you in *how* to approach the problem and then to evaluate *how well* your approach solves the problem.

The *criteria*—Software Mastery, Content, Format and Layout, and Process—represent the knowledge and skills you have gained that you can apply to solving the problem. The *levels of performance*—Professional Quality, Approaching Professional Quality, or Needs Quality Improvements—help you and your instructor evaluate your result.

	Your completed project is of Professional Quality if you:	Your completed project is Approaching Professional Quality if you:	Your completed project Needs Quality Improvements if you:
1-Software Mastery	Choose and apply the most appropriate skills, tools, and features and identify efficient methods to solve the problem.	Choose and apply some appropriate skills, tools, and features, but not in the most efficient manner.	Choose inappropriate skills, tools, or features, or are inefficient in solving the problem.
2-Content	Construct a solution that is clear and well organized, contains content that is accurate, appropriate to the audience and purpose, and is complete. Provide a solution that contains no errors of spelling, grammar, or style.	Construct a solution in which some components are unclear, poorly organized, inconsistent, or incomplete. Misjudge the needs of the audience. Have some errors in spelling, grammar, or style, but the errors do not detract from comprehension.	Construct a solution that is unclear, incomplete, or poorly organized, containing some inaccurate or inappropriate content; and contains many errors of spelling, grammar, or style. Do not solve the problem.
3-Format and Layout	Format and arrange all elements to communicate information and ideas, clarify function, illustrate relationships, and indicate relative importance.	Apply appropriate format and layout features to some elements, but not others. Overuse features, causing minor distraction.	Apply format and layout that does not communicate information or ideas clearly. Do not use format and layout features to clarify function, illustrate relationships, or indicate relative importance. Use available features excessively, causing distraction.
4-Process	Use an organized approach that integrates planning, development, self-assessment, revision, and reflection.	Demonstrate an organized approach in some areas, but not others; or, use an insufficient process of organization throughout.	Do not use an organized approach to solve the problem.

Outcomes-Based Assessments

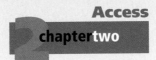
Problem Solving

Project 2K — Student Refunds

In this project, you will construct a solution by applying any combination of the skills you practiced from the Objectives in Projects 2A and 2B.

> **For Project 2K, you will need the following files:**
>
> a2K_Student_Refunds
> a2K_Student_Refunds (Word document)

You will save your database as
2K_Student_Refunds_Firstname_Lastname

Start Microsoft Word, and then from your student files, open the Word document **a2K_Student_Refunds**. Use the skills you have practiced in this chapter to assist Kathy Knudsen, the Associate Dean of Student Services, in answering questions about student refunds in your database **2K_Student_Refunds_Firstname_Lastname**. Save any queries that you create, include your name in the query title, and submit your queries as directed by your instructor. Record your answers to the questions in the Word document.

End **You have completed Project 2K** ——————

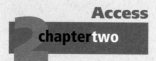

Problem Solving

Project 2L—Leave

In this project, you will construct a solution by applying any combination of the skills you practiced from the Objectives in Projects 2A and 2B.

For Project 2L, you will need the following files:

a2L_Leave
a2L_Leave (Word document)

You will save your database as
2L_Leave_Firstname_Lastname

Start Microsoft Word, and then from your student files, open the Word document **a2L_Leave**. Use the skills you have practiced in this chapter to assist Gabe Stevens, the Director of Human Resources, in answering questions about employee leave time in your database **2L_Leave_Firstname_Lastname**. Save any queries that you create, include your name in the query title, and submit your queries as directed by your instructor. Record your answers to the questions in the Word document.

 End **You have completed Project 2L** ———————

Problem Solving

Project 2M—Coaches

In this project, you will construct a solution by applying any combination of the skills you practiced from the Objectives in Projects 2A and 2B.

For Project 2M, you will need the following files:

a2M_Coaches
a2M_Coaches (Word document)

You will save your database as
2M_Coaches_Firstname_Lastname

Start Microsoft Word, and then from your student files, open the Word document **a2M_Coaches**. Use the skills you have practiced in this chapter to assist Marcus Simmons, the Athletic Director, in answering questions about the Coaches in your database **2M_Coaches_Firstname_Lastname**. Save any queries that you create, include your name in the query title, and submit your queries as directed by your instructor. Record your answers to the questions in the Word document.

End **You have completed Project 2M** ——————————

Outcomes-Based Assessments

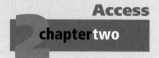
Problem Solving

Project 2N — Faculty Awards

In this project, you will construct a solution by applying any combination of the skills you practiced from the Objectives in Projects 2A and 2B.

For Project 2N, you will need the following files:

a2N_Faculty_Awards
a2N_Faculty_Awards (Word document)

You will save your database as
2N_Faculty_Awards_Firstname_Lastname

Start Microsoft Word, and then from your student files, open the Word document **a2N_Faculty_Awards**. Use the skills you have practiced in this chapter to assist Angela Ta, President of the Faculty Association, in answering questions about faculty awards in your database **2N_Faculty_Awards_Firstname_Lastname**. Save any queries that you create, include your name in the query title, and submit your queries as directed by your instructor. Record your answers to the questions in the Word document.

 You have completed Project 2N —————————

Outcomes-Based Assessments

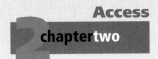
Problem Solving

Project 2O — Club Donations

In this project, you will construct a solution by applying any combination of the skills you practiced from the Objectives in Projects 2A and 2B.

For Project 2O, you will need the following files:

a2O_Club_Donations
a2O_Club_Donations (Word document)

You will save your database as
2O_Club_Donations_Firstname_Lastname

Start Microsoft Word, and then from your student files, open the Word document **a2O_Club_Donations**. Use the skills you have practiced in this chapter to assist Kathy Durbin, Director of Student Activities, in answering questions about donations to student clubs in your database **2O_Club_Donations_Firstname_Lastname**. Save any queries that you create, include your name in the query title, and submit your queries as directed by your instructor. Record your answers to the questions in the Word document.

 End You have completed Project 2O ─────────────

Outcomes-Based Assessments

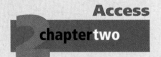 You and *GO!*

Project 2P —You and *GO!*

In this project, you will construct a solution by applying any combination of the Objectives found in Projects 2A and 2B.

From My Computer, navigate to the student files that accompany this textbook. In the folder **04_you_and_go_pg87_102**, locate and open the folder for this chapter. Open and print the instructions for this project, which are provided to you in Adobe PDF format. Follow the instructions to create queries for your personal database.

End **You have completed Project 2P** ————————

GO! with Help

Project 2Q— *GO!* with Help

There are numerous wildcards that you can use in your queries. Use the Access Help system to find out more about wildcards in Access.

1 **Start** Access. Click the **Microsoft Office Access Help** button . Click the **Search arrow**, and then under **Content from this computer**, click **Access Help**. In the **Search box**, type **wildcards** and then press Enter. Scroll the displayed list as necessary, and then click **Using Wildcard Characters in String Comparisons**. Review the information shown in this topic.

2 If you would like to keep a copy of this information, click the **Print** button . Click the **Close** button ☒ in the top right corner of the Help window to close the Help window, and then **Close** Access.

End **You have completed Project 2Q** ————————

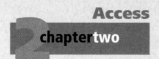

Group Business Running Case

Project 2R—Group Business Running Case

In this project, you will apply the skills you practiced from the Objectives in Projects 2A and 2B.

Your instructor may assign this group case project to your class. If your instructor assigns this project, he or she will provide you with information and instructions to work as part of a group. The group will apply the skills gained thus far to help the Bell Orchid Hotel Group achieve its business goals.

End **You have completed Project 2R** ————————————

chapterthree

Forms, Filters, and Reports

OBJECTIVES

At the end of this chapter you will be able to:

1. Create a Form
2. Use a Form To Add and Delete Records
3. Create a Form by Using the Form Wizard
4. Modify a Form in Design View and in Layout View
5. Filter Records

OUTCOMES

Mastering these objectives will enable you to:

PROJECT 3A
Create Forms To Enter and Display Data in a Database

6. Create a Report by Using the Report Tool
7. Create a Report by Using the Blank Report Tool
8. Create a Report by Using the Report Wizard
9. Modify the Design of a Report
10. Print a Report and Keep Data Together

PROJECT 3B
Create Reports To Display Database Information

Baltimore Area Job Fair

The Baltimore Area Job Fair is a nonprofit organization that brings together employers and job seekers in the Baltimore and Washington, DC metropolitan areas. Each year the organization holds a number of targeted job fairs and the annual Greater Baltimore Job Fair draws over 1,000 employers in more than 70 industries and registers more than 4,000 candidates. Candidates pay a small registration fee. Employers pay to display and present at the fairs and to have access to candidate resumes. Candidate resumes and employer postings are managed by a state-of-the-art database system, allowing participants quick and accurate access to job data and candidate qualifications.

Forms, Filters, and Reports

You can both enter and view information directly in the database tables. However, for entering and viewing information, it is usually easier to use an Access form. You can design forms to display one record at a time, with fields placed in the same order to match a paper source document. When the form on the screen matches the pattern of information on the paper form, it is easier to enter the new information. In a form or table, you can also filter records to display only a portion of the total records based on matching specific values.

When viewing information, it is usually easier to view only one record at a time. For example, your college counselor can look at your college transcript in a nicely laid out form on the screen without seeing the records of other students at the same time.

In Access, reports summarize the data in a database in a professional looking manner suitable for printing. The design of a report can be modified so that the final report is laid out in a format that is useful to the person reading it. In this chapter, you will create and modify both forms and reports for Access databases.

Project 3A Candidate Interviews

Local employers and candidates who are seeking jobs get together at the two-day Greater Baltimore Job Fair. In Activities 3.1 through 3.10, you will assist Janna Sorokin, database manager for the Job Fair, in using an Access database to track the job candidates and the job interviews they have scheduled with employers during the fair event. Your completed database objects will look similar to those in Figure 3.1.

For Project 3A, you will need the following file:

a3A_Candidate_Interviews

**You will save your database as
3A_Candidate_Interviews_Firstname_Lastname**

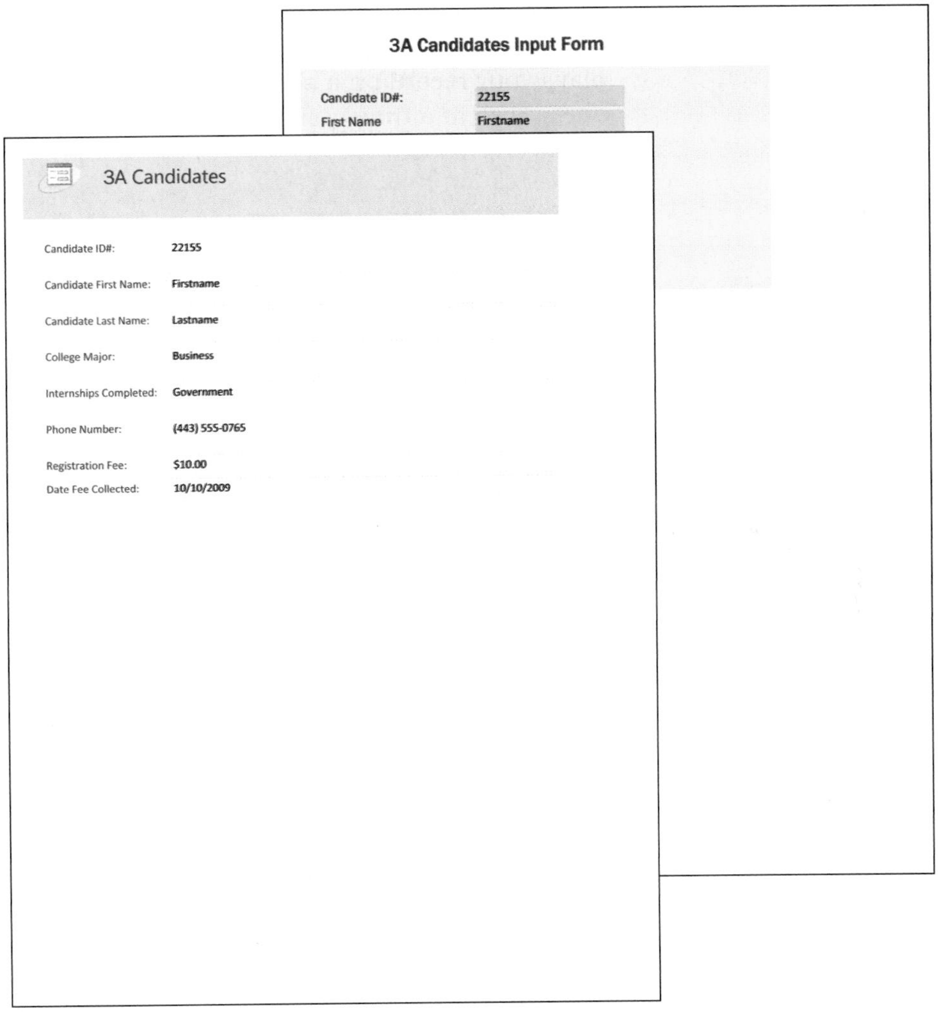

3A Candidates Input Form

Candidate ID#:	22155
First Name	Firstname

3A Candidates

Candidate ID#:	22155
Candidate First Name:	Firstname
Candidate Last Name:	Lastname
College Major:	Business
Internships Completed:	Government
Phone Number:	(443) 555-0765
Registration Fee:	$10.00
Date Fee Collected:	10/10/2009

Figure 3.1
Project 3A—Candidate Interviews

Objective 1
Create a Form

A *form* is an Access object with which you can enter, edit, or display data from a table or a query. One typical use of a form is to control access to the data. For example, in a college registration system, you could design a form for Registration Assistants who could see and enter the courses scheduled and fees paid by an individual student. However, they could not see or enter grades or other personal information in the student's record. In this manner, think of a form as a window through which others see and reach your database.

Some Access forms display only one record at a time; other form types display multiple records at the same time. A form that displays only one record at a time is useful not only to the individual who performs the *data entry*—typing in the actual records—but also to anyone who has the job of viewing information in a database. For example, when you visit the Records office at your college to obtain a transcript, someone displays your record on a screen. For the viewer, it is much easier to look at one record at a time, using a form, than to look at all the student records in the database.

Activity 3.1 Creating a Form

There are various ways to create a form in Access, but the fastest and easiest is to use the *Form tool*. With a single mouse click, all the fields from the underlying data source (table or query) are placed on the form. Then you can use the new form immediately, or you can modify it in Layout view or in Design view.

The Form tool incorporates all the information, both the field names and the individual records, from an existing table or query and then instantly creates the form for you. Records that you edit or create using a form automatically update the underlying table or tables. In this activity, you will create a form, and then use it to add new interview records to the database.

1 By using the technique you practiced in Chapter 1, open **My Computer**, and then navigate to the location where you will store your projects for this chapter. Create a new folder and name it **Access Chapter 3**.

2 From the student files that accompany this text, locate the file **a3A_Candidate_Interviews**. Copy and then paste the file to the Access Chapter 3 folder you created in Step 1. Rename the file **3A_Candidate_Interviews_Firstname_Lastname** Close **My Computer**, start Access, open your **3A_Candidate_Interviews** database, and then if necessary, enable the content.

3 Open ⟩⟩ the **Navigation Pane**. Click the **Database Tools tab**, and then in the **Show/Hide group**, click the **Relationships** button. Compare your screen with Figure 3.2.

At the Job Fair event, *one* candidate can have interviews with *many* organizations. Thus, a one-to-many relationship has been established between the 3A Candidates table and the 3A Interviews table using Candidate ID# as the common field—the field that displays in both tables.

Join line with symbols indicating one-to-many
relationship and referential integrity

Figure 3.2

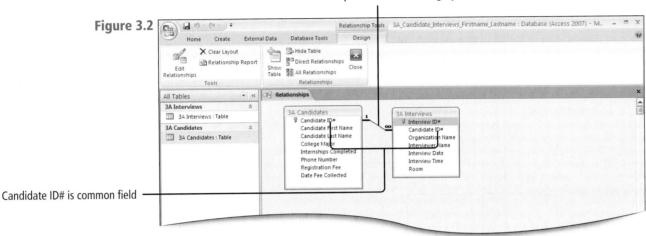

Candidate ID# is common field

4 In the **Relationships group**, click the **Close** button to close the **Relationships window**. From the **Navigation Pane**, open the **3A Interviews table**, and notice the seven fields—*Interview ID#, Candidate ID#, Organization Name, Interviewer Name, Interview Date, Interview Time,* and *Room.* **Close** ☒ the **3A Interviews table**.

5 Be sure the **3A Interviews table** is still selected in the **Navigation Pane**. Click the **Create tab**, and then in the **Forms group**, click **Form. Close** «« the **Navigation Pane**, and then compare your screen with Figure 3.3.

Access creates the form based on the currently selected object—the 3A Interviews table—and displays the form in **Layout view**. In Layout view, you can make design changes to the form while it is displaying data. For example, you can adjust the size of the text boxes to fit the data. You can use Layout view for many of the changes you might need to make to a form.

Access creates the form in a simple top-to-bottom layout, with all seven fields in the table lined up in a single column. The data for the first record in the table displays in the fields.

6 In the navigation area, click the **Next record** button ▶ four times.

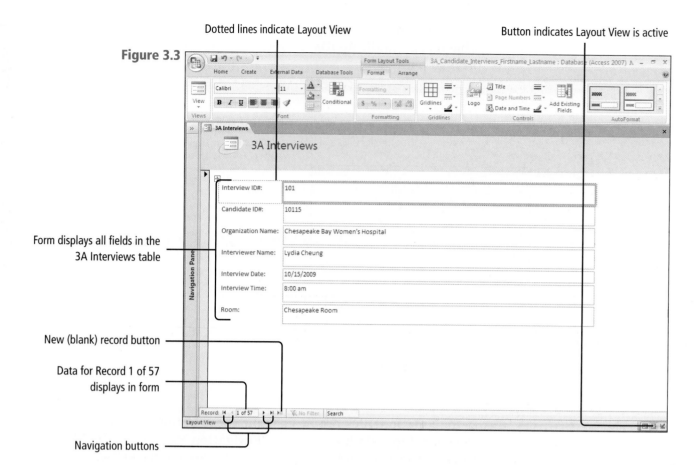

Figure 3.3

Dotted lines indicate Layout View

Button indicates Layout View is active

Form displays all fields in the 3A Interviews table

New (blank) record button

Data for Record 1 of 57 displays in form

Navigation buttons

The fifth record—for *Interview ID# 105*—displays. Use the navigation buttons to scroll among the records to display any single record you want to view.

7 In the navigation area, click the **Last record** button to display the record for *Interview ID# 157*, and then click the **First record** button to display the record for *Interview ID# 101*.

8 From the **Office** menu , click **Save** to save this form for future use. In the displayed **Save As** dialog box, edit as necessary to name the form **3A Interviews Form** and click **OK**. **Close** the form object.

9 **Open** the **Navigation Pane**, and notice that your new form displays under the table with which it is associated—the **3A Interviews table**. Notice also that your new form displays the form icon, which identifies it as a form.

10 From the **Navigation Pane**, select the **3A Candidates table**, click the **Create tab**, and then in the **Forms group**, click **Form**. **Close** the **Navigation Pane**, and then compare your screen with Figure 3.4.

If a record has related records in another table, the related records display in the form. You can scroll down and see that *Candidate ID#*

10115, for *Sally Marques*, has five interviews scheduled during the two-day Job Fair event.

Figure 3.4

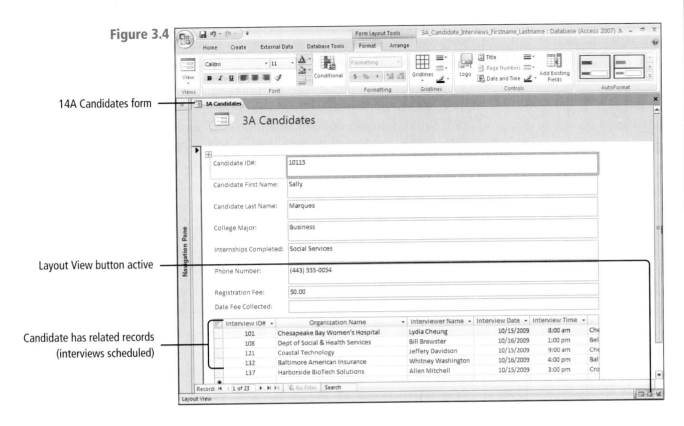

14A Candidates form

Layout View button active

Candidate has related records (interviews scheduled)

11 **Close** ❎ the **3A Candidates form**, click **Yes**, edit as necessary to name the form **3A Candidates Form** and then click **OK**.

Objective 2
Use a Form To Add and Delete Records

Adding and deleting records using a single-record form helps to prevent data entry errors, because the person performing the data entry is looking at only one record at a time. Recall that your database is useful only if the information is accurate—just like your personal address book is useful only if it contains accurate addresses and phone numbers.

Activity 3.2 Adding Records to a Table by Using a Form

Forms are based on, also referred to as **bound** to, the table where the records are stored. That is, when a record is entered in a form, the new record is added to the corresponding table. The reverse is also true—when a record is added to a table, the new record can be viewed in the corresponding form. In this activity, you will add a new record to the 3A Interviews table by using the form that you just created.

1 **Open** 〉〉 the **Navigation Pane**, and then open the **3A Interviews Form**. **Close** 〈〈 the **Navigation Pane**. In the navigation area at the bottom of the form, click the **New (blank) record** button 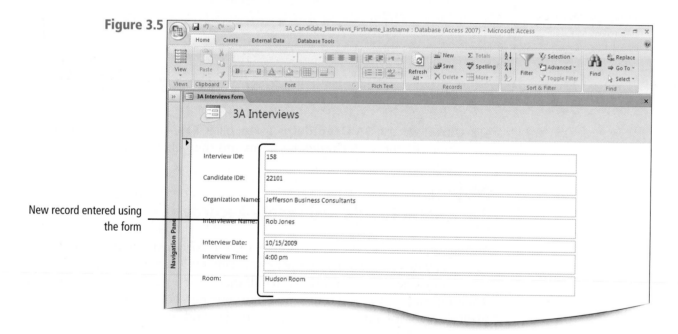.

A new blank form displays, indicated in the navigation area by *58 of 58*. Adding a new record will increase the number of records in the table to 58.

2 In the **Interview ID#** field, type **158** and then press ⎀Tab⎀.

Use the ⎀Tab⎀ key to move from field to field in a form. This is known as the ***tab order***—the order in which the insertion point moves from one field to the next on a form when you press the ⎀Tab⎀ key. After you start typing, the pencil image displays in the ***record selector*** bar at the left—the bar with which you can select an entire record.

3 Continue entering the data as shown in the following table, and then compare your screen with Figure 3.5.

Candidate ID#	Organization Name	Interviewer Name	Interview Date	Interview Time	Room
22101	Jefferson Business Consultants	Rob Jones	10/15/2009	4:00 pm	Hudson Room

Figure 3.5

New record entered using the form

4 **Close** ⊠ the **3A Interviews Form**—the new record is stored in the table. **Open** » the **Navigation Pane**, open the **3A Candidates Form**, and then **Close** « the **Navigation Pane**.

5 At the bottom of the screen, in the navigation area, click the **New (blank) record** button ⊞. In the displayed blank form, and using your own first and last name, fill in the form using the information in the following table:

Candidate ID#	Candidate First Name	Candidate Last Name	College Major	Internships Completed	Phone Number	Registration Fee	Date Fee Collected
22155	Firstname	Lastname	Business	Government	(443) 555-0765	$10.00	10/10/2009

6 **Close** ✕ the **3A Candidates Form**, **Open** ❯❯ the **Navigation Pane**, open the **3A Candidates table**, and then verify that your record as a candidate displays as the last record in the table. **Close** ✕ the table.

Activity 3.3 Deleting Records from a Table by Using a Form

You can delete records from a database table by using a form. In this activity, you will delete Interview ID# 103, because Jennifer Lee has notified Janna that she will be unable to meet with AAA Telecom at that time.

1 From the **Navigation Pane**, open the **3A Interviews Form**, click in the **Interview ID#** field, and then on the **Home tab**, in the **Find group**, click the **Find** button. Alternatively, press Ctrl + F to open the Find and Replace dialog box.

2 In the **Look In** box, notice that *Interview ID#* is indicated, and then in the **Find What** box, type **103** Click **Find Next** and then compare your screen with Figure 3.6 and confirm that the record for **Interview ID# 103** displays.

Record for *Interview ID# 103* displays

Figure 3.6

Find and Replace dialog box

Find What box—type what you want to find here

Look In box indicates Access will search the *Interview ID#* field

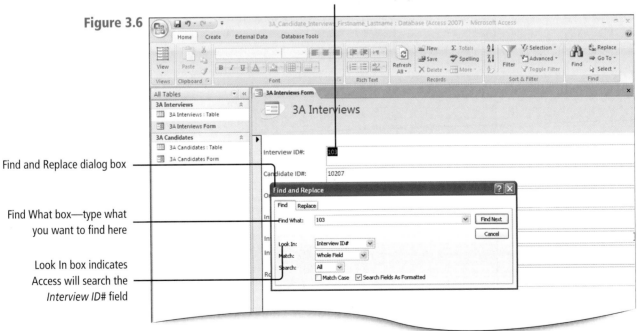

3 **Close** ☒ the **Find and Replace** dialog box.

4 On the **Home tab**, in the **Records group**, click the **Delete button arrow**, and then in the displayed list, click **Delete Record** to delete the record for Interview ID# 103. Alternatively, press ⌫ Delete on your keyboard.

The record is removed and a message displays alerting you that you are about to delete *1 record*. If you click Yes and delete the record, you cannot use the Undo button to reverse the action. If you delete a record by mistake, you must re-create the record by reentering the data.

5 Click **Yes** to delete the record, and then in the navigation area at the bottom of the screen, notice that the number of records in the table is *57*. **Close** ☒ the form object.

6 From the **Navigation Pane**, open the **3A Interviews table**.

7 Examine the table and verify that the record for *Interview ID# 103* no longer displays—by default, tables are sorted in ascending order by their primary key field, which in this table is the **Interview ID#** field. Then, scroll down and verify that the new record you added for **Interview ID# 158** is included in the table. Compare your screen with Figure 3.7.

Your actions of adding and deleting records using the 3A Interviews Form updates the records stored in this 3A Interviews table.

Figure 3.7

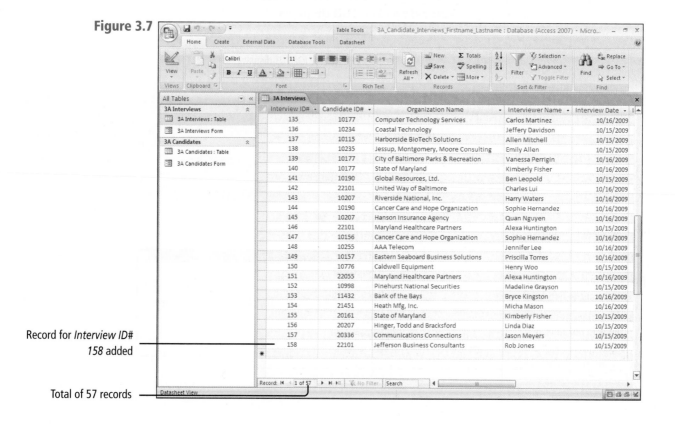

Record for *Interview ID# 158* added

Total of 57 records

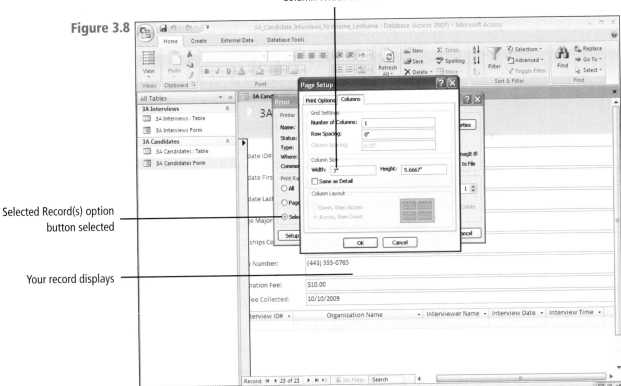

■8■ **Close** ✕ the table.

Activity 3.4 Printing a Form

Like other Access objects, forms can be printed. If you click the Print button, *all* of the records will print in the form layout that you selected.

■1■ From the **Navigation Pane**, open the **3A Candidates Form**. Press Ctrl + F to display the **Find and Replace** dialog box. In the **Find What** box, type **22155** In the **Look In** box, be sure that *Candidate ID#* is indicated, and then click **Find Next** to display the record with your name. **Close** ✕ the dialog box.

■2■ From the **Office** menu 🔳, click the **Print** button. In the displayed **Print** dialog box, under **Print Range**, click the **Selected Record(s)** option button. In the lower left corner of the dialog box, click the **Setup** button.

■3■ In the displayed **Page Setup** dialog box, click the **Columns tab**, and then under **Column Size**, in the **Width** box, delete the existing text and type **7"** Compare your screen with Figure 3.8.

Column Width set to 7"

Figure 3.8

Selected Record(s) option button selected

Your record displays

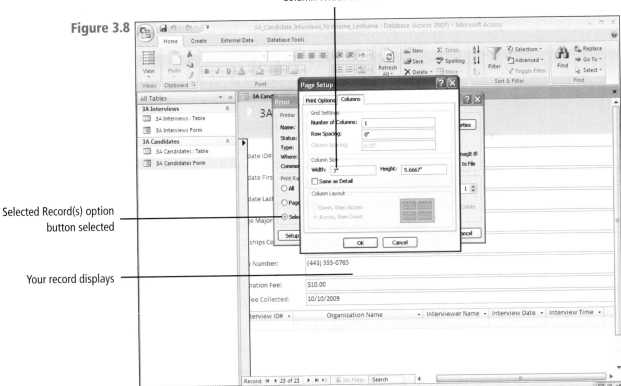

4 Click **OK** two times to print only your record in the form layout, or submit electronically as directed.

5 Close ☒ the **3A Candidates Form**, and then **Close** ⦗«⦘ the **Navigation Pane**.

Objective 3
Create a Form by Using the Form Wizard

The Form tool creates an instant form in a simple top-to-bottom layout with all the fields lined up in a single column. The Form Wizard, on the other hand, creates a form quickly, but does so in a manner that gives you more flexibility in the design, layout, and number of fields included.

The design of the form should be planned for the individuals who use the form—either for entering new records or viewing records. For example, when your college counselor displays your information to answer a question for you, it is easier for her or him to view the information spread out in a logical pattern across the screen rather than in one long column.

Activity 3.5 Creating a Form by Using the Form Wizard

By using the Form Wizard to create your form, you control how the form looks by selecting the fields to include, the style to apply, and the layout. When candidates register to attend the Job Fair and view job openings from exhibiting employers, they fill out a paper form. To make it easier to enter candidates into the database, you will create an Access form that matches the layout of the paper form. This will make it easier for the person entering the data into the database.

1 Open ⦗»⦘ the **Navigation Pane**, and then click to select the **3A Candidates table**. On the **Create tab**, in the **Forms group**, click the **More Forms** button, and then in the displayed list, click **Form Wizard**.

The Form Wizard is an Access feature that walks you step by step through a process by asking questions. In the first screen of the Form Wizard, you select which fields you want on your form, and the fields can come from more than one table or query.

2 In the text box below **Tables/Queries**, click the **arrow** to display a list of available tables and queries from which you can create the form.

There are two tables from which you can create a new form.

3 In the displayed list, click **Table: 3A Candidates**. Compare your screen with Figure 3.9.

The field names from the 3A Candidates table display in the Available Fields box.

One Field button   Next button

Figure 3.9

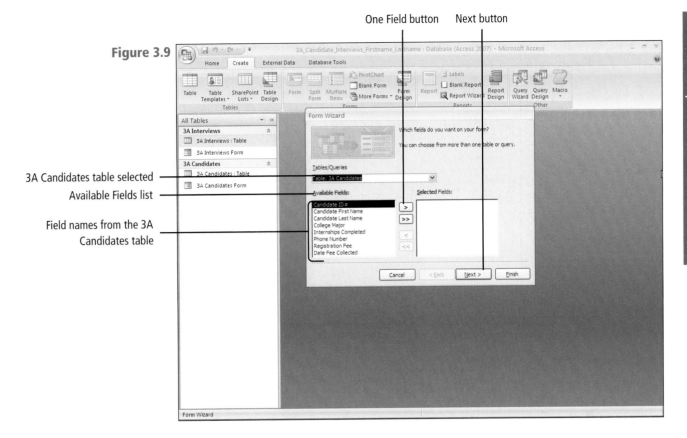

3A Candidates table selected

Available Fields list

Field names from the 3A
Candidates table

4 Using the **One Field** button [>], move the following fields to the
Selected Fields list: **Candidate First Name**, **Candidate Last Name**,
College Major, **Internships Completed**, and **Phone Number**.
Alternatively, double-click a field name to move it to the Selected
Fields box.

5 Click **Next**. Be sure **Columnar** is selected as the layout for your
form, and then click **Next**.

Here you select the style you would like for your form. The style controls the font, font size, font color, and background.

6 Click several of the styles to see how they are formatted, and then
scroll as necessary and click **Trek**. Click **Next** to move to the final
step; here you name your form. In the box at the top, edit as necessary to name the form **3A Candidates Input Form** and then click
Finish to close the wizard and create the form. Compare your screen
with Figure 3.10.

In the final step of the Form Wizard, when you name the form and
click Finish, the form is saved and added to the Navigation Pane.
Leave the new form open for the next activities.

Figure 3.10

Completed form from wizard

Candidate Sally Marques
(first record in table) displays in form

New form displays in the
Navigation Pane

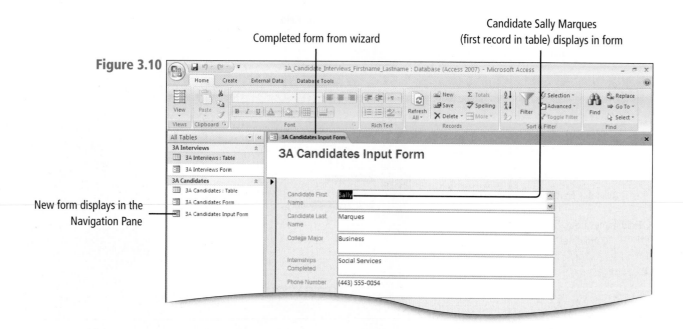

Objective 4
Modify a Form in Design View and in Layout View

After you create a form, Access provides tools with which you can make additional changes. For example, you can resize the fields on the form for easier viewing or more efficient data entry.

Activity 3.6 Modifying a Form in Design View

Design view presents a detailed view of the structure of your form. Because the form is not actually running when displayed in Design view, you cannot see the underlying data. However, some tasks, such as resizing sections, must be completed in Design view.

1 **Close** the **Navigation Pane** and be sure your **3A Candidates Input Form** displays. In the lower right corner of your screen, on the right end of the status bar, click the **Design View** button . Alternatively, in the Views group, click the View button arrow, and then click Design View. Compare your screen with Figure 3.11.

A form is divided into three sections—***Form Header***, ***Detail***, and ***Form Footer***—each designated by a bar called a ***section bar***. ***Controls*** are objects on a form that display data, perform actions, and let you view and work with information; controls make the form easier to use for the person who is either using the form to enter data or to view data.

The most commonly used control is the ***text box control***, which typically displays data from the underlying table, in which case it is referred to as a ***bound control***—its source data comes from a table or query. Access places a ***label*** to the left of a text box control, which contains descriptive information that appears on the form, usually the field names. A control that does not have a source of data, for example a label that displays the title of the form, is an ***unbound control***.

Figure 3.11

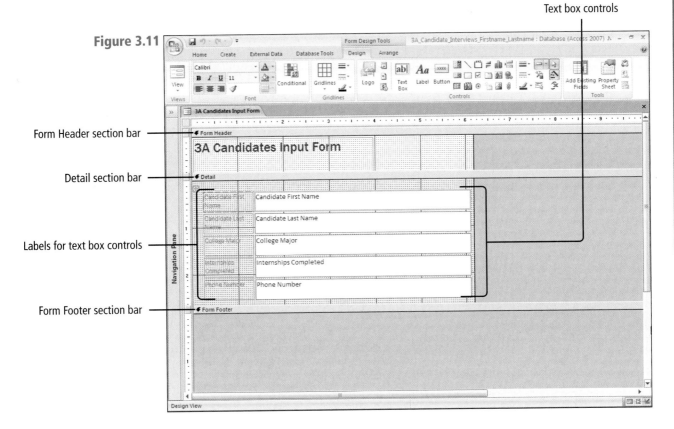

Text box controls

Form Header section bar

Detail section bar

Labels for text box controls

Form Footer section bar

Alert!   **Does the field list display?**

If the Field List pane displays on the right, in the upper right corner, click its Close button.

2 Point to upper edge of the **Detail section bar** to display the ⬍ pointer, and then drag downward approximately **0.5 inches**. Compare your screen with Figure 3.12.

The Form Header expands—do not be concerned if your expanded Form Header area does not match Figure 3.12 exactly; you will adjust it later. The background grid is dotted and divided into 1-inch squares by horizontal and vertical grid lines to help you place and align controls on the form precisely. You can also use the vertical and horizontal rulers to guide the placement of a control on the form.

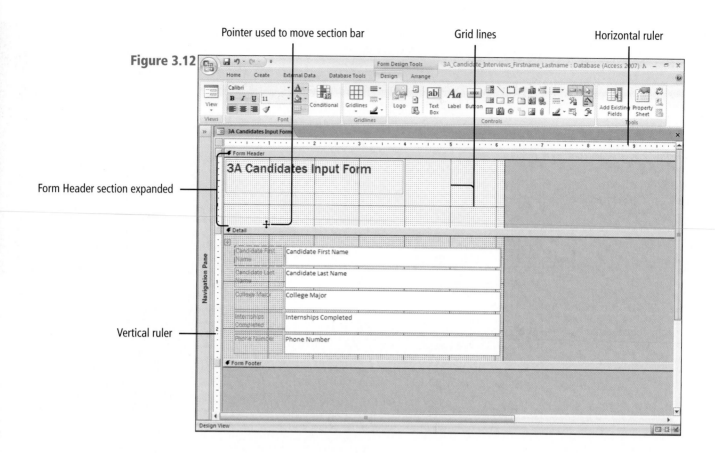

Pointer used to move section bar   Grid lines   Horizontal ruler

Figure 3.12

Form Header section expanded

Vertical ruler

3A Candidates Input Form

Candidate First Name
Candidate Last Name
College Major
Internships Completed
Phone Number

Alert!   **Are the rulers missing?**

If the horizontal and vertical rulers do not display, on the Arrange tab, in the Show/Hide group, click Ruler.

3 In the **Form Header section**, click anywhere in the title *3A Candidates Input Form* to select it. On the **Design tab**, in the **Font group**, click the **Font Size arrow** [11 ▾], and then click **18**. Click the **Bold** button [B] to add bold emphasis to the text. Click the **Font Color arrow** [A ▾], and then under **Access Theme Colors**, in the second row, click the ninth color—**Access Theme 9**.

The label is selected as indicated by the orange border surrounding it. The border displays small boxes called *sizing handles*, which are used to resize the control.

4 On the right side of the selected label control, point to the **middle sizing handle** to display the [↔] pointer—or point to one of the other sizing handles to display a resize pointer—and then double-click to adjust the size of the label control. Compare your screen with Figure 3.13.

The size of the label resizes to fit the text as it has been reformatted.

Figure 3.13

Form Header text—*3A Candidates Input Form*—modified

Sizing handles indicate label is selected

Label formatted and resized

0.50 inch on the vertical ruler

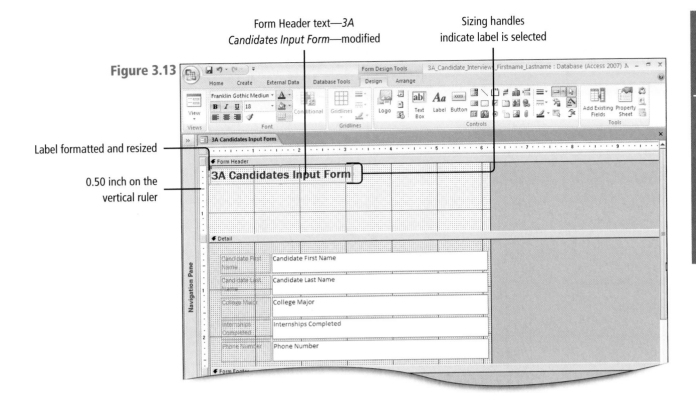

5 Point to the upper edge of the **Detail section bar** to display the ⊕ pointer, and then drag upward until the bar is at **0.50 inch on the vertical ruler**—allowing approximately two rows of dots between the lower edge of the label control border and the upper edge of the **Detail section bar**.

6 At the bottom of the form, point to the lower edge of the **Form Footer section bar** to display the ⊕ pointer, and then drag downward approximately **0.50 inch** to expand this section of the form.

7 On the **Design tab**, in the **Controls group**, click the **Label** button. Position the plus sign of the pointer ⊞A in the **Form Footer** section at approximately **0.25 inch on the horizontal ruler** and even with the top edge of the section. Drag to the right to **5 inches on the horizontal ruler**, and then downward approximately **0.25 inch**. If you are not satisfied with your result, click Undo and begin again.

8 Using your own name, type **3A Candidates Input Form Firstname Lastname** and then press Enter. Point to a sizing handle to display one of the resize pointers, and then double-click to fit the control to the text you typed. On the right end of the status bar, click the **Form View** button ▣. Compare your screen with Figure 3.14.

Form Footer text displays on the screen at the bottom of the form, and prints only on the last page when all the forms are printed as a group.

Figure 3.14

Form Header label modified

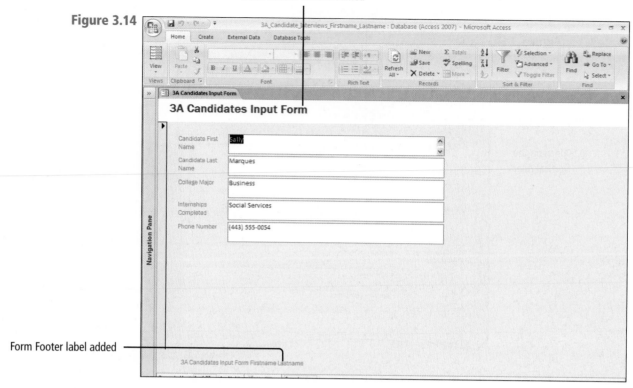

Form Footer label added ——

9 On the **Quick Access Toolbar**, click the **Save** button [icon] to save the changes you have made to the design of your form. Leave the **3A Candidates Input Form** open for the next activity.

Activity 3.7 Adding, Resizing, and Moving Controls in Layout View

Use the Layout view to change the form's ***control layout***—the grouped arrangement of controls on a form in Layout view. Use Layout view to make quick changes to the form's design by adding or moving controls.

1 In the lower right corner of your screen, at the right end of the status bar, click the **Layout View** button [icon].

On the Ribbon, the Format tab is selected. A dotted line surrounds the first control—label and text box—and the white text box is surrounded by a solid orange border. In the upper left corner, the ***layout selector*** displays, with which you can select and move the entire group of controls in this view.

2 In the **Controls group**, click the **Add Existing Fields** button to display the **Field List** pane. Compare your screen with Figure 3.15.

Figure 3.15

First label and control selected

Field List pane displays

Layout selector

Layout View button in status bar selected

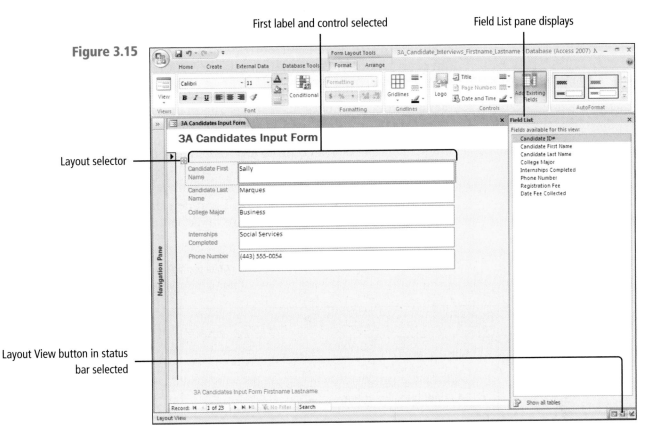

In the displayed **Field List**, point to **Candidate ID#**, hold down the left mouse button, and then drag until the pointer is in the upper portion of the *Candidate First Name* text box control and a thick orange line displays above the control. Release the mouse button, and then compare your screen with Figure 3.16. If you are not satisfied with your result, click Undo and begin again.

The Candidate ID# text box control is added to the form; recall that Access also places a label to the left of the text box. In this manner you can add a bound text box to a form by dragging a field from the Field List pane.

Candidate ID# text box control added to the form

Figure 3.16

Access adds label to the text box control

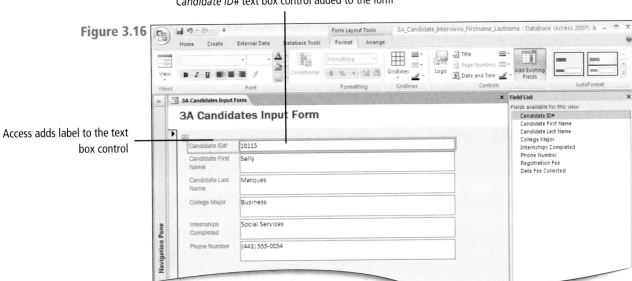

4 **Close** ✕ the **Field List** pane. Click the white text box control for **Candidate ID#**, which currently displays *10115*, to surround it with an orange border. Point to the right edge of the white text box control until the ⟷ pointer displays, and then drag to the left until all the white text box controls align under the *m* in the form title above. Compare your screen with Figure 3.17.

All six white text box controls are resized simultaneously. By decreasing the width of the text box controls, you have more space in which to rearrange the various form controls. In Layout view, because you can see your data, you can determine visually that the space you have allotted is adequate to display all records.

White text box controls align under *m* in form title

Figure 3.17

Horizontal resize pointer

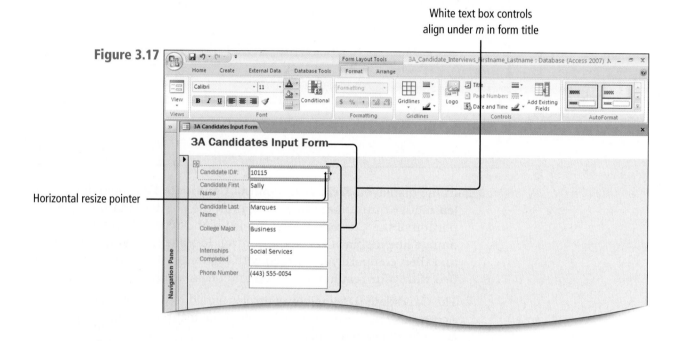

5 Click the white text box control for **Phone Number**, which currently displays *(443) 555-0054*. With both the label and the text box control selected, point to the white text box control until the 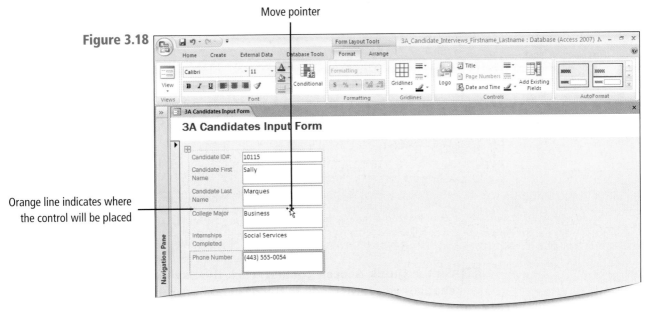 pointer displays, and then drag upward until a thick orange line displays above the text *College Major* as shown in Figure 3.18.

Move pointer

Figure 3.18

Orange line indicates where
the control will be placed

6 Release the mouse button to place the **Phone Number control** above the **College Major control**.

7 Click the **Candidate First Name label** to select it. Click to the left of the word *First* to place the insertion point in the control, and then press ←Bksp as necessary to delete the text *Candidate* so that the label indicates *First Name*.

With the insertion point placed in the label, you can edit the label. The form label text does not have to match the field name of the associated table.

8 Using the technique you just practiced, edit the **Candidate Last Name label** to indicate *Last Name*. Then, click in a shaded area of the form so that no controls are selected and compare your screen with Figure 3.19.

Figure 3.19

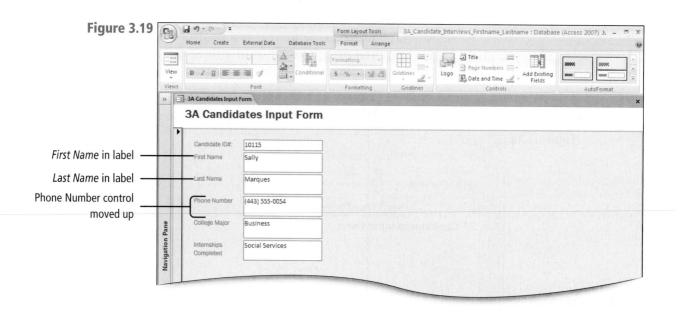

First Name in label ——
Last Name in label ——
Phone Number control moved up ——

9 On the **Quick Access Toolbar**, click the **Save** button to save the changes you have made to the design of your form in Layout view.

Activity 3.8 Formatting and Aligning Controls in Layout View

1 With the form still displayed in Layout view, hold down ⇧ Shift, and then click each of the **white text box controls**.

2 With the six text box controls selected, on the **Format tab**, in

Alert!	**Do your controls change order when selecting?**
	If, when selecting all the controls, the controls change order, click Undo and select the controls again.

the **Font group**, click the **Fill/Back Color button arrow**. Under **Access Theme Colors**, in the second row, click the fourth color—**Access Theme 4**. Click the **Font Size button arrow** [11 ▾], and then click **12**.

3 Click in a shaded area of the screen to deselect all the **text box controls**. Hold down ⇧ Shift, and then click each of the six labels to the left of the text box controls. With the six label controls selected, change the **Font Size** [11 ▾] to **12**, change the **Font Color** [A ▾] to

Access Theme 9, and then apply **Bold** [B]. Click in a shaded area to deselect, and then compare your screen with Figure 3.20.

Text box controls formatted with Font Size 12 and Access Theme 4 fill color

Figure 3.20

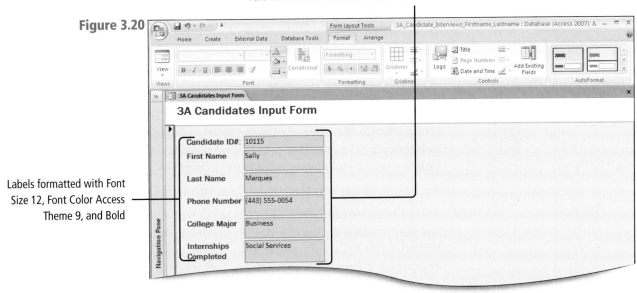

Labels formatted with Font Size 12, Font Color Access Theme 9, and Bold

4 Click the label **Internships Completed**. On the Ribbon, click the **Arrange tab**, and then in the **Tools group**, click the **Property Sheet** button. Compare your screen with Figure 3.21.

The **Property Sheet** for the selected label displays. Each control has an associated Property Sheet where you can make precision changes to the properties—characteristics—of selected controls.

Property Sheet button in Tools group

Arrange tab selected

Figure 3.21

Property Sheet for label

Label selected

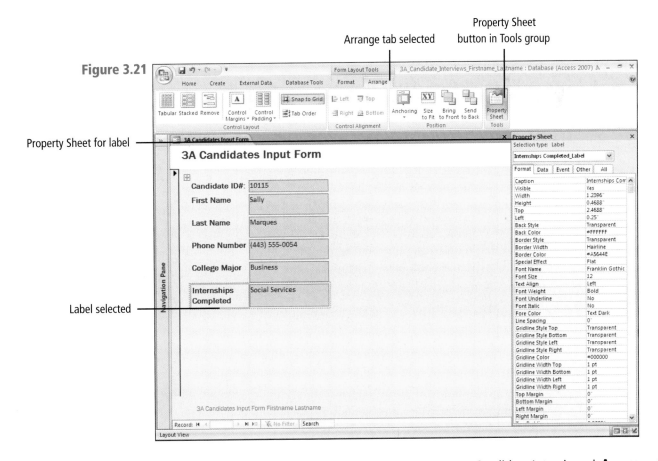

5 In the displayed **Property Sheet**, be sure the **Format tab** is selected. In the **Width** property box, point to the word *Width* and click to select its value to the right. Type **2** to replace the value, and then press Enter.

The width of all the labels changes to 2 inches.

6 Click in the shaded area to deselect the label. Hold down ⇧Shift, and then click to select the blue text box controls for **First Name**, **Last Name**, **Phone Number**, **College Major**, and **Internships Completed**. With the five text boxes selected, in the **Property Sheet**, click the word *Height*, type **0.3** and then press Enter.

The height of the selected text box controls decreases.

7 In the **Form Footer section**, click to select the label with your name that you created earlier. In the displayed **Property Sheet**, point to the text *Left* and click to select the value, and then change the **Left** property to **1** Press Enter to align the left edge of the label at 1 inch.

8 In the **Form Header section**, click anywhere in the title label text *3A Candidates Input Form*. In the **Property Sheet**, on the **Format tab**, change the **Left** property to **1** and then press Enter. Compare your screen with Figure 3.22.

Recall that each control has an associated Property Sheet on which you can change the properties—characteristics—of the control. Because this is a label that was added to the form, Access assigns it a number. The number on your property sheet may differ. The left edge of the label moves so that its left edge aligns at 1 inch. In this manner you can place a control in a specific location on the form.

Height of five controls
modified to 0.3 inch

Figure 3.22

Width of labels modified
to 2 inches

Form Header label left
aligned at 1 inch

Form Footer label left aligned
at 1 inch

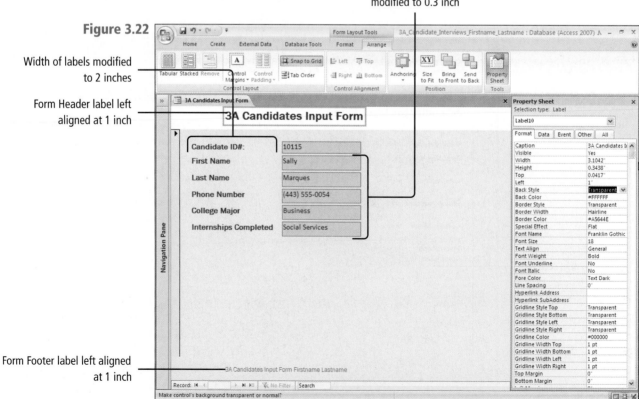

9 In the upper right corner of the **Property Sheet**, click the **Close** button ☒. On the right side of the status bar, click the **Form View** 📧 button. Compare your screen with Figure 3.23.

The form displays in Form view. Using these techniques, you can make a form attractive and easy to use for those who must use the form to view and enter records on a screen.

Figure 3.23

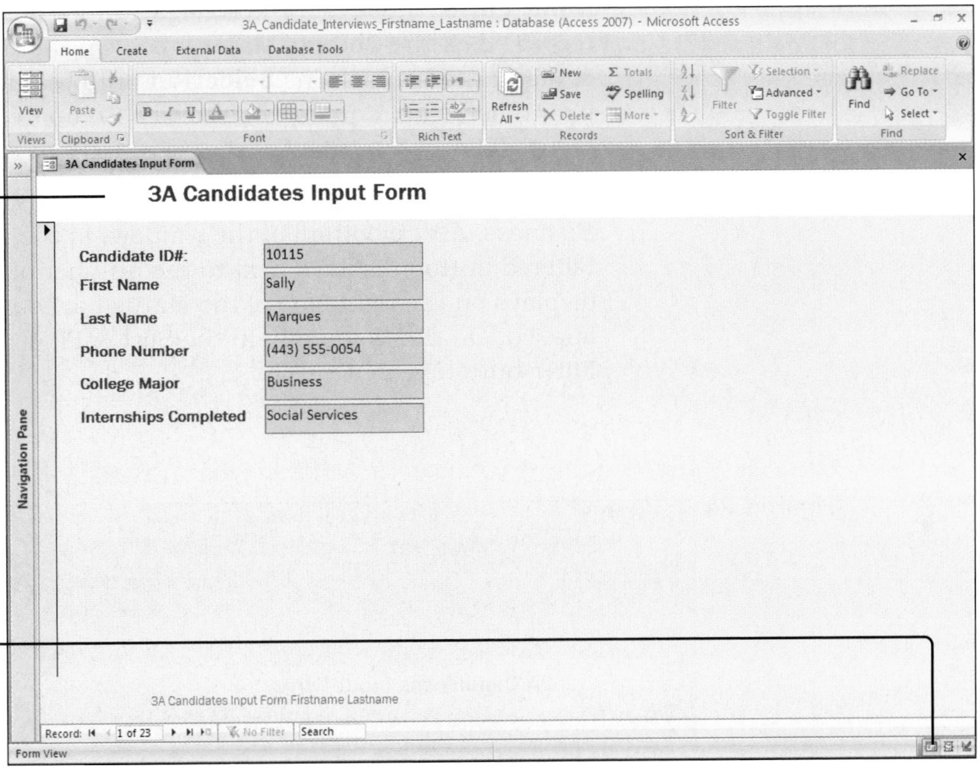

Form displays in Form view —————

3A Candidates Input Form

Candidate ID#:	10115
First Name	Sally
Last Name	Marques
Phone Number	(443) 555-0054
College Major	Business
Internships Completed	Social Services

3A Candidates Input Form Firstname Lastname

Record: 1 of 23

Form View button on status bar —————

10 On the **Quick Access Toolbar**, click the **Save** button 🔲 to save the changes you have made to your form's design. In the navigation area, click the **Last record** button ▶️ to display the record containing your name. Then, from the **Office** menu 🔘, click **Print**. In the displayed **Print** dialog box, under **Print Range**, click the **Selected Record(s)** option button. Click **OK** to print, or submit electronically as directed.

11 **Close** ☒ the form, and if necessary, click **Yes** to save the changes.

Objective 5
Filter Records

Filtering records in a form is the process of displaying only a portion of the total records—a *subset*—based on matching specific values. Filters are commonly used to provide a quick answer, and the result is not generally saved for future use. For example, by filtering records in a form, you can quickly display a subset of records for students majoring in Business.

Activity 3.9 Filtering Data by Selection on One Field

Several interviewers at the Baltimore Job Fair would like to see records for candidates who are majoring in Business. Use the *Filter By Selection* command—which retrieves only the records that contain the value in the selected field—to temporarily remove the records that do *not* contain the value in the selected field.

1 Open 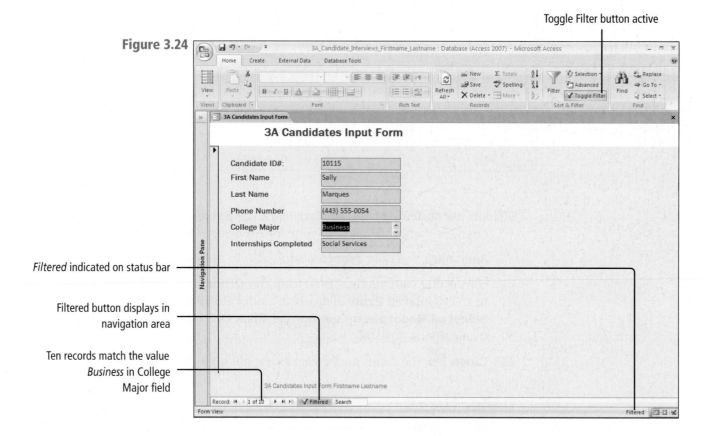 the **Navigation Pane**, and then open the **3A Candidates Input Form**. **Close** the **Navigation Pane**. In the displayed first record, click the **College Major** label. On the **Home tab**, in the **Sort & Filter group**, click the **Selection** button, and then in the displayed list, click **Equals "Business"**. Compare your screen with Figure 3.24.

Ten records match the contents of the selected College Major field—*Business*. At the bottom of the window, in the navigation area, a Filtered button displays next to the number of records. *Filtered* also displays on the right side of the status bar to indicate that a filter is applied. On the Home tab, in the Sort & Filter group, the Toggle Filter button is active.

Toggle Filter button active

Figure 3.24

Filtered indicated on status bar

Filtered button displays in navigation area

Ten records match the value *Business* in College Major field

2 On the **Home tab**, in the **Sort & Filter group**, click the **Toggle Filter** button to remove the filter and activate all 23 records. Notice the **Unfiltered** button in the navigation area. Alternatively, click the Filtered button in the navigation area to remove a filter.

3 Be sure the first record—for Sally Marques—displays, and then click to place the insertion point in the blue **College Major** text box control to display up and down arrows. On the **Home tab**, in the **Sort & Filter group**, click the **Toggle Filter** button to reapply the filter, and then in the navigation area, click the **Last record** button ⏭ to display the last of the ten records that match *Business*.

The record for *Candidate ID# 22155* displays—the record with your name.

4 In the **Sort & Filter group**, click the **Toggle Filter** button to remove the filter and activate all of the records. In the navigation area, click the **Next record** button ▶ one time to move to **Record 2**. In the **Phone Number** field, select the text *(410)* including the parentheses, which is the Area Code. On the **Home tab**, in the **Sort & Filter group**, click the **Selection** button, and then click **Begins with "(410)"**.

A new filter is applied that retrieves the fourteen records in which the *Phone Number* contains the (410) Area Code.

5 On the **Home tab**, in the **Sort & Filter group**, click the **Toggle Filter** button to remove the filter and activate all of the records.

Activity 3.10 Using Filter by Form

Use the *Filter By Form* command to filter the records in a form based on one or more fields, or based on more than one *value* in the same field. The Filter By Form command offers greater flexibility than the Filter by Selection command when you want an answer to a question that requires matching multiple values. In this activity, you will help Janna Sorokin determine how many candidates have a major of *Communications* or *Graphic Arts*, because several interviewers are interested in candidates with one of those two backgrounds.

1 With the **3A Candidates Input Form** still open, on the **Home tab**, in the **Sort & Filter group**, click the **Advanced** button, and then in the displayed list, click **Filter By Form**. Click the **Advanced** button again, and then click **Clear Grid**. Compare your screen with Figure 3.25.

The Filter by Form window displays; all the field names are included, but without any data. In the empty text box for each field, you can type a value or choose from a list of available values. The *Look for* and *Or* tabs display at the bottom.

Figure 3.25

Data is cleared

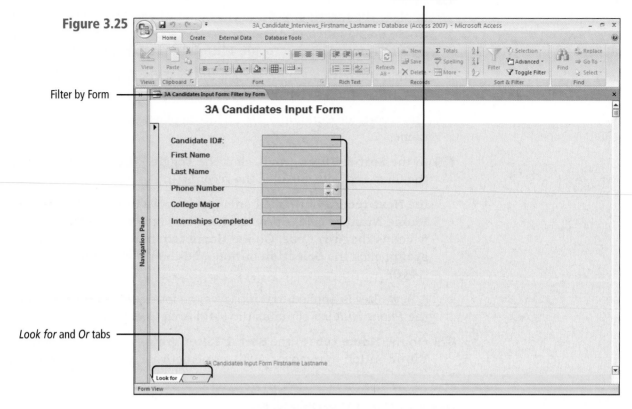

Filter by Form

3A Candidates Input Form

Candidate ID#:

First Name

Last Name

Phone Number

College Major

Internships Completed

Look for and *Or* tabs

3A Candidates Input Form Firstname Lastname

Look for   Or

Form View

2 Click the blue **College Major** text box control. At the far right edge of the text box, click the larger **down arrow**, and then in the displayed list, click **Communications**. In the **Sort & Filter group**, click the **Toggle Filter** button, and then compare your screen with Figure 3.26.

As indicated in the navigation area, six candidate records indicate a College Major of *Communications*.

Figure 3.26

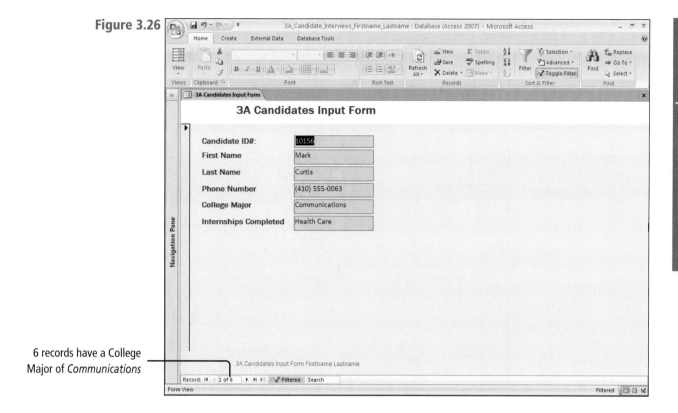

6 records have a College Major of *Communications*

Note — Toggle Filter Button

On the Home tab, the Toggle Filter button is used to apply or remove a filter. If no filter has been created, the button is not active—it is dimmed. After a filter is created, this button becomes active. Because it is a toggle button used to apply or remove filters, the ScreenTip that displays for this button will alternate between Apply Filter—when a filter has been created but is not currently applied—and Remove Filter—when a filter has been applied.

3 Click in the blue **College Major** text box control again. In the **Sort & Filter group**, click the **Filter** button. From the displayed menu, click to select the **Graphic Arts** check box, and then click **OK**.

As indicated in the navigation area, eight candidate records have a College Major in either Communications *or* Graphic Arts. You have created an *OR condition*; that is, only records where one of two values—Communications *or* Graphic Arts—is present in the selected field are activated.

4 Click in the blue **College Major** text box control. In the **Sort & Filter group**, click the **Advanced** button, and then from the displayed menu, click **Clear All Filters**. Click the **Advanced** button again, and then from the displayed menu, click **Advanced Filter/Sort**. Use the ⬉ pointer to expand the field list so that you can view all of the field names. Compare your screen with Figure 3.27.

The Advanced Filter design grid displays. The design grid is similar to the query design grid.

Figure 3.27

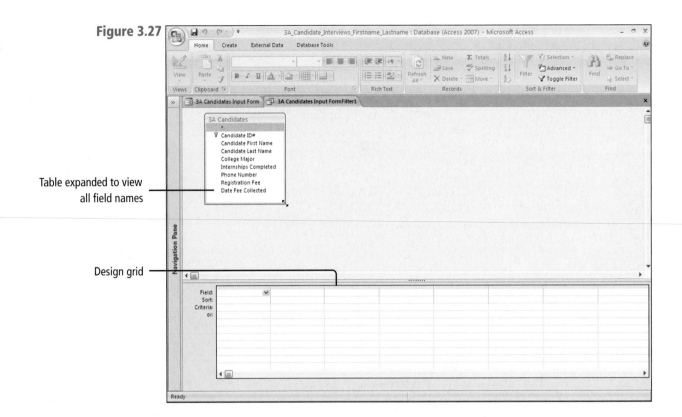

Table expanded to view all field names

Design grid

From the **3A Candidates table**, double-click the **College Major** field to add it to the design grid. Then, add the **Internships Completed** field to the design grid. In the **Criteria** row, in the **College Major** field, type **Business** In the **Criteria** row, in the **Internships Completed** field, type **Finance** and then press Enter. In the **Sort & Filter group**, click **Toggle Filter**. Compare your screen with Figure 3.28.

As indicated in the navigation area, three records match the criteria. You have created an *AND condition*; that is, only records where both values—Business *and* Finance—are present in the selected fields display. There are three Business majors who have completed an internship in Finance.

Figure 3.28

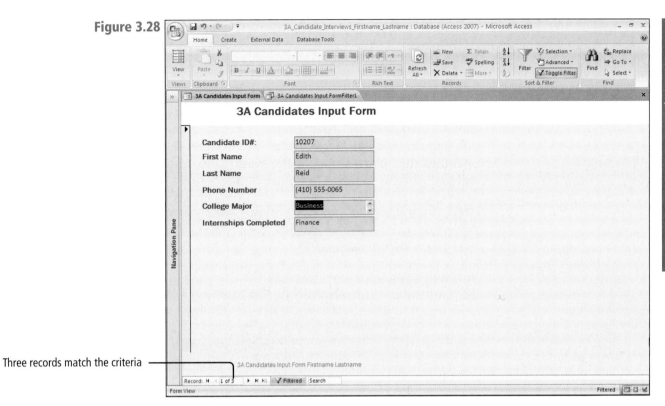

Three records match the criteria

6 In the **Sort & Filter group**, click the **Toggle Filter** button to unfilter the records. Close all open objects, from the **Office** menu close the database, and then **Close** Access.

End **You have completed Project 3A**

Project 3B Employers and Job Openings

At the Job Fair event, employers post job openings and candidates can request interviews for jobs in which they are interested. In Activities 3.11 though 3.16, you will assist Janna Sorokin, database manager for the Job Fair, in using an Access database to track the employers and the job openings they plan to post at the event. Your completed database objects will look similar to those in Figure 3.29.

For Project 3B, you will need the following file:

a3B_Employers_Job_Openings

You will save your database as
3B_Employers_Job_Openings_Firstname_Lastname

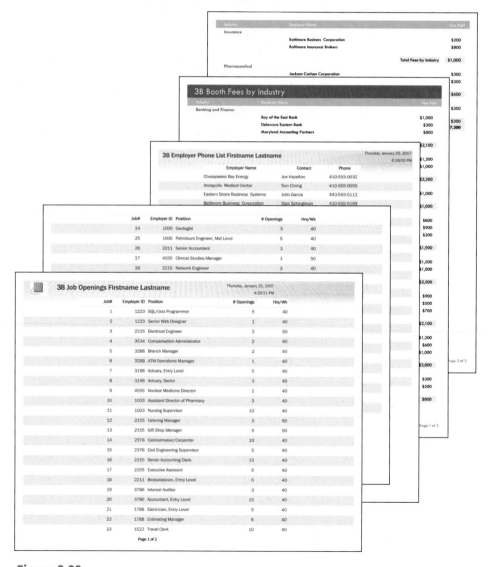

Figure 3.29
Project 3B—Employers and Job Openings

Objective 6
Create a Report by Using the Report Tool

A **report** is a database object that summarizes the fields and records from a table, or from a query, in an easy-to-read format suitable for printing. The report consists of information pulled from tables or queries, as well as information that is stored with the report's design, for example labels, headings, and graphics.

The tables or queries that provide the underlying data for a report are referred to as the report's **record source**. If the fields that you want to include in your report all come from the same table, then you can use the table as the report's record source.

Access provides three ways to create a report: by using the Report tool, the Blank Report tool, or the Report Wizard. After you create a report, you can modify the report in Layout view or in Design view.

Activity 3.11 Creating and Modifying a Report by Using the Report Tool and Layout View

The **Report tool**, which is the fastest way to create a report, generates a report immediately by displaying all the fields and records from the record source that you choose—the underlying table or query. This method of creating a report is useful as a way to quickly look at the underlying data in an easy-to-read format, after which you can save the report and then modify it in Layout view or in Design view.

In this activity, you will use the Report tool to create a report for Janna Sorokin that lists all the employers who are participating in the Job Fair, modify the report in Layout view, and then print the report.

1 Open **My Computer**. From the student files that accompany this text, locate the file **a3B_Employers_Job_Openings**. Copy and then paste the file to your Access Chapter 3 folder. Rename the file as **3B_Employers_Job_Openings_Firstname_Lastname** Close **My Computer**, start Access, open your **3B_Employers_Job_Openings** database, and then if necessary enable the content.

2 Click the **Database Tools tab**, and then in the **Show/Hide group**, click the **Relationships** button. Compare your screen with Figure 3.30.

At the Job Fair event, *one* employer can have *many* job openings. Thus, a one-to-many relationship has been established between the 3B Employers table and the 3B Job Openings table using Employer ID# as the common field—the field that displays in both tables.

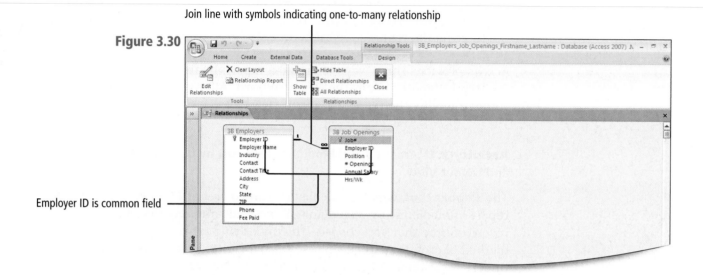

Join line with symbols indicating one-to-many relationship

Figure 3.30

Employer ID is common field

3 In the **Relationships group**, click the **Close** button to close the **Relationships** window.

4 **Open** [»] the **Navigation Pane**, click to select the **3B Job Openings table**, and then on the **Create tab**, in the **Reports group**, point to the **Report** button and read its ScreenTip. Click the **Report** button, and then **Close** [«] the **Navigation Pane**. Compare your screen with Figure 3.31.

Access creates the 3B Job Openings report and displays it in Layout view. The report includes all the fields and all the records in the table. In Layout view, you can see the margins and page breaks in the report as the pages are currently set up.

All fields from table display in report

Figure 3.31

Dotted lines indicate margins

All records from table display in report

Report displays in Layout view

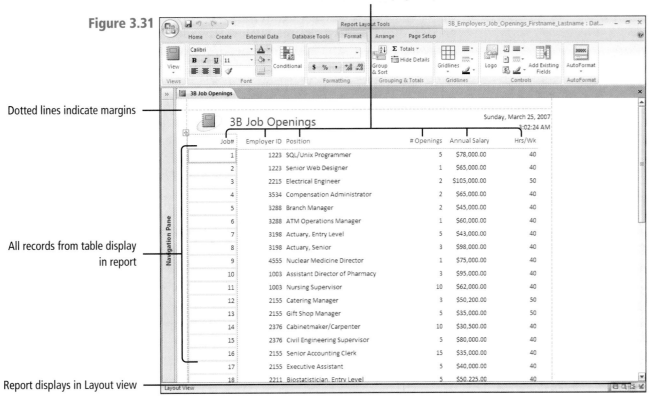

5 Click to select the field name **Annual Salary** to surround it with an orange border and to select the entire column. Right-click over the selected name, and then from the displayed shortcut menu, click **Delete**.

The Annual Salary field is deleted from the report.

6 Click to select the field name **# Openings** to surround it with an orange border and to select the entire column. On the **Format tab**, in the **Grouping & Totals group**, click the **Totals** button. In the displayed list, click **Sum**. Scroll down to view the last line of the report, and notice that Access summed the numbers in the field and that the total number of job openings is *182*.

Use Layout view in this manner to make quick changes to a report created with the Report tool. The Report tool is not intended to create a perfectly formatted formal report, but rather it is a way to quickly summarize the data in a table or query in an easy-to-read format suitable for printing and reading.

7 Click the **Page Setup tab**, and then in the **Page Layout group**, click the **Landscape** button. Click the **Format tab**, and then in the **AutoFormat group**, click the **AutoFormat** button. From the displayed gallery of formats, locate, and then click the **Trek** AutoFormat.

AutoFormat enables you to apply a predefined format to a report, which is another way to give a professional look to a report created quickly with the Report tool. Apply AutoFormat before performing other editing to the text of your report.

8 In the **Report Header** at the top of the screen, click the text *3B Job Openings*, and then click again to position the insertion point in the header. Alternatively, double-click the header. Edit as necessary to add your name to the end of the header text. On the **Format tab**, in the **Font group**, change the **Font Size** [11 ▾] to **16**.

9 Click any field in the report. In the upper left corner of the report, click the small brown **layout selector** button ⊞, and then drag it to the right until the ⊞ pointer is positioned approximately below the *O* in the word *Openings*. Compare your screen with Figure 3.32.

Recall that by using the layout selector button, you can move the entire layout of the labels and text box controls. In this manner, you can easily center the entire layout on the page visually, instead of opening and manipulating the controls in Design view.

Your name displays in Report Header

Trek AutoFormat applied

Figure 3.32

Report Header Font Size changed to 16 pt.

Layout centered horizontally on the page

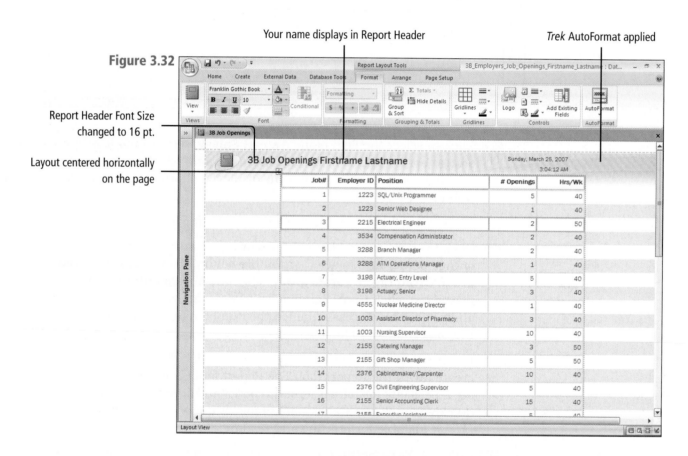

10 In the lower right corner of the screen, at the right edge of the status bar, click the **Print Preview** button ▣. On the **Print Preview tab**, in the **Zoom group**, click the **Two Pages** button to view the two pages of your report.

11 To print your report, on the **Print Preview tab**, in the **Print group**, click **Print** to print the report. Or, submit electronically as directed.

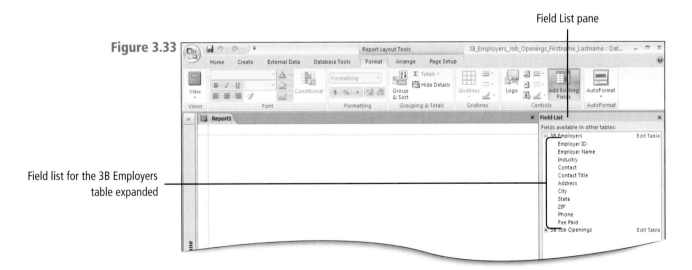

12 On the **Print Preview tab**, in the **Close Preview group**, click the **Close Print Preview** button, and then **Close** ✗ the **3B Job Openings report**. In the displayed message box, click **Yes** to save changes to the design of the report. In the **Save As** dialog box, click **OK** to accept the default name—*3B Job Openings*.

Objective 7
Create a Report by Using the Blank Report Tool

Activity 3.12 Creating a Report by Using the Blank Report Tool

Use the ***Blank Report tool*** to create a report from scratch. This is an efficient way to create a report, especially if you plan to include only a few fields in your report.

In this activity, you will use the Blank Report tool to build a report that lists only the Employer Name, Contact, and Phone fields, which Janna will use as a quick reference for phoning various employers to verify the details of their Job Fair participation.

1 On the **Create tab**, in the **Reports group**, click the **Blank Report** button.

A blank report displays in Layout view, and the Field List pane displays.

2 In the **Field List** pane, if necessary click **Show all tables**, and then click the **plus sign (+)** next to the **3B Employers table**. Compare your screen with Figure 3.33.

The list of fields in the 3B Employers table displays.

Figure 3.33

Field List pane

Field list for the 3B Employers table expanded

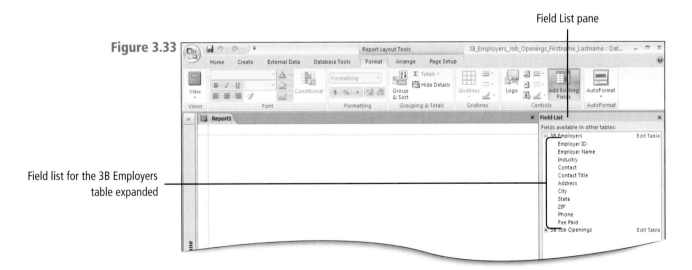

3 Point to the **Employer Name** field, right-click, and then click **Add Field to View**.

The Employer Name field and its associated records display as the first column of the report. In this manner, you build the report field by field, in the order you want the fields to display.

4 From the **Field List** pane, drag the **Contact** field into the blank report—anywhere to the right of **Employer Name**. Double-click the **Phone** field to add it as the third field in the report. Compare your screen with Figure 3.34.

You can use any of the techniques you just practiced when you want to include fields in a blank report.

Three fields added to the report

Figure 3.34

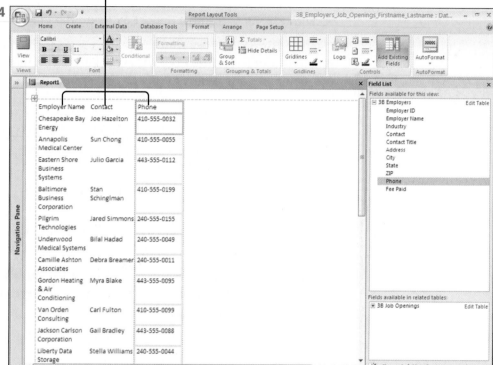

5 **Close** [×] the **Field List** pane. Click the field name **Employer Name** to surround it with an orange border and to select the column. Point to the right edge of the orange border to display the [↔] pointer, and then drag to the right until the name for *Baltimore Management Association* (toward the bottom of the list) displays on one line and there is a small amount of space between the name and the next column.

6 Using the technique you just practiced, widen the **Contact** field so that all the names display on one line and some space is allowed between the end of the longest name and the beginning of the next column. Compare your screen with Figure Figure 3.35.

Figure 3.35

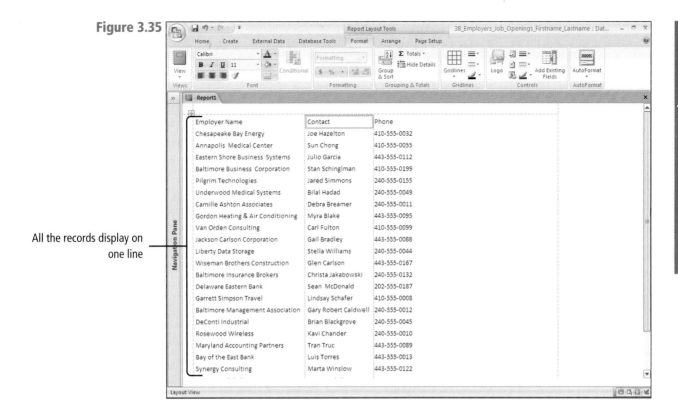

All the records display on one line

7 On the **Format tab**, in the **Controls group**, click the **Date & Time** button . In the displayed **Date and Time** dialog box, click **OK**.

In the **Controls group**, click the **Title** button , and then using your own name, type **3B Employer Phone List Firstname Lastname** In the **AutoFormat group**, click the **AutoFormat** button, and then apply the **Trek** AutoFormat. With the title still selected, in the **Font group**, change the **Font Size** 11 to **14**.

8 Click the field name **Employer Name** to select it, hold down ⇧ Shift, and then click the **Contact** field name and the **Phone** field name. On the **Format tab**, in the **Font group**, click the **Center** button .

9 In the upper left corner of the report, click the small brown **layout selector** button , and then drag it to the right until the pointer is positioned approximately below the *P* in the word *Phone*—or to whatever position appears to center the group of controls horizontally between the dotted margin lines. Compare your screen with Figure 3.36.

Apply the AutoFormat first, and then edit other formatting. Recall that by using the layout selector button, you can move the entire

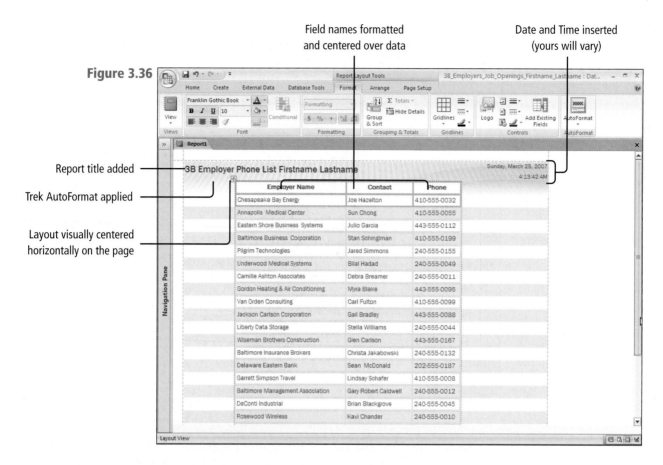

Figure 3.36

Field names formatted and centered over data

Date and Time inserted (yours will vary)

Report title added

Trek AutoFormat applied

Layout visually centered horizontally on the page

layout of the label and text box controls to easily center the entire layout on the page visually.

10 To print your report, on the status bar, click the **Print Preview** button ![Print Preview icon]. On the **Print Preview tab**, in the **Print group**, click **Print** to print the report. Or, submit electronically as directed.

11 On the **Print Preview tab**, in the **Close Preview group**, click the **Close Print Preview** button, and then **Close** ![X] the report. In the displayed message box, click **Yes** to save the changes to the design of the report. In the **Save As** dialog box, type **3B Employer Phone List** and then click **OK**.

12 **Open** ![>>] the **Navigation Pane**. Notice that in this Navigation Pane arrangement—Tables and Related Views—reports display below the table with which they are associated. Notice also that report objects display a small green notebook icon, which visually identifies them as reports. **Close** ![<<] the **Navigation Pane**.

Objective 8
Create a Report by Using the Report Wizard

Use the **_Report Wizard_** when you need flexibility and want to control the report content and design. The Report Wizard enables you to specify how the data is grouped and sorted, and you can use fields from more than one table or query, provided you have specified the relationships between the tables and queries beforehand.

The Report Wizard is similar to the Form Wizard; it creates a report by asking you a series of questions and then designs the report based on your answers.

Activity 3.13 Creating a Report by Using the Report Wizard

The Greater Baltimore Area Job Fair database includes data regarding employment information such as industry sectors, employers, job openings, and annual salaries. Based on the data that has been collected, Janna would like to have a report that shows groupings by industry, employer, and the total fees paid by employers for renting a booth at the Job Fair.

1 On the **Create tab**, in the **Reports group**, click **Report Wizard**.

The Report Wizard displays with its first question. Here you select the tables or queries from which you want to get information, and then select the fields that you want to include in the report. You can also choose from more than one table or query.

2 Click the **Tables/Queries arrow**, and then click **Table: 3B Employers**. Using either the **One Field** button $>$ or by double-clicking the field name, move the following fields to the **Selected Fields** list in the order given: **Industry**, **Employer Name**, and **Fee Paid** (scroll down as necessary to find the *Fee Paid* field). Click **Next**.

The Report Wizard displays its second question. Here you decide if you want to add any grouping levels.

3 With **Industry** selected, click the **One Field** $>$ button, and then compare your screen with Figure 3.37.

Figure 3.37

Report will be grouped by Industry

Employer Name and Fee Paid will display left to right

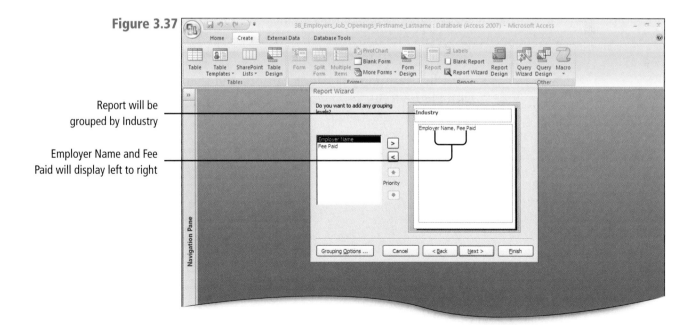

Grouping data helps you organize and summarize the data in your report. Grouping data in a report places all of the records that have the same data in a field together as a group—in this instance, each *Industry* will display as a group.

4 Click **Next**. In the **1** box, on the right, click the **arrow**, and then click **Employer Name**. Compare your screen with Figure 3.38.

Here you decide how you want to sort and summarize the information. You can sort on up to four fields. The Summary Options button displays because the data is grouped and contains numerical or

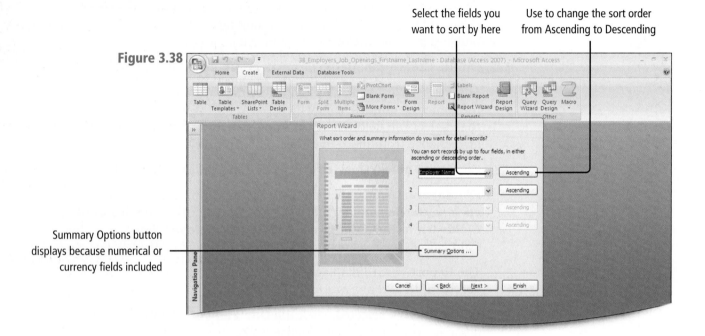

Figure 3.38

Select the fields you want to sort by here

Use to change the sort order from Ascending to Descending

Summary Options button displays because numerical or currency fields included

currency data. This action will cause the records in the report to be sorted alphabetically by Employer Name within the grouping option specified, which is *Industry*. Sorting records in a report presents a more organized report.

5 Click the **Summary Options** button, and then compare your screen with Figure 3.39.

Figure 3.39

Choose to show details and
summary or only summary information

Choose how you want to
summarize the data

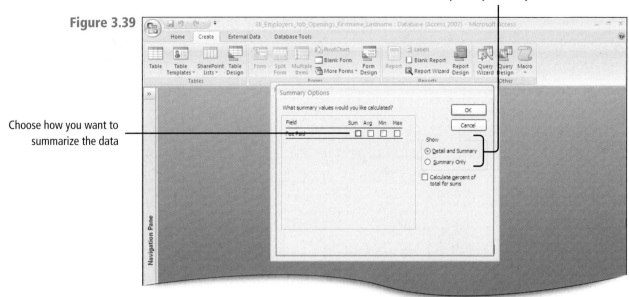

The Summary Options dialog box displays. Here you can choose to
display only summary information or to display both details—each
record—and the summary information. The Fee Paid field can be
summarized by selecting one of the four options displayed—Sum,
Avg, Min, or Max.

6 To the right of **Fee Paid**, select the **Sum** check box. Under **Show**, be
sure the **Detail and Summary** option button is selected, and then
click **OK**. Click **Next**.

Here you select the layout and the page orientation. The box on the
left displays a preview of the currently selected layout.

7 Click each **Layout** option button and view the options, and then
click the **Stepped** option button to select it as the layout for your
report. On the right side of the dialog box, under **Orientation**, be
sure **Portrait** is selected, and at the bottom be sure the **Adjust the
field width so all fields fit on a page** check box is selected.

8 Click **Next**. In the displayed list of styles, click one or more styles to
view the preview to the right.

9 Click the **Median** style, and then click the **Next** button. In the **What
title do you want for your report?** text box, name the report **3B
Booth Fees by Industry** and then click the **Finish** button. Compare
your screen with Figure 3.40.

The report is named and displays in Print Preview. This step also
saves the report with the name that you entered as the report title.

Each of the specifications you defined in the Report Wizard is
reflected in the report, although some data is not completely visible.
The records are grouped by Industry, and then within each Industry,

the Employer Names are alphabetized. In a manner similar to an Excel spreadsheet, numeric data that does not fit into the space may display as a series of # signs. Within each Industry grouping, the Fee Paid is summarized—the word *Sum* displays at the end of the grouping. However, some information is not fully displayed.

indicates data too wide for field

Figure 3.40

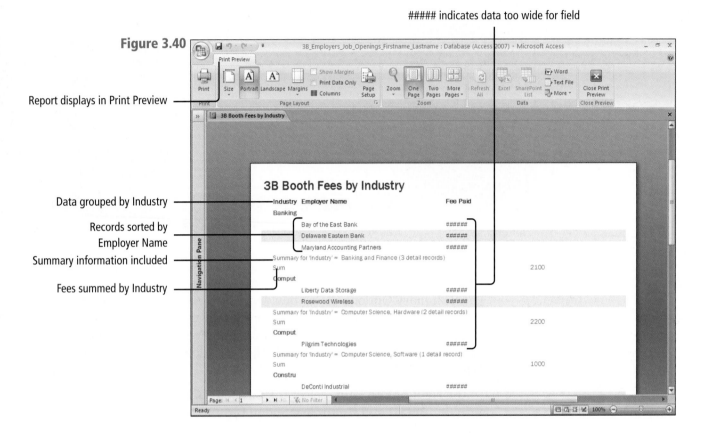

Report displays in Print Preview

Data grouped by Industry

Records sorted by Employer Name

Summary information included

Fees summed by Industry

10 In the **Zoom group**, click the **Two Pages** button.

As currently formatted, the report will print on two pages.

11 In the lower right corner of your screen, on the status bar, click the **Layout View** button 🔲 to switch to Layout view, and leave the report open in this view for the next activity.

Objective 9
Modify the Design of a Report

After a report is created, you can modify its design by using tools and techniques similar to those you used to modify the design of a form. You can change the format of controls, add controls, remove controls, or change the placement of controls in the report. Most report modifications can be made in Layout view.

Activity 3.14 Modifying a Report in Layout View

In your *3B Booth Fees by Industry* report, under the *Industry* heading, several of the industry names are truncated—not fully displayed.

Likewise, some of the amounts under Fee Paid are not fully displayed and display as # signs. You can modify the controls on a report to accommodate the data that displays.

In this activity, you will adjust the size and position of the controls so that the data is visible and attractively presented.

1 Be sure that your **3B Booth Fees by Industry** report displays in Layout view; if necessary click the Layout View button 🔲 on the status bar.

2 In the upper left corner of the report, click to select the **Industry label control** to surround it with an orange border and to select the column. Point to the right side of the selected label control to display

Fees not fully displayed and display as ####

Figure 3.41

Industry controls expanded

Industry names display fully

Layout View button active

the ↔ pointer, and then drag to the right until the right edge is aligned under the *I* in *Industry* in the Report Header above. Compare your screen with Figure 3.41.

3 Click to select the **Fee Paid label control**, and then drag its right edge to the right just slightly inside the dotted margin. Then drag the left side of the control to the right to shorten the control and leave a

Figure 3.42

Left side of
control shortened

Right side of control
moved to right margin

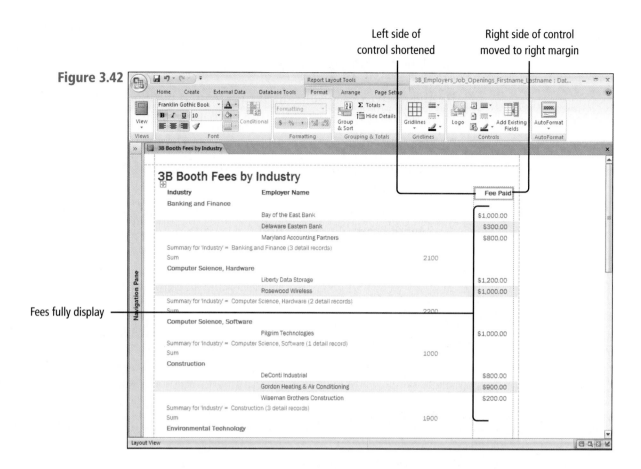

Fees fully display

small amount of space to the left of the dollar signs ($) in the fees.
Compare your screen with Figure 3.42.

The # signs are removed and the fee amounts display fully.

4 Within each Industry grouping, notice the **Summary for 'Industry'**
information.

Access includes a summary line that details what is being summarized (summed) and how many records are included in the total. Now
that Janna has viewed the report, she has decided this information
is not necessary and can be removed.

5 Click any of the **Summary for 'Industry' controls**.

The control that you clicked is surrounded by an orange border and
all the others are surrounded by paler borders to indicate that all are
selected.

6 Right-click any of the selected controls, and then from the displayed
shortcut menu, click **Delete**. Alternatively, press Del.

7 In the **Fee Paid** field, click any of the fee amounts to select these
controls. Right-click any of the selected controls, and then from the
displayed shortcut menu, click **Properties**. In the displayed
Property Sheet, click the **Format tab**.

Property Sheet

Figure 3.43

Format tab

Controls selected

Decimal Places property box

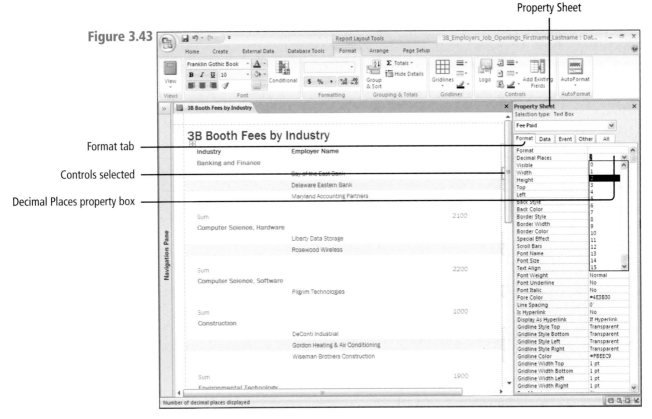

8 In the **Property Sheet**, on the **Format tab**, click the name of the second property—**Decimal Places**—and then click the **arrow** that displays. Compare your screen with Figure 3.43.

9 In the displayed list, click **0. Close** ☒ the **Property Sheet**.

The fees display with no decimal places.

10 In the **Banking and Finance grouping** of the report, to the right of the word *Sum*, click **2100** to select these controls. Point to any of the selected controls, right-click, and then from the displayed shortcut menu, click **Properties**.

These amounts would be more relevant if they included currency formatting to indicate that they are the sum of the fees paid within each industry grouping.

The summary controls are examples of *calculated controls*—controls that contain an expression—often a formula—that uses one or more fields from the underlying table or query.

11 In the **Property Sheet**, on the **Format tab**, click the name of the first property—**Format**—and then click the arrow that displays to the right.

12 In the displayed list of formats, click **Currency**. Click the **Decimal Places** property box, click the **arrow** that displays, and then click **0**. **Close** ☒ the **Property Sheet**.

13 With the ↔ pointer, drag the right side of any of the selected controls to the right, just inside the dotted margin line. After you release the mouse button adjust as necessary so that the summed amounts

Controls selected

Figure 3.44

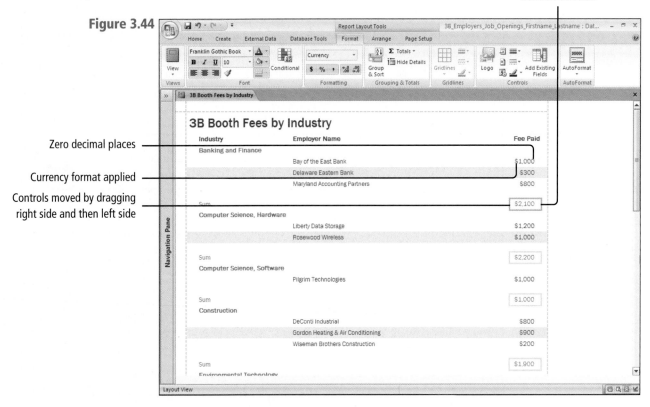

Zero decimal places

Currency format applied

Controls moved by dragging
right side and then left side

display directly under the fees above. Then, shorten the control by dragging the left side to the right with just enough space to accommodate the data. Compare your screen with Figure 3.44.

14 On the left side of the report, click one of the **Sum** controls to select these controls, and then click again to place the insertion point inside the selected control. Alternatively, double-click to place the insertion point inside the control.

15 Delete the text, type **Total Fees by Industry** and then press Enter. Notice that the label is on the left side of the page, but the Fee Paid to which it refers is on the right.

The new text more clearly states what is being summed, however, the label would be more useful positioned next to the summary value.

16 Use the pointer to lengthen the right side of the control so that it

Figure 3.45

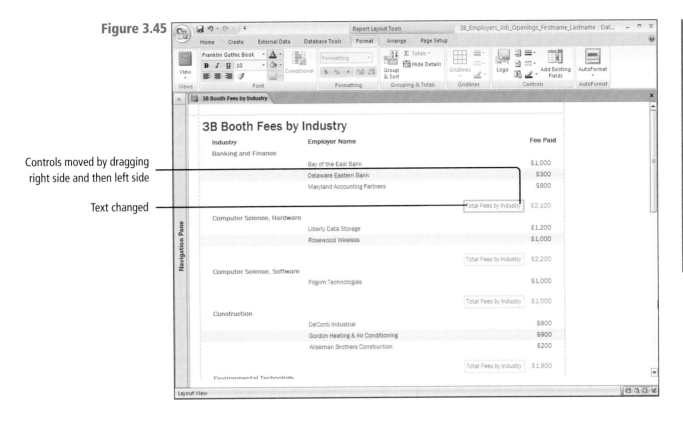

Controls moved by dragging
right side and then left side

Text changed

is slightly to the left of the total amount, and then shorten the left
side so that the control accommodates the text with no extra space.
Compare your screen with Figure 3.45.

17 At the top of your report, click to select the **Industry label control**,
hold down ⟨⇧ Shift⟩, and then click the **Employer Name label control**
and the **Fee Paid label control**. In the **Font group**, click the **Italic**
button $\boxed{I}$, and then click the **Bold** button $\boxed{B}$.

18 Scroll downward to view the end of the report. Click to select the
sum **17300**, which is the Grand Total for all fees paid. Using the
techniques you have practiced, display the **Property Sheet** for this
control and change its format to **Currency** with **0 Decimal Places**.
Close $\boxed{\times}$ the **Property Sheet**, and then adjust each side of the control to position it below the other fees.

19 By adjusting the right and left sides of the control, move the text
Grand Total to the immediate left of **$17,300**. Compare your screen
with Figure 3.46.

The *Grand Total* amount is the **report footer** and displays at the end
of the data. The current date and the page number information that
display on the bottom of the page is the **page footer**.

Figure 3.46

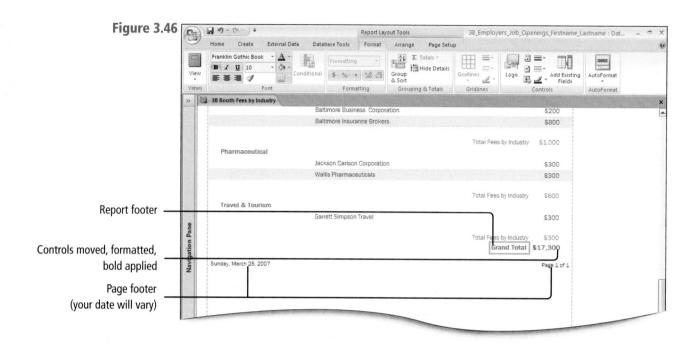

Report footer

Controls moved, formatted,
bold applied

Page footer
(your date will vary)

The report footer displays one time at the end of the data, and displays items such as report totals. It displays *only* if the data has been summarized. A page footer displays at the bottom of every page of the report.

20 On the **Quick Access Toolbar**, click **Save**. Leave your report open in Layout view for the next activity.

Activity 3.15 Modifying a Report in Design View

Design view gives you a more detailed view of the structure of your report. You can see the header and footer bands for the report, for the page, and for groups. In Design view, your report is not actually running, so you cannot see the underlying data while you are working. However some tasks, such as adding labels and images, are accomplished in Design view. In this activity you will add a label to the Page Footer section of your *3B Booth Fees by Industry* report and insert identifying information there.

1 Be sure that your **3B Booth Fees by Industry** report is displayed in Layout view. Press Ctrl + Home to display the top of the report. On the right end of the status bar, click the **Design View** button ☑. Compare your screen with Figure 3.47.

You can see that the Design view for a report is similar to the Design view of a form. You can also modify the layout of the report here, and use the dotted grid pattern to align controls. This report contains a **Report Header**, a **Page Header**, a **Group Header**, which in this instance is the *Industry* grouping, a Detail section that displays the data, a **Group Footer** (Industry), a Page Footer, and a Report Footer.

The Report Header displays information at the top of the *first page* of a report. The Page Header displays information at the top of *every page* of a report. The Group Header and Group Footer displays the field label by which the data has been grouped—*Industry* in this

Figure 3.47

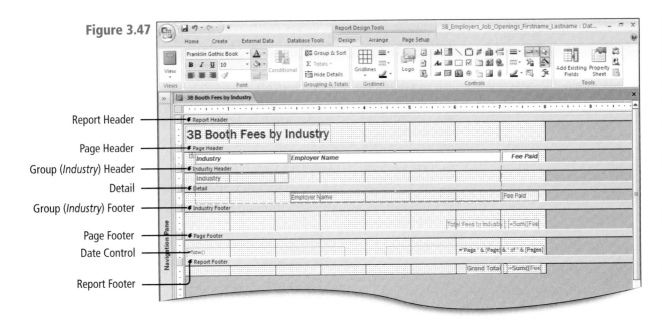

Report Header —

Page Header —

Group (*Industry*) Header —

Detail —

Group (*Industry*) Footer —

Page Footer —

Date Control —

Report Footer —

instance. If you do not group data in a report, the Group Header does not display. Similarly, if you do not summarize data, the Group Footer does not display.

2 Locate the **Page Footer** section of the report and examine the two controls in this section.

The **date control** on the left, identified as *=Now( )*, inserts the current date each time the report is opened. The **page number control** on the right, identified as *="Page" & [Page] & "of"" & [Pages]*, inserts the page number, for example Page 1 of 2, in the report when the report is displayed in Print Preview or when you print the report. Both of these are examples of programming code that is used by Access to create controls in a report.

3 In the **Page Footer** section, click to select the **date control**. Shorten this control by dragging the right sizing handle to the left to **1.75 inches on the horizontal ruler**.

The Page Footer displays information at the bottom of *every page* in the report, including the page number and the current date inserted by those controls.

4 Click the **page number control** on the right. Shorten this control by dragging the left sizing handle to the right to **5.5 inches on the horizontal ruler**.

5 On the **Design tab**, in the **Controls group**, click the **Label** button ***Aa***, and then in the **Page Footer** section, position the + portion of the pointer vertically in the middle of the section and horizontally at **2 inches on the horizontal ruler**. Click one time, and then using your own name, type **3B Booth Fees by Industry Firstname Lastname** Press Enter to select the control. If necessary, hold down Ctrl, and then press ↑ to align the top edge even with the other two controls, but do not be concerned if this control overlaps the page number control. Compare your screen with Figure 3.48.

As you type, the label expands to accommodate your typing. The Error Checking Options button displays to the left of the label. The Error Checking Options button displays when Access detects a potential problem. In this instance, the control you have added is a new unassociated label. If you clicked the Error Checking Options button, a list of options would display, one of which is to associate— attach—the new label to another control so the two controls could be treated as one unit for the purpose of moving the controls. This label should not be attached to another control so you can ignore this

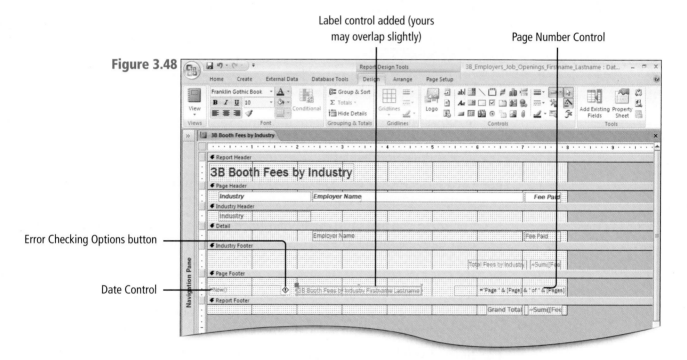

Figure 3.48

Label control added (yours may overlap slightly)

Page Number Control

Error Checking Options button

Date Control

option button. A green triangle displays in the upper left corner of the affected control.

6 With the label control selected, on the **Design tab**, in the **Font group**, click the **Font Color button arrow** , and then under **Access Theme Colors**, click **Access Theme 1**. On the **Quick Access Toolbar**, click **Save** . At the right edge of the status bar, click the **Report View** button . Scroll to the bottom of the page and compare your screen with Figure 3.49.

Figure 3.49

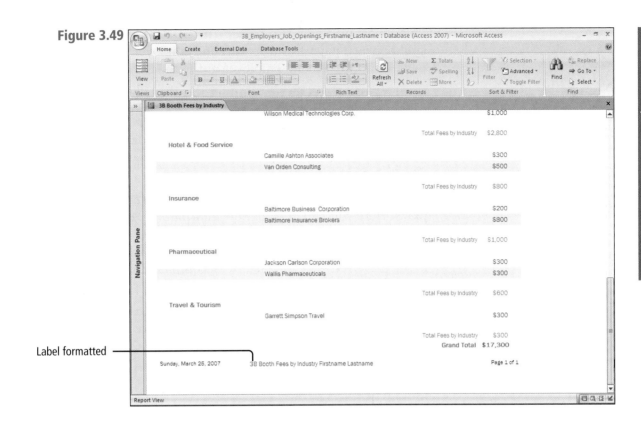

Label formatted

The new label displays with your name and the font color.

Objective 10
Print a Report and Keep Data Together

Before you print a report, examine the preview of the report to ensure that all of the labels and data are fully displayed, and to make sure that all of the data is properly grouped. Sometimes a page break occurs in the middle of a group of data, leaving the labels on one page and the data or totals on another page.

Activity 3.16 Keeping Data Together and Printing a Report

It is possible to keep the data in a group together so it does not break across a page unless, of course, the data itself exceeds the length of a page.

1 From the **Office** menu, point to the **Print** button, and then click **Print Preview**. In the **Zoom group**, click the **One Page** button. Click the **Zoom button arrow**, and then click **Zoom 100%**. Scroll to the bottom of the report to see where the first page ends, and then at the bottom of the screen, click the **Next Page** button and scroll to view the top of **Page 2**. Alternatively, in the Zoom group, click the Two Pages button to see a reduced view of the pages side by side.

This report prints on two pages. The data in the *Insurance* group is split between page 1 and 2, with one employer at the bottom of page 1 and the second employer at the top of page 2.

2 On the **Print Preview tab**, in the **Close Preview group**, click **Close Print Preview**. Click the **Layout View** button 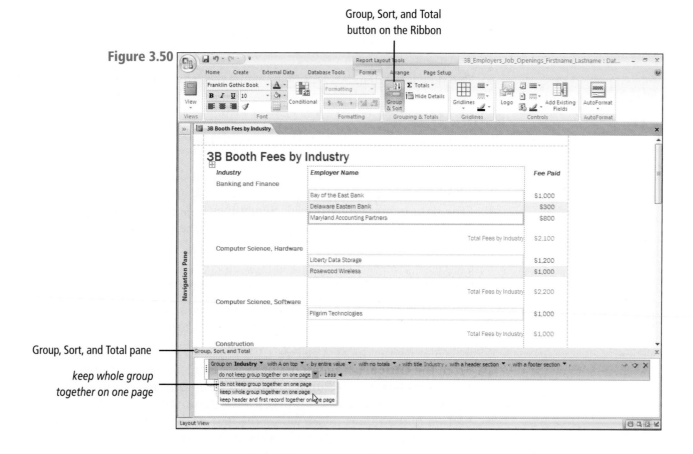 on the status bar. On the **Format tab**, in the **Grouping and Totals group**, point to the **Group & Sort** button, and then read its ScreenTip. Then click the **Group & Sort** button.

At the bottom of your screen, the ***Group, Sort, and Total pane*** displays. Here you can control how information is sorted and grouped. This pane gives you the most flexibility when you want to add or modify groups, sort orders, or totals options on a report. Layout view is the preferred view in which to accomplish such tasks, because you can see how your changes affect the display of the data.

3 In the **Group, Sort, and Total** pane, on the **Group on Industry bar**, click the **More** button, click the **arrow** to the right of **do not keep**

Group, Sort, and Total
button on the Ribbon

Figure 3.50

Group, Sort, and Total pane

keep whole group together on one page

group together on one page, and then point to **keep whole group together on one page**. Compare your screen with Figure 3.50.

4 Click **keep whole group together on one page**, and then click the **with A on top arrow**. In the displayed list, click **with A on top,** which indicates this field is sorting in ascending order. Compare your screen with Figure 3.51.

Figure 3.51

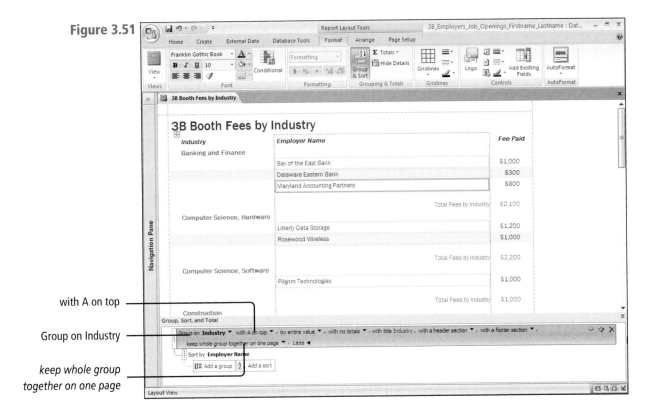

with A on top

Group on Industry

keep whole group together on one page

The *keep whole group together on one page* command will keep each employer together as a group, from the name in the group header, through the summary in the group footer.

5 On the Ribbon, in the **Grouping & Totals group**, click the **Group & Sort** button again to close the **Group, Sort & Total** pane. From the **Office** menu, point to the **Print** button, and then click **Print Preview**. Display the top of **Page 2** to verify that the two records and total for the **Insurance** group display together as a group.

6 On the **Print Preview tab**, in the **Print group**, click the **Print** button to print the report. Or, submit electronically as directed.

7 On the **Print Preview tab**, in the **Close Preview group**, click the **Close Print Preview** button. **Close** the report, and then click **Yes** to save the changes to the design of your report. **Close** the database and close Access.

End You have completed Project 3B ——————

There's More You Can Do!

From My Computer, navigate to the student files that accompany this textbook. In the folder **02_theres_more_you_can_do_pg1_36**, locate and open the folder for this chapter. Open and print the instructions for this project, which are provided to you in Adobe PDF format.

Try IT! 1—Insert a Logo into a Form or a Report

In this Try IT! exercise, you will insert a logo into an Access form.

Content-Based Assessments

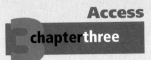

Summary

A form is a tool for either entering or viewing information in a database. Although you can both enter and view database information in the database table itself, using a form is easier because it can display one record at a time. The Form tool creates an instant form based on the fields in the table. Using the Form Wizard, you can create a customized form. Once created, a form can be modified in Layout view or in Design View.

Reports in Access summarize the data in a database in a professional-looking manner suitable for printing. The Report tool, the Blank Report tool, and the Report Wizard assist in report creation. The design of a report can be modified so that the final report is laid out in a format that is useful for the person reading it.

Key Terms

Content-Based Assessments

Matching

Match each term in the second column with its correct definition in the first column by writing the letter of the term on the blank line in front of the correct definition.

_____ **1.** An Access object with which you can enter, edit, or display data from a table or a query; a window for displaying and collecting information.

_____ **2.** The action of typing a record into a database.

_____ **3.** The Access tool that creates a form with a single mouse click, and that includes all the fields from the underlying data source (table or query).

_____ **4.** The Access view in which you can make changes to a form or to a report while the form is running, and in which the data from the underlying record source displays.

_____ **5.** The term used to describe objects and controls that are based on data that is stored in tables.

_____ **6.** The order in which the insertion point moves from one field to the next in a form when you press the Tab key.

_____ **7.** The bar on the left side of a form with which you can select the entire record.

_____ **8.** The detailed structured view of a form or report, and the view in which some tasks must be performed; only the controls, and not the data, are visible in this view.

_____ **9.** Information, such as a form's title, which displays at the top of the screen in Form view, and that is printed at the top of the first page when records are printed as forms.

_____ **10.** The section of a form or report that displays the records from the underlying table or query.

_____ **11.** Information at the bottom of the screen in Form view that is printed after the last detail section on the last page.

_____ **12.** In Design view, a gray bar in a form or report that identifies and separates one section from another; used to select the section and to change the size of the adjacent section.

_____ **13.** Objects on a form or report that display data, perform actions, and let you view and work with information.

_____ **14.** The graphical object on a form or report that displays the data from the underlying table or query.

_____ **15.** A control on a form or report that contains descriptive information, typically a field name.

A Bound

B Controls

C Data entry

D Design view

E Detail section

F Form

G Form footer

H Form header

I Form tool

J Label

K Layout view

L Record selector

M Section bar

N Tab order

O Text box control

Fill in the Blank

Write the correct answer in the space provided.

1. A control that does not have a source of data is an _____ control.

2. The small boxes around the edge of a control indicating the control is selected and that can be adjusted to resize the selected control are _____ handles.

3. The grouped arrangement of controls on a form or report is referred to as the _____ layout.

4. A small symbol that displays in the upper left corner of a selected control layout, and with which you can move the entire group of controls is the _____ _____.

5. A list of characteristics for controls on a form or report in which you can make precision changes to each control is the _____ Sheet.

6. The process of displaying only a portion of the total records (a subset) based on matching specific values is called _____.

7. An Access command that retrieves only the records that contain the value in the selected field is called _____ _____ _____.

8. An Access command that filters the records in a form based on one or more fields, or based on more than one value in the same field is called _____ _____ _____.

9. A condition in which only records where one of two values is present in the selected field is the _____ condition.

10. A condition in which only records where both specified values are present in the selected fields is a(n) _____ condition.

11. A database object that summarizes the fields and records from a table, or from a query, in an easy-to-read format suitable for printing is a(n) _____.

12. The tables or queries that provide the underlying data for a report are referred to as the _____ _____.

13. The Access feature that creates a report with one mouse click, and which displays all the fields and records from the record source that you choose is the _____ _____.

Content-Based Assessments

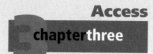

Fill in the Blank

14. An Access feature with which you can create a report from scratch by adding the fields you want in the order you want them to appear is the _____ _____ _____.

15. A control whose source of data is an expression—typically a formula—rather than a field is called a _____ control.

Content-Based Assessments

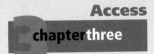
Project 3C—Counseling Sessions

In this project, you will apply the skills you practiced from the Objectives in Project 3A.

Objectives: 1. *Create a Form;* **2.** *Use a Form To Add and Delete Records;* **3.** *Create a Form by Using the Form Wizard;* **4.** *Modify a Form in Design View and in Layout View;* **5.** *Filter Records.*

At the Job Fair, various professional organizations schedule personal one-on-one counseling sessions with interested candidates to give them advice about opportunities in the fields they represent. Janna Sorokin, the database manager, has a database in which she is tracking the counseling sessions that have been scheduled thus far. Your completed database objects will look similar to those in Figure 3.52.

For Project 3C, you will need the following file:

a3C_Counseling_Sessions

You will save your database as 3C_Counseling_Sessions_Firstname_Lastname

Figure 3.52

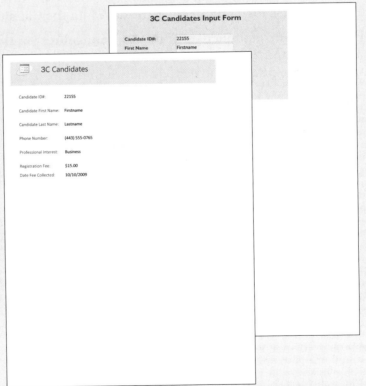

(Project 3C–Counseling Sessions continues on the next page)

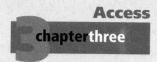

Skills Review

(Project 3C–Counseling Sessions continued)

1. Open **My Computer** and navigate to the location where the student files that accompany this textbook are located. Click once to select the file **a3C_Counseling_Sessions**; copy and then paste the file to your chapter folder. Rename the file **3C_Counseling_Sessions_Firstname_Lastname**

2. Close **My Computer**, start Access, and then open your **3C_Counseling_Sessions** database. If necessary, enable the content. Click the **Database Tools tab**, and then in the **Show/Hide group**, click the **Relationships** button. Examine the one-to-many relationship, and then **Close** the Relationships window. *One* candidate can attend *many* counseling sessions.

3. From the **Navigation Pane**, select the **3C Counseling Sessions table**, and then on the **Create tab**, in the **Forms group**, click **Form**. **Close** the **Navigation Pane**. Click the **Next record** button four times to display the record for *Session ID# 105*. Click the **Last record** button to display the record for *Session ID# 132*, and then click the **First record** button to display the record for *Session ID# 101*. Recall that you can view records one at a time in this manner by using a form. On the **Quick Access Toolbar**, click the **Save** button. In the displayed **Save As** dialog box, edit as necessary to name the form **3C Counseling Sessions Form** and then click **OK**. As additional candidates schedule sessions, you can use this form to enter the data into the 3C Counseling Sessions table. **Close** the form object.

4. From the **Navigation Pane**, select the **3C Candidates table**, click the **Create tab**, and then in the **Forms group**, click **Form**. **Close** the **Navigation Pane**. Notice that the form displays the scheduled sessions for the first candidate's record. On the **Quick Access Toolbar**, click **Save**, name the form **3C Candidates Form** and then click **OK**. **Close** the form object. As new candidates register, you can use this form to enter the data into the Candidates table.

5. **Open** the Navigation Pane, and then open the **3C Counseling Sessions Form**. **Close** the **Navigation Pane**. Click the **New (blank) record** button. In the **Session ID#** field, type **133** and then press Tab. Continue entering the data as shown in the following table:

Candidate ID#	Counseling Session Host	Counselor
10776	Graphic Arts Professionals	Connie Rogers

6. **Close** the 3C Counseling Sessions Form—the record is added to the associated table. **Open** the **Navigation Pane**, open the **3C Candidates Form**, and then **Close** the **Navigation Pane**. Click the **New (blank) record** button. Using your own first and last name, fill in the form using the information in the following table:

Candidate ID#	Candidate First Name	Candidate Last Name	Phone Number	Professional Interest	Registration Fee	Date Fee Collected
22155	Firstname	Lastname	(443) 555-0765	Business	$15.00	10/10/2009

7. **Close** the 3C Candidates form, **Open** the **Navigation Pane**, open the **3C Candidates table**, and then verify that your record as a candidate displays as the last record in the table. **Close** the table.

(Project 3C–Counseling Sessions continues on the next page)

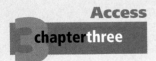
(Project 3C–Counseling Sessions continued)

8. From the **Navigation Pane**, open the **3C Counseling Sessions Form**. **Close** the **Navigation Pane**. Click in the **Session ID#** field, and then on the **Home tab**, in the **Find group**, click the **Find** button. In the **Look In** box, notice that *Session ID#* is indicated, and then in the **Find What** box, type **106** Click **Find Next**, and then confirm that the record for **Session ID# 106** displays. **Close** the **Find and Replace** dialog box.

9. On the **Home tab**, in the **Records group**, click the **Delete button arrow**, and then in the displayed list, click **Delete Record**. Click **Yes** to delete the record, and notice that the number of records in the table is *32*. **Close** the form object.

10. From the **Navigation Pane**, open the **3C Counseling Sessions table**. Examine the table and verify that the record for *Session ID# 106* no longer displays. Then, verify that the new record you added for **Session ID# 133** is included in the table. **Close** the table.

11. From the **Navigation Pane**, open the **3C Candidates Form**. **Close** the **Navigation Pane**. Press Ctrl + F to display the **Find and Replace** dialog box. In the **Find What** box, type **22155** In the **Look In** box, be sure that *Candidate ID#* is indicated, and then click **Find Next** to display the record with your name. **Close** the dialog box. With this record displayed, from the **Office** menu, click **Print**. In the displayed **Print** dialog box, under **Print Range**, click the **Selected Record(s)** option button. Click the **Setup** button, click the **Columns tab**, and then under **Column Size**, in the **Width** box, delete the existing text and type **7"** Click **OK** two times to print only your record in the form layout, or submit electronically as directed. **Close** the **3C Candidates form**.

12. **Open** the **Navigation Pane**, and then select the **3C Candidates table**. On the **Create tab**, in the **Forms group**, click the **More Forms button**, and then in the displayed list, click **Form Wizard**. Click the **Tables/Queries arrow**, and then in the displayed list, click **Table: 3C Candidates**. Move the following fields to the **Selected Fields** list in the order given: **Candidate First Name**, **Candidate Last Name**, **Professional Interest**, and **Phone Number**. Click **Next**. Be sure **Columnar** is selected, and then click **Next**. Click **Solstice**, click **Next**, name the form **3C Candidates Input Form** and then click **Finish** to close the wizard and create the form.

13. **Close** the **Navigation Pane** and be sure your **3C Candidates Input Form** displays. Click the **Design View** button; if necessary close the Field List pane. Point to the upper edge of the **Detail section bar** to display the ⊕ pointer, and then drag downward approximately **0.5 inch**. In the **Form Header section**, click in the title *3C Candidates Input Form* to select it. On the **Design tab**, in the **Font group**, click the **Font Size arrow**, and then click **18**. Click the **Bold** button. Click the **Font Color arrow**, and then under **Access Theme Colors**, click **Access Theme 9**.

14. Point to any **sizing handle** and double-click to fit the size of the label. Point to the upper edge of the **Detail section bar**, and then by using the ⊕ pointer, drag upward until the bar is at **0.50 inch** on the vertical ruler.

(Project 3C–Counseling Sessions continues on the next page)

Content-Based Assessments

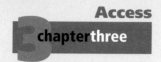
(Project 3C–Counseling Sessions continued)

15. Expand the lower edge of the **Form Footer section bar** approximately **0.50 inch**. On the **Design tab,** in the **Controls group**, click the **Label** button. Position the plus sign of the pointer in the **Form Footer** section at approximately **0.25 inch on the horizontal ruler** and even with the top edge of the section. Drag to the right to **5 inches on the horizontal ruler**, and then downward approximately **0.25 inch**. Using your own name, type **3C Candidates Input Form Firstname Lastname** and then press Enter. Double-click a sizing handle to fit the label to the text you typed. On the status bar, click the **Form View** button. On the **Quick Access Toolbar**, **Save** the changes you have made thus far.

16. On the status bar, click the **Layout View** button. In the **Controls group**, click the **Add Existing Fields** button to display the **Field List** pane. Point to **Candidate ID#**, and then drag to position the pointer in the upper portion of the white **Candidate First Name** text box control until a thick orange line displays above the control. Release the mouse button. **Close** the **Field List** pane. Click the white text box control for **Candidate ID#**, which currently displays *10115*, to surround it with an orange border. Point to the right edge of the white text box control, and then drag to the left until all of the white text box controls align under the *m* in the form title above.

17. Click the white text box control for **Phone Number**, which currently displays *(443) 555-0054*.

With the control selected, drag upward with the pointer until a thick orange line displays above **Professional Interest**. Release the mouse button to place the **Phone Number control** above the **Professional Interest control**. Click the **Candidate First Name label** to select it, and then click again to place the insertion point in the control. Edit the **Candidate First Name** and **Candidate Last Name** labels so that the labels indicate *First Name* and *Last Name*. On the **Quick Access Toolbar**, **Save** the changes you have made.

18. Click in a shaded area of the form to deselect any controls. Hold down ⇧ Shift, and then click to select each of the five **white text box controls**. On the **Format tab**, in the **Font group**, click the **Fill/Back Color** button arrow. Under **Access Theme Colors**, click **Access Theme 3**. Click the **Font Size button arrow,** and then click **12**. Click in a shaded area of the screen to deselect all the controls. Using the technique you just practiced, select the five labels, change the **Font Size** to **11**, change the **Font Color** to **Access Theme 9**, and then apply **Bold**.

19. Click the **Professional Interest** label, right-click, and then click **Properties**. In the **Property Sheet**, on the **Format tab**, click **Width**, and then change the width to **1.75** Click in a shaded area to deselect. Hold down ⇧ Shift, and then select the blue **First Name**, **Last Name**, **Phone Number**, and **Professional Interest** text box controls. In the Property Sheet, change the Height to **0.3** and then press Enter.

20. In the **Form Footer** section, click to select the label with your name. In the displayed **Property Sheet**, change the **Left** property to **1** and then press Enter. In the **Form Header** section, click anywhere in the label text *3C Candidates Input Form*. In the **Property Sheet**, change the **Left** property to **1** and then press Enter. **Close** the **Property Sheet**. On the status bar, click the **Form View** button. Click the **Last record** button to display the record containing your name. Then, from the **Office** menu, click **Print**. Under **Print Range**, click the

(Project 3C–Counseling Sessions continues on the next page)

Content-Based Assessments

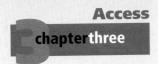
(Project 3C–Counseling Sessions continued)

Selected Record(s) option button. Click **OK** to print, or submit electronically as directed. **Close** the form, and then click **Yes** to save the changes you have made.

21. From the **Navigation Pane**, open the **3C Candidates Input Form**. **Close** the **Navigation Pane**. In the displayed first record, click the **Professional Interest** label. On the **Home tab**, in the **Sort & Filter group**, click the **Selection** button, and then in the displayed list, click **Equals "Business"**. Ten records indicate *Business* in the Professional Interest field. On the **Home tab**, in the **Sort & Filter group**, click **Toggle Filter** to remove the filter and activate all 22 records. Notice the **Unfiltered** button in the navigation area.

22. Be sure the first record displays, and then click to place the insertion point in the **Professional Interest** text box control. On the **Home tab**, in the **Sort & Filter group**, click the **Toggle Filter** button to reapply the filter. In the navigation area, click the **Last record** button to display the tenth record that matches *Business*. In the **Sort & Filter group**, click the **Toggle Filter** button to reactivate all of the records. In the navigation area, click the **Next record** button one time to move to **Record 2**. In the **Phone Number** field, select the Area Code text *(443)* including the parentheses. On the **Home tab**, in the **Sort & Filter group**, click the **Selection** button, and then click **Begins With "(443)"**. Nine records contain this Area Code. On the **Home tab**, in the **Sort & Filter group**, click the **Toggle Filter** button to remove the filter and reactivate all 22 records.

23. With the **3C Candidates Input Form** still open, on the **Home tab**, in the **Sort & Filter group**, click the **Advanced** button, and then click **Filter By Form**. Click the **Advanced** button again, and then click **Clear Grid**. Click the **Professional Interest** text box control, click the **arrow** at the far right edge of the control, and then click **Nursing**. In the **Sort & Filter group**, click the **Toggle Filter** button. Click in the **Professional Interest** text box again. In the **Sort & Filter group**, click the **Filter** button. Click to select the **Biology** check box, and then click **OK**. Five records meet the OR condition; that is, five candidates have a Professional Interest of either Nursing *or* Biology.

24. Click the **Toggle Filter** button to remove all filters. Close the form object, close the database, and then close Access.

 End **You have completed Project 3C**

Content-Based Assessments

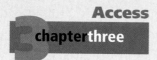
Project 3D — Workshops and Rooms

In this project, you will apply the skills you practiced from the Objectives in Project 3B.

Objectives: 6. *Create a Report by Using the Report Tool;* **7.** *Create a Report by Using the Blank Report Tool;* **8.** *Create a Report by Using the Report Wizard;* **9.** *Modify the Design of a Report;* **10.** *Print a Report and Keep Data Together.*

In the following Skills Review, you will create, modify, and print reports for Janna Sorokin regarding details about the Workshop rooms for the Job Fair. Your completed database objects will look similar to Figure 3.53.

For Project 3D, you will need the following file:

a3D_Workshops_Rooms

You will save your database as
3D_Workshops_Rooms_Firstname_Lastname

Figure 3.53

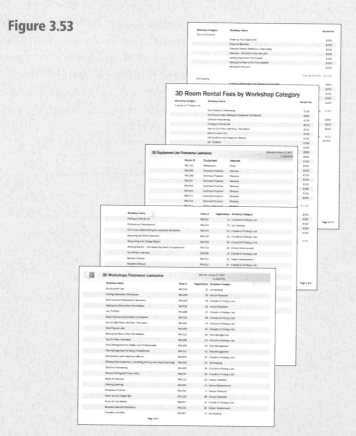

(Project 3D–Workshops and Rooms continues on the next page)

Content-Based Assessments

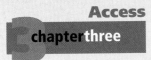
(Project 3D–Workshops and Rooms continued)

1. From the student files that accompany this text, locate the file **a3D_Workshops_Rooms**. Copy and then paste the file to your Access Chapter 3 folder. Rename the file as **3D_Workshops_Rooms_Firstname_Lastname** **Start** Access and open your **3D_Workshops_Rooms** database. If necessary, enable the content. Click the **Database Tools tab**, and then in the **Show/Hide group**, click the **Relationships** button to view the relationship between the two tables; one room can have many workshops. **Close** the Relationships window.

2. From the **Navigation Pane**, select the **3D Workshops table**. On the **Create tab**, in the **Reports group**, click the **Report** button, and then **Close** the **Navigation Pane**. Click to select the field name **Workshop #**, right-click over the selected name, and then click **Delete**. Click the **Rental Fee** field, and then delete it. Click to select the field name **Registrations**. On the **Format tab**, in the **Grouping & Totals group**, click the **Totals** button. In the displayed list, click **Sum**. Scroll to the bottom of the report; the total registrations for the various workshops is *988*.

3. Click the **Page Setup tab**, and then in the **Page Layout group**, click **Landscape**. Click the **Format tab**, and then in the **AutoFormat group**, click the **AutoFormat** button. Locate, and then click the **Trek** AutoFormat. In the **Report Header** at the top of the screen, double-click the header text *3D Workshops* to position the insertion point in the header. Edit as necessary to add your name to the end of the header text, and then on the **Format tab**, in the **Font group**, change the **Font Size** to **16**.

4. Click the **Workshop Name** field name, point to the right edge of the orange border to display the ↔ pointer, and then drag to the right until each name displays on one line. Click the **Room #** field name, point to the right edge of the orange border to display the ↔ pointer, and then drag to the left to set the column width to accommodate the longest entry with a small amount of space to the right. Click any record in the report. In the upper left corner of the report, click the small brown **layout selector** button, and then drag it to the right until the pointer is positioned approximately below the *D* in *3D* of the report header.

5. In the lower right corner of the screen, at the right edge of the status bar, click the **Print Preview** button. On the **Print Preview tab**, in the **Zoom group**, click the **Two Pages** button to view the two pages of your report. To print your report, on the **Print Preview tab**, in the **Print group**, click **Print** to print the report. Or, submit electronically as directed. On the **Print Preview tab**, in the **Close Preview group**, click the **Close Print Preview** button, and then **Close** the **3D Workshops** report. In the displayed message box, click **Yes** to save changes to the design of the report. In the **Save As** dialog box, edit the Report Name to indicate **3D Workshop Attendance Report** and then click **OK**.

6. On the **Create tab**, in the **Reports group**, click the **Blank Report** button. In the **Field List** pane, click **Show all tables**, and then click the **plus sign (+)** next to the **3D Rooms table**. Point to the **Room #** field, right-click, and then click **Add Field to View**. In the **Field List** pane, drag the **Equipment** field into the blank report—

(Project 3D–Workshops and Rooms continues on the next page)

Content-Based Assessments

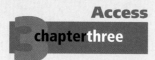

(Project 3D—Workshops and Rooms continued)

anywhere to the right of **Room #**. Double-click the **Internet** field to add it as the third field in the report. **Close** the **Field List** pane.

7. Click the **Equipment** field name, point to the right edge of the orange border to display the $\leftrightarrow$ pointer, and then drag to the right until the text *Overhead Projector* displays on one line and there is a small amount of space between the name and the next column. On the **Format tab**, in the **Controls group**, click the **Date & Time** button. In the displayed **Date and Time** dialog box, click **OK**. In the **Controls group**, click the **Title** button, and then using your own name, type 3D Equipment List Firstname Lastname In the **AutoFormat group**, click the **AutoFormat** button, and then apply the **Trek** AutoFormat. With the title still selected, in the **Font group**, change the **Font Size** to **14**.

8. Click the field name **Room#**, hold down (⇧ Shift), click the **Equipment** and **Internet** field names, and then with the three field names selected, change the **Font Size** to **12** and apply **Bold**. By using the **layout selector** button, move the group of controls until the pointer is positioned approximately below the *t* in the word *List*—or to whatever position appears to be horizontally centered between the margins. From the status bar, click **Print Preview**, and then print the report or submit electronically as directed. **Close Print Preview**, and then **Close** the report. In the displayed message box, click **Yes** to save the changes to the design of the report. In the **Save As** dialog box, type 3D Equipment List and then click **OK**.

9. On the **Create tab**, in the **Reports group**, click **Report Wizard**. Click the **Tables/Queries arrow**, and then click **Table: 3D Workshops**. Use the **One Field** button to move the following fields to the **Selected Fields** list in the order given: **Workshop Category**, **Workshop Name**, and **Rental Fee**. Click **Next**. With **Workshop Category** selected, click the **One Field** button to group the report by this field. Click **Next**. In the **1** box, on the right, click the **arrow**, and then click **Workshop Name** to sort by the name of the workshop. Click the **Summary Options** button. To the right of **Rental Fee**, select the **Sum** check box. Under **Show**, be sure the **Detail and Summary** option button is selected, and then click **OK**.

10. Click **Next**. Click the **Stepped** option button. On the right side of the dialog box, under **Orientation**, be sure **Portrait** is selected, and at the bottom be sure the **Adjust the field width so all fields fit on a page** check box is selected. Click **Next**. In the displayed list of styles, click the **Trek** style, and then click the **Next** button. In the **What title do you want for your report?** text box, name the report 3D Room Rental Fees by Workshop Category and then click the **Finish** button. In the **Zoom Group**, click the **Two Pages** button, and then examine the report as currently formatted. Then, in the lower right corner of your screen, on the status bar, click the **Layout View** button.

11. Select the **Workshop Category label control**, and then widen the right side of the controls to align under the *t* in *Rental* in the Report Header above. Widen the right side of the **Rental Fee label**

(Project 3D—Workshops and Rooms continues on the next page)

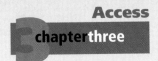
(Project 3D–Workshops and Rooms continued)

controls to just slightly inside the dotted margin. Then drag the left side of the control to the right to shorten the control and leave a small amount of space to accommodate the data.

12. Within each **Workshop Category group**, notice the **Summary for 'Workshop Category'** information. Click any of the **Summary for 'Workshop Category'** controls. Right-click any of the selected controls, and then from the displayed shortcut menu, click **Delete**. In the **Rental Fee** field, click any of the fee amounts to select these controls. Right-click any of the selected controls, and then from the displayed shortcut menu, click **Properties**. In the displayed **Property Sheet**, click the **Format tab**. In the **Property Sheet**, on the **Format tab**, click the name of the second property—**Decimal Places**—and then click the **arrow** that displays to the right of *Auto*. In the displayed list, click **0**. **Close** the **Property Sheet**. In any of the **Workshop Category groupings** of the report, to the right of the word *Sum*, click the dollar amount to select these controls. Point to any of the selected controls, right-click, and then from the displayed shortcut menu, click **Properties**. Change the number of decimal places to **0**, and then **Close** the **Property Sheet**.

13. By using the ⟷ pointer, move the right and then the left border to position the summed amounts directly under the fees above with just enough space to accommodate the data. On the left side of the report, click one of the **Sum** controls to select these controls, and then click again to place the insertion point inside the selected control. Alternatively, double-click to place the insertion point inside the control. Delete the text, type **Total Rental Fees**

and then press Enter. Move the controls to the immediate left of the summed amounts.

14. At the top of your report, click to select the **Workshop Category label control**, hold down ⇧ Shift, and then click the **Workshop Name**, and the **Rental Fee label control**. Apply **Italic**. Scroll down to view the end of the report. Click to select the sum **6400.00**, which is the Grand Total for all the rental fees. Display the **Property Sheet** for this control and change its format to **0 Decimal Places**. **Close** the **Property Sheet**, and then adjust each side of the control to position it below the other fees. From the **Format tab**, apply **Bold** formatting. By adjusting the right and left sides of the control, move the text *Grand Total* to the immediate left of **$6,400**, and then apply **Bold**. On the **Quick Access Toolbar**, click **Save** to save the changes you have made to your report thus far.

15. Press Ctrl + Home to display the top of the report, and then on the right end of the status bar, click the **Design View** button. Drag the upper edge of the **Page Header section bar** downward approximately **0.5 inch**. Click the **Report Header** *3D Room Rental Fees by Workshop Category*, and then change the **Font Size** to **26**. Double-click a sizing handle to fit the control to the larger text. Drag the **Page Header section bar** upward slightly to approximately **0.5 inch on the vertical ruler**.

16. In the **Page Footer** section, click to select the **date control**. Shorten this control by dragging the right sizing handle to the left to **1.75 inches on the horizontal ruler**. Click the **page number control** on the right. Shorten this control by dragging the

(Project 3D–Workshops and Rooms continues on the next page)

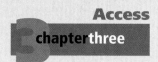
(Project 3D–Workshops and Rooms continued)

left sizing handle to the right to **5.5 inches on the horizontal ruler**. On the **Design tab**, in the **Controls group**, click the **Label** button, and then in the **Page Footer** section, position the plus sign portion of the pointer vertically in the middle of the section and horizontally at **2 inches on the horizontal ruler**. Click one time, and then using your own name, type **3D Rental Fees by Category Firstname Lastname** Press Enter to select the control. If necessary, hold down Ctrl, and then press ↑ to align the top edge even with the other two controls, but do not be concerned if this control overlaps the page number control. With the label control selected, on the **Design tab**, in the **Font group**, click the **Font Color button arrow**, and then under **Access Theme Colors**, click **Access Theme 9**. On the **Quick Access Toolbar**, click **Save**. Click the **Layout View** button.

 17. On the status bar, click the **Print Preview** button. In the **Zoom group**, click the **Two Pages** button to view how your report is currently laid out. Notice that the bottom of **Page 1** does not break at the end of a category. **Close** the **Print Preview**.

18. On the **Format tab**, in the **Grouping and Totals group**, click the **Group & Sort** button. In the **Group**, **Sort**, **and Total** pane, on the **Group on Workshop Category bar**, click the **More** button, click the arrow to the right of **do not keep group together on one page**, and then click **keep whole group together on one page**. Click the **with A on top arrow**. In the displayed list, click **with A on top**, which indicates this field is sorting in ascending order. In the **Grouping & Totals group**, click the **Group & Sort** button again to close the **Group**, **Sort & Total** pane.

19. On the status bar, click the **Print Preview** button. Print the report, or submit electronically as directed. **Close** the report, click **Yes** to save the changes to the design of your report. Close the database, and then close Access.

End **You have completed Project 3D**

Content-Based Assessments

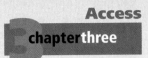
Mastering Access

Project 3E — Booth Duty

In this project, you will apply the skills you practiced from the Objectives in Project 3A.

Objectives: 1. *Create a Form;* **2.** *Use a Form To Add and Delete Records;* **3.** *Create a Form by Using the Form Wizard;* **4.** *Modify a Form in Design View and in Layout View;* **5.** *Filter Records.*

In the following Mastering Access assessment, you will assist Janna Sorokin, database manager for the Greater Baltimore Area Job Fair, in using a database to track the staff and booth duty schedule during the fair event. Your completed database objects will look similar to Figure 3.54.

For Project 3E, you will need the following file:

a3E_Booth_Duty

**You will save your database as
3E_Booth_Duty_Firstname_Lastname**

Figure 3.54

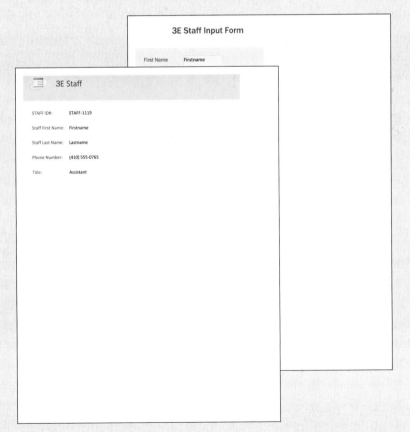

(Project 3E–Booth Duty continues on the next page)

Content-Based Assessments

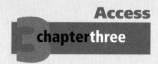

Mastering Access

(Project 3E–Booth Duty continued)

1. From the student files that accompany this textbook, locate the file **a3E_Booth_Duty**. Copy and paste the file to your Access Chapter 3 folder. Rename the file **3E_Booth_Duty_Firstname_Lastname Start** Access and open your **3E_Booth_Duty** database. Enable the content. On the **Database Tools tab**, view the table relationships, and then **Close** the window. One staff member can be assigned many booth duties during the Job Fair event.

2. Based on the **3E Booth Duty table**, use the **Form** tool to create a new form. From the status bar, switch to Form view. Scroll through the records, and then after verifying that you can view the 48 records, **Save** and name the form 3E Booth Duty Form Use the form to add the following new record:

Booth Duty ID#	BOOTH	STAFF ID#	Time Slot	Booth Location	Day
BD-49	BOOTH-I	STAFF-1109	8-12	South Hall	Day 1

3. Close the form, and then based on the **3E Staff table**, use the **Form** tool to create a new form. Switch to Form view, **Save** the form, name it **3E Staff Form** and then using your own first and last name, add the following new record:

STAFF ID#	Staff First Name	Staff Last Name	Phone Number	Title
STAFF-1119	Firstname	Lastname	(410) 555-0765	Assistant

4. After adding the record, display the **Print** dialog box, click the **Selected Record(s)** option button, click the **Setup** button, click the **Columns tab**, and then under **Column Size**, in the **Width** box, type 7" Click **OK** two times to print only your record in the form layout, or submit electronically as directed. Close the **3E Staff Form**.

5. Open the **3E Staff table**, verify that your record as a staff member displays as the last record in the table, and then close the table. Open the **3E Booth Duty Form**. Display the **Find and Replace** dialog box, locate, and then delete the record for **Booth Duty ID# BD-06** Close the form. Open the **3E Booth Duty table**. Examine the table and verify that the record for **Booth Duty ID# BD-06** no longer displays. Then, look at the last record in the table, and verify that the new record that you added for **BOOTH-I** is included in the table. Close the table.

6. Based on the **3E Staff table**, use the **Form Wizard** to create a form. Add the following fields to the **Selected Fields** list in the order listed: **Staff First Name, Staff Last Name, Title**, and **Phone Number**. Select the **Columnar** layout and the **Trek** style for the form. Edit the title as necessary to name the form **3E Staff Input Form** and then click **Finish**.

(Project 3E–Booth Duty continues on the next page)

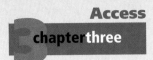

Mastering Access

(Project 3E–Booth Duty continued)

7. Switch to Design view. Expand the lower edge of the **Form Footer section bar** approximately **0.50 inch**, and then in the expanded **Form Footer section**, create a label, beginning at approximately **0.25 inch on the horizontal ruler** and even with upper edge of the section. Drag to the right to **5 inches on the horizontal ruler**, and then downward approximately **0.25 inch**. Using your own name, type **3E Staff Input Form Firstname Lastname** and then press Enter. Double-click a sizing handle to fit the control to the text you typed.

8. Switch to Layout view. Display the **Field List** pane, and then drag the **Staff ID#** field into the form slightly below the **Phone Number control**. Close the **Field List** pane. Adjust the white text box controls to align under the *m* in the form title. Move the **Phone Number** control above the **Title** control. Edit the **Staff First Name** and **Staff Last Name** labels to indicate *First Name* and *Last Name*.

9. Deselect all controls. Then, hold down ⇧ Shift and select all five **text box controls**. Apply a **Fill/Back Color** using **Access Theme 2**. Change the font size to **12**, and if necessary, widen the controls so that the phone number displays on one line. Deselect all the controls. Select all the labels, change the font size to **12**, change the font color to **Access Theme 8**, and then apply **Bold**.

10. Deselect all controls, and then select all the labels. From the **Arrange tab**, display the **Property Sheet**. Change the **Width** property for all of the labels to **1.25** Select all the text box controls, and then change the **Height** property for all the text box controls to **0.35** and the **Width** property to **1.25** Select the **Form Footer label**, hold down ⇧ Shift and click the **Form Header label**, and then change the **Left** property to **1** Close the **Property Sheet**. Switch to Form view. Click the **Last record** button to display the record containing your name. Display the **Print** dialog box, click the **Selected Record(s)** option button, and then click **OK** to print; or submit electronically as directed. **Close** the form and save the changes.

11. Open the **3E Staff Input Form**. In the displayed first record, click the **Title** label. In the **Sort & Filter group**, click the **Selection** button, and then in the displayed list, click **Equals "Associate"**. Six records contain the title *Associate*. In the **Sort & Filter group**, click **Toggle Filter** to remove the filter and activate all 19 records. Be sure the first record displays, and then click to place the insertion point in the **Title** text box control. Click the **Toggle Filter** to reapply the filter, and then in the navigation area, click the **Last record** button to display **Record 6**. In the **Phone Number** field, select the Area Code text *(410)*. Click the **Selection** button, and then click **Begins with "(410)"**. Four records meet the condition. Click the **Toggle Filter** button to remove the filter and reactivate all of the records. Close all the open objects, close the database, and then close Access.

 You have completed Project 3E ⎯⎯⎯⎯⎯⎯⎯⎯⎯⎯⎯⎯⎯⎯⎯⎯

Content-Based Assessments

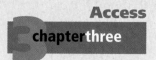

Access

chapterthree

Mastering Access

Project 3F—Lectures and Presenters

In this project, you will apply the skills you practiced from the Objectives in Project 3B.

Objectives: 6. *Create a Report by Using the Report Tool;* **7.** *Create a Report by Using the Blank Report Tool;* **8.** *Create a Report by Using the Report Wizard;* **9.** *Modify the Design of a Report;* **10.** *Print a Report and Keep Data Together.*

In the following Mastering Access assessment, you will create reports for Janna Sorokin regarding information about the various informational lectures and presenters that will be conducted during the Job Fair event. Your completed database objects will look similar to Figure 3.55.

For Project 3F, you will need the following file:

a3F_Lectures_Presenters

You will save your database as
3F_Lectures_Presenters_Firstname_Lastname

Figure 3.55

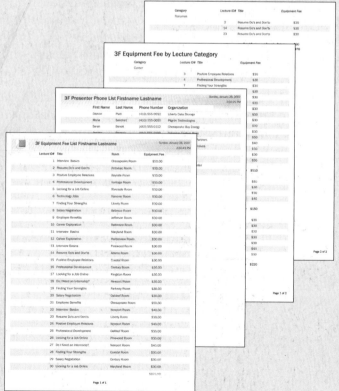

(Project 3F–Lectures and Presenters continues on the next page)

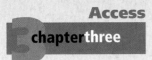
(Project 3F–Lectures and Presenters continued)

1. From the student files that accompany this textbook, locate the file **a3F_Lectures_Presenters**. Copy and then paste the file to your Access Chapter 3 folder. Rename the file as **3F_Lectures_Presenters_Firstname_Lastname Start** Access, and then open your **3F_ Lectures_Presenters** database. Enable the content. On the **Database Tools tab**, view the table relationships, and then **Close** the window. One presenter can give many lectures during the Job Fair event.

2. Based on the **3F Lectures table**, use the **Report** tool to create a new report. Delete the following fields from the report: **Presenter ID**, **Lecture Date**, **Lecture Time**, and **Category**. At the bottom of the **Equipment Fee** column, notice that the Report tool automatically summed the column; the total is *$970.00*. Apply the **Trek** AutoFormat. Edit the Report Header text to indicate **3F Equipment Fee List Firstname Lastname** and then change the font size to **3**. Shorten the right side of the **Room** field leaving a small amount of space between the columns. Use the **layout selector** button to visually center the entire layout horizontally between the margins. Click the **Print Preview** button, click the **One Page** button, check your centering. Print the report, or submit electronically as directed. Close Print Preview, close the report, save, and then name the report **3F Equipment Fee List**

3. Based on the **3F Presenters table**, create a **Blank Report**. Add the following fields: **First Name**, **Last Name**, **Phone Number**, and **Organization**. Widen the **Organization** field until all the names display on one line. Click the **Date & Time** and **Title** buttons, and type **3F Presenter Phone List Firstname Lastname** as the report title. Apply the **Trek** AutoFormat, and then with the title still selected, change the

title's font size to **16**. Select the four field names, change the font size to **12**. Center the layout horizontally on the page. Check the layout in **Print Preview**. Print the report, or submit electronically as directed. Close Print Preview, close the report, save, and then name the report **3F Presenter Phone List**

4. Based on the **3F Lectures** table, create a report by using the **Report Wizard**, and then add the following fields in the order listed: **Category**, **Lecture ID#**, **Title**, and **Equipment Fee**. Group the report by **Category**, sort by **Lecture ID#** in **Ascending order**, and **Sum** the **Equipment Fee** field. Select the **Stepped** option, **Portrait** orientation, and **Trek** style. For the report title, type **3F Equipment Fee by Lecture Category** In **Print Preview**, click the **Two Pages** button, and notice that one category is split between two pages.

5. Switch to Layout view. Widen the right side of the **Category** field to accommodate the longest category name, which is *Job Search Techniques*. Shorten the right side of the **Title** field to accommodate the longest line with just a small amount of space between the columns. Click any of the **Lecture ID#** numbers, and in the **Font group**, click the **Center** button. Select the four field names, center them, and then apply **Italic**. By using the **layout selector** button, visually center the entire layout horizontally on the page.

6. Select and delete the **Summary for 'Category'** controls. In the **Career** grouping of the report, to the right of the word *Sum*, click **$510.00** to select these controls, right-click, and then click **Properties**. Change the number of **Decimal Places** to **0**.

(Project 3F–Lectures and Presenters continues on the next page)

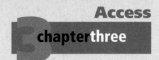

Mastering Access

(Project 3F–Lectures and Presenters continued)

7. Select one of the amounts in the **Equipment Fee** field, display the **Property Sheet**, and then change the number of **Decimal Places** to **0**. Select the summed amount of **$510**, and then adjust as necessary so that the summed amounts display directly under the fee above with just enough space to accommodate the data. Change the font color to **Access Theme 10**. Select one of the **Sum** controls, place the insertion point inside the control, delete the text, type **Total Equipment Fees by Category** change the font color to **Access Theme 10**, and then press Enter. Position theses controls to the immediate left of the total amount.

8. At the end of the report, select the sum **$970.00**, which is the Grand Total for all equipment fees, change the number of decimal places to **0**, apply **Bold**, and then change the font color to **Access Theme 10**. Position the total directly below the other totals. Apply the same formatting to the text *Grand Total*, and then position this label to the immediate left of the total amount. **Save** the changes you have made to your report thus far.

9. Switch to Design view. In the **Page Footer** section, shorten the date control by moving its right edge to **1.75 inches on the**

horizontal ruler. Shorten the **page number control** by moving its left edge to **5.5 inches on the horizontal ruler**. In the **Page Footer section**, create a label, and then position the pointer at **2 inches on the horizontal ruler** and in the vertical center of the section. Click one time, and then using your own name, type **3F Equipment Fees by Category Firstname Lastname** and then press Enter. Double-click a sizing handle to fit the control. With the label control selected, change the font color to **Access Theme 9**.

10. Display the **Print Preview** in the **Two Pages** arrangement, notice the bottom of **Page 1**, and then close the Print Preview. Switch to Layout view. In the **Grouping and Totals group**, click the **Group & Sort** button. From the **Group, Sort, and Total** pane, choose to **keep whole group together on one page** and **with A on top arrow**. Close the pane, click **Print Preview**, display **Two Pages**, and then verify that the entire *Resumes* group displays at the top of **Page 2**.

11. Print the report or submit electronically as directed. Close the report, save your changes, close the database, and then close Access.

End **You have completed Project 3F**

Content-Based Assessments

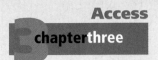

Access

chapterthree

Mastering Access

Project 3G — Raffle Sponsors

In this project, you will apply skills you practiced from the Objectives in Projects 3A and 3B.

Objectives: 1. *Create a Form;* **2.** *Use a Form To Add and Delete Records;* **6.** *Create a Report by Using the Report Tool;* **7.** *Create a Report by Using the Blank Report Tool;* **10.** *Print a Report and Keep Data Together.*

In the following Mastering Access Assessment, you will assist Janna Sorokin, database manager for the Greater Baltimore Area Job Fair, in using a database to track raffle items and sponsors for the fair event. Your completed form and report will look similar to Figure 3.56.

For Project 3G, you will need the following file:

a3G_Raffle_Sponsors

You will save your database as 3G_Raffle_Sponsors_Firstname_Lastname

Figure 3.56

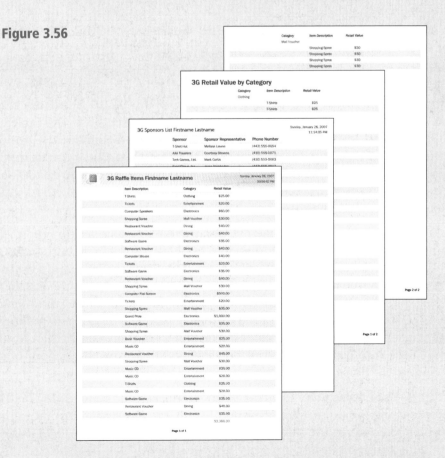

(Project 3G–Raffle Sponsors continues on the next page)

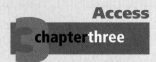

Access

Mastering Access

(Project 3G–Raffle Sponsors continued)

1. From the student files that accompany this textbook, locate the file **a3G_Raffle_Sponsors**. Copy and then paste the file to your Access Chapter 3 folder. Rename the file **3G_Raffle_Sponsors_Firstname_Lastname Start** Access, and then open your **3G_Raffle_Sponsors** database. Enable the content. On the **Database Tools tab**, view the table relationships, and then **Close** the window. One sponsor can provide many raffle items during the Job Fair event.

2. Based on the **3G Raffle Items table**, use the **Form** tool to create a form. Switch to Form view and scroll through the records. Add a new record as follows:

Raffle Item ID#	Item Description	Sponsor ID#	Provider's Item Code	Category	Retail Value
RAFF-31	Software Game	SP-1203	TG-79044	Electronics	35

3. Close the form, and then save it as **3G Raffle Items Form** Based on the **3G Sponsors table**, use the **Form** tool to create a form. Switch to Form view, and then scroll through the records. Add a new record as follows, using your own first and last name:

Sponsor ID#	Sponsor	Phone Number	Sponsor Representative
SP-1211	Baltimore Sweets	(410) 555-0765	Firstname Lastname

4. Close the form, and then save it as **3G Sponsors Form** Open the **3G Sponsors table**, verify that your record as a sponsor representative displays as the last record in the table, and then close the table. Open the **3G Raffle Items Form**. Use the **Find and Replace** dialog box to locate the record for **RAFF-02**, **Delete** the record for **RAFF-02**, and then **Close** the form. Open the **3G Raffle Items table**. Examine the table and verify that the record for *RAFF-02* no longer displays. Then scroll to **Record 31** and verify that the new record you added for **Sponsor ID# SP-1203** is included in the table. Close the table.

5. Based on the **3G Raffle Items** table, use the **Report** tool to create a new report. Apply the **Trek** AutoFormat to the report; recall that you should apply the AutoFormat first, and then edit other formatting. Delete the following fields: **Raffle Item ID#**, **Sponsor ID#**, and **Provider's Item Code**. At the bottom of the report, notice that the Report tool summed the **Retail Value** field; the total is *$2,380.00*. Add your name to the end of the Report Header text, and then change the font size to **16**. Shorten the right side of the **Category** field leaving a small amount of space between the columns. Use the **layout selector** button to visually center the layout horizontally on the page. Check your centering in print preview, and then print the report, or submit electronically as directed. Close, and then name the report **3G Retail Value List**

6. Based on the **3G Sponsors table**, create a **Blank Report**. Add the following fields: **Sponsor**, **Sponsor Representative**, and **Phone Number**. Apply the **Trek** AutoFormat to the report; recall that you should apply the AutoFormat first, and then edit other formatting. Widen

(Project 3G–Raffle Sponsors continues on the next page)

Content-Based Assessments

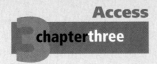

Access

chapter three

Mastering Access

(Project 3G–Raffle Sponsors continued)

the **Sponsor** field until all the names display on one line. Click the **Date & Time** and **Title** buttons, and then as the report title, type **3G Sponsors List Firstname Lastname** Change the title's font size to **14**. Select the three field names, and then change the font size to **12**. Visually center the layout horizontally on the page. Check your centering in print preview, and then print the report; or, submit electronically as directed. Close, save, and then name the report **3G Sponsors List**

7. Based on the **3G Raffle Items** table, create a report by using the **Report Wizard**, and then add the following fields in the order listed: **Category**, **Item Description**, and **Retail Value**. Group the report by **Category**, sort by **Item Description** in **Ascending order**, and **Sum** the **Retail Value** field. Select the **Stepped** option, **Portrait** orientation, and **Trek** style. As the report title, type **3G Retail Value by Category** In **Print Preview**, click the **Two Pages** button, and then examine how the records break across the two pages.

8. Switch to Layout view. Widen the right side of the **Category controls** to accommodate the longest category name. Shorten the right side of the **Item Description controls** to accommodate the longest line and leave a small amount of space between the columns. Select the three field names and apply **Italic**. Visually center the layout horizontally.

9. Select, and then delete the **Summary for 'Category'** controls. Select any value in the **Retail Value** field, and then from the **Property Sheet**, change the **Decimal Places** to **0**. In the **Clothing** grouping of the report, to the right of the word *Sum*, click **$50.00** to select these controls. Change the number of **Decimal Places** to **0**, change the font color to **Access Theme 10**, and then align the total under the values above.

10. Select one of the **Sum** controls, change the text to **Total Retail Value by Category** align this control to the immediate left of the amount, and then change its font color to **Access Theme 10**.

11. At the end of the report, select the Grand Total **$2,380.00**, change the number of decimal places to **0**, apply **Bold**, and then change the font color to **Access Theme 10**. Position the total directly below the other totals. Apply the same formatting to the text *Grand Total*, and then position this label to the immediate left of the total amount. **Save** the changes you have made thus far.

12. Switch to Design view. In the **Page Footer** section, shorten the date control by moving its right edge to **1.75 inches on the horizontal ruler**. Shorten the **page number control** by moving its left edge to **5.5 inches on the horizontal ruler**. In the **Page Footer section**, create a label, and then position the pointer at **2 inches on the horizontal ruler** and in the vertical center of the section. Click one time, and then using your own name, type **3G Retail Values by Category Firstname Lastname** and then press (Enter). Double-click a sizing handle to fit the control. With the label control selected, change the font color to **Access Theme 9**.

13. Display the **Print Preview** in the **Two Pages** arrangement, notice the bottom of **Page 1**, and then close the Print Preview. Switch to Layout view. In the **Grouping and Totals group**, click the **Group & Sort** button. From the **Group, Sort, and Total** pane, choose to **keep whole group together on one page** and **with A on top arrow**. Close the pane, display the print

(Project 3G–Raffle Sponsors continues on the next page)

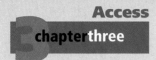

Access

chapterthree   Mastering Access

(Project 3G–Raffle Sponsors continued)

preview, display **Two Pages**, and then verify that the entire *Mall Voucher* group displays at the top of **Page 2**.

14. Print the report or submit electronically as directed. Close the report, save your changes, close the database, and then close Access.

End **You have completed Project 3G** ————————————————

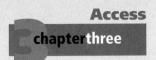

Mastering Access

Project 3H — Contractors and Facility Services

In this project, you will apply skills you practiced from the Objectives in Projects 3A and 3B.

Objectives: 1. *Create a Form;* **2.** *Use a Form To Add and Delete Records;* **6.** *Create a Report by Using Report Tool;* **7.** *Create a Report by Using the Blank Report Tool;* **8.** *Create a Report by Using the Report Wizard;* **10.** *Print a Report and Keep Data Together;* **9.** *Modify the Design of a Report*

In the following Mastering Access assessment, you will assist Janna Sorokin, database manager for the Greater Baltimore Area Job Fair, in using a database to track facility and staff services for the fair event. Your completed objects will look similar to Figure 3.57.

For Project 3H, you will need the following file:

a3H_Contractors_Facility_Services

You will save your database as
3H_Contractors_Facility_Services_Firstname_Lastname

Figure 3.57

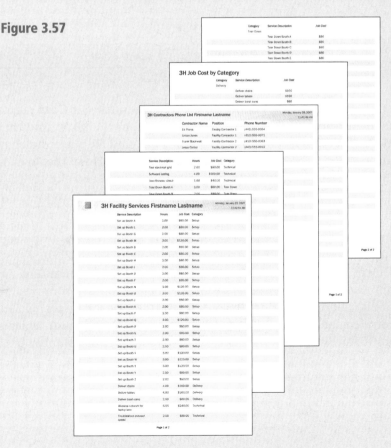

(Project 3H–Contractors and Facility Services continues on the next page)

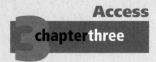

(Project 3H—Contractors and Facility Services continued)

1. From the student files that accompany this textbook, locate the file **a3H_Contractors_Facility_Services**. Copy and then paste the file to your Access Chapter 3 folder. Rename the file **3H_Contractors_Facility_Services_Firstname_Lastname Start** Access, and then open your **3H_Contractors_Facility_Services** database. Enable the content. On the **Database Tools tab**, view the table relationships, and then **Close** the window. One contractor can provide many facility services during the Job Fair event.

2. Based on the **3H Facility Services table**, use the **Form** tool to create a form. Switch to Form view, and then scroll through some of the 60 records. Add a new record as follows:

Job#	Date	Service Description	Contractor ID#	Hours	Job Cost	Category
JB-061	4/11/2009	Set up workroom	CO-3009	2	$80.00	Setup

3. Close the form, and then save it as **3H Facility Services Form** Based on the **3H Contractors table**, use the **Form** tool to create a form. Switch to Form view, and then scroll through the some of the 15 records. Add a new record as follows, using your own first and last name:

Contractor ID#	Contractor Name	Position	Phone Number
CO-3016	Firstname Lastname	Facility Contractor 1	(410) 555-0765

4. Close the form, and then save it as **3H Contractors Form** Open the **3H Contractors table**, verify that your record as a contractor displays as the last record in the table, and then close the table. Open the **3H Facility Services Form**. Use the **Find and Replace** dialog box to locate the record for **JB-003**, **Delete** the record for **JB-003**, and then **Close** the form. Open the **3H Facility Services table**. Examine the table and verify that the record for *JB-003* no longer displays. Then, scroll to the end of the table and verify that the new record you added for **JB-061** is included in the table. Close the table.

5. Based on the **3H Facility Services** table, use the **Report** tool to create a new report. Apply the **Trek** AutoFormat to the report; recall that you should apply the AutoFormat first, and then edit other formatting. Delete the following fields: **Job#**, **Date**, and **Contractor ID#**. At the bottom of the **Job Cost** column, notice that the total job cost is *$5,440.00*. Add your name to the end of the Report Header text. Shorten the right side of the **Service Description** field leaving a small amount of space between the columns (longest line is toward the bottom). Shorten the right side of the **Category** field to accommodate the data. Use the **layout selector** button to visually center the controls horizontally on the page. Display the **Print Preview** to check your centering. Print the report, or submit electronically as directed. Close, and then name the report **3H Job Cost List Firstname Lastname**

(Project 3H—Contractors and Facility Services continues on the next page)

Content-Based Assessments

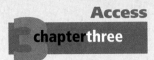

(Project 3H–Contractors and Facility Services continued)

6. Based on the **3H Contractors table**, create a **Blank Report**. Add the following fields: **Contractor Name**, **Position**, and **Phone Number**. Widen the **Position** field until all the positions display on one line. Click the **Date & Time** and **Title** buttons, and then as the title, type **3H Contractors Phone List Firstname Lastname** With the title still selected, apply the **Trek** AutoFormat, and then change the title's font size to **14**. Select the three field names, and then change the font size to **12**. Visually center the controls horizontally on the page. Display **Print Preview** to check your centering. Print the report, or submit electronically as directed. Close, and then name the report **3H Contractors Phone List Firstname Lastname**

7. Based on the **3H Facility Services table**, create a report by using the **Report Wizard**. Select the following fields in the order given: **Category**, **Service Description**, and **Job Cost**. Group the report by **Category**, sort by **Service Description** in **Ascending order**, and **Sum** the **Job Cost** field. Select the **Stepped** option, **Portrait** orientation, and **Trek** style. For the report title, type **3H Job Cost by Category** In **Print Preview**, click the **Two Pages** button and examine your report.

8. Switch to Layout view. Widen the right side of the **Category controls** to accommodate the longest category name, which is *Technical*. Shorten the right side of the **Service Description controls** to accommodate the longest line, and leave a small amount of space between the columns (the longest line is at the bottom of the list). Select the three field names, and then apply **Italic**. Visually center the layout horizontally.

9. Select, and then delete the **Summary for 'Category'** controls. Select any value in the **Job Cost** field, right-click, click **Properties**, and then change the number of **Decimal Places** to **0**. In the **Delivery** grouping of the report, to the right of the word *Sum*, click the value displayed as ##### to select these controls. Change the number of **Decimal Places** to **0**, change the font color to **Access Theme 10**, and then align the total under the values above.

10. Select one of the **Sum** controls, place the insertion point inside the control, delete the text, type **Total Job Cost by Category** and then press [Enter]. Align this control to the immediate left of the amount, and then change its font color to **Access Theme 10**. Be sure you have aligned the amount properly so that each Category's amount displays completely.

11. At the end of the report, expand if necessary, and then select the Grand Total sum that displays as #####, change the number of decimal places to **0**, apply **Bold**, and then change the font color to **Access Theme 10**. Position the total directly below the other totals. Apply the same formatting to the text *Grand Total*, and then position this label to the immediate left of the total amount. **Save** the changes you have made thus far.

12. Switch to Design view. In the **Page Footer** section, shorten the date control by moving its right edge to **1.75 inches on the horizontal ruler**. Shorten the **page number control** by moving its left edge to **5.5 inches on the horizontal ruler**. In the **Page Footer section**, create a label, and then position the pointer at **2 inches on the horizontal ruler** and in the vertical center of the section. Using your own name, type **3H Job Cost by Category Firstname Lastname** and then press [Enter]. Double-click a sizing handle to fit the control. With the label control selected, change the font color to **Access Theme 9**.

(Project 3H–Contractors and Facility Services continues on the next page)

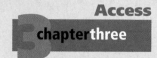

(Project 3H–Contractors and Facility Services continued)

13. Display the **Print Preview** in the **Two Pages** arrangement, notice how the groups flow from the bottom of **Page 1**, and then close the Print Preview. Switch to Layout view. In the **Grouping and Totals group**, click the **Group & Sort** button. From the **Group, Sort, and Total** pane, choose to **keep whole group together on one page** and **with A on top arrow**. View the Print Preview again, display **Two Pages**, and then verify that the entire *Tear Down* group displays on **Page 2**.

14. Print the report or submit electronically as directed. Close the Print Preview, close the report, save your changes, close the database, and then close Access.

End **You have completed Project 3H**

Content-Based Assessments

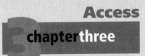

Mastering Access

Project 3I—Career Bookstore

In this project, you will apply all the skills you practiced from the Objectives in Projects 3A and 3B.

Objectives: 1. *Create a Form;* **2.** *Use a Form To Add and Delete Records;* **3.** *Create a Form by Using the Form Wizard;* **4.** *Modify a Form in Design View and in Layout View;* **5.** *Filter Records;* **6.** *Create a Report by Using the Report Tool;* **7.** *Create a Report by Using the Blank Report Tool;* **8.** *Create a Report by Using the Report Wizard;* **9.** *Modify the Design of a Report;* **10.** *Print a Report and Keep Data Together.*

In the following Mastering Access assessment, you will assist Janna Sorokin, database manager for the Greater Baltimore Area Job Fair, in using a database to track publishers and book titles for the books that are for sale at the Career Bookstore during the Job Fair event. Your completed objects will look similar to Figure 3.58.

For Project 3I, you will need the following file:

a3I_Career_Bookstore

**You will save your database as
3I_Career_Bookstore_Firstname_Lastname**

Figure 3.58

(Project 3I–Career Bookstore continues on the next page)

Content-Based Assessments

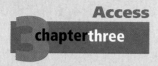

Mastering Access

(Project 3I–Career Bookstore continued)

1. From the student files that accompany this textbook, locate the file **a3I_Career_Bookstore**. Copy and then paste the file to your Access Chapter 3 folder. Rename the file **3I_Career_Bookstore_Firstname_Lastname Start** Access, and then open your **3I_Career_Bookstore** database. Enable the content. Examine the data in the two tables. On the **Database Tools tab**, view the table relationships, and then **Close** the window. One publisher can provide many career book titles during the Job Fair event.

2. Based on the **3I Career Book Titles table**, use the **Form** tool to create a form. Switch to Form view, and then scroll through the records. Add a new record as follows:

Title ID #	Title	Author	Publisher ID#	Category	Price	Total Sales
T-33	Effective Networking	Jean Flowers	PUB-100	Job Search	20	200

3. Close the form, and then save it as **3I Career Book Titles Form** Based on the **3I Publishers table**, use the **Form** tool to create a form. Switch to Form view, and then scroll through the records. Add a new record as follows, using your own first and last name:

Publisher ID#	Phone Number	Sales Representative	Company Name	Title
PUB-111	(410) 555-0765	Firstname Lastname	Associated Publishers	Sales Associate

4. Close the form, and then save it as **3I Publishers Form** Open the **3I Publishers table**, verify that your record as a Sales Associate displays as the last record in the table, and then close the table. Open the **3I Career Book Titles Form**. Use the **Find and Replace** dialog box to locate the record for **T-05**, **Delete** the record for **T-05**, and then close the form. Open the **3I Career Book Titles table**. Examine the table and verify that the record for *T-05* no longer displays. Then scroll to **Record 33** and verify that the new record you added for **Title ID# T-33** is included in the table. Close the table.

5. Based on the **3I Career Book Titles table**, use the **Report** tool to create a new report. Apply the **Trek** AutoFormat to the report; recall that you should apply the AutoFormat first, and then edit other formatting. Delete the following fields: **Title ID#**, **Author**, and **Publisher ID#**. At the bottom of the report, notice that the Report tool summed the **Total Sales** field, the total is *$9,945.00*. Add your name to the end of the Report Header text, and then change the font size to **16**. Shorten the right side of the **Category** field leaving a small amount of space between the columns. Use the **layout selector** button to visually center the layout horizontally on the page. Click the **Print Preview** button to check your centering. Print the report, or submit electronically as directed. Close, and then name the report **3I Total Sales**

6. Based on the **3I Publishers table**, create a **Blank Report**. Add the following fields: **Company Name**, **Sales Representative**, and **Phone Number**. Widen the **Company Name** field until all the names display on one line. Click the **Date & Time** and **Title** buttons, and then as the

(Project 3I–Career Bookstore continues on the next page)

Content-Based Assessments

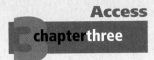
(Project 3I–Career Bookstore continued)

report title, type **3I Publishers List Firstname Lastname** With the title still selected, apply the **Trek** AutoFormat, and then change the title's font size to **14**. Select the three field names, change the font size to **12**. Check your centering in print preview, and then print the report; or, submit electronically as directed. Close, save, and then name the report **3I Publishers List**

7. Based on the **3I Career Book Titles table**, create a report by using the **Report Wizard**, and add the following fields in the order listed: **Category**, **Title**, and **Total Sales**. Group the report by **Category**, sort by **Title** in **Ascending order**, and then **Sum** the **Total Sales** field. Select the **Stepped** option, **Portrait** orientation, and **Trek** style. As the report title, type **3I Total Sales by Category** In **Print Preview**, click the **Two Pages** button, and then examine how the records break across the two pages.

8. Switch to Layout view. Widen the right side of the **Category controls** to accommodate the longest category name. Shorten the right side of the **Title controls** to accommodate the longest line and leave a small amount of space between the columns. Select the three field names and apply **Italic**. Visually center the layout horizontally.

9. Select, and then delete the **Summary for 'Category'** controls. Select any value in the **Total Sales** field, right-click, click **Properties**, and then change the **Decimal Places** to **0**. In the **Interviewing Strategies** grouping of the report, to the right of the word *Sum*, click **$3,600.00** to select these controls. Change the number of **Decimal Places** to **0**, change the font color to **Access Theme 10**, and then align the total under the values above.

10. Select one of the **Sum** controls, change the text to **Total Sales by Category** align this control to the immediate left of the amount, and then change its font color to **Access Theme 10**.

11. At the end of the report, select the sum **$9,945.00**, which is the Grand Total, change the number of decimal places to **0**, apply **Bold**, and then change the font color to **Access Theme 10**. Position the Grand Total directly below the other totals. Apply the same formatting to the text *Grand Total*, and then position this label to the immediate left of the Grand Total amount. **Save** the changes you have made to your report thus far.

12. Switch to Design view. In the **Page Footer** section, shorten the date control by moving its right edge to **1.75 inches on the horizontal ruler**. Shorten the **page number control** by moving its left edge to **5.5 inches on the horizontal ruler**. In the **Page Footer section**, create a label, and then position the pointer at **2 inches on the horizontal ruler** and in the vertical center of the section. Click one time, and then using your own name, type **3I Total Sales by Category Firstname Lastname** and then press Enter. Double-click a sizing handle to fit the control. With the label control selected, change the font color to **Access Theme 9**.

13. Display the **Print Preview** in the **Two Pages** arrangement, notice the flow between the bottom of **Page 1** and the top of **Page 2**, and then close the Print Preview. Switch to Layout view. In the **Grouping and Totals group**, click the **Group & Sort** button. From the **Group, Sort, and Total** pane, choose to **keep whole group together on one page** and **with A on top arrow**. Close the pane, click **Print Preview**, display **Two Pages**, and then verify that the entire *Resumes* group displays at the top of **Page 2**. Print the report or submit electronically as directed. Close, and then save the report.

(Project 3I–Career Bookstore continues on the next page)

Content-Based Assessments

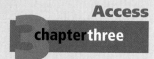

(Project 3I–Career Bookstore continued)

14. Open the **3I Publishers Form**. In the displayed first record, click the **Title** label. In the **Sort & Filter group**, click the **Selection** button, and then in the displayed list, click **Equals "Sales Representative"**. Six records contain the title *Sales Representative*. In the **Sort & Filter group**, click **Toggle Filter** to remove the filter and activate all 12 records. Be sure the first record displays, and then click to place the insertion point in the **Title** text box control. Click the **Toggle Filter** to reapply the filter, and then in the navigation area, click the **Last record** button to display the sixth record in the filtered group. In the **Phone Number** field, select the Area Code text *(443)*. Click the **Selection** button, and then click **Begins with "(443)"**. Four records meet the condition. Click the **Toggle Filter** button to remove the filter and reactivate all of the records. Close all the open objects, close the database, and then close Access.

End **You have completed Project 3I**

Content-Based Assessments

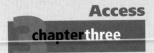
Project 3J — Business Running Case

In this project, you will apply the skills you practiced in Projects 3A and 3B.

From My Computer, navigate to the student files that accompany this textbook. In the folder **03_business_running_case_pg37_86**, locate and open the folder for this chapter. Open and print the instructions for this project, which are provided to you in Adobe PDF format. Follow the instructions and use the skills you have gained thus far to assist Jennifer Nelson in meeting the challenges of owning and running her business.

 You have completed Project 3J ————————

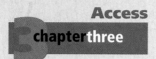

Rubric

The following outcomes-based assessments are *open-ended assessments*. That is, there is no specific correct result; your result will depend on your approach to the information provided. Make *Professional Quality* your goal. Use the following scoring rubric to guide you in *how* to approach the problem and then to evaluate *how well* your approach solves the problem.

The *criteria*—Software Mastery, Content, Format and Layout, and Process—represent the knowledge and skills you have gained that you can apply to solving the problem. The *levels of performance*—Professional Quality, Approaching Professional Quality, or Needs Quality Improvements—help you and your instructor evaluate your result.

	Your completed project is of Professional Quality if you:	Your completed project is Approaching Professional Quality if you:	Your completed project Needs Quality Improvements if you:
1-Software Mastery	Choose and apply the most appropriate skills, tools, and features and identify efficient methods to solve the problem.	Choose and apply some appropriate skills, tools, and features, but not in the most efficient manner.	Choose inappropriate skills, tools, or features, or are inefficient in solving the problem.
2-Content	Construct a solution that is clear and well organized, contains content that is accurate, appropriate to the audience and purpose, and is complete. Provide a solution that contains no errors of spelling, grammar, or style.	Construct a solution in which some components are unclear, poorly organized, inconsistent, or incomplete. Misjudge the needs of the audience. Have some errors in spelling, grammar, or style, but the errors do not detract from comprehension.	Construct a solution that is unclear, incomplete, or poorly organized, containing some inaccurate or inappropriate content; and contains many errors of spelling, grammar, or style. Do not solve the problem.
3-Format and Layout	Format and arrange all elements to communicate information and ideas, clarify function, illustrate relationships, and indicate relative importance.	Apply appropriate format and layout features to some elements, but not others. Overuse features, causing minor distraction.	Apply format and layout that does not communicate information or ideas clearly. Do not use format and layout features to clarify function, illustrate relationships, or indicate relative importance. Use available features excessively, causing distraction.
4-Process	Use an organized approach that integrates planning, development, self-assessment, revision, and reflection.	Demonstrate an organized approach in some areas, but not others; or, use an insufficient process of organization throughout.	Do not use an organized approach to solve the problem.

Outcomes-Based Assessments

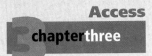

Problem Solving

Project 3K — Candidates and Offers

In this project, you will construct a solution by applying any combination of the Objectives found in Projects 3A and 3B.

For Project 3K, you will need the following file:

a3K_Candidates_Offers

You will save your database as
3K_Candidates_Offers_Firstname_Lastname

Copy the student file **a3K_Candidates_Offers** to your Access Chapter 3 folder and rename it **3K_Candidates_Offers_Firstname_Lastname** Michael Dawson, Executive Director of the Baltimore Area Job Fair, would like one form and two reports created from the Job Fair database. Mr. Dawson wants a report listing the Organization Name and Offer Amount of each job offered to a candidate as a result of the Job Fair. Create and save the report as **3K Offers Firstname Lastname** Print the report or submit electronically as directed. Mr. Dawson also wants a report of the names, college majors, and phone numbers of the candidates. Save the report as **3K Candidates Firstname Lastname** Print the report or submit electronically as directed. Using the skills you have practiced in this chapter, create an attractive, easy-to-follow input form that can be used to update candidate records. Using your own information, add a new record as Candidate ID# 22102. Save the form as **3K Candidate Update Firstname Lastname** For the report that you added, print or submit electronically.

 End **You have completed Project 3K** ──────────

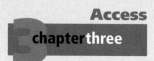

Problem Solving

Project 3L — Applicants and Job Openings

In this project, you will construct a solution by applying any combination of the Objectives found in Projects 3A and 3B.

For Project 3L, you will need the following file:

a3L_Applicants_Job_Openings

You will save your database as
3L_Applicants_Job_Openings_Firstname_Lastname

Copy the file **a3L_Applicants_Job_Openings** to your Access Chapter 3 folder and rename it **3L_Applicants_Job_Openings_Firstname_ Lastname** Janice Strickland, Employer Coordinator, wants to know which types of positions have the most openings so she can highlight them on the Job Fair Web site. Sort the records in the table so you can provide Janice with the appropriate information, print the table in the sorted order, save the table as **3L Table Sort Firstname Lastname** or submit electronically; save the changes to the table's design. Janice also needs an input form for Job Fair applicants so she can update the database if needed. Save the form as **3L Applicant Input Form Firstname Lastname** Print the form, or submit electronically. Create an Applicant input form, and using your own information, add a new record as Applicant ID# 4600. Janice needs a report with applicant contact information so she can send updates about new job openings. Create an attractive, easy-to-read applicant contact information report. Include a Report Header with **3L Applicant Contact Information Firstname Lastname** Save and print the report, or submit electronically.

End **You have completed Project 3L** ——————

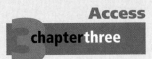

Problem Solving

Project 3M—Candidates and Activities

In this project, you will construct a solution by applying any combination of the Objectives found in Projects 3A and 3B.

> ### For Project 3M, you will need the following file:
>
> a3M_Candidates_Activities

You will save your database as
3M_Candidates_Activities_Firstname_Lastname

Copy the file **a3M_Candidates_Activities** to your Access Chapter 3 folder and rename it **3M_Candidates_Activities_Firstname_Lastname** Janice Strickland, Employer Coordinator, wants a report that shows the room where each activity is being held so that she can give the Activity Coordinators their room assignments. Create an attractive, easy-to-read report that shows the Meeting Room for each Activity. Include your name in the report heading, save the report as **3M Activity Meeting Rooms Firstname Lastname** and then print the report or submit electronically. Then create a Candidate Input Form for adding information for new candidates. Using your own information, as STU-2049 add a new record to the form. Save as **3M Candidate Input Form Firstname Lastname** and then print the STU-2049 record or submit electronically.

 End **You have completed Project 3M** ————————

Outcomes-Based Assessments

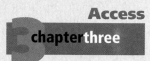
Problem Solving

Project 3N—Donors and Gifts

In this project, you will construct a solution by applying any combination of the Objectives found in Projects 3A and 3B.

> **For Project 3N, you will need the following file:**
>
> a3N_Donors_Gifts

You will save your database as
3N_Donors_Gifts_Firstname_Lastname

Copy the file **a3N_Donors_Gifts** to your Access Chapter 3 folder and rename it **3N_Donors_Gifts_Firstname_Lastname** Michael Dawson, Executive Director of the Baltimore Area Job Fair, wants a Donor Gifts Report so he can determine the total retail value of gift items distributed during the Job Fair. Create a report grouped by Category and sorted by Item Description that includes the Retail Value totals. Include the Grand Total of the Retail Value of the gift items. Create a footer with the project name (3N Donors and Gifts) and your name in the footer. Save the report as **3N Gift Retail Value Firstname Lastname** Mr. Dawson also needs a donor list with phone numbers so he can call the donor representatives and thank them for participating in the Job Fair. Create a report with the date and a report title that includes the project name and your name. Save the report as **3N Donor List Firstname Lastname** Print or submit the reports electronically.

End You have completed Project 3N —————

Outcomes-Based Assessments

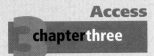
Problem Solving

Project 3O — Food Services Staffing

In this project, you will construct a solution by applying any combination of the Objectives found in Projects 3A and 3B.

For Project 3O, you will need the following file:

a3O_Food_Services_Staffing

You will save your database as
3O_Food_Services_Staffing_Firstname_Lastname

Copy the file **a3O_Food_Services_Staffing** to your Access Chapter 3 folder and rename it **3O_Food_Services_Staffing_Firstname_Lastname** Roy McLean, Food Services Manager for the Baltimore Area Job Fair, would like a report created with Food Service staff contact information. He needs the report for calling staff members when the schedule changes. Create an attractive, easy-to-read staff contact report. Include the project name (3O Food Services Staffing) and your name in the report heading. Save the report as **3O Staff Contact Firstname Lastname** Print or submit electronically.

End **You have completed Project 3O** ———————

Outcomes-Based Assessments

You and *GO!*

Project 3P—You and *GO!*

In this project, you will construct a solution by applying any combination of the skills you practiced from the Objectives in Projects 3A and 3B.

From My Computer, navigate to the student files that accompany this textbook. In the folder **04_you_and_go_pg87_102**, locate and open the folder for this chapter. Open and print the instructions for this project, which are provided to you in Adobe PDF format. Follow the instructions to create forms and reports for your personal database.

End **You have completed Project 3P** ————————

GO! with Help

Project 3Q— *GO!* with Help

In addition to creating single-record forms, you can create a multiple items form. Use the Access Help system to find out how to create a form that displays multiple records.

1 **Start** Access. Click the **Microsoft Office Access Help**

button . Click the **Search arrow**, and then under **Content from this computer**, click **Access Help**. In the **Search box**, type **create a form** and then press Enter. Scroll the displayed list as necessary, and then click **Create a form**. Under **What do you want to do?**, click **Create a form that displays multiple records by using the Multiple Items tool**.

2 If you would like to keep a copy of this information, click the **Print**

button . Click the **Close** button ☒ in the top right corner of the Help window to close the Help window, and then close Access.

End **You have completed Project 3Q** ————————

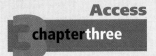

Access

chapterthree

Group Business Running Case

Project 3R—Group Business Running Case

In this project, you will apply the skills you practiced from the Objectives in Projects 3A and 3B.

Your instructor may assign this group case project to your class. If your instructor assigns this project, he or she will provide you with information and instructions to work as part of a group. The group will apply the skills gained thus far to help the Bell Orchid Hotel Group achieve its business goals.

 End **You have completed Project 3R** ——————

Glossary

Aggregate functions Calculations that are performed on a group of records.

AND condition A condition in which only records where both specified values are present in the selected fields.

Ascending order A sorting order that arranges text in alphabetical order (A to Z) or numbers from the lowest to highest number.

AutoNumber An Access feature that sequentially numbers entered records creating a unique number for each record; useful for data that has no distinct field that could be considered unique.

Between . . . And operator A comparison operator that looks for values within a range.

Blank database A database that has no data and has no database tools; you create the data and the tools as you need them.

Blank Report tool An Access feature with which you can create a report from scratch by adding the fields you want in the order you want them to appear.

Bound The term used to describe objects and controls that are based on data that is stored in tables.

Calculated controls Controls whose source of data is an expression—typically a formula—rather than a field.

Cell The box formed by the intersection of a row and a column in a datasheet.

Common fields Fields that contain the same data in more than one table.

Comparison operators Symbols that evaluate each field value to determine if it is the same (=), greater than (>), less than (<), or in between a range of values as specified by the criteria.

Compound criteria Multiple conditions in a query or filter.

Control Objects on a form or report that display data, perform actions, and let you view and work with information.

Control layout The grouped arrangement of controls on a form or report.

Criteria Conditions that identify the specific records you are looking for.

Data Facts about people, events, things, or ideas.

Data entry The action of typing the record data into a database.

Data source The table or tables from which a query gets its data.

Data type The characteristic that defines the kind of data that can be entered into a field, such as numbers, text, or dates.

Database An organized collection of facts about people, events, things, or ideas related to a particular topic or purpose.

Datasheet view The Access view that displays an object organized in a format of columns and rows similar to an Excel spreadsheet.

Date control A control on a form or report that inserts the current date each time the form or report is opened.

DBMS An acronym for database management system.

Descending order A sorting order that arranges text in reverse alphabetical (Z to A) order or numbers from the highest to the lowest number.

Design grid The lower pane of the Query window, which displays the design of the query.

Design view The Access view that displays the underlying structure of an object.

Detail section The section of a form or report that displays the records from the underlying table or query.

Dialog box A window containing commands or that asks you to make a decision.

Field A category that describes each piece of data stored in a table.

Field list A list of the field names in a table.

Field properties Characteristics of a field that control how the field will display and how the data can be entered in the field.

Filter By Form An Access command that filters the records in a form based on one or more fields, or based on more than one value in the same field.

Filter By Selection An Access command that retrieves only the records that contain the value in the selected field.

Filtering The process of displaying only a portion of the total records (a subset) based on matching specific value.

Foreign key The field that is included in the related table so that it can be joined to the primary key in another table for the purpose of creating a relationship.

Form An Access object with which you can enter, edit, or display data from a table or a query; a window for displaying and collecting information.

Form footer Information at the bottom of the screen in Form view that is printed after the last detail section on the last page.

Form header Information, such as a form's title, which displays at the top of the screen in Form view, and that is printed at the top of the first page when records are printed as forms.

Form tool The Access tool that creates a form with a single mouse click, and that includes all the fields from the underlying data source (table or query).

Group footer Displays the field label by which the summarized data has been grouped.

Group header Information printed at the beginning of each new group of records, for example the group name.

Group, Sort, and Total pane A pane that opens at the bottom of your screen in which you can control how information is sorted and grouped in a report; provides the most flexibility for adding or modifying groups, sort orders, or totals options on a report.

Information Data that has been organized in a useful manner.

Innermost sort field When sorting on multiple fields in datasheet view, the field that will be used for the second level of sorting.

Is Not Null A criteria that searches for fields that are not empty.

Is Null A criteria that searches for fields that are empty.

Join line In the Relationships window, the line joining two tables that visually indicates the related field and the type of relationship.

Label control A control on a form or report that contains descriptive information, typically a field name.

Landscape orientation A print layout in which the printed page is wider than it is tall.

Layout selector A small symbol that displays in the upper left corner of a selected control layout, and with which you can move the entire group of controls.

Layout view The Access view in which you can make changes to a form or to a report while the form is running—the data from the underlying record source displays.

Logical operators (Access) The criteria of AND and OR used to enter criteria for the same field or different fields; AND requires that both conditions be met and OR requires that either condition be met.

Message Bar The area directly below the Ribbon that displays information such as security alerts when there is potentially unsafe, active content in an Office 2007 document that you open.

Multiple items form A form in which multiple records can be entered into or displayed from a table.

Navigation Pane The area of the Access window that displays and organizes the names of the objects in a database; from here you open objects for use.

Object window The portion of the Access window that displays open objects.

Objects The basic parts of a database, which includes tables, forms, queries, reports, and macros.

OLE An abbreviation for *object linking and embedding*, a technology for transferring and sharing information among applications.

One-to-many relationship A relationship between two tables where one record in the first table corresponds to many records in the second table—the most common type of relationship in Access.

OR condition A condition in which only records where one of two values is present in the selected field.

Outermost sort field When sorting on multiple fields in datasheet view, the field that will be used for the first level of sorting.

Page footer Information printed at the end of every page in a report; used to print page numbers or other information that you want to appear at the bottom of every report page.

Page header Information printed at the top of every page of a report.

Page number control A control on a form or report that inserts the page numbers of the pages when displayed in Print Preview or when printed.

Populate The action of filling a database table with records.

Portrait orientation A print layout in which the printed page is taller than it is wide.

Primary key The field that uniquely identifies a record in a table—for example, a Student ID number at a college.

Property sheet A list of characteristics—properties —for controls on a form or report in which you can make precision changes to each property associated with the control.

Query A database object that retrieves specific data from one or more tables and then displays the specified data in datasheet view.

Record All of the categories of data pertaining to one person, place, thing, event, or idea.

Record selector The bar on the left side of a form with which you can select the entire record.

Record selector box The small box at the left of a record in datasheet view which, when clicked, selects the entire record.

Record source The tables or queries that provide the underlying data for a report.

Referential integrity A set of rules that Access uses to ensure that the data between related tables is valid.

Relational database A type of database in which the tables in the database can relate or connect to other tables through common fields.

Relationship An association that is established between two tables using common fields.

Report A database object that summarizes the fields and records from a table, or from a query, in an easy-to-read format suitable for printing.

Report footer Information that is printed once at the end of a report; used to print report totals or other summary information for the entire report.

Report header Information printed once at the beginning of a report; used for logos, titles, and dates.

Report tool The Access feature that creates a report with one mouse click, and which displays all the fields and records from the record source that you choose—a quick way to look at the underlying data.

Report Wizard An Access feature with which you can create a report by answering a series of questions; Access designs the report based on your answers.

Run The process in which Access searches the records in the table(s) included in a query design, finds the records that match the specified criteria, and then displays those records in a datasheet; only the fields that have been included in the query design display.

Section bar A gray bar in a form or report that identifies and separates one section from another; used to select the section and to change the size of the adjacent section.

Select Query A database object that retrieves (selects) specific data from one or more tables and then displays the specified data in datasheet view.

Simple select query Another name for a select query.

Sizing handles The small boxes around the edge of a control indicating the control is selected and that can be adjusted to resize the selected control.

Sorting The process of arranging data in a specific order based on the value in each field.

Spotlight The area in the opening Access program screen that displays content from Microsoft's Web site.

Subset A portion of the total records available.

Tab order The order in which the insertion point moves from one field to the next in a form when you press the Tab key.

Table The Access object that stores your data organized in an arrangement of columns and rows.

Table area The upper pane of the Query window, which displays the field lists for tables that are used in the query.

Table design The number of fields, and the type of content within each field, in an Access table.

Table template A pre-built table format for common topics such as contacts, issues, and tasks.

Tables and Views category An arrangement of objects in the Navigation Pane in which the objects are grouped by the table to which they are related.

Template A pre-formatted database designed for a specific purpose.

Text box control The graphical object on a form or report that displays the data from the underlying table or query; a text box control is known as a bound control because its source data comes from a table or a query.

Text string A sequence of characters, which when used in query criteria, much be matched.

Trust Center (Access) An area of the Access program where you can view the security and privacy settings for your Access installation.

Unbound control A term used to describe a control that does not have a source of data.

Wildcard character In a query, a character that serves as a placeholder for one or more unknown characters in your criteria.

Wizard A feature in Microsoft Office programs that walks you step by step through a process.

Zoom The action of increasing or decreasing the viewing area of the screen.

Index

SINGLE PC LICENSE AGREEMENT AND LIMITED WARRANTY

READ THIS LICENSE CAREFULLY BEFORE OPENING THIS PACKAGE. BY OPENING THIS PACKAGE, YOU ARE AGREEING TO THE TERMS AND CONDITIONS OF THIS LICENSE. IF YOU DO NOT AGREE, DO NOT OPEN THE PACKAGE. PROMPTLY RETURN THE UNOPENED PACKAGE AND ALL ACCOMPANYING ITEMS TO THE PLACE YOU OBTAINED THEM. *THESE TERMS APPLY TO ALL LICENSED SOFTWARE ON THE DISK EXCEPT THAT THE TERMS FOR USE OF ANY SHAREWARE OR FREEWARE ON THE DISKETTES ARE AS SET FORTH IN THE ELECTRONIC LICENSE LOCATED ON THE DISK:*

1. GRANT OF LICENSE and OWNERSHIP: The enclosed computer programs ("Software") are licensed, not sold, to you by Prentice-Hall, Inc. ("We" or the "Company") and in consideration of your purchase or adoption of the accompanying Company textbooks and/or other materials, and your agreement to these terms. We reserve any rights not granted to you. You own only the disk(s) but we and/or our licensors own the Software itself. This license allows you to use and display your copy of the Software on a single computer (i.e., with a single CPU) at a single location for academic use only, so long as you comply with the terms of this Agreement. You may make one copy for back up, or transfer your copy to another CPU, provided that the Software is usable on only one computer.

2. RESTRICTIONS: You may not transfer or distribute the Software or documentation to anyone else. Except for backup, you may not copy the documentation or the Software. You may not network the Software or otherwise use it on more than one computer or computer terminal at the same time. You may not reverse engineer, disassemble, decompile, modify, adapt, translate, or create derivative works based on the Software or the Documentation. You may be held legally responsible for any copying or copyright infringement which is caused by your failure to abide by the terms of these restrictions.

3. TERMINATION: This license is effective until terminated. This license will terminate automatically without notice from the Company if you fail to comply with any provisions or limitations of this license. Upon termination, you shall destroy the Documentation and all copies of the Software. All provisions of this Agreement as to limitation and disclaimer of warranties, limitation of liability, remedies or damages, and our ownership rights shall survive termination.

4. DISCLAIMER OF WARRANTY: THE COMPANY AND ITS LICENSORS MAKE NO WARRANTIES ABOUT THE SOFTWARE, WHICH IS PROVIDED "AS-IS." IF THE DISK IS DEFECTIVE IN MATERIALS OR WORKMANSHIP, YOUR ONLY REMEDY IS TO RETURN IT TO THE COMPANY WITHIN 30 DAYS FOR REPLACEMENT UNLESS THE COMPANY DETERMINES IN GOOD FAITH THAT THE DISK HAS BEEN MISUSED OR IMPROPERLY INSTALLED, REPAIRED, ALTERED OR DAMAGED. THE COMPANY DISCLAIMS ALL WARRANTIES, EXPRESS OR IMPLIED, INCLUDING WITHOUT LIMITATION, THE IMPLIED WARRANTIES OF MERCHANTABILITY AND FITNESS FOR A PARTICULAR PURPOSE. THE COMPANY DOES NOT WARRANT, GUARANTEE OR MAKE ANY REPRESENTATION REGARDING THE ACCURACY, RELIABILITY, CURRENTNESS, USE, OR RESULTS OF USE, OF THE SOFTWARE.

5. LIMITATION OF REMEDIES AND DAMAGES: IN NO EVENT, SHALL THE COMPANY OR ITS EMPLOYEES, AGENTS, LICENSORS OR CONTRACTORS BE LIABLE FOR ANY INCIDENTAL, INDIRECT, SPECIAL OR CONSEQUENTIAL DAMAGES ARISING OUT OF OR IN CONNECTION WITH THIS LICENSE OR THE SOFTWARE, INCLUDING, WITHOUT LIMITATION, LOSS OF USE, LOSS OF DATA, LOSS OF INCOME OR PROFIT, OR OTHER LOSSES SUSTAINED AS A RESULT OF INJURY TO ANY PERSON, OR LOSS OF OR DAMAGE TO PROPERTY, OR CLAIMS OF THIRD PARTIES, EVEN IF THE COMPANY OR AN AUTHORIZED REPRESENTATIVE OF THE COMPANY HAS BEEN ADVISED OF THE POSSIBILITY OF SUCH DAMAGES. SOME JURISDICTIONS DO NOT ALLOW THE LIMITATION OF DAMAGES IN CERTAIN CIRCUMSTANCES, SO THE ABOVE LIMITATIONS MAY NOT ALWAYS APPLY.

6. GENERAL: THIS AGREEMENT SHALL BE CONSTRUED IN ACCORDANCE WITH THE LAWS OF THE UNITED STATES OF AMERICA AND THE STATE OF NEW YORK, APPLICABLE TO CONTRACTS MADE IN NEW YORK, AND SHALL BENEFIT THE COMPANY, ITS AFFILIATES AND ASSIGNEES. This Agreement is the complete and exclusive statement of the agreement between you and the Company and supersedes all proposals, prior agreements, oral or written, and any other communications between you and the company or any of its representatives relating to the subject matter. If you are a U.S. Government user, this Software is licensed with "restricted rights" as set forth in subparagraphs (a)-(d) of the Commercial Computer-Restricted Rights clause at FAR 52.227-19 or in subparagraphs (c)(1)(ii) of the Rights in Technical Data and Computer Software clause at DFARS 252.227-7013, and similar clauses, as applicable.

Should you have any questions concerning this agreement or if you wish to contact the Company for any reason, please contact in writing:

Multimedia Production
Higher Education Division
Prentice-Hall, Inc.
1 Lake Street
Upper Saddle River NJ 07458